WESTERN EUROPE:
geographical perspectives
SECOND EDITION

ICELAND
Reykjavik

SWEDEN

FINLAND

NORWAY
Helsinki

Oslo
Stockholm

DENMARK

IRELAND
Dublin

NETHERLANDS

UNITED
KINGDOM
The
Hague
Copenhagen

London
Brussels
Bonn

BELGIUM
LUXEMBOURG

Paris
WEST
GERMANY

Vienna

FRANCE
Berne
AUSTRIA
SWITZERLAND

ITALY

PORTUGAL
Madrid
Rome

Lisbon
SPAIN

GREECE

Athens

0   Km   500

WESTERN EUROPE:

geographical perspectives

SECOND EDITION

HUGH CLOUT
MARK BLACKSELL
RUSSELL KING
DAVID PINDER

Longman
Scientific &
Technical

Copublished in the United States with
John Wiley & Sons, Inc., New York

Longman Scientific & Technical.
Longman Group UK Limited,
Longman House, Burnt Mill, Harlow
Essex CM20 2JE, England
and Associated Companies throughout the world.

Copublished in the United States with
John Wiley & Sons, Inc., 605 Third Avenue, New York, NY
10158
© Longman Group Limited 1985
This edition © Longman Group UK Limited 1989

First published 1985
Second edition 1989

British Library Cataloguing in Publication Data
Western Europe: geographical perspectives.
 – 2nd ed.
 1. Western Europe. Social conditions,
 1980–1989. Geographical aspects
 I. Clout, Hugh, *1944 –*
 940.55'8

ISBN 0-582-01772-6

Library of Congress Cataloging-in-Publication Data
Western Europe: geographical perspectives/Hugh Clout
. . . [et al.].
 – 2nd ed.
  p.   cm.
  Bibliography: p.
  Includes index.
  ISBN 0-470-21193-8 (Wiley, USA only).
  1. Europe – Economic conditions – 1945– 2. Europe
 – Social conditions. 3. Europe – Politics and government
 – 1945– 4. Regional planning – Europe. I. Clout, Hugh
 D.
 HC240.W434   1989
 940.55 – dc19   88-18733
                                 CIP

Set in Linotron 202 9/11pt Times

Produced by Longman Singapore Publishers (Pte) Ltd.
Printed in Singapore

Contents

List of figures

List of tables

Preface

At the beginning of this century, Paul Vidal de la Blache (1903) observed that the land of France resembled a medal, struck in the likeness of its people. In so doing, he introduced a methodology for comprehending both the inter-relationship of man and nature and the spatial differentiation of long-settled countries of Europe. His approach was to prove long lasting and influenced generations of geographers who produced highly detailed textbooks that explored the intricacies of place. Major works dealing with component parts of Europe were produced by British geographers (e.g. Houston 1964; Monkhouse 1959; Mutton 1961), while writers in North America tended to embrace a country-by-country approach to cover the continent of Europe as a whole (e.g. Gottmann 1950; Hoffmann 1953; Pounds 1953). These and other comparable texts went through several editions and fashioned the education of countless students.

Then came a phase in the late 1960s and 1970s when geographers tended to cast their thoughts about European area studies within a frame of applied (or applicable) geography and examined economic trends, social processes and management problems in the context of individual nation-states or official planning regions (e.g. House 1978; Thompson 1970). By emphasizing the importance of process, rather than accentuating the uniqueness of place, the legacy of the past or the endowments of nature, this approach was much more problem-orientated than that which preceded it. Geographers stressed the role of planners and the activities of planning institutions and their writings reflected the belief that wise management could manipulate resources in the best interests of society at large. Such assumptions had, of course, to be rethought in the light of the depression that followed the oil crisis of 1973. It became clear that cheap energy, low unemployment, political compromise and racial harmony no longer formed the scenario against which the human geography of Western

Europe was enacted. Authors subsequently recast their thoughts in a more pessimistic way (e.g. Clout 1981a) and sometimes adopted a much more political approach to regional problems (e.g. Carney, Hudson and Lewis 1980).

The present book does not propose such an overtly political standpoint but has certainly been written with the economic and social challenges of the 1980s in mind. It is presented in a thematic way and, rather than emphasizing the uniqueness of each of the eighteen nation-states of Western Europe, attempts to draw out common characteristics and shared problems, while always recognizing spatial variations in their expression. Geography, whatever else it may be, remains the study of areal differentiation; and hence maps and case studies represent important features of this book. The essays within it have been written by four university geographers who have wide experience of teaching and researching European matters. Three obtained their doctorates for research in Continental Europe and each has his own distinctive areal, linguistic and thematic expertise. The collection is edited by Hugh Clout, who also wrote the introduction and dealt with population and social change, tertiary activities, urban conditions and regional development. Mark Blacksell authored the sections on political evolution, recreation and conservation, and marine resources; Russell King wrote on migration and on agricultural matters; while David Pinder covered energy and manufacturing.

It has to be stressed that the book has been written in a selective, generalized way and at an introductory level, with a British undergraduate audience in mind. Only a minority of bibliographical items in languages other than English have been included. Each essay is concluded with some suggestions for further reading, while the consolidated bibliography at the end of the book lists a much fuller range. Place names are normally expressed in their conventional English form, except where they refer to planning regions (e.g. Bretagne) rather than broader geographical areas (e.g. Brittany). Likewise, 'West Germany' and 'East Germany' have been used rather than the 'Federal Republic of Germany' and the 'German Democratic Republic'. All the illustrations have been drawn by Tim Aspden, Claire Bourne, Anne Mason and Alick Newman in the Cartographic Unit at University College London, while manuscripts have been typed by many hands in different cities. The authors express their thanks to all involved for their assistance; to their students, for their criticisms, and to the Longman staff for their advice and encouragement in preparing this revised and enlarged edition.

Acknowledgements

We are grateful to the following for permission to reproduce copyright material:

Almqvist and Wiksell International our fig. 10.1 redrawn from fig. 1 (Kariel 1982); *Annales de Geographie* and the author, Prof. Alain Metton for fig. 7.4 (redrawn from Metton 1982). The author, Mrs. Marianne Carey for fig. 9.1 (Van Valkenburg and Held 1952); the Délégation à l'Aménagement du Territoire et à l'Action Régionale, Paris for fig. 7.5 (redrawn from DATAR originals); *The Economist* for figs. 3.5, 3.6 & 3.7 (each redrawn) and table 11.2 from *The Economist* (1.5.82, 20.2.82, 18.4.87, 6.11.82); the Controller of Her Majesty's Stationery Office for table 6.5 (Health & Safety Exec. 1979); the Organization for Economic Cooperation and Development, Paris for tables 5.12 & 5.13 (OECD Energy Statistics 1970–85), 4.1, 5.9, 6.3, 6.4, 10.3, 10.4 & 11.1; the Population Council for fig. 4.5 redrawn from a figure p. 35 (Bourgeois-Pichat 1981).

1

From Optimism to Uncertainty

Fundamental features

More attention has been devoted by geographers to Europe than to any similarly-sized portion of the earth's surface. Generations of scholars have described and analysed its diverse natural environment, the numerous human activities that it sustains and the complex imprints that they impart to its evolving cultural landscapes. Research monographs, textbooks and learned articles, replete with maps and statistical series, record these facts and interpretations in every language in use across the continent. The majority of these works are expressed at the scale of the nation-state, the region or the precise locality; only rarely do authors look to wider horizons and try to capture the fundamental essence of Europe (Mellor and Smith 1979).

Long and intimate knowledge of the continent and penetrating understanding of the minds of its geographers enabled W.R. Mead (1982) to produce such a distillation in a challenging and wide-ranging essay entitled 'The discovery of Europe'. It is his belief that the distinctiveness of Europe as a whole derives from an amalgam of physical geography, ethnography, technology, values and territorial organization. The physical resource base of this continent of peninsulas, isthmuses and islands, stretching from Mediterranean latitudes to beyond the Arctic Circle, is intricate and remarkably diverse, with localized resources often complementing those available in neighbouring areas. The assembled interdigitation of land and sea, successions of mountains, plains and valleys, arrays of soils, and gradations from maritime to continental climatic regimes are without parallel.

Nowhere else in the world is there comparable cultural complexity across such a relatively compact area, whether this is expressed with regard to tangible features, such as traditional house styles or field patterns, or in terms of language or religious tradition

(Fig. 1.1). In this respect, sharp lines on maps must be recognized as deceptive, since significant minority groups are to be found within apparently homogeneous cultural domains. Migration flows during many centuries have produced far more complicated meshes of language and religious tradition than Fig. 1.1 could possibly convey, with the recent arrival of migrants from North Africa, Asia and many other distant parts of the world providing striking examples.

Over the past two centuries, Europe has been the focus of technological innovation, cradling the 'industrial revolution', diffusing technical skills throughout the world, and experiencing the emergence of post-industrial civilization more intensely than elsewhere. Europeans flourished by virtue of their technical acumen and commercial expertise, with several nations amassing great empires by land or sea. The fruits of technology, colonialism and trade added even more advantages to those enjoyed by the dwellers of this already well-endowed part of the globe. Imperialism and commerce ensured that methods and techniques developed in Europe were adopted widely thoughout the world. The same processes contributed to the diffusion of shared European values, including inventiveness and democracy.

In addition, Europe bears the distinctiveness of an intense proliferation of nation-states of varying ethno-political status, ranging from one-nation federations (such as Austria and West Germany) and multi-ethnic units (such as Belgium and Switzerland) to one-nation states (such as France and Italy) (Fig. 1.1c). However, several one-nation states contain areas with autonomous status (e.g. Alto Adige, Sardinia, Sicily and the Val d'Aosta in Italy) or with special status with regard to bilingualism (e.g. Friesland in the Netherlands) or legal system (e.g Scotland in the UK). Europe's nation-states and their boundaries have undergone complex evolution through time, with the territorial imperative being at the heart of hundreds of the

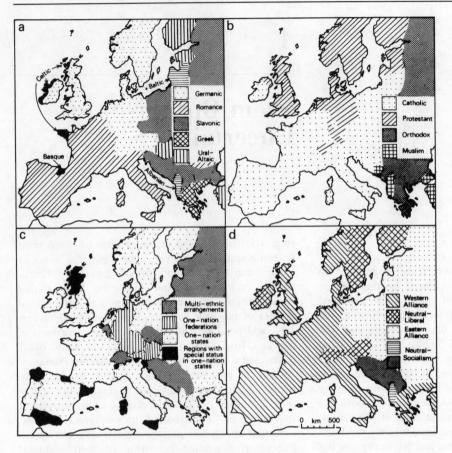

Fig. 1.1
Cultural indicators: (a)
language groups; (b) religious
tradition; (c) ethno-political
situation; (d) political blocs.

continent's wars, including the two world wars of our own century. Europe has a more elaborate patchwork of political boundaries and national 'systems' of administration and organization of ordinary life than any other continent (Jenkins 1986).

Nationality implies peripherality as well as centrality and Europe is endowed with areas of marginality along all of its political boundaries. None of these is sharper or harsher than the line that partitions nation-states and component regions of the old continent, stretching from the Atlantic to the Urals, into two fundamental blocs: the eastern and western alliances, with relatively few countries maintaining neutral positions (Fig. 1.1d). Of course, the east/west divide is not impervious, western travellers and tourists visit Eastern Europe, but significantly fewer East Europeans travel westwards. Radio and television are no respecters of political boundaries and television programmes transmitted in West Germany and Austria reach substantial parts of East Germany, Czechoslovakia, Hungary and Yugoslavia, while western radio programmes are received much further eastward. Nonetheless, in many respects the 'real

division of Europe' is between territories that look ultimately to Moscow or to Washington DC and is given most acute expression along the line of the 'Iron Curtain', regardless of whether that is composed of brick, concrete, barbed wire or minefield (Fontaine 1971). The chapters in this book concern themselves exclusively with economic and social conditions in the eighteen states located to the west of that critical line and with the lives of the 354 million Europeans who inhabit them.

Seen from the global perspective, Western Europe is composed of a set of 'old', predominantly urbanized and industrialized nations which are served by dense networks of transport and communication (Jordan 1973). Indeed, the population of Western Europe is older than that of any other continent, with West Germany and Denmark having the lowest fertility rate in the entire world. In West Germany there are already more than four pensioners for every ten workers; by the year 2030 their numbers may well be almost equal. West Europeans are rich, well-fed (even over-fed) and well educated. They live long, healthy and relatively comfortable lives, and display low levels

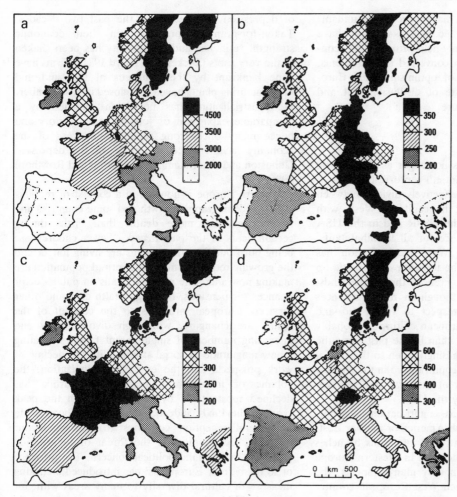

Fig. 1.2
Indicators of well-being:
(a) consumption of energy
(tonnes of oil equivalent/per
capita), 1984; (b) motor cars
per thousand population,
1984; (c) television sets per
thousand population, 1984;
(d) telephones per thousand
population, 1984.

of natural increase. Their agricultural systems are highly productive, regularly generating 'mountains' of surplus butter, grain and fruit and 'lakes' of surplus milk and wine which could relieve the suffering of the world's under-fed millions.

While acknowledging the general validity of this array of facts and perceptions, the mythical 'average' West European would insist that attention be drawn to at least three major qualifications. First, the countries to the west of the Iron Curtain display important spatial differences with regard to the affluence and well-being of their inhabitants (Ilbery 1986). Such features emerge clearly from analyses of per capita income, energy consumption, housing quality, health care, car ownership and a host of other indicators (Fig. 1.2). The broad dimensions of these differences are well known, with an affluent West European 'core' contrasting with a poorer Atlantic and Mediterranean 'periphery' (Ilbery 1984).

Second, these differences are simply spatially-packaged expressions of social differences with regard to employment, class and access to financial resources, educational capital and political power. 'Regional problems' do not exist of themselves, in splendid spatial isolation; they are just geographical expressions of more deeply-rooted social conditions which have grown in each specific political economy (Massey 1979). In the case of Western Europe, they cannot be divorced from the workings of capitalism in the late twentieth century (Carney, Hudson and Lewis 1980; Peet 1980; Williams 1987).

Third, many of the indicators that defined the strength and general well-being of Western Europe in the eyes of the world have undergone a drastic reversal in recent years. The 1950s and 1960s had been a period of unprecedented economic growth and political stability and West Europeans had been swept along in a tide of rising expectations, generally believing that they would enjoy even greater affluence in the years to come (Landes 1969). In the past two decades, such assumptions have become redundant. Widely-accepted facts of economic strength have become fables and commonly-held principles of economic supremacy have been converted into problems. After a protracted phase of optimism, West Europeans have entered a time of disillusionment and uncertainty about their future.

Changing conditions

In many ways the world is no longer as Eurocentric as it was earlier in the twentieth century. In terms of global strategy, Europe is effectively divided between the communist East and the capitalist West, with policy decisions taken in the USSR and in the USA being of ultimate significance for all its inhabitants. Since the Second World War, decolonization has brought independence to the territories that made up the empires of Belgium, France, the Netherlands, Portugal and the UK, although in many instances significant contacts with respect to trade, aid and education still survive. European culture is probably less unified and distinctive than in the past since the continent has become increasingly open to the rest of the world and the western countries are in the shadow of a partner and protector of vast size and unprecedented importance, namely the USA.

In the economic context, multi-national corporations, often based in North America or the Far East, have come to exercise control of numerous branches of manufacturing and business life in Western Europe (Lee and Ogden 1976). In very many respects, the dominating influence in each West European country in the post-war years has been that of the USA, rather than that of another European country or of Europe as a whole (Aron 1964). Dramatic changes in the world energy market since the end of 1973 have driven home even more forcibly the fact that West European nations are no longer the masters of their own destinies. As Sampson (1968) had stressed just a few years earlier, Europe was more than ever at the mercy of events, discoveries and decisions outside its frontiers. The decision by the Organization of Petroleum Exporting Countries (OPEC) members to abandon price-fixing arrangements with international oil corporations brought the era of cheap oil to an end. Crude oil prices tripled immediately and world-wide inflation began its dizzy course, ultimately producing recession in Western Europe and elsewhere in the oil-importing world.

After a phase of recovery following the Second World War and a remarkable period of low-cost growth in the 1950s and 1960s, the economies of Western Europe have been thrown into a condition of depression and decline in the past two decades. Taken-for-granted confidence in their economic strength, resilience and adaptability has been shaken to the very roots (Dicken and Lloyd 1981). Firms have gone bankrupt by the hundreds of thousand and manufacturing plants have been closed in vast number. De-industrialization has not been matched by a comparable expansion of jobs in other sectors and hence many once-strong regions and areas of the economy have entered the ranks of the depressed (Johnston and Doornkamp 1982; Martin and Rowthorn 1986).

Western Europe is now set in a context of remarkably low demographic growth and some countries and regions recorded more deaths than births during certain years in the past decade. Fewer children are being born but West Europeans are living longer and the growing requirements of the retired population are making new and quite necessary calls on public-sector finances for pensions, housing, health care and other services. European attitudes to the concept of the family are changing, with high divorce rates and increasing numbers of single-parent families creating a new magnitude of social strain. With the decline of work prospects and the end of decolonization, the volume of immigration to Western Europe has declined substantially by comparison with the peak years of the 1960s; indeed, attempts have been made by several reception countries to redirect labour migrants back home and the threat of repatriation gives rise to profound political concern. The presence of so many 'new Europeans' has introduced a striking measure of cultural diversity to many areas with, for example, Islam becoming an important new component in the religious complexion of Western Europe (Trébous 1980). To some extent the countries of the West have already become significantly multi-cultural, but this on-going process continues to be surrounded by serious social tensions which have their most painful expressions in inner-city environments.

It may be argued that West Europeans have become more politically conscious than in earlier decades and certainly there is an increasing trend for all aspects of planning and public administration to be enveloped in political challenge and debate. A growing number of people are expressing their concern for social justice and are attempting to exercise their political muscle in order to change the distribution of scarce resources to the benefit of those in need. Concern for the rights (actual or claimed) of specific sectors of society and for regional minority groups is being expressed more forcefully and sometimes violently. The rise of 'green' political parties, whose aims are imbued with the principles of ecology and conservation, reflects a growing concern for the world at large; and the critical moral issues surrounding the use of nuclear energy and the possession of nuclear deterrents are receiving wider public debate than ever before.

In the late 1980s, Western Europe finds itself in the apparently paradoxical situation of becoming both more united and more fragmented at the same time. The European Community has enlarged from the six original signatories of the Treaty of Rome (1957) to twelve member states, with Portugal and Spain joining in 1986, Turkey having applied and other Mediterranean states expressing interest. However, similarities of habit and behaviour are also accompanied by profound antagonisms and the Community is sharply divided over numerous budgetary and policy issues. At least one major political party is committed to withdrawal from the EC. Undoubtedly the Community of the Ten was not only a larger but a more problematical entity than the compact and rather more homogeneous Common Market of the Six. Certainly the entry of the Iberian nations in 1986, extending the Ten to the Twelve, has unleashed a formidable range of new difficulties.

Within individual nation-states many territorial minorities (the so-called 'old nations' of Europe) are expressing their desire for greater power for the management of their own affairs (Williams 1980). The very existence of such organizations manifests a basic lack of faith in the ability of national political systems to perceive and cope with economic, social and cultural questions in the outer regions during the painful transition to post-industrial conditions (De Rougement 1979). Autonomist or nationalist sentiments have emerged from Basques, Bretons, Catalans, Corsicans, Flemings, Scots, Walloons, Welshmen and from members of various other groups. It may be argued that recent trends for regionalization and devolution of power in Belgium, France and Spain have reduced the grasp of some centralized national administrations in some respects, but demands for greater regional power continue to be pressed in many parts of Western Europe and the problems of Northern Ireland remain particularly desperate (Boal and Douglas 1982). Repeated outbreaks of violence in Corsica since the early 1980s reflect the divergence of views between relatively liberal members of the island's new regional assembly and those held by political extremists belonging to the now outlawed liberation front. In Spain, the violent activities of ETA, the armed wing of the Basque separatist movement, have provoked widespread public outrage. French authorities have made serious efforts to dislodge suspected Basque guerillas from their traditional sanctuaries in neighbouring parts of the French Basque country along the Pyrenean border (see Fig. 2.2).

In many ways, Western Europe is more open and accessible than in the past. West Europeans now travel to neighbouring countries more easily than before, with growing prosperity, improved holiday benefits for workers, cheap air travel, package holidays and rising rates of car ownership in the 1950s and 1960s having guided the trend (see Ch. 10). Indeed, despite recent economic and social ills, the number of cars in Western Europe continued to rise from 68.9 million in 1971 to 116.9 million in 1984 (+ 70 per cent) at a rate that equalled the world average. This was surpassed substantially in the newly acquisitive societies of Greece, Portugal and Spain, while rates less than half the world average characterized the fairly 'saturated' car-owning societies of Denmark, Sweden and the UK.

Despite unemployment and profound economic difficulties, the number of tourists visiting the countries of Western Europe continued to rise each year during the 1970s, and in some respects tourism may be considered as one of the few growth activities in the current recession. The environments of many localities continue to undergo drastic remodelling to cater for the needs of tourists and many regional economies are highly dependent on their presence and purchasing power (Naylon 1967; Morris 1985; Morris and Dickinson 1987). Over 3 per cent of the workforce of the EC depends entirely on tourism for its livelihood and a further 7 per cent derives seasonal or part-time employment from it. However, it must be admitted that in the last few years there has been a noticeable trend for visitors to economize on their holiday budgets and to satisfy themselves with destinations closer to home than an extrapolation of the outward-thrusting trends of the 1960s might have led one to expect (Williams and Zelinsky 1970). Even so, 56 per cent of the citizens of the EC went away on holiday at least once during 1985 when tourism represented 5.5 per cent of the GDP of the nations of the Twelve.

In 1981, Italy, Spain and France occupied the leading places among the top ten West European nations for the arrival of foreign tourists and together accounted for 68 per cent of foreign inflows (Fig. 1.3). Some 26 per cent of tourists travelling to a destination in the top ten countries came from West Germany, with a further 21 per cent originating in France. Many tourist trips tend to be dominated by a dual quest for sunshine and 'the familiar' (especially in matters of food) but, nonetheless, each generation of West Europeans is undoubtedly visiting (if not always really experiencing) other parts of its native continent more

Millions of tourist
arrivals 1981

45
30
15
5

More than 1 million
arrivals from;

Rest of Europe	Eu
Rest of World	W
Great Britain	GB
Netherlands	N
W. Germany	D
Switzerland	CH
Portugal	P
Belgium	B
Austria	A
France	F
U.S.A.	US
Spain	Es

0   km   500

Fig. 1.3
Top ten West European
nations for the arrival of
foreign tourists, 1981.

frequently than members of every generation that preceded it. The European Commission is keen to assist further development of tourism in the Twelve by easing border checks, improving transport facilities, extending traditional holiday 'seasons', and encouraging rural, cultural and other less-familiar types of tourism, thereby boosting this form of activity in localities where economic initiatives are greatly needed.

The harsher than expected economic, social and political realities that many West Europeans are undergoing at this time of recession are literally brought into our gaze and into our living rooms by news and current affairs reporting on television and in the columns of the more serious newspapers. The geographical background to the European news of the day forms the substance of the chapters in this book. They do not claim to be all-embracing thematically,

nor can they dwell on the specificities of place or of organizational system in the eighteen countries of the West. Instead, they are written at a higher level of generalization, in full recognition of both the advantages and the limitations of such an approach.

Further reading

Carney J, Hudson R, Lewis J (eds) 1980 *Regions in Crisis*. Croom Helm, London

Hudson R, Rhind D, Mounsey H 1984 *An Atlas of EEC Affairs*. Methuen, London

Lee R, Ogden P E (eds) 1976 *Economy and Society in the EEC*. Saxon House, Farnborough

Mead W R 1982 The discovery of Europe. *Geography* **67**: 193–202

Williams A 1987 *The Western European Economy*. Hutchinson, London

2

Political evolution

Security, democracy and trade

For most of the twentieth century, the political geography of Western Europe has been undergoing a series of dramatic upheavals as the empires that were so dominant over the previous two hundred years gradually disintegrated (Tilly 1975). The fragmentation of the Austro-Hungarian, the German and the Ottoman Empires into a multitude of independent nation-states, not to mention the subsequent loss of world-wide colonial territories by Belgium, Britain, France, Germany, Italy, the Netherlands, Spain and Portugal, made a fundamental realignment and reassessment of Europe's global role in the latter half of the twentieth century inevitable (Smith 1978; Harris 1977).

Since 1945, the most obvious manifestation of these changed circumstances has been the ideological schism which has resulted in the continent being physically divided into two by the Iron Curtain. Western Europe is now allied closely to the political and economic ideals championed by the USA, while Eastern Europe is entirely under the influence of the communist ideology of the USSR. For more than a generation this division has stood seemingly immutable, although within each of the two spheres of influence evolution has been rapid, particularly in Western Europe.

Politically, the west has been guided by three overwhelming concerns. First, in the years immediately after the end of the Second World War when the Cold War was at its height, the need for collective security against both a resurgent Germany and the rapacious expansionism of the USSR was the prime objective. Despite some subsequent relaxation in the tensions caused by the threat of imminent attack, the need for collective security remains a powerful cohesive force throughout Europe, in the east as well as in the west (Gorbachev 1987).

Second, and linked closely to this joint response to a common threat, is a widespread desire to see democratic governments in all the individual states in Western Europe (Everling 1980). Great care was taken to ensure that democratic institutions replaced the paraphernalia of the Fascist dictatorships in both Germany and Italy after 1945, and the Western European nations as a group have sought successfully to exert pressure on any of their number with a totalitarian regime so as to ensure its demise. In Portugal, the successive dictatorships of Salazar and Caetano were overthrown by a military coup in 1974, to be followed rapidly by free elections, and in Spain the death of Franco in 1975 was the signal for an almost immediate return to democracy. In both cases, a desire to end the isolation imposed by their West European neighbours was important in contributing to the change. Equally in Greece where, after a coup in 1967, a military junta ruled until 1974, international disapproval and actual exclusion from most areas of European decision making in the European Community, the Council of Europe and the North Atlantic Treaty Organization were critical factors in ensuring that the suspension of democratic rule was only an interlude (Georgakopoulos 1980). Subsequently, in Turkey, where there was a successful *coup d'état* in 1980, intense international pressure eventually persuaded the government to hold democratic elections.

The third of the cohesive forces has been a general determination to reduce and, if possible, abolish the multiplicity of trade quotas and tariffs that existed between European states in the years immediately after the end of the Second World War. Throughout the 1950s and 1960s, negotiations were entered into at a number of different levels within the framework of the General Agreement on Tariffs and Trade, the Organization for Economic Cooperation and Development (and its predecessor the Organization for European Economic Cooperation), the European Economic Community and the European Free Trade

Association with the result that by the 1970s there was almost completely free movement of industrial goods within Western Europe and, indeed, among all the major western trading nations (Hechter and Brustein 1980). So long as the economies of all the individual countries were generally expanding in the affluent years during the 1960s, successful extensions of the principles of free trade were relatively easy to achieve. But it is indicative of the strength of the commitment to this principle that even in the recession of the late 1970s and early 1980s, triggered initially by the trebling of the price of crude oil in 1973, the fundamental structure of free trade within Western Europe remained virtually unscathed. Indeed, within the European Community, commitment to it is stronger than ever, with a single internal market embracing all twelve member states realistically in prospect by 1992.

To describe the desire for collective security, democracy and free trade as three separate forces is in some respects misleading: essentially they are different manifestations of a remarkable sense of purpose that has broadly united Western Europe in the recent past. The major political test now facing this region is to see whether it is possible to extend the close economic cooperation that has been achieved among the northern industrialized nations to the less developed agricultural societies in the Mediterranean Basin (Tovias 1979). Success will almost certainly lead to an even greater degree of political and economic integration, but failure could result in a deepening split between rich and poor nations, ultimately encouraging political rivalry and dissension.

The North Atlantic Treaty Organization and collective security

NATO is the embodiment of the desire throughout Western Europe for a common defence front against any threat, either external or internal, to the democratically-elected governments in the region. The prime danger has always been seen as the USSR and this continues to be the case, but in the late 1940s and early 1950s a subsidiary objective was also to guard against the possibility, however remote, of renewed totalitarian aggression in Germany, or indeed anywhere else in Western Europe.

Somewhat surprisingly, given the ferocity and destruction of the Second World War, the need for a formal expression in the shape of a common defence treaty was not immediately apparent to the victorious western allies in 1945. In the euphoria that prevailed at the end of six years of conflict it was rather naively assumed that the United Nations and its Charter, to which all the European states were signatories,

provided sufficient guarantees of protection. Such hopes were, of course, short-lived; the repeated attempts at destabilization by the Communist Party, not only in what are now generally referred to as the countries of Eastern Europe, but also in Greece and Turkey and even Belgium and France, caused great alarm both in Western Europe and in the USA and evoked a decisive strategic response. The United States Congress accepted the Truman Doctrine in 1947, thus pledging American support for free peoples anywhere who were resisting subjugation by armed minorities or outside pressure. The first beneficiaries of this new commitment were Greece and Turkey, where communist putsches were effectively extinguished thanks to military and economic aid from the USA. In north-west Europe, Belgium, France, Luxembourg, the Netherlands and the UK signed the Brussels Treaty in 1948, guaranteeing the support of all should any one of their number be attacked.

Wherever the Communist Party had tried to secure support in free elections, as in Berlin in 1946, it had fared badly and this fact, together with the initiatives described above, drove the USSR into taking unilateral action. On 24 June 1948, it imposed the Berlin Blockade and threatened to precipitate just the kind of confrontation that the Brussels Treaty had been designed to combat. For their part, the Americans sought to widen the concept of collective security beyond Western Europe so that it would include Canada and the USA as well and thus encompass the whole of the North Atlantic area. The idea was widely welcomed and NATO was born in the spring of 1949. The original members were the five signatories of the Brussels Treaty, together with the USA and Canada and five additional European nations: Denmark, Iceland, Italy, Norway and Portugal. In 1952, Greece and Turkey were admitted, along with West Germany in 1955. Since then, membership has changed little. France withdrew from the military committee, though not the alliance itself, in 1966 and Spain became a full member in 1981 (Fig. 2.1).

NATO has always been first and foremost a military alliance, built around the concept of collective security. An armed attack against any one of the signatories in either Europe or North America would be considered as an attack against them all. The geographical scope of the treaty is defined very precisely as the territory of any of the member nations and islands administered by them north of the Tropic of Cancer. It also covers attacks on ships and aircraft in the North Atlantic and Mediterranean areas.

The organization is, however, more than just a military pact: it provides for cooperation in a much wider field and has always been seen as a means of

Fig. 2.1
European institutions.

defending a way of life, not only by military might, but also by joint action in political, social and economic matters. One of the most important instances of such cooperation was the attitude of the organization to the membership of West Germany. When agreement was reached in 1954 that the new state should be allowed to join as a full member, the other signatories to the treaty also implicitly accepted the Federal Republic's own controversial view of its status as the only legitimate German state with the right of representation for the whole of the German nation, whether in Western or Eastern Europe. This meant that the German Democratic Republic (East Germany) was not recognized in any shape or form and was a crucial factor in formalizing the political confrontation in Europe and the influence of the Iron Curtain between west and east (Blacksell 1982).

Until the middle of the 1960s, NATO was overwhelmingly concerned with containing the political and military threat posed by the USSR. There was little open dissension among the member states and private misgivings were put aside in the face of brutal acts of repression, such as the invasion of Hungary by Soviet troops in 1956. This unity was extremely important, because it supported the prevailing orthodoxy that world politics in the middle of the twentieth century was a matter for negotiation between the two super powers – the USA and the USSR.

Nevertheless, there was always a degree of unease in Western Europe about the wisdom of identifying so closely with the USA, and gradually a view began to gain ground that NATO was a positive impediment to the relaxation of international tension. Pre-eminent among the doubters was France under the strong leadership of its President De Gaulle. He had an alternative vision of the distribution of political power, preferring a European axis linking Paris to Moscow, rather than what he saw as the Anglo-Saxon domination of NATO. In March 1966, when all French forces were withdrawn from the NATO command, even though France formally remained a member of the alliance, the administrative facilities in France had to be moved, the military headquarters going to Brussels, the Defence College to Rome and the Central European Command to Brassum in the Netherlands. Although French disenchantment had been apparent for some years, the actual withdrawal came as a shock to the other members, undermining the fundamental unity of purpose and weakening the self-confidence of the whole alliance.

Further evidence of reassessment elsewhere in Western Europe was provided by the Ostpolitik of the SPD/FDP coalition headed by Chancellor Willi Brandt, which came to power in 1969 in West Germany (Sallnow and John 1982; Blacksell and Brown 1983). It was the first time that the socialists had ever been the party of government and they were eager to demonstrate both their independence and their capacity for new initiatives. A whole series of treaties and non-aggression pacts were negotiated with the countries of Eastern Europe, including one with the USSR in 1972. A dialogue was also started with East Germany which led to the signing of a Basic Treaty (Grundvertag), the first step in normalizing diplomatic relations between the two states. While it was always strenuously denied that these developments were intended in any way to undermine the status of NATO, inevitably they represented a softening of the antagonistic stance that had prevailed hitherto towards Eastern Europe.

It is probable that NATO's cohesion would have been more seriously undermined had it not been for the invasion of Czechoslovakia in 1968 by armies from the Warsaw Treaty Organization. The ruthless suppression of the tentative attempts by the Czechs to broaden their contacts with their Western European neighbours was a sharp reminder to the NATO allies that talk of political and military realignment in Europe as a whole was still very premature.

Even so, the 1970s were still the era of the alliance's greatest weakness. The military junta that took power by force in Greece in 1967 severely dented the general belief in the ultimate, inevitable triumph of democracy. It also meant that Greece was no longer able to play a full part in NATO's defensive commitments. In 1976, a rumbling territorial dispute between Greece and Turkey over Cyprus and various other islands in the Aegean Sea was only narrowly prevented from erupting into war (Rustow and Penrose 1981). It was another crack in the facade of unity, which had been such a feature of the early years of the alliance. Further, more minor evidence of internal conflict was the so-called Cod War of 1972–73 over fishing rights in territorial waters between Iceland, the UK and to

a lesser degree West Germany (Mitchell 1976). Perhaps the most serious blow to NATO's prestige, however, was in the form of increasingly frequent negotiations between the USSR and the USA over reductions in nuclear armaments, which took place outside the framework of the alliance. At the time it was organized in 1975, the European Security Conference in Helsinki was heralded as the greatest single step towards military detente in Europe during this century.

Recently, NATO has enjoyed a considerable and rather unexpected revival. The invasion by the USSR of Afghanistan in 1980 and its shadowy and sinister role in the imposition of martial law in Poland in 1981 succeeded in reawakening many of the fears of the Cold War in relations between Western and Eastern Europe and certainly rekindled interest in the health of NATO among its member countries. A measure of the revival was the fact that Spain, after much agonizing, became the thirteenth member in May 1981 (Minet, Siotis and Tsakaloyannis 1981). Such a move had been debated ever since the end of the Franco dictatorship in 1975, but fears of being too closely identified with the foreign policy of the USA had always caused the government to draw back from actually signing the treaty. The growing tension in the relations between east and west finally decided the Spanish government in favour of joining and, although subsequently there has been a referendum on the issue, Spain remains a full member of the alliance. Ironically, the renewed interest in agreement between the USA and the USSR on nuclear disarmament, which has to date produced a treaty limiting medium-range missiles, has only served to strengthen NATO. Modern conventional forces, organized collectively within Western Europe, are now, more than ever, seen as the key to long-term security.

NATO remains, after nearly forty years, one of the most influential of the international groupings in Western Europe (Russett 1971). The individual states have little option but to depend for their defence on a collective security agreement, and NATO is the only realistic alternative. Even so there are a number of countries that choose not to join. Malta and Cyprus are too small to have their own armed forces and therefore would have little to contribute to the organization. Switzerland, Sweden and the Republic of Ireland have all historically pursued a policy of neutrality and feel that membership would compromise their stance (Fig. 1.1d). Finland and Austria are both required to be neutral as part of the agreement which enabled them to emerge as independent states from occupation at the end of the Second World War. Despite these exceptions and continuing doubts in some Mediterranean countries, notably Greece and Spain, NATO is still a strong unifying force providing a thread of cohesion and a sense of identity of purpose throughout the region.

A common culture and the search for a European identity

The Council of Europe

Fear of Soviet aggression is not the only pressure drawing the countries of Western Europe closer together; in the latter half of the twentieth century there has been a strong sense of the need to develop a European identity and to stress the positive features of a shared culture. The movement has developed a number of institutional forms over the last four decades, with varying degrees of success. Most have been primarily concerned with economic cooperation, but some have taken wider terms of reference. The most ambitious conceptually is the Council of Europe which was set up in 1949 with a view to achieving unity between its members so as to safeguard their common heritage and facilitate social and economic progress. The original members were Belgium, Denmark, France, Italy, Luxembourg, the Netherlands, Norway, the Republic of Ireland, Sweden and the UK, but they were joined subsequently by Greece (1949), Iceland, Turkey, the Saar and West Germany (1950), Austria (1956), Cyprus (1961), Switzerland (1963), Malta (1965), Portugal (1976), Spain (1977) and Liechtenstein (1978), so that the Council now encompasses the whole of Western Europe with the exception of Finland and the microstates of Andorra, Monaco and the Vatican (Catudal 1975) (Fig. 2.1).

The broad scope of the Council is one of its strengths, for it can truly claim to speak for Western Europe as a whole, but it has also proved one of its severest limitations, for among twenty-one members the areas of agreement and cooperation tend, almost inevitably, to be general and unspecific, making difficult the formulation of detailed policies. There is, however, universal acceptance of the need for democracy and the protection of individual human rights, and states have proved to be surprisingly sensitive to censure by the Council in these matters. Greece's membership was suspended between 1969 and 1974 while the country was ruled by the military junta and neither Portugal nor Spain were able to join so long as they were governed by dictatorships. Equally, violations of human rights are regularly investigated and if necessary criticized by the European Court of Human Rights established in 1958, and in most instances member countries have been quick to remedy any shortcomings identified.

The progress made by the Council towards institutional initiatives leading to formal integration has been disappointing and in recent years has caused the organization to be edged out of the mainstream of political reorganization in Western Europe. The Council has never acted as a forum, let alone a focus, for the debate about economic cooperation, and the sensitivity of some members about any reference to national defence resulted in the subject being the only one specifically excluded from consideration by the founding statute. This was in deference to the same neutral nations – Austria, the Republic of Ireland, Sweden and Switzerland – which found it impossible to join NATO and would have refused to have anything to do with the Council of Europe had there been the slightest suspicion that it might encompass military matters. The lack of agreement about a substantive agenda for discussion and the tacit acceptance that controversial matters should not be debated if there was a chance that they might cause members to leave have been the main limitations on the Council's effectiveness. On the other hand, it has meant that there has always been a forum in Western Europe where any state could air its concerns at governmental level, a virtue well-illustrated by the Council's unwavering support for democracy in Greece.

Nordic initiatives

For the four Scandinavian states – Denmark, Finland, Norway and Sweden – together with Iceland, the Council of Europe has never offered a wholly satisfactory answer to their desire for closer political cooperation (Smidelius and Wiklund 1979). Nordic unity has a sporadic history reaching back to the late fourteenth century, but it really acquired popular appeal, if not tangible success, in the nineteenth century. The first really significant recent development was the setting up of the Nordic Council in 1952. It was a loose-built ministerial forum that was convened about once a year and most of its achievements have been the result of the endeavours of permanent committees of civil servants working under the Council's general guidance. Not surprisingly, the most progress has been made on detailed issues such as customs control, railway freight tariffs, vehicle insurance and the free movement of labour; larger and politically more sensitive issues have proved much more intractable. Nevertheless, citizens of all five member countries can move freely throughout any part of Scandinavia and have the right to seek work wherever they wish. For unskilled and semi-skilled jobs, this principle was quickly established but, in common with other parts of Europe, it proved much more difficult to gain agreement about the inter-changeability of professional qualifications. It was not until the late 1960s that all restrictions were finally removed (Turner and Nordquist 1982).

Even within this relatively homogeneous group of countries with a long history of cooperation, progress towards integration has not always been smooth (Smidelius and Wiklund 1979). The political constraints placed upon Finland as part of the price for the ending of Soviet wartime occupation prevented it from joining the Nordic Council until 1955. More recently there have been considerable problems raised by the differing approaches adopted by the Scandinavian countries towards closer economic cooperation with the rest of Europe and the European Community.

In the 1960s, when all but Iceland belonged to the European Free Trade Association but none to the European Community, a separate customs union in Scandinavia seemed a desirable and an achievable objective. Nordek was agreed in principle in 1969, but as the details began to be debated the whole idea lost favour as the disadvantages of economic union to individual countries began to be apparent. Eventually, Finland withdrew in 1970 and the concept foundered when Denmark became a member of, and all the other Scandinavian countries concluded separate trade agreements with, the European Community in 1973.

Despite the disappointment of Nordek, Scandinavian cooperation continued and alternative initiatives were sought. In 1971, a Nordic Council of Ministers was set up under the terms of the Helsinki Treaty and one of its first acts was to secure agreement that each member country would follow the existing Danish example and appoint a Minister for Nordic Affairs. Although these appointments have been of fairly low rank in the majority of cases, there is still a solid list of achievements for the corporate approach. Progress on commercial and legal harmonization has continued: there is a joint policy on development aid; and electricity production and distribution throughout Scandinavia are coordinated through a single body (Nordel). Finally in 1976, after long and difficult negotiations about how much each country should contribute, the Nordic Investment Bank was established. Forty-five per cent of the capital has been put up by Sweden, 22 per cent by Denmark, 16 per cent each from Norway and Finland, and 1 per cent from Iceland. By the end of 1985 it had provided loans of more than $500 million for investment projects ranging from a plant to produce glue for a chipboard factory in eastern Finland to the restructuring of the aluminium industry in Norway and Sweden. The amount of money involved is not large when compared with the combined GNP of the five countries, but it does represent a tangible token of a genuine desire for closer cooperation.

Regional groups, borders and languages

Undoubtedly the predominant trend in Western Europe in the recent past has been towards closer cooperation, but this has not been exclusively the case. Given the large number of small states and the turbulent history of the region in the nineteenth and early twentieth centuries, it would have been surprising had the political boundaries and resulting allegiances been universally accepted without dissent and this was far from being the case (Williams 1980). Minority languages such as Welsh, Breton and Flemish have acted as the catalyst for a number of struggles to prevent cultural identities being swamped by the seductive attractions of large-scale political groupings (Stephens 1978; Teumis 1978). It is worth emphasizing too that many such regional groups, as for example the Scots in Scotland, represent populations and areas larger than some of the independent states in Western Europe (Webb 1978). Even so, most of the disagreements have been relatively trivial in the context of the political changes taking place in the continent as a whole, though not of course to the particular groups involved.

The aftermath of the Second World War left a number of unresolved border issues in its wake, though all those in Western Europe now appear to have been settled amicably (Fig. 2.2). It was uncertain whether the Saar should be incorporated into France or West Germany; whether the South Tyrol should be part of Austria or Italy; and where the boundary between Italy and Yugoslavia should run. Eventually, after a plebiscite, the population of the Saar elected to become part of West Germany; after a number of years of intermittent guerilla activity, the existing boundary between Austria and Italy in the Tyrol was accepted; and in 1979 a final line was agreed for the boundary between Italy and Yugoslavia ensuring that the much disputed city of Trieste was incorporated into Italy.

There are a number of other disputes which are of longer standing, have deeper roots and for which, in most cases, a lasting solution has proved more elusive. Most involve a small minority in a state with the remnants of a distinctive culture and language in danger of being swamped by the domineering majority. In the northern part of Belgium, the population is predomi-

Fig. 2.2
Selected regional minorities
in Western Europe.

nantly Flemish speaking, but in the south French is the norm (Ashworth 1980). Although the state is officially bilingual, the conflict between the two factions has been extremely acrimonious and on several occasions in recent years has threatened the stability of the national government (Stephenson 1972; Hill 1974).

The United Kingdom, as its name implies, is an amalgam of various national groups, and the Scots, the Welsh and the Irish have all at times felt that their interests and their culture have been poorly served by the predominantly English government in London. In Northern Ireland the division is particularly serious, because there is an overlay of bitter religious conflict between the Roman Catholic minority and the Protestant majority, a problem unresolved by the partition of Ireland in 1922. Since the late 1960s, there has been an intermittent state of undeclared war in the province but, somewhat ironically, the short-term result has been to tie Northern Ireland even more closely to the central government in London. For fifty years it exer-

cised autonomy over most of its internal affairs, but the growing civil unrest caused nearly all these powers to be suspended in 1972 in favour of direct rule from London. Since then, repeated attempts to restore a devolved government have been frustrated by the continuing conflict (Boal and Douglas 1982).

In Scotland and Wales, power has never been devolved in the same way, but in the 1970s there was strong political pressure for greater autonomy. At one time it seemed probable that regional assemblies, not unlike the one which had once existed in Northern Ireland, would be set up, but in 1978 the proposals for such a change were defeated in regional referenda, in Wales overwhelmingly so.

The fact that such changes were eventually shown to lack general public support is not of great significance in the wider context of Western Europe as a whole, but their rejection did re-emphasize the widespread support for integration as opposed to fragmentation. Nor was this expression of opinion restricted to the UK. In France, Breton nationalism had briefly threatened to become an important political force, but here too a short period of ascendancy was followed by a rapid decline. Nonetheless, nationalist objectives continue to give rise to serious problems in Corsica (Kofman 1982).

Spain is another country in Western Europe where, at the present time, regional divisions seem unlikely to be solved either peacefully or quickly. The return of democratic government in 1975 after more than forty years of Franco's dictatorship revived the political aspirations of several of the country's regions (Ling 1973). In north-western Spain the people of the Basque country have long hankered after independence and have pursued a persistent and often violent campaign to gain acceptance for their cause. Similar, though less well-organized, movements have also begun to flourish in Catalonia in north-eastern Spain and in Andalusia in the south.

If their cases are to come to general attention at all, minority groups have to exploit every possible means of attracting publicity for their causes. As a result it is often easy to overestimate their true significance or the extent of their popular support. In Western Europe as a whole, governments over the past four decades have been at pains to pursue an ultimate goal of European unity, believing presumably that the things binding the various countries together are stronger and more important then those that divide them.

Free trade and the road to economic integration

Early moves

If cultural unity in the sense that Jean Monnet used the term when he was trying to gain support for his concept of a United States of Europe in the 1940s has remained elusive, real progress has been at the rather more prosaic level of economic integration. In the late 1940s there was widespread frustration and dissatisfaction with the complex network of tariffs and quotas which seriously inhibited trade, and a general consensus emerged that if they could be dismantled and replaced by a system of free trade, then this would provide the stimulus for a much-needed economic revival.

In fact, the dissatisfaction and general recognition of the need for change can be traced back to well before the outbreak of the Second World War, but it was only in its aftermath that significant progress began to be made. Throughout the years of conflict the USA had poured aid across the Atlantic with a

view to freeing Europe as a whole rather than any individual country. Despite some initial reluctance and hesitation, the American government also agreed with an almost overwhelming generosity to secure the peace, as it had financed the war, by continuing the flow of economic aid in the form of both money and raw materials. The main instrument was the European Recovery Programme, widely referred to as the Marshall Plan, mooted in 1947 and put into operation the following year. Between 1948 and 1952, the equivalent of $13 500 million were distributed under the aegis of the programme and eventually these resources did provide the intended stimulus necessary for the revival of the shattered industrial economies of Western Europe (Blacksell 1981).

Initially, however, considerable problems were raised by the American gesture, because no Europe-wide institution existed for managing the distribution of monies among the individual states. The impasse was finally broken by the creation of the Organization for European Economic Cooperation (OEEC) (Fig. 2.1), the main initial task of which was to devise a formula for sharing out Marshall Aid. In common with virtually all the other umbrella organizations founded at this time, the OEEC also had a broader and more grandiose objective of recreating a sound and viable European economy. It sought to achieve this by facilitating free trade and, as far as possible, removing all barriers to the movement of goods among its member countries. The strategy had two distinct, though closely linked, aspects: the removal of tariffs and quotas on trade and the maintenance of stable currency exchange rates.

Progress on both was spectacular and by the late 1950s there was almost total free trade in industrial goods and the currencies of all the member states were freely convertible. The latter in particular was a momentous achievement, due almost entirely to the success of a subsidiary of the OEEC, the European Payments Union (EPU), which provided for the multilateral settlement of trading accounts and also provided guarantees to ensure the stability of the weaker currencies. In practice, the EPU meant that rather than each state having to settle every trade transaction with any other in an acceptable (hard) currency, it could calculate the sum of all its transactions with the whole group and settle the account on a monthly basis. The problems caused by fluctuations in the value of individual European currencies were overcome by the EPU guarantees. The system provided precisely the kind of stability and reduction in bureaucracy which enabled international trade in an expanding economy to flourish. The average increase in the volume of trade in real terms throughout the

OEEC countries in the decade 1950 to 1960 was 47 per cent, and all the members, except for Iceland and Turkey, shared in the improvement. There was, however, considerable variation, with West Germany (182 per cent) and Austria (104 per cent) recording increases well above the norm. There is little doubt that the success of the EPU was one of the outstanding achievements in the whole process of political and economic integration, and the speed and lack of acrimony with which it was created contrast starkly with the wrangling and long drawn-out argument that has preceded many later developments.

By the end of the 1950s, the OEEC had accomplished all its major objectives and its exclusively West European orientation was coming to be something of an impediment. The member countries wanted to see the principles of free trade extended world-wide and to be in a position to deal with the other major western trading nations on a more equal footing. In 1958 the EPU was superseded by the European Monetary Agreement which extended the scope of the EPU arrangement beyond Europe to the whole of the pound sterling and French franc areas and, at the same time, most West European currencies became freely convertible with the US dollar. The changes meant that barriers to international trade between all the main industrial nations of the non-communist world were reduced to a level that had never previously been possible. In 1961, the OEEC itself was wound up and replaced by the Organization for Economic Cooperation and Development (OECD), which eventually numbered the USA, Finland, Canada, Japan and Australia among its members. This new organization provided the framework for sustaining economic growth through trade and sought to spread the benefits of industrialization to the developing world by drawing the economically less-developed countries more closely into the system of international trade. Throughout the 1960s the OECD was generally judged to be highly successful, but in the last decade it has not proved so effective at protecting developing countries from the effects of economic depression in the industrial nations and at ensuring a fairer distribution of wealth between rich and poor countries. The OECD is also not an exclusively European organization; the focus of its work is global, rather than concentrating on promoting the economic health of one particular area.

It would be misleading to give the impression that the enthusiasm for European integration came mainly from the USA, because it wanted to see economic recovery without the political complications of having to deal with a multiplicity of different governments. The attractions of closer cooperation have been obvious to most shades of European opinion for a long time, and the Western European governments themselves have made by far the most significant long-term contribution to integration in the form of the European Community.

The seeds of this initiative go back as far as 1921 when the Belgium and Luxembourg governments agreed to remove all restrictions on trade and commerce between their two countries. In 1944, the Dutch government in exile in London decided to join the arrangement, although the decision did not take effect until 1948, well after the end of the Second World War. The Benelux agreement, as it was called, was only a small beginning among three of the smallest states in Western Europe, but it was nevertheless of considerable importance. The emphasis on free trade, primarily in industrial goods, did much to set the tone of the subsequent more comprehensive initiatives which flourished in the general atmosphere of economic buoyancy and expansion that pervaded the 1950s and 1960s.

The European Community

Preliminaries

The origins of the European Community as such have their roots in the chaotic political and economic aftermath of the Second World War. The industrial nations of north-west Europe had been severely disrupted by the conflict and one of the essential prerequisites for revival was the creation of a more integrated and mutually interdependent industrial structure. The critical stumbling block was finding an acceptable way of readmitting Germany to the industrial system without allowing it to develop the political means once more to threaten the peace. The urgency of finding a solution was increased, because by 1950 the USA was heavily involved in another war under the auspices of the United Nations in Korea, and there was a world-wide shortage of steel for manufacturing military supplies. In this situation it was somewhat perverse not to be exploiting German and other European capacity to the full for rather doctrinaire political reasons.

The deadlock was broken by the French, a number of whose leading politicians had been advocating greater political and economic integration in Europe for a number of years. Their Foreign Minister, Robert Schuman, proposed the setting up of a European Coal and Steel Community (ECSC) in 1950, primarily to manage jointly the coal, iron and steel production of France and Germany, but open to any of the industrial countries in north-west Europe. Enthusiasm for the

plan varied. The newly-formed Federal Republic of
Germany (West Germany) was very enthusiastic, as
it rightly considered that membership of such an
organization would confer a measure of much-needed
political respectability. The Benelux countries all
welcomed the idea as an extension of their own supranational initiatives. Italy was also more than ready to
take part because of the implied international
approval that membership would bring in its wake. On
the other hand, the UK, then the largest industrial
country in Europe, was distinctly luke-warm fearing,
in particular, that its recently nationalized coal and
steel industries might find difficulty in adjusting to
such an ambitious multilateral venture.

Despite the reservations of the UK, the ECSC was
set up by the Treaty of Paris, with Belgium, France,
West Germany, Italy, Luxembourg and the Netherlands as members, and came into operation on 1
August 1952. It rapidly set about removing restrictions
on production and trade in coal and iron and steel
products and watched over a rapid expansion in the
volume of trade in all the industries involved. There
is considerable doubt about the extent to which the
ECSC actually managed the revival of heavy industry
or was simply a mechanism for formally removing
barriers to trade which would have fallen in any case.
Certainly the organization found it difficult to resist
protective measures used by member governments
who felt that 'free trade' in their own products would
benefit from judicious subsidies. Freight rates on the
mainly nationalized European railway systems were
and are regularly manipulated to confer advantages on
domestic industries. Equally, price fixing among the
major producers was also difficult both to detect and
to control. In the latter part of the 1950s, the apparent
inability of the ECSC to manage the declining markets
for coal, iron and steel in the member countries and
its failure to take remedial measures of sufficient scale
to avoid the consequences of depression in the traditional heavy industrial regions, such as the Borinage
in Belgium and the Nord-Pas de Calais in France,
raised serious doubts about its true effectiveness.

In the early 1950s, however, the initial expansion
of both production and trade led to something
approaching euphoria among the member states and
a desire to see further steps towards European integration. Their attention turned to defence and the
possibility of establishing a European Defence
Community but, after a first flush of enthusiasm for
the idea in 1952, political objections to such a pooling
of strategic resources began to multiply. Eventually,
both Italy and France, the prime mover of the original
proposal, failed to ratify the draft treaty and the whole
project was abandoned in 1954.

The Treaties of Rome

The collapse of the European Defence Community
was a serious blow and at the time it appeared that
the prospects for progress towards unity were dim, yet
within two years a much more ambitious set of
proposals was agreed. In 1957, the six members of the
ECSC signed two Treaties of Rome to take effect
from 1 January 1958, one creating the European
Economic Community (EEC), the other the European
Atomic Energy Community (Euratom). Once again,
overtures to the UK to join had proved unsuccessful
and the Communities therefore retained their rather
narrow geographical focus.

Of the two new organizations, one, the EEC, was
to provide the springboard for a process of integration, both economic and political, that is still in full
spate. The other, Euratom, was to prove something
of an irrelevance as the early promise of nuclear
energy was beset with technical problems and
burgeoning competition from oil.

As its name suggests, the EEC was concerned
primarily with reducing still further the barriers to
trade within Western Europe and, like the ECSC, was
born as much out of the immediate economic requirements of France and West Germany as out of any
more lofty commitment to the ideal of integration.
France was eager to have freer access for its large
farming industry to the markets in the industrial cities
of Germany, while the Federal Republic wanted a
larger share of the French consumer market for its
manufactured goods. The Treaty of Rome reflects
these interests, but contains a very wide range of
provisions for creating a broadly-based, integrated
economy in the Community, covering such matters as
a customs union, common policies for agriculture and
transport, joint initiatives for social security and development aid, and the harmonization of the different
legal systems. In the event, however, it was in the
promotion of free trade and the formulation of a
common agricultural policy that the EEC was most
active in its early years.

Trade

In striving for the abolition of tariffs and quotas within
the EEC, the members were only reflecting the more
general moves to free trade that were being pursued
simultaneously in Western Europe as a whole by the
OEEC and on an even wider global basis by the
General Agreement on Tariffs and Trade. The EEC
policy was, however, much more comprehensive in
that its objective was a customs union, which meant
that not only would restrictions on trade within the

Community be abolished, but also that there would also be a common tariff wall to the world outside. As far as industrial goods were concerned, the common tariff posed little problem because of the more general moves to reduce restrictions, but where agricultural products were concerned the situation was very different. The majority of West European countries had traditionally enacted strong measures to protect their domestic farming economies and anything approaching free trade would have wrought havoc with this carefully manipulated section of the economy. For this reason the creation of the customs union had to go hand in hand with the formulation and implementation of a common agricultural policy.

The initial timetable agreed by the EEC suggested that the customs union should be introduced in a series of stages and be fully operational by the beginning of 1970. The problem was that after a good start, the parallel agreement on a common agricultural policy proved much more difficult to achieve. Rather than simply removing a set of restrictions, in the case of agriculture it was necessary to agree a framework of subsidy and support for farmers in six different countries and to devise a policy for imports and exports for the whole Community. For the French, who laid the greatest store by a common agricultural policy, the delays caused first frustration and then fury, and in 1965 they threatened to withdraw from the EEC completely if agreement was not reached. The threat was obviously effective, because by the middle of 1967 common guaranteed price levels were in operation for most of the major agricultural products. The impasse was solved by the relatively simple stratagem of agreeing guaranteed minimum price levels for all products no less than the highest minimum price guarantees previously operating in any individual country. It was to prove an effective but extremely expensive solution which, although it ensured the continued survival of the EEC, meant that the bulk of the budget was committed to agricultural support. Inevitably, this in turn meant that other positive policies had little chance of becoming successfully established, a fact that in the long term has seriously blunted the effectiveness of the European Community as a whole (Inglehart 1971).

Once agreement on agriculture had been reached, the implementation of the customs union posed few problems and by 1 July 1968 all tariffs within the Community had been completely abolished, eighteen months ahead of the original timetable. The EEC was by this juncture far more than just a statement of intent by six countries since they had transferred major aspects of their economic policy-making from a national to a Community level. It was not surprising that there should have been a concurrent desire to strengthen the structure of the organization and, on 1 July 1967, the ruling authorities of all three communities (the ECSC, the EEC and Euratom) were merged into a single European Community (the EC), thus tightening yet further the bonds between the member countries.

Beyond the Community

Elsewhere in Western Europe, the emerging cohesion of the European Community was watched with a mixture of concern and envy. While other countries had chosen not to join rather than being directly excluded, the success of the new organization clearly altered their relationship both with the Community's members and with each other (Puchala 1971). Largely to counter the diversion of trade that seemed likely to result from the establishment of the customs union, a second group of countries constituted themselves as the European Free Trade Association (EFTA) in 1960. The driving force behind the initiative was the UK which, though it had declined to join the European Community for a combination of political and economic reasons, was nonetheless alarmed at the prospective consequences of being excluded from European markets. EFTA was a body with a single overriding objective of stimulating free trade between its members. It was not interested in creating a customs union or interfering in any other way with the relationships of member countries towards other states and it claimed to have no supranational ambitions. This enabled it to embrace a wide spectrum of opinion, from countries like Sweden, Switzerland and Austria which were politically neutral, to the UK which had long-standing preferential trade agreements for agricultural products with non-European Commonwealth countries. EFTA was also able to accept easily small countries, such as Norway and Denmark, even if their economies were only poorly developed, as in the case of Portugal, because the association was only concerned with free trade in industrial goods among the members, who were therefore free to protect their economies from other sources of competition. Through the ploy of devising Associate Member status, it was even possible to include Finland in the agreement, despite the fact that it was extremely constrained when it came to joining any international agreement as a result of its treaty obligations with the USSR.

Given the scale of the realignments implied by the new groupings and the somewhat arbitrary political and economic logic behind the actual membership of the two organizations, it is hardly surprising that there have subsequently been significant changes. The UK, faced with rapid dissolution of many of its economic ties with the Commonwealth, became increasingly eager to play a central role in European affairs and quickly found that EFTA did not provide an adequate vehicle. In 1961 and 1967, it made two attempts to join the EC, but on both occasions was not accepted, largely at the instigation of the French, who probably felt that it would never be possible to reach agreement on a common agricultural policy if the negotiations became any more complex. Certainly the French President, De Gaulle, did not relish having to cede any of his influence in the Community to the British.

New members of the European Community

Once the mould of the EC had been set, it became easier for it to countenance an expansion of membership, as any newcomers would inevitably have to accept the organization on its own terms. In 1971 the UK, together with Denmark, the Republic of Ireland and Norway, applied to join and all were successful, although Norway subsequently withdrew its application. From 1 January 1973, therefore, the Community had nine members and had to begin to adjust to a new set of political and economic pressures. The UK, in particular, wanted to see much more scope for positive economic intervention in the form of a comprehensive regional policy, rather than the somewhat narrow and overwhelming concentration on agriculture. It is a measure of how firmly the EC had become set in its ways during the 1960s that while lip service has been paid to the need for a regional policy in the form of the European Regional Development Fund (ERDF), little fundamental alteration has occurred in the general pattern of expenditure (Croxford et al 1987).

The effect on EFTA of Denmark and the UK joining the EC was, of course, traumatic. Well over half the customers covered by the free trade agreement were suddenly removed and the loss was hardly compensated for by the acquisition of a new member, Iceland, in 1970. As a matter of urgency, the EFTA members had to negotiate a formal agreement with the EC and because of the association's lack of any institutional structure, each had to do so separately. To some extent this undermined the authority of EFTA, for every agreement was slightly different and underlined the impossibility of it ever evolving into a more cohesive organization. Indeed, since 1973, while EFTA has continued its work, it has become very much a peripheral part of the political and economic infrastructure of Western Europe.

The greatest weakness of the EC at this time was

that it was only as strong as its most reluctant member allowed it to be. All major decisions were subject to veto and it derived its political power from the national governments rather than any elected European body. In an attempt to overcome this and strengthen its institutional base, direct elections to a European Parliament were organized in 1979, but so far the 518 European Members of Parliament have not succeeded in organizing themselves as an effective force, capable of standing up to the national governments and creating a genuine base for Community decisions. A potentially most important development was achieved in 1986 with agreement on the Single European Act (Brewin 1987). Among other things, the Act commits the member states of the EC to creating a single internal market, free of all restrictions on the movement of goods, persons and services by 1992. This ideal was part of the original Treaty of Rome and making it an effective reality will substantially strengthen the EC at the expense of national governments. The transfer of power will also be further facilitated by the clause in the Act which extends majority voting to all deliberations, thus virtually removing all scope for national vetoes (House of Lords 1986).

In its first twenty years, the whole tenor of the EC was that of an organization geared primarily to serving the development needs of the industrial nations of Western Europe and it has frequently been upbraided for not showing sufficient concern for the problems facing both the less advanced parts of Europe and the Third World. Although treaties of association were concluded with Greece, Turkey, Malta and Cyprus in the early 1960s, these fell far short of even a form of associate membership of the Community itself. None of these countries enjoyed much protection from the barriers to free trade with their industrial neighbours created by the customs union and neither did they receive significant amounts of aid to help them modernize their economies so that they would be in a position to compete on a more equal footing (Commission of the European Communities 1982). Much the same has been true of developing countries outside Europe as well. A series of conventions has been signed, mainly with former colonial territories, but the effect of these has been to protect traditional markets for these countries' raw material exports in Europe, rather than providing a vehicle for redistributing wealth between the industrial and developing worlds. In fairness, it should be said that all these agreements were eagerly sought after by the countries concerned and they were always keen to renegotiate when any particular programme came to an end. There has also been a marked, if not a fundamental, change of policy on the part of the Community itself. The latest series of agreements, the Lomé Conventions, the third of which came into operation in 1986, are very much more concerned with providing resources to improve the structure of the economies of those developing nations that are party to it, though the scale of what is proposed is still small in relation to the enormity of the task.

Within Europe, political considerations have forced the Community, albeit reluctantly, to adopt a more radical stance (Lambert 1971). Under the terms of the Treaty of Rome, any European country has the right to apply for membership and in the 1970s a number of Mediterranean nations did so. Indeed, they would have applied earlier, but it was made quite clear that the weakness of their economies alone would have precluded acceptance (Deubner 1980). Gradually, however, it became clear that one of the best ways of preserving the fragile new democratic governments in Greece, Spain and Portugal was by drawing them more closely into the institutional framework of Western Europe (Pepelasis et al 1980). In other words, the EC was faced with the very real prospect that to reject their overtures would simply herald the return of some form of totalitarian regime (Leigh and Van Praag 1978). Greece applied to join immediately after the military junta was deposed in 1974 and became the tenth member in 1981. After the overthrow of their dictatorships, Spain and Portugal made similar applications and both became full members in 1986. Still more nations are seriously considering applications to join. Turkey has been exploring the possibility for some years and, faced with the prospect of a unified internal market in the EC after 1992, the EFTA countries are looking to reopen talks which may lead to full membership for some or all of them in due course.

Heart-warming as these developments may be, there is no disguising the difficulties that the expansion has caused the EC economically (Commission of the European Communities 1982). All the Mediterranean countries are much more heavily dependent on agriculture than the original members of the Community and their incomes are some 40 per cent lower. They open up the very worrying prospect of the markets of the industrial nations of Europe being swamped by uncontrollable amounts of food which are unwanted and largely unsaleable elsewhere in the world. The result will be even more pressure on the common agricultural policy at a time when the

Community is still seeking to reduce its significance and the amount of money it absorbs. Nor are the problems confined to agriculture: Greece, Portugal and Spain all have large fishing fleets, whose catches compete strongly in the already declining Community market; and the same applies to many of the manufacturing industries, such as textiles and food processing. For these reasons, the negotiations to expand the membership of the Community to the Mediterranean countries were slow and fraught with difficulty, but eventually the political benefits have outweighed the undoubted economic problems. This is in sharp contrast to the early years of the Community, when economic arguments seemed to dictate its every move, and is a measure of the changing nature of European integration (Williams 1984).

The political evolution of Western Europe in recent decades has been spectacular. From a deeply-divided, warring group of small industrial states has emerged what can best be described as a strong confederation (Von Krosigk 1971). There is not a single country that is not party to at least one pan-European economic grouping and most also support a common defence policy. There is also a spontaneous unanimity about cultural values which has been enormously strengthened by day-to-day contact in the European economic and military institutions. Despite understandable concern about the economic advisability of such close and one-sided commitment to Europe which has led some in the UK to question in the past whether it ought to remain a full member of the EC, it is now inconceivable that the fundamental bonds forged since 1945 will be seriously weakened and the degree of commitment, as evidenced by the Single European Act is greater than ever.

Further reading

Blacksell M 1981 *Post-war Europe: a political geography* 2nd edn. Hutchinson, London

Blacksell M 1982 Reunification and the political geography of the Federal Republic of Germany. *Geography* 67: 310–19

Brewin C 1987 The European Community – a union without unity of government. *Journal of Common Market Studies* 26: 1–23

Williams A M (ed) 1984 *Southern Europe Transformed*. Harper and Row, London

Williams A M 1987 *The West European Economy*. Hutchinson, London

3

Demographic and social change

Population

From growth to stagnation

Since the Second World War, the population of Western Europe has undergone a complicated transformation with regard to numbers, distribution and composition. The many marriages contracted soon after hostilities ended in 1945 produced a veritable 'baby boom' that was strikingly different from the demographic depression of the 1930s and the massive loss of life that occurred between 1939 and 1945 as a direct result of fighting or because of general disruption and poor conditions among the civilian population. Parts of the political map of Europe were redrawn once war had ended and consequently the second half of the 1940s witnessed an important redistribution of people. For example, in 1950, refugees from the Sudetenland, former eastern provinces of Germany, and from minority areas in Eastern Europe made up 16 per cent of the population of what was to become West Germany, and regional figures were as high as 21 per cent in Bayern, 27 per cent in Niedersachsen and 33 per cent in Schleswig-Holstein (George 1972). Indeed, a comparable process was to take place during the 1960s as roughly 2 million people moved from East Germany to the west. Even in the late 1980s, the arrival of refugees, usually from non-European countries, poses severe problems for some West European governments.

By mid-century, the eighteen countries of Western Europe contained 284.7 million people, some 11.3 per cent of the world total. Their demographic growth continued during the 1950s and 1960s, albeit with decreasing vigour. By contrast, the labour-hungry economies of Western Europe were growing fast during those decades and large numbers of labour migrants had to be enlisted from elsewhere since the products of the late 1940s baby boom were not yet old enough to enter the labour market. In addition, the processes of decolonization and repatriation, together with major changes in world affairs, dispatched yet more migrants to swell Western Europe's total. For example, decolonization and especially the granting of independence to Algeria in 1962 resulted in the repatriation of 1 160 000 French nationals between 1954 and 1963. A miniature baby boom did occur in some countries of Western Europe in the mid-1960s but the general tendency during that decade was for natural increase to decline and continuing population growth to become increasingly reliant on immigration.

In the 1970s, the relationship between demographic factors and migration was modified again. Economic recession, with consequent job loss on a massive scale, and the presence of the baby-boom generation on the labour market meant that new supplies of foreign labour were not needed. Many 'guestworkers' were in fact sent home as soon as their short-term work permits expired. At the same time, rates of natural increase continued to fall in most of Western Europe, even reaching the point of more deaths than births being recorded in some countries and especially so during the mid-1970s. Fertility picked up fractionally in a few areas in the late 1970s and early 1980s, but there is no doubt that Western Europe has now entered (or to be more accurate, re-entered) a population cycle that displays only modest growth and will soon be characterized by stability or even decline. The present chapter will focus on demographic trends and attendant modifications in employment and society; migratory processes will be examined in Chapter 4 and discussion of the massive urbanization of Western Europe since the Second World War will be reserved until Chapter 8.

Facts and figures

Outworking of the broad trends described above

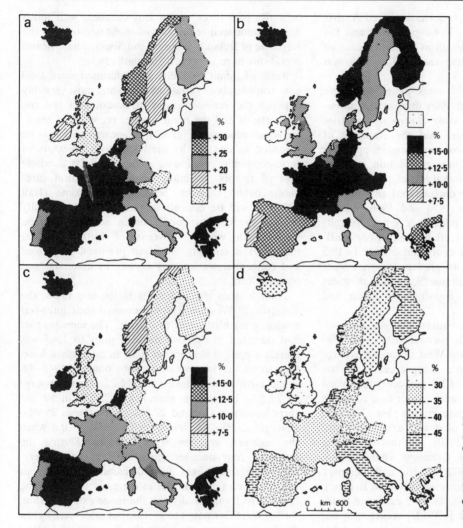

Fig. 3.1
Aspects of population
change: (a) total growth,
1950–86 (%); (b) change,
1950–66 (%); (c) change,
1966–86 (%); (d) decline in
crude birth rates
1945/49–1986 (%).

meant that by 1966 the population of Western Europe had risen by 14.2 per cent from its 1950 figure, to reach a total of 325.2 million. In the following twenty years the rate of growth decelerated very sharply to produce a total of 353.9 million in 1986 (i.e. an increase of 24 per cent since 1950) but accounted for only 7.2 per cent of the world's greatly enlarged population. The interplay of differing rates of natural change and net migration generated enormous variations in this trend of growth both between countries and within them. During the three and a half decades, net increases of more than 30 per cent were recorded in the Netherlands (+43.9 per cent), Switzerland (+32.6 per cent), Spain (+37.9 per cent), France (+32.6 per cent) and Greece (+30.5 per cent), but the relationship of demographic and migratory processes

in those five countries was far from uniform (Fig. 3.1a).

Some of these nations displayed impressive rates of natural growth, but while the Netherlands received substantial numbers of repatriates and guestworkers, Spain dispatched large numbers of migrants to labour-hungry France and other industrial countries. Switzerland was the destination for large contingents of migrants, coming especially from Italy. Spain's relative growth in population was certainly very high, but its absolute increase of 10.6 million in thirty-five years was equalled by Italy and overtaken by West Germany (+11.1 million) and France (+13.6 million). Absolute increases of this kind of magnitude between 1950 and 1986 surpassed the individual totals of no less than a dozen West European countries in 1986. At the other extreme, modest rates of growth characterized Austria (+9.6 per cent), Belgium (+14.7 per cent) and the UK (+12.5 per cent), although in the latter case an absolute increase of no less than 6.3 million was involved.

Not surprisingly, national rates of growth were stronger between 1950 and 1966 than in the subsequent fifteen years in all West European countries save the Netherlands, Spain and the Republic of Ireland, with the latter country, long sapped by emigration and having official prohibition of birth control, switching from an initial loss of population to the fastest rate of increase encountered anywhere in Western Europe. Between 1950 and 1966, natural increase, immigration and policies of labour recruitment combined to give Switzerland (+29.8 per cent), West Germany (+19.6 per cent) and France (+18.5 per cent) the fastest rates of growth and they were followed closely by some of the Scandinavian states and the labour-exporting countries of Spain and Greece (Fig. 3.1b).

After the mid-1960s the pattern changed dramatically, with rates of growth between 1966 and 1986 falling to half the much lower West European average (+8.8 per cent) in Belgium (+3.8 per cent), Austria (+3.6 per cent), the UK (+3.4 per cent) and West Germany (+2.2 per cent), and a further four countries also displaying below average growth (Fig. 3.1c). In five countries the number of deaths exceeded births for some period during the 1970s, with this trend being most pronounced in West Germany where natural decrease commenced in 1972. Austria and Denmark now also display natural decrease, while in Belgium, Luxembourg and the UK deaths have exceeded births in some years since the mid-1970s. By contrast, Spain, with 6.6 million more inhabitants in 1986 than in 1966, and the Republic of Ireland, with an additional 650 000, stood out as new foci of dynamic growth.

Deaths and births

Death rates in Western Europe have declined since the beginning of this century in response to continued medical progress and are now remarkably similar in the eighteen countries (Fig. 3.2). Higher rates now tend to reflect the sucess of health services in allowing populations to live longer rather than the existence of seriously inadequate medical provision, although there is always scope for improvement (Table 3.1). Thus in the UK, West Germany and the countries of Scandinavia, death rates for 1986 were fractionally higher than in the late 1940s simply because national populations had become more elderly. In most other parts of Western Europe, a slight decline was in evidence

over the past three and a half decades, with much more pronounced reductions of about one-third in the Republic of Ireland, Portugal and Spain, where health conditions have improved substantially.

Rates of infant mortality have declined since 1950 but considerable variations remain, most notably between the very low rates of Scandinavia and the Netherlands and the higher values recorded in Mediterranean countries (Fig. 3.2). Infant mortality may be regarded as one of the most sensitive indicators of socio-economic conditions, since it reflects a whole host of factors, including quality of medical care, public health services, housing and income (Hall 1976). It will be difficult to reduce infant mortality beyond the current conditions in northern Europe since death within 4 weeks of birth (neonatal mortality) is strongly linked to pre-natal conditions and congenital weaknesses as well as antenatal and obstetric care.

After a steep rise in fertility in the late 1940s, the countries of Western Europe resumed their inter-war tendency for birth rates to decline. The increase that had occurred in the two decades prior to 1965 was merely a cyclical shift rather than an established long-term trend. At the peak of the baby boom of 1945–49, crude birth rates ranged from 14.2‰ (Luxembourg) to 27.2‰, but values were below 22.5‰ in all but three countries (Iceland 27.2‰, Netherlands 25.9‰, Portugal 25.6‰) to yield a mean index of 20.8 when the eighteen averages were summed. During the following four decades, birth rates declined everywhere, although slight upward fluctuations had been recorded in a few countries in the early 1960s and the late 1970s. By the mid-1980s the range extended from 9.6‰ (West Germany) to 18.1‰, but rates were below 16.0‰ everywhere except in the Republic of Ireland (18.1) and Iceland (17.2) (Fig. 3.2). The mean index was 12.7‰, one-third lower than in the late 1940s, with the strongest rates of decline in Finland, the Netherlands, Denmark, Italy, West Germany, Norway and Switzerland (Fig. 3.1d).

Smaller families

The human situation summarized by these bald statistics is one of declining fertility and contracting family size throughout Western Europe. The proportion of couples with one child each or without children is increasing, while the share of families with several children is on the decline, and is particularly evident in the case of couples with four or more children. Calculations derived from recent patterns of family formation in West Germany estimated that a quarter of marriages in that country in the late 1970s would

Fig. 3.2
Demographic indicators,
1986, and measures of
urbanization.

produce no children, a quarter would produce one child, 30 per cent two children and the remaining 20 per cent three or more children (Schubnell 1978). Associated with this trend, the proportion of births to women aged 35 and over is falling, but contrasting behaviour is in evidence for birth patterns to younger women. Some complete family production by their mid-twenties and then return to employment; others first pursue their careers and postpone starting a family until they are well into their twenties.

No other demographic development in Western Europe has been so uniform in such a short period as this decline in fertility since the mid-1960s. During this time a range of contraceptive techniques has been widely diffused in most countries to allow the number and spacing of births to be planned more effectively. The economic, social and psychological processes at work to enable family planning to be widely accepted are complicated in the extreme but must include the following considerations. Traditional rural societies, in which large families were raised to supply farm labour and ensure security for parents in their old age, have largely disappeared as the agricultural workforce has declined throughout Western Europe. Nonetheless,

Table 3.1 Demographic characteristics, 1986

	Total population (mill.)	Projection for 2000 (mill.)	Density /km²	Death rate (‰)	Infant mortality rate (‰)	Birth rate (‰)
Austria	7.560	7.629	90	11.8	11.0	11.5
Belgium	9.861	9.630	323	11.2	9.4	11.6
Denmark	5.116	5.114	119	11.4	7.7	10.6
Finland	4.911	5.073	15	9.8	6.5	12.9
France	55.288	57.882	101	10.0	8.1	13.9
West Germany	61.020	59.198	246	11.5	8.9	9.6
Greece	9.920	10.435	75	8.9	14.3	12.7
Iceland	0.240	0.255	2	6.6	6.1	17.2
Republic of Ireland	3.550	4.123	51	9.1	9.8	18.1
Italy	57.202	57.925	189	9.6	11.1	10.3
Luxembourg	0.366	0.373	141	11.1	11.7	11.5
Netherlands	14.530	15.147	350	8.5	8.0	12.3
Norway	4.159	4.319	13	10.6	8.3	12.4
Portugal	10.192	11.012	110	9.6	16.7	12.8
Spain	38.494	40.975	76	7.8	10.5	12.5
Sweden	8.358	8.329	19	11.3	6.4	11.8
Switzerland	6.487	5.889	156	9.2	7.1	11.5
United Kingdom	56.590	57.684	231	11.8	9.4	13.2

many regions that remain quite strongly dependent on agricultural employment have been less affected by the general decline in fertility and still tend to display relatively high birth rates. Rural–urban migration has continued apace, as has the reach of mass communications, and it is clear that the role of the family is viewed differently by couples in urbanized, welfare-state societies than in peasant economies. Traditional imperatives no longer hold sway and having children is increasingly seen as a way of 'completing the family', ensuring biological survival and finding new companionship. Many urban couples feel that cramped apartments or houses are quite unsuitable for raising more than a small family (of, say, one or two children); and, in any case, having more children involves added expenses which family allowances do little to compensate.

Even more important than these environmental and economic considerations is the evolving status of women in European society. The education and professional training of girls has improved substantially since the Second World War and their aspiration for an identity outside the home has been reflected by increased employment of women, with or without children, in industry and more especially in the service sector of the economy. Motherhood has become just one of several feminine roles and for many women pursuit of a career has taken preference to child

rearing. Adherence to religious traditions which proscribe family limitation tends to encourage larger families although many 'religious' West Europeans have adopted liberal attitudes to the organization of family life. Social and material objectives for personal fulfilment and well-being are now likely to be dominant in the minds of most couples.

The operation of factors such as these produced interesting fluctuations in national birth rates during the mid and late 1960s, by which time the baby boom of 1945–50 had reached reproductive age. In some countries (e.g. West Germany, Italy, Sweden, the UK) a second baby boom duly occurred but did not happen in others. The reasons for this difference were related in part to shortage of accommodation and other environmental factors, but the fundamental explanation was probably to do with young women having taken new opportunities to pursue careers, postponing both marriage and child bearing in consequence. Various social factors were also advanced for the slight upturn in the birth rate in the UK that commenced in the late 1970s. Women born shortly after the Second World War and still in their early thirties were catching up just as younger women born in the late 1950s were having their children. Many older mothers had postponed child bearing until their careers were well under way; others had been divorced and were starting new families with new partners. Other hypotheses included the fact that fewer British women were taking the contraceptive pill, preferring other less reliable methods after a medical report had linked deaths from thrombosis with the pill; and that many couples waited until they were better off and settled in their own home before embarking on reproduction.

Population policies

National policies regarding population vary both in broad terms and in highly significant details among the countries of Western Europe. At one extreme stands the Republic of Ireland where regulations indicate a pro-natalist attitude, while at the other extreme West Germany and the Netherlands have adopted policies aimed at stabilizing population numbers. The other countries occupy various positions in the middle ground, either having no particular point of view or else remaining neutral and leaving such matters up to individuals. Official attitudes have become increasingly liberal in many of these middle-ground countries, as in France where legislation banning contraception was repeated in 1967 and abortion reform came in 1975, a year ahead of West Germany but nine years after Denmark and England and Wales (Ardagh 1988). The French anti-contraception law of 1920 had been devised for demographic purposes: to help compensate the deaths of 1914–18. It prohibited publicity for birth control and advisory clinics, and forbad the sale of contraceptives, except for a number of defined medical reasons. Nonetheless, many French couples exercised their will power and resorted to time-honoured means of birth control or turned to clandestine abortion.

It is probably impossible to establish a clear relationship between fertility trends and the myriad laws regarding contraception, abortion, sterilization, family benefits and medical care in the eighteen countries of Western Europe, since the marital behaviour of individuals depends on a complex web of social, cultural and economic variables rather than the dictates of law. However, that is not to deny that relative permissiveness or harshness of laws on family matters does condition general availability of information on family planning, provision of necessary materials for birth control, or procurement of safe abortions. For example, the situation in the Republic of Ireland, where artificial contraception is forbidden by both state and church and there is a strict interdiction on abortion, contrasts with that in Denmark, West Germany, Sweden or the UK where the means of birth control are readily available and abortion, within certain periods of pregnancy, is legal. The remaining countries display various but generally increasing degrees of liberality on such matters.

Nonetheless, national differences in legislation have been sufficiently great to generate 'abortion tourism' and smuggling of quantities of contraceptives into less liberal countries. Indeed, the latter practice continues into the Republic of Ireland to this day. During the early 1970s, about a quarter of abortions performed in England and Wales involved non-residents who came mainly from France and West Germany, prior to changes in their legislation in 1975 and 1976 respectively. Clinics in Denmark and the Netherlands were visited by large numbers of German and Belgian women, while London's clinics continue to form one of the 'tourist attractions' for some Spanish women spending a short time in the UK. In recent years some 30 000 women went abroad each year for terminations; however, in 1983 the Spanish parliament approved a fiercely debated bill to permit abortion in cases where the mother's health is endangered or the foetus deformed. 'Abortion tourism' involves social discrimination since women with low incomes do not have this option open to them and are likely to attempt self-induced abortion or choose other forms of dangerous and, of course, illegal operations. Estimates on the incidence of illicit terminations in the 1960s and early 1970s varied enormously. The average for Western Europe as a whole was thought to equal between 25 and 50 per cent of the number of live births, with annual estimates being in the order of 30 000–200 000 for Belgium, over 400 000 for France, and over 650 000 for Italy. Estimates for West Germany suggested one abortion for every live birth, while in the Netherlands about 15 per cent of pregnancies were terminated illegally (Hall 1976). Recent reports suggest that each year some 300 000 Spanish women risk physical damage, infection and religious excommunication by having illegal terminations which are usually performed by unqualified abortionists.

Despite important national differences in legislation and significant variations in marital behaviour between socio-economic groups, a number of common trends have emerged in Western Europe and are likely to continue to operate in the future. Greater social and spatial mobility, together with the impact of mass communications, has brought about greater individualization of behaviour patterns and this trait will probably continue. More and more couples will plan the number and spacing of their offspring and it has been suggested that increased recourse to family planning may reduce the incidence of abortion. Wider education will encourage more women to seek employment outside the home and to try to continue economic activity after the birth of children. Conjugal fertility is likely to level out even further in all regions and through all social strata, so that the small family with one or two children will predominate throughout Western Europe. Life expectancies will probably not increase much more. The net result will be low rates of population growth for the remainder of the century, with recent projections from the European Community raising the West European total for 1986 by a mere 1.0 per cent to 361 million in 2 000. The outcome of recent demographic trends will mean that the number of people of working age will begin to decline in the 1990s.

Social characteristics

An ageing population

Widespread advances in living standards, combined with improved housing provision and medical and social services, are enabling more West Europeans to live longer while, at the same time, birth rates are much lower than in the 1940s and 1950s. The total population has become not only more numerous but also substantially older than at mid-century. At mid-century, only 9 per cent of the population was aged 65 or over, but by 1986 the share had risen to 13.4 per cent, with the proportion of under 15-year-olds declining from 27.5 to 19.8 per cent over the same span of thirty-five years. Sweden now has 17.1 per cent of its population aged 65 or over, with Norway (15.6 per cent) and Denmark (14.9 per cent) close behind (Fig. 3.3a). By contrast, less than 12 per cent of the population of Iceland, the Netherlands, the Republic of Ireland, Spain or Portugal is aged 65 or more.

Life expectancy at birth (i.e. including infant mortality) now ranges from 69 years in Belgium, Finland and West Germany to 72 years in Denmark and the Netherlands. These figures represent considerable advances since 1950 and incorporate additional expectancies that range from 1.4 years in the Netherlands and 3.0 years in the UK to 6.8 years in France, 7.2 years in Belgium and a remarkable 10.6 years in Spain. The average difference in male (71 years) and female (78 years) expectancy among West Europeans has widened by 2–3 years over the past four decades, with the lower increase for men being partly due to an upsurge of mortality rates in certain age groups associated with pathogenic behaviour and increased risk of accident.

A clear tendency is for more people to live into their eighties and, by virtue of the differences in life expectancy and the higher impact of wartime mortality on the male population, this means the survival of a growing number of elderly women. The decline of the traditional multi-generation household in urbanized Western Europe means that most elderly people live by themselves and may endure considerable social isolation. Many are in failing physical and mental health and depend on pensions and other forms of transfer payment for their survival. National pension schemes vary enormously in entitlement and amount but, despite the efforts made by some governments to provide all elderly people with an adequate minimum income, old folk who have no personal resources to supplement these minimum amounts must be recognized as being among the most deprived people in Western Europe. The worst off include the very old, who have contributed to pensions for only part of their working lives; widows who have never worked; and

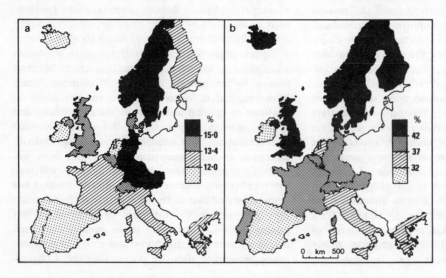

Fig. 3.3
Population characteristics, 1986: (a) proportion aged 65 years and over (%); (b) women as proportion of civilian employment (%).

members of occupational categories that had no pension schemes until recently.

The need to provide and manage a range of types of accommodation for the elderly, according to their varying health requirements, is already one of the most urgent problems in Western Europe and will certainly grow in magnitude in the immediate future. One estimate suggested that by 1990 one half of the much enlarged population aged over 65 would in fact be over 80 years of age (Anon. 1981). The dimensions of the problem associated with an ageing society have only just started to be comprehended and it is to our collective shame that West European families and nations in general have shown themselves badly prepared to cope with a larger share of elderly people. This fundamental challenge remains very largely unmet (Warnes 1982). Clearly the consequences of an ageing population are very great. Business activities will have to adapt to meeting the requirements of the elderly; the health service and the caring professions will need to make profound adjustments; some forms of leisure or free-time activity may expand substantially; and builders and housing departments will have to construct more small houses and apartments for elderly households, as well as providing 'sheltered housing' (with staff always on the premises) and special residential homes.

Changing household structure

The presence of greater numbers of old folk, the fact that different adult generations tend no longer to live together, and the decline in the average number of children per family represent important explanatory factors behind a general reduction in household size. Other causes include an increasing tendency for young people to move away from the parental home, as well as the dramatic increases in the number of divorces and one-parent families in recent years. In 1960, the average West European household contained 3.3 people, but by 1970 the figure had declined to 3.0 and has fallen further since then. In the mid-1980s, two-person households represented the most common size category in most countries except for two groups. In the Republic of Ireland, larger households were most numerous (comprising 5 persons), while one-person households formed the largest size category in Norway (where they made up 41 per cent of the total), Sweden (33 per cent), Finland (27 per cent), West Germany (31 per cent) and Austria (26 per cent). Taking Western Europe as a whole, 24 per cent of households in the mid-1980s were made up of lone persons compared with 18.2 per cent two decades earlier.

Information on divorce rates is far from complete, but there is clear evidence that numbers increased rapidly after 1960 in response to changes in national legislation. Little is known about broken marriages in strongly Roman Catholic nations, but for a dozen countries of Western Europe data are available which relate the annual number of divorces to each hundred marriages conducted during the year. We should observe at this point that, as the population has aged and attitudes to formal marriage have changed, the trend has been for the number of marriages to decline with time. In 1965, the range was from 5.9 divorces per hundred marriages in Scotland to 18.2 in Denmark, with Sweden (17.8) and Austria (14.5) also displaying high ratios. In 1985 the values ranged from 28.5 divorces per hundred marriages in the Netherlands to 45.4 in Sweden, 45.1 in Denmark and 40.4 in England and Wales.

In contrast with these figures, there are also signs of continuing attachment to 'family life', although such attachment is being expressed in other than conventional ways, for example remarriage after divorce of one or both partners and the fact that growing numbers of couples of the opposite sex and indeed the same sex are choosing to 'live together'. These trends may well represent a change in the concept and form of 'family life' rather than a rejection of the family as such. In any case, sizeable numbers of West Europeans, adults and children alike, are experiencing other kinds of tie. In some countries, alternatives to formal marriage have become widespread and this is especially so in northern Europe where, for example, two births in every five in Sweden were illegitimate in the early 1980s and long-established unmarried couples are by no means exceptional (Roussel 1987). In France and West Germany, roughly one birth in ten was outside formal marriage and in the UK one in every five. Demographers suggest that there seems to be a growing reluctance to marry, even when children are involved; age at marriage is rising and, failing substantial numbers of deferred marriages taking place, there will probably be a notable increase in one-person households in Sweden in the near future (Guilmot 1978). Similar tendencies are now in evidence in many other parts of Western Europe.

Life styles within families have changed considerably in response to the growing trend for women as well as their partners to take jobs outside the home. Since grandparents rarely live close at hand, this trend can cause problems in caring for young children and coping with domestic duties, but it has also had the very positive effect of playing down the rigid sex-stereotyped roles that past generations of husbands and wives were expected to perform. To some extent, male and female roles are converging; many women are spending less time than before on bringing up children and many men are willing to undertake domestic chores (Schmid 1982).

By virtue of the increasing occurrence of divorce and a host of other factors, the number of single-parent families has risen greatly so that in Belgium, Denmark, West Germany, the UK and the Scandinavian countries they now account for more than 15 per cent of all families with dependent children. In four cases out of five the single parent is a woman. In several countries the number of single-parent families is growing more rapidly than the number of 'complete' families. Unmarried mothers, divorced or separated women and widows tend to work more than married mothers, but their jobs are often insecure and badly paid. They depend heavily on child allowances and supplements of various kinds to meet family needs and it is no surprise that single-parent families make up a disproportionate share of all low-income households. They deserve specialist assistance of various kinds, including nursery schools and a range of community facilities for older children.

Health and disease

West Europeans are certainly living longer and, in general terms, are healthier than ever before. Deaths from infectious diseases have declined dramatically since mid-century so that heart disease and cancer now form the leading causes. The rising impact of socially-induced disease gives rise to mounting concern; for example, chronic alcoholism occupies third position in the list of causes of serious illness. Death from cirrhosis of the liver is the most usual cause and its incidence has risen sharply among men aged 35–54 years. It must also be recognized that 'problem drinking' is also affecting growing numbers of women and young people; indeed, in several countries more than 5 per cent of the population is considered to be alcoholic (Anon. 1981). In addition, alcohol consumption represents an important risk factor in all kinds of accident, especially those on the roads. On an encouraging note, the total number of road accidents involving death or personal injury declined slightly during the 1970s even though the number of cars on the roads of Western Europe rose from 69 million in 1972 to 117 million in 1984. Speed restrictions and the wearing of safety belts may have helped this general reduction. Unfortunately, the number of young people involved in traffic accidents rose sharply and death on the road is now the main cause of premature death for the 15–24 age group. The steep rise in the number of motor bicycles is part of this tragic story.

A higher proportion of West Europeans now smoke than they did in the 1950s with one man in every two and one women in every three being a regular smoker, despite the fact that smoking is a significant risk factor in the development of certain cancers and cardio-vascular diseases. A heavy smoker may be considered to have 8–10 years trimmed off his or her life expectancy, with lung cancer being a growing cause of death among women as well as men in the 45–54 age group. Drug misuse represents a third form of socially-induced disease and this has increased disturbingly in Western Europe since the 1960s, spreading from one area and social group to another and extending from young adults to juvenile age groups. Drug control poses major problems by virtue of the wide range of commodities involved and the fact that many medicines – which may be used as drugs – can be purchased across a pharmacist's counter. The link between certain forms of drug abuse and the incidence of AIDS is well known. Far from being a 'gay plague', AIDS can affect straight and gay, married and single, rich and poor. It is no respecter of age, class, gender or sexuality, and as such is surely the greatest challenge that medical science, welfare services and West European society at large will have to face in the final years of the twentieth century.

Employment

Sectors and classes

Long-established forms of employment, such as agriculture, mining and traditional branches of manufacturing, have contracted massively during the past three decades as the balance of Western Europe's economy has been transformed by the emergence of modern industries, office work and a wide range of service activities. At mid-century there were highly important spatial variations in employment structure, with the agricultural economies of southern Europe contrasting with the greater development of manufacturing in the north-west, and urban economies everywhere being very different from those in the countryside. One-quarter of the total workforce was in farming and forestry, roughly one-third in manufacturing and the remaining two-fifths in services of various kinds.

Thirty-five years later, the relative proportions had changed to less than one-tenth, one-third and substantially more than half of the much enlarged workforce (Williams 1987). Commensurate with this structural shift away from farming and workshop industry to jobs in factories and offices has been a decline in the number of employers, self-employed and family workers. Wage and salary earners now make up four-fifths of civilian employment throughout Western Europe, surpassing 90 per cent in the UK and Scandinavia but standing at less than 70 per cent in the Mediterranean economies of Spain, Portugal and especially Greece. At the same time, the conventional classification into primary, secondary and tertiary sectors of the economy has become blurred, with the separation between some modern forms of manufacturing and of service generation being particularly indistinct (Bailly 1987a, b).

Traditional rural societies have been drained by out-migration and have virtually disappeared. The remaining population in the countryside has acquired new status and occupational characteristics and makes up the rural strata of wider industrial and increasingly post-industrial societies (Archer and Giner 1971). Urbanization and industrialization have seen the rise of an increasingly complex working class, while the middle classes of Western Europe have been enlarged and modified by the growing presence of managerial staff, bureaucrats, higher-grade clerical workers and teachers, all of whom represent 'hinge groups' in the processes of upward social mobility and typify the transition from industrial to post-industrial society (Mallet 1975). In the 1950s, many social scientists believed that West European countries were moving towards a condition in which class differences would be much less marked, barriers between classes less formidable, opposition between them less acute, and the consciousness of class membership itself less intense (Bottomore 1971). Some even maintained that classes were virtually disappearing in response to rising living standards, changes in technology, the wider spread of education and the impact of the welfare state, which served to redistribute a proportion of wealth through the taxation system.

Wisdom of hindsight suggests that these views were probably misplaced; social conflict has surely intensified since the late 1960s rather than declined. In most countries of Western Europe, access to really meaningful financial, cultural and educational capital has remained essentially in the hands of the 'establishment' (Marceau 1977). The socio-cultural influence of upper classes and a range of elite groups has endured during the post-war years and represents one of the most impermeable barriers to meaningful social mobility in Western Europe. The real and often limited significance of indices of social change needs to be appreciated; 'continuity' might be a more appropriate word to describe social relations in Western Europe over the past four decades rather than 'change'.

The changing workforce

It is arguable that the distribution of power in society may not have shifted substantially; however, the structure of the workforce has most certainly been modified by the recruitment of large numbers of guestworkers to perform less appealing jobs in every branch of work. For example, in West Germany, foreign workers comprise one-quarter of the underground workforce in the coal industry, one-half of the shiftworkers in foundries, one-quarter of the workforce in hotels and catering, and one-tenth of nurses and hospital staff. A controversial television programme attempted to determine what would happen to factories and public services in Stuttgart without guestworkers. It displayed pictures of streets piled high with refuse, factories and transport systems at a standstill, restaurants without service, and hospitals unable to function. Exactly the same kind of result would be produced in hundreds of cities throughout Western Europe. In addition, the presence of guestworkers and their families has introduced striking aspects of cultural and religious diversity in each of the reception countries, but such mass immigration has not occurred without tension arising.

Secondly, there has been a sharp rise in the number of women taking on paid employment, especially in modern branches of industry and in service activities. Women made up 39 per cent of the total workforce of Western Europe in 1985 but national proportions varied considerably from 29–33 per cent in rather more traditional societies such as Greece, Spain and the Republic of Ireland, where older generations believed a woman's place to be in the home, to 47 and 48 per cent in the more liberal societies of Sweden and Finland (Fig. 3.3b). In Scandinavia, two-thirds of all married women have paid employment and in several countries the proportion is almost one-half, but in the more traditional countries mentioned above and in the Netherlands far fewer women continue in paid employment after marriage. Expressed another way, some four-fifths of all women aged 25–54 years hold jobs in Sweden (83 per cent) and Finland (78 per cent), while the proportion is very much smaller in Italy (36 per cent), Greece (33 per cent), Spain (33 per cent), the Netherlands (32 per cent) and the Republic of Ireland (27 per cent). However, it should not be forgotten that a notable proportion of female workers are engaged in part-time jobs that are neither secure nor well paid.

Other changes in the West European labour force involve a marked decline in participation by young adults, since many more pursue higher education than in earlier decades; and the widespread introduction of old-age pensions has brought in the concept of retirement and removed older workers from the labour force. Efforts have been made in Scandinavia and to a lesser extent elsewhere to replace the brutal break from work to retirement by a more gradual transition during which elderly staff work fewer hours and have the opportunity to prepare for their years after the world of work. Unfortunately, the mounting pace of job losses in recent years has overtaken many of these laudable initiatives.

The world of work

During the 1970s, the employed population of Western Europe became more emphatically 'post-industrial', with 57.8 per cent of the workforce in service jobs in 1985 by comparison with 43.5 per cent 15 years previously (Fig. 3.4a). In absolute terms, this meant an increase in the service-sector workforce of 20 million people, roughly equal to the combined population of Greece and Portugal! Italy employed 4.5 million more people in the service sector in 1985 than in 1970, with increases in excess of 3 million being recorded in France and the UK. By 1985, the Benelux countries, Scandinavia and the UK were the most strongly service orientated, with over 65 per cent of their workforce in that sector, being closely followed by France (60.4 per cent). Service employment lagged behind the West European average especially in Portugal (42.2 per cent), Greece (43.7 per cent), Spain (50.9 per cent) and the Republic of Ireland (55.1 per cent), which still engaged important proportions of their workforces in agriculture, and in Austria (52.9

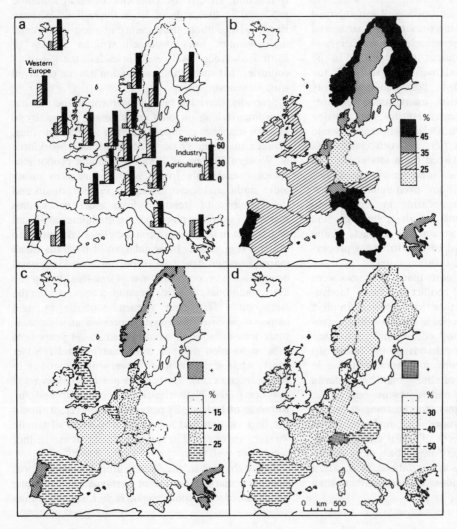

Fig. 3.4
Workforce characteristics:
(a) employment by sector, 1985; (b) evolution of numbers in service employment, 1970–85 (%); (c) in industrial employment; (d) in agricultural employment.

Table 3.2 Civilian employment by main sectors of economic activity (%), 1985

	Primary	Secondary	Tertiary
Austria	9.0	38.1	52.9
Belgium	3.0	29.9	67.1
Denmark	7.1	26.8	66.0
Finland	11.5	31.9	56.5
France	7.6	32.0	60.4
West Germany	5.6	41.0	53.4
Greece	28.9	27.4	43.7
Iceland	15.3	32.1	52.6
Republic of Ireland	16.0	28.9	55.1
Italy	11.2	33.6	55.2
Luxembourg	4.2	33.4	62.3
Netherlands	4.9	28.1	67.0
Norway	7.2	27.8	65.0
Portugal	23.9	33.9	42.2
Spain	16.9	32.1	50.9
Sweden	4.8	29.9	65.3
Switzerland	6.6	37.7	55.7
United Kingdom	2.6	32.4	65.0

per cent) and West Germany (53.4 per cent), both of which had above average proportions of their employees in manufacturing (Table 3.2).

The industrial share of Western Europe's workforce declined by 11.7 million between 1970 and 1985, falling from 42.8 to 33.8 per cent of the total, not only because of the dynamism of the service sector but also in response to the severe economic difficulties experienced in so many branches of manufacturing. In Denmark, West Germany and France the industrial workforce declined by just over 20 per cent and in Spain (−28 per cent), the UK (−30 per cent) and Belgium (−36 per cent) the rate of loss was much greater, being roughly half as large again as the West European average (20.3 per cent) (Fig. 3.4c). The UK trimmed its manufacturing workforce by 3.3 million and the losses in West Germany amounted to almost 3 million. By 1985, West Germany (41.0 per cent), Austria (38.1 per cent) and Switzerland (37.7 per cent) were the only countries to employ substantially more than the average proportion of their workforce in manufacturing. Contrary to the West European trend, both Greece (+19 per cent) and Portugal (+27 per cent) increased their manufacturing workforces between 1970 and 1985.

Employment in agriculture and forestry retreated by over 7 million between 1970 and 1985, and the primary sector of the workforce declined from 13.7 per cent to 8.4 per cent. In Spain and Austria the agricultural workforce fell by one-half, while in Finland,

France, Greece and the Republic of Ireland the loss was in excess of 40 per cent (Fig. 3.4d). In absolute terms, the really big losses in farmworkers were in Spain (1.9 million), Italy (1.4 million), France (1.2 million), West Germany and Greece (each 800 000). Nonetheless, in Greece (28.9 per cent) and Portugal (23.9 per cent), roughly three times as much employment was provided in farming as in Western Europe as a whole, while in Spain (16.9 per cent) and the Republic of Ireland (16.0 per cent) the proportion was roughly double.

In short, by the mid-1980s, Western Europe was no longer composed of predominantly industrial neighbours; while, more frighteningly, a much larger number of workers were on the unemployment registers than held jobs in farming. In addition, it had become very clear that manufacturing some kinds of goods and generating some kinds of services represented a convergence of productive processes rather than a clear line of separation between distinctive sectors in the economy.

The quality of life

Just as the nature of work has changed, so has its pattern and duration. Overtime practices vary enormously from country to country, but the general trend has been for a reduction in the number of hours worked by each employee. After a period of very little change in the 1950s, increases in the duration of paid holidays, creation of part-time jobs and introduction of shorter working weeks all contributed to the same general trend. Employees now work a 38 to 40-hour, 5-day week in most countries, although 35 hours is usual in Scandinavia. In Belgium, Denmark, Italy and Norway the number of hours worked by a jobholder in 1980 represented a 30 per cent reduction on comparable figures for 1950. Flexitime, shortened lunch hours, three or four 'long' working days per week, and a number of short holidays during the year rather than one long break all represent substantial modifications to work patterns and enable workers to participate more fully in family and community life. The presence of so many married women on the labour market and the recent rise in unemployment have contributed to a rapid rise in part-time jobs. Four-fifths of such jobs are held by women and three-quarters of the total are in the service sector. In addition the incidence of shiftwork has doubled since the 1950s and has spread from manual work to computing, welfare services and many other sectors which employ large numbers of women. The growth of a 'black' or a 'shadow' economy, that goes unrecorded in official employment and tax statistics, reflects both this fundamental sectoral shift and the rise of unemployment. Economists have investigated multiple jobholding and what in the Third World would be called the 'informal sector' which carries no tax or social welfare obligations. They conclude that the black economy has grown in all West European countries since the mid-1960s and usually accounts for 7–10 per cent of the GDP of individual nations but stands at more than double that share in Italy and Spain.

Despite the undeniable hardship endured by some, the mythical 'average West European' now enjoys a much higher living standard than he or she did at mid-century simply in response to the fact that the average real GDP more than tripled during the four intervening decades. Family incomes have risen substantially and have given rise to a consumer society in which a declining proportion of income is spent on food and clothing, and a rising share on luxury goods, commercial services and holidays. Most houses are much better equipped than ever before, with nine out of ten households having a refrigerator, nearly half possessing a television set and over two-thirds having a car. The messages of the mass media and the greatly enhanced personal mobility afforded by car ownership offer the possibility of opening our minds to quantities of information and opinion and enriching our lives by new experiences in ways that earlier generations would have held inconceivable. Unfortunately, other features of the quality of life are less positive: violent crime is on the increase, especially offences against private property, as is juvenile delinquency. Equally disturbing is the fact that an ever-increasing share of West European households depends on social security transfers in the form of old-age pensions, unemployment monies and supplementary payments of various kinds to single-parent families and to the poor, who are most certainly still with us.

Unemployment

The numbers

At the start of 1986, some 15.8 million people were registered as unemployed in the European Community – a figure very much greater than the 11.5 million in agricultural work at the time. For more than two decades after the Second World War, it seemed that mass unemployment had become a thing of the past over the greater part of Western Europe. Buoyant economic growth gave rise to millions of new jobs on building sites, in factories and in offices to employ an adult population that was expanding as the baby-boom

generation came on to the labour market and guest-workers were recruited in vast numbers. Demographic and migratory processes interacted to raise the 15–64 years age group to some 200 million in 1980 (Jallade 1981). In addition, many more women took paid employment and increased the potential labour force substantially. In the countries of the Nine, only about 2.2 per cent of the rapidly growing workforce was unemployed during the 1950s and 1960s, with the annual average falling to 1.9 per cent for 1964–66. In the eighteen countries of Western Europe, the proportion was a mere 1.4 per cent and a notable element in that figure was due to frictional unemployment in the short interval between jobs.

There were, of course, substantial national and regional deviations from these figures for the mid-1960s, with unemployment rates in the Republic of Ireland (4.5 per cent) and Italy (5.7 per cent) standing at more than double the average for the Nine. By contrast, unemployment involved less than 0.8 per cent of the workforce in Luxembourg, West Germany, the Netherlands, Denmark and France. The *Report on the Regional Problems of the Enlarged Community* (1973) showed that in the mid-1960s unemployment rates exceeded 6 per cent in a range of old industrial areas and more remote rural localities; namely, the southern half of Italy and the islands, the rural west of Ireland, Ulster, North Wales, the Highlands and Islands of Scotland, northern Jutland and parts of southern Belgium. Underemployment in traditional agriculture dampened down official rates in several of these regions and the same was undoubtedly true for Iberia and Greece. All 'old' industrial areas in Belgium and the UK, together with the remainder of the Irish Republic and Jutland, had between 4 and 6 per cent of their workforces unemployed but, by contrast, the general job picture in France, West Germany, the Netherlands and south-east England was unquestionably healthy.

By 1970, the West European total had risen to 2.5 million (1.8 per cent) and conditions deteriorated drastically after 1973–74, with the average unemployment rate for the Community in 1975 (4.3 per cent) being double that for the mid-1960s and the average more than doubling again to reach 12.0 per cent at the start of 1986, when 15.8 million were registered as being out of work in the Community – a figure somewhat greater than the total population of the Netherlands! In January 1982, the crude total of unemployed in the UK topped the 3 million mark for the first time since the 1930s, reached 3.2 million in August of that year and stood at 3.3 million in early 1986.

Definitions of unemployment and methods of

collecting figures vary considerably between the countries of Western Europe but it is widely accepted that official figures underestimate the real situation. Household surveys and censuses reveal another large group of people – especially married women – who regard themselves as unemployed and would like to find work but are not on the formal unemployment register. When the 'hidden unemployed' and those on temporary job-creation schemes were included, the British total rose closer to 4 million people at the beginning of 1982. (Incidentally, undercounting also scales down the number of job vacancies.)

Unlike the pattern of the mid-1960s, Spain (with 22.1 per cent officially unemployed) and the Republic of Ireland (18.0 per cent) stood at the top of the list at the start of 1986, with Belgium (13.6 per cent), the Netherlands (13.3 per cent) and Italy (12.9 per cent) also recording above average rates. Unemployment in the mid-1980s had become a very different and much more diffuse phenomenon than that experienced in earlier years. It is no longer confined to the rural 'fringes' and the 'old' industrial areas of Europe. Nor is it experienced mainly by men, by the unqualified and those used to manual jobs. It is no longer a short-term problem but has become a generalized, long-term feature affecting many sectors of the labour force and all parts of Western Europe, albeit with differing degrees of intensity.

It is also a changing phenomenon, since job losses in any one sector of the economy do not necessarily imply higher unemployment on the whole. Even when gross domestic product is declining, some new jobs are being created and at least a proportion of workers are changing jobs within and between sectors all the time. For example, jobs in service activities in the UK rose from 12.5 million in 1971 to 15.6 million in 1986, while employment in manufacturing contracted from 11.1 million to 7.8 million and in primary activities from 665 000 to 620 000. Because of differing dynamism in the varying sectors of the economy, the unemployed are not always made up of the same types of worker. The harsh truth of that statement is becoming increasingly apparent as redundancies are striking white-collar and professional workers who had come to regard their jobs as 'safe'.

The reasons

The conditions that have given rise to this crisis are both numerous and complex. At the heart of the problem stands the world recession which requires greater economic efficiency from high-cost producers such as the countries of Western Europe. In addition, West European industry is experiencing fundamental

structural changes, which are resulting from the transfer to low-cost developing countries of competitive advantages in production of low-technology and labour-intensive goods. By way of illustration, in 1980, hourly compensation in manufacturing industry was under US$1.50 in Hong Kong, Singapore, South Korea and Taiwan, while rates were $7.10 in the UK and $9.00 in Italy, rising sharply through the other nations of north-western Europe to reach $13.20 in Belgium and even higher in Scandinavia.

Industrial firms in Western Europe have responded in various ways in their attempts to render themselves more competitive: by closing down capacity (newly recognized as being surplus to requirements), trimming costly labour inputs while reorientating production, and adopting new forms of industrial technology and marketing (Massey and Meegan 1982). In other instances, firms have ceased production completely. The net result has been the same: fewer jobs in manufacturing and in ancillary services as well. Routine paper work is also retreating as a source of employment as new computerized techniques of information processing are being applied to office jobs. Micro-electronics is poised to bring about a veritable revolution in this sector of the economy which has been the backbone of many formerly healthy urban regions, where large numbers of white-collar workers, especially women, were taken on in the 1960s and 1970s.

Another major cause of employment problems is the fact that the workforce has been swollen by the arrival on to the labour force of the largest-ever generation of school leavers (Fig. 3.5). In every major West European country the number of children born rose each year from 1955 to 1964. From 1964 onwards the number declined, except in France and the Republic of Ireland. By the early 1980s the number of young people in their late teens and early twenties looking for their first jobs had reached an all-time

Fig. 3.5
Trend in births in four West European countries, 1955–86 (after *The Economist*).

peak, but this fell slowly as the decade progressed. But large numbers of young people continued to flood on to the labour market in the Republic of Ireland and they now face formidable problems as they look for work. For many of them, the choice is stark: emigrate or be unemployed. Thus in the early 1980s net migration losses involved about 1 000 each year; in the late 1980s the annual figure is more like 30 000. The Irish birth rate remains the highest in Western Europe and, at 2.4 births per woman, the fertility rate has declined but is still very substantial.

A further contribution to widespread unemployment is the fact that over the past quarter century growing numbers of married women throughout Western Europe have sought paid work outside the home, often in the form of part-time employment which fits in with home-based activities. As we have seen, there are important variations in female participation rates between the more liberal societies of northern Europe and their more traditional Mediterranean counterparts. For example, only 30 per cent of Spanish women of working age have a job or want one (half the proportion in the UK). But that situation is changing fast as better-educated young women with fewer children are swelling the labour force and will surely inflate Spain's unemployment rate which is already in excess of 20 per cent. These two inputs have created severe strains in a situation where many employment opportunities are shrinking and are certainly failing to keep up with growing demand.

Even more controversial is the question of whether generous social security payments discourage people from seeking work. It certainly has to be admitted that some nations are more benevolent than others in this respect. For example, the Dutch have developed a range of imaginative, caring but undoubtedly costly extensions of welfare payments. Thus an unemployed person in the Netherlands does not have to take a job paying less than his or her former salary, or involving a different skill, or in a place more than 30 km from home. Until 1985 that person would have received unemployment pay worth four-fifths of his or her previous salary for six months, followed by payments at 75 per cent of the old salary for a further two years. With high labour costs, high unemployment rates and a high proportion of women in paid employment, it is not surprising that some Dutch politicians are urging a tougher line.

Social welfare and economic policy are bound together inextricably, but each nation in Western Europe ties the knots in a different way and with varying degrees of tension.

Those hardest hit

Four groups have traditionally been worst affected by unemployment: those living in depressed regions, the long-term unemployed, the unskilled and the young. They will continue to represent the core of the problem in the future, but it is clear that unemployment is spreading to all regions and to many sectors of the economy that have been recognized as buoyant until recently. In addition, women are bearing an increasing share of the unemployment burden and in most countries suffer a higher rate of unemployment than men. For a while, female workers were protected from the first effects of recession since they were heavily concentrated in less-affected sectors of the economy such as service activities, but that period of grace did not last. Despite recent improvements in education, women are still less well trained than men and for a relatively narrow range of 'feminine' occupations; now they are faced with fewer opportunities even in these fields.

Old industrial regions with a legacy of declining 'sunset' industries typically display high unemployment rates. Textiles in north-west England and northern France, shipbuilding in north-east England and central Scotland, coal extraction in many European mining districts, all fit into that mould. In addition, relatively new industries in other regions have suffered the same fate in recent years, as the decline of the West Midlands' motor and engineering industries in the late 1970s and early 1980s bears clear witness. After displaying an unemployment rate of 0.5 per cent in 1955 (when the British average was 1.2 per cent) and one that conformed exactly to the national average in the mid-1970s, this region lost jobs on a massive scale and displayed a rate that was about a quarter above the national average in the early months of 1982 (Fig. 3.6).

The old industrial regions of Northern Ireland (18.1 per cent), Wales (14.9 per cent) and the north of England still had very high rates of jobless, but their plight appeared rather differently as the average for the UK was inflated by the collapse of the West Midlands (14.3 per cent). Scotland managed to improve its relative unemployment record during the late 1970s because of North Sea oil and its spin-off industries, coupled with newly-attracted high-technology electronics firms. At the other extreme, south-east England, with the highest proportion of jobs in service industries, still has the lowest regional rate in the country even though localized 'black spots' display very high rates. Unfortunately, the continuing application of computerized technology to routine

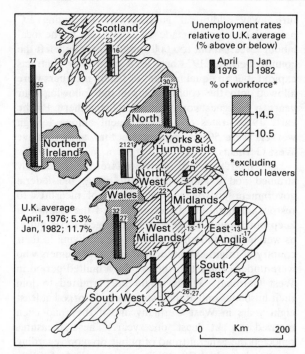

Fig. 3.6
United Kingdom unemployment, 1976 and 1982, by region
(after *The Economist*).

office work threatens south-east England with serious unemployment in the future, and similar problems loom in comparable service-based regions throughout Western Europe. At a finer scale of analysis, inner cities have already been added to the list of areas with high unemployment, and suburbia and small-town Europe is being hit by redundancies as well.

Numbers of long-term unemployed have increased substantially in recent years and the longer a worker remains out of a job the more difficult it becomes to obtain one. For example, in the UK, those on the autumn unemployment register for less than a month decreased from 33 per cent of all unemployed in 1974 to 17 per cent in 1977 and 10 per cent in 1981. At the other end of the scale, those registered for 6 months or more rose from 30 to 38 per cent (557 000) and 49 per cent (1.4 million) over the same span of years. Surveys in the late 1970s offered a sombre picture of workers who had been out of work for 12 months or more. About three-quarters were semi-skilled or unskilled manual workers; few had any formal qualifications; most came from declining industries; and many were in the older age range of the workforce and felt that their age told against them when they went in search of jobs. There is every reason to believe that the situation has deteriorated since then

by the addition of younger, more qualified workers to the list of the long-term jobless. Thus at the end of 1986, 52 per cent of the unemployed in the EC had been jobless for more than 12 months, with the proportion ranging from one-third in Denmark to two-thirds in Belgium, Italy and the Republic of Ireland. Dutch employers have been distressed to find that some people out of work for a year or more become so demoralized and disenchanted with work that they are no longer worth hiring. The hard truth is that a high long-term unemployment rate is dispiriting socially and useless economically; the longer someone is unemployed, the less able he or she is to compete for work.

Finally, and most tragically, there is the problem of youth unemployment which comprises school leavers, those who pursued higher education and other young people who, for one reason or another, failed to obtain permanent employment. Not only are the cohorts of young people who flood on to the labour market remaining substantial each summer, but it is taking their members longer to find jobs. Individual countries have devised strikingly different formulae for organizing the lives of their young people. In each state of Western Europe, save the UK, young men undergo 'national' service for varying lenghts of time. This normally involves military service but, under some circumstances, social or educational service may be undertaken and there are always grounds for exemption. Systems of apprenticeship and further and higher education also vary greatly from country to country. For example, young workers aged 16–18 in West Germany, Switzerland and Austria undertake apprenticeships on low pay for three years, while they continue education on a compulsory day-release basis in order to work towards a formal certificate of competence. Thus 70 per cent of all school leavers in West Germany are absorbed by apprenticeship schemes, and two out of every five apprentices are girls. Teachers, manpower authorities and employers have clearly defined responsibilities in this process. Such an approach does not apply in the UK, where some teenagers on the open market receive higher rates of pay than their German counterparts. This economic fact works against the interests of British school leavers since many employers are reluctant to take on 'expensive' and inexperienced young workers at this time of financial stringency. Youth training schemes do provide some opportunity for government-subsidized work experience for up to two years in the UK; however, many offer no formal qualification or promise of future employment.

Throughout Western Europe, older workers tend to be protected by job security laws, collective bargaining agreements and personnel practices which function to the relative disadvantage of the young. Unemployment rates among young people are normally in inverse relationship to their level of education or training. In broad terms that point still remains true but, for the first time in several decades well-educated, middle-class young people are experiencing spells of unemployment and the sense of powerlessness and lack of control over their lives that has long been suffered by less-educated members of society. Indeed, for almost everyone, prolonged unemployment is a seriously destructive experience that undermines personality and weakens the will and capacity to work (Sinfield 1981).

As well as the four groups identified above, relatively recent immigrants and their children often experience high rates of joblessness. That problem, together with institutionalized discrimination, is shared by Surinamese and Antillans in the Netherlands, Turks in West Germany, North Africans in France, and 'Black Britons' in the UK. But the legal status of these people is highly varied: some are technically foreigners, others have acquired the citizenship of a West European country, while others have held such status since birth. Unfortunately, all too many Europeans only see differences in skin colour and fail to appreciate complexities of legal status and all that this implies for right of abode.

Palliatives

Numerous attempts are being made to minimize the problem, including national measures to facilitate migration of workers to areas where appropriate jobs may still be available, artificial job-creation schemes, and a host of programmes for postponing the arrival of young people on the job market and perhaps even reducing the total supply of labour. Conscription and mass higher education are traditional and widely-accepted mechanisms for keeping young people off the unemployment register and they are being supplemented by a host of special training schemes throughout Western Europe.

Repatriation of foreign workers when their work contracts come to an end is an effective way of trimming a workforce that has no permanent right of abode in a particular country. Thus in West Germany, recruitment of new foreign workers was suspended in November 1973 and renewal of work permits was made increasingly difficult in cases where it was felt that guestworkers were competing directly with German nationals for jobs. Laws were enacted which imposed strict penalties on illegal immigration and a ruling of April 1975 entitled West German cities to

turn away additional guestworkers (excluding EC nationals) once they made up 12 per cent of the local labour force. About 650 000 guestworkers duly left the country between 1973 and 1977 when their contracts expired, but an equal number of family members were allowed into the country during the following four years to join guestworkers already living there. By the early 1980s, rates of unemployment among foreign workers were 50 per cent higher than among native West Germans.

Late in 1981, with social-welfare funds severely strained and unemployment still rising, the federal government approved a new batch of measures to restrict immigration. It recommended the *Länder* to keep out foreign workers' children aged 16 or more, as well as all children who had a parent living in their country of origin and all dependents of foreigners who were under contract to spend only a limited period in West Germany. Wives would be permitted to join their husbands only if their spouses had worked at least eight years in West Germany and if they had been married for at least one year. These measures reflected the general trend of public opinion regarding guestworkers. In 1978, public opinion polls had shown that one-third of West Germans were in favour of sending foreign workers home; by the summer of 1982 the proportion had risen to two-thirds. In 1981, two-thirds of those questioned said they would support a ban on the entry of guestworkers' dependents; in mid-1982, 90 per cent wanted such a ban. Early in that year, financial incentives were proposed to encourage guestworkers and their families to return to their home countries. West Germany then contained 4.6 million foreigners (comprising some 2 million workers and a rather larger total of dependents), or 7.7 per cent of the total population, while in West Berlin, Frankfurt, Munich and Stuttgart the proportion exceeded 20 per cent (O'Loughlin 1980).

In France, a provisional halt to labour migration was called in 1974 and was extended in 1975. Efforts to stop illegal immigration were stepped up and in 1977 the government introduced the offer of a special financial bonus plus a one-way air ticket for each guestworker who agreed to return home. By the summer of 1980 only 41 000 of the country's 1.8 million foreign workers had risen to the bait, with Portuguese making up more than half of that small total. One-third of the jobs thus vacated were taken by French workers, another third by previously unemployed foreign workers, while the remaining jobs were not filled. Belgium also banned further immigration of non-EEC nationals (with the exception of certain skills), while Dutch authorities were forced to interpret work permit regulations very strictly and discourage the relatives of Mediterranean guestworkers from settling in the Netherlands. Dutch problems had been exacerbated by the arrival in 1974–75 of 120 000 migrants from Surinam who have fared less well on the labour market than the 300 000 who preceded them in the 1950s. The scope for continuing the politically-sensitive process of repatriation is limited and could not be envisaged for workers and family members who possess residence permits. By contrast, West European governments have found scope for further curtailment of non-European immigration and in recent years have tightened their regulations on both entry and residence.

Early retirement schemes offer the possibility of opening jobs for younger people, but pensions need to be financially attractive if such an approach is to work on a voluntary basis. The recent appearance of 'grey power' in the USA is a salutary manifestation of people's desire to continue working beyond retirement age. Limiting or prohibiting overtime, and working shorter days, weeks or even years offer ways of sharing out available work more widely, but schemes of this kind require adequate wages or social-security payments for living standards to be maintained. Part-time work is already widespread in Scandinavia and the UK and the idea of job sharing has received considerable discussion but companies that have experimented with it have encountered problems. Daf, the Dutch vehicle firm, found that women staff in secretarial, medical and other service posts adapted well to work sharing and found that they could suit both their own and their employer's interests. Middle-aged, male factory workers in the southern Netherlands reacted less positively and resented being deprived of their full wage-earner status and having to bring home a slimmed-down wage packet, especially if their wives were fully employed. By contrast, the prejudice associated with this aspect of sexual stereotyping is breaking down among young workers of both sexes in the Netherlands and especially the open-minded citizens of Amsterdam. The hard truth is that fear of unemployment is a powerful stimulus for changing one's work routine. Doubtless this helps explain a surge of interest in flexible working arrangements by employees, companies and governments in the mid-1980s.

Whatever policies may be adopted to alleviate the hardships of unemployment and improve the chances of the long-term unemployed, the fact remains that there are insufficient jobs to absorb the total working population, while the supply of labour will continue to increase more rapidly than demand for workers during the rest of the 1980s. The impact of 'new technology' will continue to exacerbate the problem when

demographic pressures start t
In short, the age of full employ
social history. Unemployment is n
scroungers; it extends throughout so
executives, long-serving craftsmen, d
grammers and all other walks of life so
is secure. It will have to be recognized as a
of everyday life for a large and growing sectio
adult population in Western Europe during
remainder of the twentieth century. That condi
will require a social revolution in attitudes, behaviou
and self-esteem of almost unfathomable magnitude.

Looking further ahead, the decline in the birth rate over recent years may mean that some parts of Western Europe may be labour-hungry again in the early years of the twenty-first century. For example, West Germany may be fretting over labour shortages and may have to look to the nations of North Africa or Asia; but that demographic projection is of no consolation to those West Europeans who cannot find work now.

Inequalities

Poverty

The grinding, starving poverty of the inter-war years barely exists in Western Europe in the late 1980s but one-tenth of all families in the European Community (roughly 35 million people) have incomes sufficiently below average national earnings to bring them within a relative poverty line, defined as a margin that excludes individuals from the 'minimum acceptable way of life' in the member state in which they live. Rates of unemployment are still rising in some areas and among some groups, with social-service provision in every country proving inadequate to cope with needs. The European Commission's report on the *First Programme to Combat Poverty* (1981) stressed that certain groups or categories of people – notably the elderly, immigrants, households headed by women, one-parent families, large households and the handicapped – were most vulnerable to relative poverty regardless of where they lived.

The evidence showed that economic growth did not of itself eliminate poverty, not even when accompanied by increased spending on welfare services. Thirty years ago, spending on these services in countries that were to become the Community of the Nine ranged from 8 to 15 per cent of GNP; by 1980 the corresponding proportions were 20 to 30 per cent. Spending on education rose from less than 4 per cent to 5–7 per cent of GNP and many programmes were developed

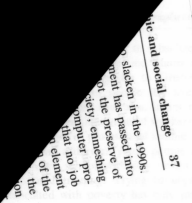

housing for the
...d resettlement
Despite these
... sub-standard
...tality rates in
... still twice as
...d between an
...ember coun-
...ifications or
...h problems
...un and the
...ss adults, more
...ore one-parent families renders
...even more difficult.

Xenophobia

Rising unemployment rates have also served to stir up xenophobic tendencies among many West Europeans who fear that jobs which they believe should have been theirs have been purloined by guestworkers. For example, in 1964 the millionth guestworker to arrive in West Germany received a celebrity's welcome at Cologne station; now the talk is of *Überfremdung* – too many foreigners. Hundreds of thousands of second- and third-generation 'foreigners' have been born in West Germany and the birth rate among immigrant families is twice that among native Germans. The death rate is currently six times lower since at present there are few elderly foreigners in that country. Nonetheless, in 1982, 15 per cent of guest-workers had been in West Germany for more than 15 years and a further 40 per cent for 10–15 years. Statisticians estimate that foreigners and their children could make up 11 per cent of the probably static national population by the year 2000 and 20 per cent by 2030.

In summer 1982, West Germany contained approximately equal numbers of Yugoslavs (637 000) and Italians (624 000), but the 1.5 million Turks comprised by far the largest single group of foreigners and have a strikingly different culture, religion and way of life from their hosts; only a tiny fraction are interested in acquiring German nationality. They have experienced violent xenophobic attacks in some cities and graffiti such as 'Germany for the Germans', 'Foreigners out' and 'Turkish-occupied zone' have become increasingly commonplace.

At the start of 1986, France contained about 4 million foreigners, with that figure having contracted from 4.4. million in 1983 because of return migration and naturalization. Portuguese (765 000) form the most numerous group, but it is North Africans (Moroccans 494 200, Tunisians 200 780, and especially Algerians 535 000) who are the most frequent targets of racial attacks. As in other West European countries, many of the 'foreigners' are in France to stay. The earlier phases of labour migration by lone males and later arrivals of wives and children have long passed (Castles 1984). Now the key issues are integration and assimilation of whole families, including many young people actually born in France and perhaps holding French nationality.

The popularity of Jean-Marie Le Pen and the Front National is a worrying demonstration of racism not only among the working class but also among some middle-class elements who respond to a philosophy of the purity of the French nation and of keeping France for the French. Le Pen insists that all illegal immigrants should be sent home and even those in jobs should be encouraged to go, thereby helping to reduce unemployment among the 'French-French'. The Front National receives sizeable votes in de-industrializing working-class districts (with high unemployment and large immigrant communities), in southern towns (where many Europeans settled after leaving newly-independent Algeria in 1962), and in bourgeois neighbourhoods in Paris and other large cities. After a honeymoon of goodwill towards foreigners in the early 1980s, major political parties of both right and left are now adopting a tougher line in policies regarding immigrants from non-EC countries.

Guestworkers have different origins in Belgium, the Netherlands, Switzerland and the UK but a walk through the back streets of any major city in Western Europe and a casual reading of graffiti reveals a wide-spread demonstration of racist attitudes. The slogans are expressed in various languages and daubed in differing colours, but the sentiments and the fundamental problems are very much the same. Even Brussels, arguably the 'capital' of Western Europe, is not immune. In three inner-city districts, poorer foreigners from the Mediterranean states, Asia and Africa make up between one-third and one-half of the total population and there the slogans are as embittered as anything to be seen in working-class Paris, London's East End or the poorer districts of West Berlin. The immigration issue dominated campaigning during the 1985 election and some local authorities in the Belgian capital refuse to grant residence permits to new arrivals from Turkey or North Africa.

Asylum?

The latest part in this complicated story involves the arrival of non-European refugees who are seeking asylum in north-west Europe for fear of persecution in their home country on grounds of race, religion,

Swe. 4975	Belg. 1780
Den. 4370	Fran. 1310
Switz. 4000	Neths. 990
W.Ger. 3350	Norw. 945
Aust. 2965	U.K. 240

1984
1985
1986

Fig. 3.7
Asylum seekers in main West European countries –
columns indicate annual arrivals in thousands (after *The
Economist*).

social group or political opinion. Over 750 000 have
arrived since 1977, including 200 000 in 1986 alone,
and all at a time of mounting unemployment and
xenophobia (Fig. 3.7). During 1984, 1985 and 1986,
Sweden accepted about 5 000 refugees for every

million inhabitants, Denmark and Switzerland took in
over 4 000 per million and West Germany 3 350, but
the UK only 240 per million. West European governments have failed to agree a policy on refugees, partly
because of the difficulty of judging the genuineness of
asylum seekers, including 50 000 Tamils arriving from
Sri Lanka (1984–86), 40 000 Iranians (mostly young
men avoiding military service) and thousands more
from Ghana, Ethiopia, Pakistan, Zaire and the
Lebanon.

Increasingly, Austria, Greece and Italy have functioned as places of transit for those seeking asylum in
the supposedly more comfortable and generous
welfare states of north-west Europe. Each destination
country operates in its own way with regard to refugees but all now attempt to discourage further arrivals.
For example, once-generous West Germany prevents
non-European refugees from taking work for five
years and requires them to live in camps. Agreement
with East Germany has halted the flow of Asians and
Africans who had been arriving by plane to East
Berlin and then been allowed to pass through the
Wall. Belgium, France, the UK and formerly open-
hearted Switzerland, Sweden and Denmark are tightening their border controls to ensure that asylum
seekers who lack genuine claims are dispatched elsewhere or sent home. Fining airlines that bring them
to Western Europe is the latest tactic.

Further reading

Archer M S, Giner S (eds) 1971 *Contemporary Europe: class,
status and power*. Routledge and Kegan Paul, London
Castles S 1984 *Here for Good: Western Europe's new ethnic
minorities*. Pluto, London
Kosiński L 1970 *The Population of Europe*. Longman,
London
Warnes A M (ed.) 1982 *Geographical Perspectives on the
Elderly*. Wiley, London

4
Migration

Migration in context

Migration is the main factor changing the demographic map of post-war Europe. As birth and death rates converge, migration becomes the key element in explaining regional variations in population change. Not only that, migration also lies at the root of, or is heavily involved in, several major trends shaping the contemporary human geography of Western Europe: processes like urbanization and counterurbanization, regional economic growth and decline, rural depopulation and repopulation, inner-city decline and gentrification – to name but a few.

Human mobility can be classified in many ways. Generally, there is a broad correlation between distance moved and frequency of the movement. A continuum exists, ranging from short-distance daily commuting and weekly flows to second homes, through annual holiday trips and seasonal farm labour moves, to more permanent residential shifts which may be local, inter-regional or international in character. Before 1914, there were enormous outpourings of European population to the New World, chiefly the Americas. Since 1945 there have been large-scale transfers of migrants into the industrial countries of north-west Europe from the continent's Mediterranean fringe and from former 'colonial' territories like Algeria, the West Indies, India and Pakistan. In all, a bewildering variety of types and scales of movements!

This chapter is mainly concerned with migration *within* Western Europe. Historical migrations of Europeans overseas and recent immigration waves originating from non-European countries are mentioned only in passing. We shall also not dwell on local-scale intra-urban residential movement. The two main types of migration to be dealt with are intra-European international migration and inter-regional migration within individual countries.

As with many other socio-economic phenomena in Western Europe, the story of migration reached a kind of threshold in late 1973 with the onset of the oil crisis. The discussion is therefore structured around this 'tipping-point', although it will be shown that economic deterioration was by no means the only factor accounting for the sharp change in migratory trends in the early 1970s. The chapter contains three main parts. First, the evolution of international migration is traced up to 1973. Secondly, we examine the effects of the oil crisis on migratory patterns, with the freezing of new movements, the switch to the consolidation of foreign migrant stocks and the trend to return migration. The final section explores trends in internal migration and makes a special study of France, which is the most instructive country to consider because of the variety of its internal migration processes. It is, however, worth noting that, with twelve of the eighteen major countries of Western Europe participating in the EC, the distinction between internal and international migration may become increasingly irrelevant.

International migration: the picture to 1973

Two major influences lie behind international migration: political and economic. Much of Western Europe's twentieth-century cross-national movement has been politically inspired, associated with the two world wars. Since 1945, economic reasons have taken over. The search for better jobs and higher incomes has guided millions of southern Europeans, Irish and Finns, mostly from rural backgrounds, to the great industrial conurbations and capital cities of north-west Europe. Most recently of all, in 'post-industrial' Europe, complex flows of high-level manpower have arisen between highly-urbanized countries.

Kosiński (1970) has traced the earlier waves of European mobility and has shown how emigration has been a persistent theme in Europe's demography. Between 1820 and 1940 an estimated 55–60 million people left Europe for overseas, the annual rate peaking at over 1 million in the years immediately preceding the First World War. Most migrants – 38 million during 1820–1940 – were destined for the USA. Initially, they came from 'old' emigration countries like Great Britain, Germany and Scandinavia but by the end of the century the centre of gravity had shifted south: Italy alone was sending 400 000 a year by 1910.

Intra-European movements were also under way before 1940. In the nineteenth century, industrializing nations drew workers from neighbouring countries, the Irish moving to Britain, Italians to France and Central Europeans to the German Empire. Later, Kosiński (1970) estimated that 7.7 million Europeans were involved in 'political migrations' associated with the First World War. The German census of 1925 recorded that 770 000 persons had moved into Germany from German-conquered territories such as Alsace-Lorraine, northern Schleswig and Eupen-Malmédy when they reverted to their original countries (France, Denmark and Belgium, respectively). Regional wars provoked large transfers of population between Greece and Turkey, and an estimated 300 000 Spaniards moved to France during and after the Spanish Civil War. Political migrations continued in the late 1930s with the *Volksdeutsche*, the 'gathering in' of ethnic Germans attracted by pan-German propaganda and economic prosperity in pre-war Germany.

The Second World War was accompanied by further massive shifts of population across national frontiers which were themselves changing. One estimate gives 25 million people moving (Kosiński 1970), the majority of them (13 million) Germans. Most of the remaining displacements were in Eastern Europe. Germans drafted for military service were replaced by foreign workers recruited from conquered lands. Amounting to 7 million, of whom 5 million were civilians and 2 million were prisoners-of-war, they accounted for 20 per cent of the German workforce by the end of the war.

At the end of the war, further *Volksdeutsche* took place from the Baltic states, Ukraine, Romania, Bulgaria and from different parts of dismembered Yugoslavia. As a result of an agreement with Italy, Germans from the Bolzano region were given a chance to emigrate to Germany. About one-third of them, around 100 000, actually moved. Six million Germans emigrated from Poland, Czechoslovakia and Hungary during 1945–49, 485 000 Finns were repatriated in two waves in 1939 and 1944 during the Soviet–Finnish wars, and about 200 000 Italians left

Istria when the It[...]
the end of the [...]

This descri[...]
skeletal, is [...]
omic' mi[...]
a sudde[...]
which is s[...]
country of th[...]
900 000 members [...]
1931. Italian prisoners [...]
had an important influenc[...]
Italian settlement there [...]
Germany there were 9.8 millio[...]
('expelled from homes') recorded i[...]
their young age structure (2.5 million [...]
20 years of age in 1964), they contributed [...]
the labour supply, holding down wages and a[...]
a key factor in the West German economic mira[...]
before the subsequent influxes of non-German migrants from southern Europe (Kosiński 1970).

Later, politically-stimulated migrations resulted from decolonization processes in the Maghreb and elsewhere. The most dramatic among this group were the 1 million *pieds noirs* from Algeria who were re-patriated to France after the Treaty of Evian in 1962. Most of the *pieds noirs* settled in the Midi or in Paris; by 1973, 80 per cent were living in towns, mostly large ones, and 60 per cent had settled in a belt stretching between Bordeaux and Nice. The settlers opting for southern France were mostly the poorer classes among the repatriates; the numerically-fewer civil servants and professionals tended to head for Paris and the north (Baillet 1975). Overall, repatriates lacked the training to fill the technical and industrial jobs then available in France, a fact which partly explains the geographical distribution of their settlement and their reluctance to go to those regions where the French government wanted them (McDonald 1965).

General character of post-war labour migration

The post-war labour migrations from southern European villages to northern European towns and cities are the world's most massive in recent decades. Estimates vary as to the numbers involved because of the considerable quantity of clandestine movers and the large amount of fluid temporary movement which goes partially unrecorded. The various countries have different ways of recording migrants based partly on different definitions of exactly what constitutes a migrant. Switzerland differentiates 'permanent', 'annual', 'seasonal' and 'frontier' migrants, whereas France has a much more lax recording system. Official statistics indicate that at the eve of the recession in

bout 7 million migrant workers in
companied by a further 5 million
larging the figures to account for
oves and for non-EC countries like
Switzerland yields 'guesstimates' of
illion for workers and perhaps 15 million
al migrant population (most of the unre-
ovement consists of unaccompanied people).
ghly, we may say that 1 in 10 workers in the
cross-national migrants and about 1 in 10 of
orkers in the main Mediterranean sending coun-
(Portugal, Spain, Italy, Yugoslavia, Greece,
rkey, Tunisia, Algeria and Morocco) earns his
ving in industrial Europe. Again, this may be an
underestimate. Implicit in the title of Berger and
Mohr's classic documentary *A Seventh Man* (1975) is
the proportion of 1 in 7, though this probably refers
to manual workers. In Switzerland and Luxembourg
the proportion is more like 1 in 3. In fact, the migrant
workers of Europe may be likened to an invisible thirteenth member of the EC, in population terms equivalent in size to Belgium or Greece.

What distinguishes this migration from others in the
past is its essential *temporary* character. At least to
start with, neither the migrant himself nor the reception country had any ambitions for permanent settlement, although in recent years this has been changing.
The migrants came basically to sell their labour where
there was a labour shortage. The jobs they filled had
certain common characteristics: poorly paid, insecure,
unpleasant, boring and heavy. Until recently, non-EC
migrants had few rights or claims outside the reality
of their jobs. Berger and Mohr (1975) wrote that it
was not men who migrated but machine-minders,
sweepers, diggers, cement mixers, etc.

There is no doubt that the recruitment of foreign
workers became a central plank for the growth and
prosperity of the members of the EC and of other
European industrial countries between the 1950s and
the early 1970s. What was initially regarded as a
temporary expedient to ease labour shortages has
become something close to a necessity, a permanent
structural feature of the EC space economy. The 'self-
feeding' process of labour migration has seen the
penetration of migrants into other sectors of the
economy (Böhning 1972). To a certain extent this is
because of a natural process of upward mobility that
some migrants enjoy through their drive and perhaps
their ability to adapt and to learn a new language
quickly. In other cases the existence of a migrant
community provides its own opportunities for entre-
preneurship to flourish within the 'ethnic economy'.
A good example of this is the Cypriot community in
London which is almost completely self-sufficient with

its own housing market, eating places, lawyers, travel
agents, shops and other services (Constantinides
1977). The occupational and economic mobility of
Cypriots in London is quite striking. Most have been
in a range of jobs and business enterprises and a
substantial proportion are now self-employed, not
only in the traditional Cypriot activities of catering
and clothing manufacture but also in a wide range of
other, mostly service concerns. As the pattern of
Cypriot residence has moved out from the original
'heartland' in inner north London, so has this proliferation of small businesses (King and Bridal 1982).
Now Cypriot restaurants which originally served
Cypriot workers in the 1950s cater largely for a British
clientele which has 'discovered' Greek and Turkish
food. In this way an immigrant group is able to *market*
its ethnicity, something that the Italians (in catering
and hairdressing) and the Chinese (in take-away food)
have also done in Britain since the war.

Expansion of migrants into other job fields also
takes place as rising standards of living induce a flight
on the part of the native population from employment
types that are perceived as undesirable. Labour migration thus has two inter-related but very different
effects: it ensures a plentiful supply of cheap, low-
grade labour; and it acts as an agent for the social
promotion – the *embourgeoisement* – of the indigenous
workforce.

In very general terms, labour migration into
Western Europe's industrial heartland has well-
defined characteristics (Salt 1976). Most migrants are
male, unmarried and unskilled, departing in their
twenties. The temporary nature of the movement is
partially governed by the nature of the work contracts,
which rarely last for more than a year or two, though
most are renewable. This 'rotation' of migrant workers
found its most overt expression in West Germany in
the 1960s where the policy of *Konjunkturpuffer* was
a clear attempt to use migrant labourers as an industrial 'reserve army' to be hired and dismissed
according to the dictates of the economy's fluctuations, thereby protecting the host country's own
workers from the unemployment effects of cyclical
recession (Castles and Kosack 1985). Berger and
Mohr (1975) cynically expose the exploitative
character of migration and the way industrialized
countries benefit from it. They explain that the
migrant's labour power is ready-made. Production in
the industrialized country is going to benefit, but that
country has not supported the cost of creating that
labour power. So far as the economy of the industrial
country is concerned, it is as if migrant workers are
'immortal' because they are continually interchange-
able. 'They are not born: they are not brought up:

they do not age: they do not get tired: they do not die. They have a single function – to work' (p. 64).

Nevertheless, the fundamental ambiguity of the European migrant worker situation must be recognized. It is a paradox that millions of people are living in foreign countries in Europe but are not designated as immigrants. The concept of 'immigrant' is cryptically paraphrased by the use of such terms as 'guest-worker' (*Gastarbeiter*), 'foreign employee' and 'migrant labourer'. Yugoslavian emigrants are termed 'Yugoslav residents in temporary employment abroad' by the sending country: a clear if clumsy refusal by the Yugoslav government to acknowledge that the emigrants might not return. A consequence of this collective denial of the objective existence of emigrants and immigrants and of emigration and immigration countries is that no clearly-defined migration policies have been developed, even in those countries which have been receiving post-war migrants for forty years. The migrants' status remains permanently provisional – a situation which is as paradoxical as it is absurd and ultimately inhumane (Hoffmann-Nowotny 1978).

Institutional background

Articles 48 and 49 of the Treaty of Rome provide for the free movement of labour within the EC and for the abolition of discrimination between Community nationals with regard to employment, pay and other rights of work and civic life. The free movement provisions were ushered in between 1961 and 1968. The articles have been described as little more than a liberal–capitalist prescription for bringing manpower shortages and surpluses into balance within a given trade area (Böhning 1972). They were inserted at the prompting of Italy, the Common Market country then most affected by labour surpluses, but the provisions were also actively supported by industrial countries whose governments and large employers wanted a flexible and non-permanent labour supply to perform the least desirable job functions during periods of rapid economic growth and labour shortage.

In practice, the 'free movement' policy had negligible effects. Migration between EC countries actually declined over the period of free movement, a paradoxical situation which is partly explained by the growth of the Italian economy in the 1960s and the diversion of southern Italian migration from Europe to northern Italy. This, however, is not the whole story, for Italian emigration to Switzerland continued to grow and in most years during the 1960s more Italians migrated to Switzerland than to the entire EC. In fact, Articles 48 and 49 failed to halt a trend that

was already established before 1961 – the decline of intra-EC movement as a proportion of all migration into the EC (65 per cent in 1958, 51 per cent in 1961, 28 per cent in 1964). In the same year as the free movement provisions came into force, West Germany concluded bilateral agreements with Spain, Greece and Turkey for labour importation under German controls. An agreement with Yugoslavia followed soon after. As Italian migration to West Germany tailed off (141 000 in 1960; 30 000 in 1970), the Yugoslavian and Turkish streams swelled to account for over half of West Germany's annual intake of *Gastarbeiter* by 1970.

In short, the 'liberal–capitalist prescription' had failed: labour movements had not equalized income and prosperity differentials within the Community – if anything, regional disparities became accentuated. Labour migration had shown itself to be one of the most powerful links binding the economic core of Europe to an ever-widening periphery (King 1982).

Geographical pattern of flows

Figure 4.1 shows the spatial pattern of international migration into the major receiving countries of the EC at the eve of the recession. The pattern has a certain spatial symmetry, the magnet of the 'core' attracting inflows from the periphery. France drew most of its migrants from the south and south-west (Spain, Portugal and Algeria), while West Germany's hinterland lay to the south-east in Yugoslavia, Greece and Turkey. Italy has sent large numbers of migrants to both France and West Germany, as well as to Switzerland. Britain has drawn mainly from the Irish periphery as well as from New Commonwealth territories, while in the far north (not shown on Fig. 4.1) the Nordic Common Labour Market, dating from 1954, has enabled many Finns to migrate across the Gulf of Bothnia to Sweden.

Post-war European labour migration has evolved in a series of stages, with different sending and receiving countries dominant at different times. During the late 1940s and the 1950s, France, Belgium, Switzerland, Sweden and the UK were the principal destination countries; Italy, the Republic of Ireland and Finland were the main suppliers. West Germany still drew labour from territories to the east, but this changed in 1961 when the East German source was shut off. The period 1961–73 saw the rise of West Germany as the major destination for southern European migrants. At the same time, the Italian source began to dry up, to be replaced by Greeks, Yugoslavs and Turks in West Germany and by Spaniards, Portuguese and North Africans in France. Details of the Italian post-

No of established
foreign workers, 1973
Less than 100000

1971 flow to E.C.
with main destination   41776:Fr

7,500
Danes

471,000
Irish in U.K.

183,000
E.C. in U.K.

46,000
British in E.C.

98,000
Dutch

74,000
Belgians

81,000
Germans

582,000
Turks
126213:Ger

1,348,000
from other
Countries

93,000
French

535,000
Yugoslavs
128144:
Ger

469,000
Portuguese
87 492:Fr

527,000
Spaniards
60173: Fr & Ger

858,000
Italians
197 546:Ger

332,000
Greeks
42 738:
Ger

701,000
North Africans
41776:Fr

0   km   500

Fig. 4.1
Labour migration in the
European Community in the
early 1970s.

war flow to Europe can be seen in Fig. 4.2. The four
triennia were chosen for their representativeness in
charting the changing pattern and volume of flow. In
the 1950s, France and Switzerland dominated the
exodus, although over 20 000 were going each year to
the Benelux countries (mostly to Belgium) and over
10 000 to Great Britain. Five years later, the West
German and Swiss flows had risen to dominance; the
British flow was maintained but the Belgian and
French were halved. The early 1970s and the triennium 1979–81 reveal contraction across all major
destination countries, especially marked being the fall-
off to France.

The overall tendency has been for the EC's main
labour demand countries, France and West Germany,
to recruit from further and further afield. By the mid-
1960s the whole of the EC, Mediterranean Europe,
Turkey and the Maghreb had been incorporated into
one huge labour market. Manpower decisions taken
in one country, such as France or West Germany, had
immediate bearing on employment levels in half a
dozen others, as was made clear by the West German
recession of 1966–67 when reduced inflows and accel-

erated outflows provided a brief foretaste of things to
come seven years later. As Salt (1976) pointed out,
migration flows could be quickened, slowed or
reversed by the twist of a tap.

Although the sending countries share common
features of relàtive overpopulation, underemployment
and underdevelopment (Finland is something of an
exception), their individual migration profiles vary.
Some were 'old' emigration countries whose post-war
flows to Europe represented the deflection of streams
which had headed mainly for the New World (Greeks
and Italians to America, Portuguese to Brazil and
Angola). For other countries, like Yugoslavia and
Turkey, emigration was an almost completely new
phenomenon, lacking significant precedents. This
notion of the 'maturity' of migration flows is also
important in that it affected the character of the
migration that resulted, a character which, according
to Böhning (1972), proceeds through four stages.

In the first phase, migrants are short-stay workers,
primarily young, single males from the more urbanized and industrialized parts of their countries, the
innovatory 'grapevine' of migration not having yet

Fig. 4.2
Emigration from Italy to
European countries.

penetrated the remote rural regions. In the second
phase, the migration stream ages slightly with married
males (usually leaving their wives and children at
home) joining the single workers. Duration of stay
increases slightly. Returnees set in motion a diffusion
process which extends the areas of origin into small
towns and some surrounding rural regions. The third
stage sees a continuation of the ageing of the migration stream and a change in its character as wives and
families are sent for. Length of stay increases further,
especially for families; turnover decreases accordingly.
The remaining areas of the sending country are drawn
into the migration stream, although this depresses its
skill content, with untrained rural workers predominant. The final phase is reached when the migratory
presence becomes self-feeding and creates its own
demands for infrastructures, consumer goods and
further employment related to the development of the
ethnic community. Family reunion dominates the
migration streams and returns are few. This is the
stage that many migrant groups in Europe are
reaching in the 1980s.

Although analytically distinct, these four stages are
historically intertwined so that at any point in time
different supply countries' migration streams exhibit
different characteristics according to the maturity of
the stream. In the early 1960s, for instance, the
Turkish flow was in its first phase, whereas the Spanish
and Italian flows were already approaching maturity.
Even as late as 1971, 98.5 per cent of Turks entering
France were male; 55 per cent were in their twenties
and, although four-fifths of the migrants were married,
only one in twenty had their families with them
(Gokalp 1973).

Böhning's four stages also help to explain regional
differences in the intensity of outmigration within the
individual supply countries. In Portugal, Spain, Italy
and Greece, emigration during the 1960s was heaviest
from overpopulated, rural, upland districts like Tras-
os-Montes, Galicia, Andalusia, the southern Apennines, Epirus and Thrace. For Yugoslavia and Turkey,
the pattern was the opposite, with heaviest outmigration from the more urbanized regions of Slov-
enia, Croatia and Istanbul (see the map in King 1976,

...rresponds to the difference ...' emigration countries. More ...1973 Yugoslavia and Turkey ...igration from regions like ...Yugoslavia and Anatolia in ...case also demonstrates how ...specialized links with certain ...maps presented by Baučić (1973) show that the pattern of outmigration to France, concentrated in Serbia, is the complete opposite to the pattern for outmigration to West Germany. The Turkish case, on the other hand, reveals that many migrants move internally before emigrating abroad. Although few figures exist to verify this trend, it seems that a large number of rural Turks acclimatize themselves first in the shanty-towns of Istanbul, Izmir and Ankara before setting off for Europe.

The flows of labour migrants that built up during the 1960s were matched by invisible, reverse flows of money. Remittances are held to be the principal advantage emigration brings to the sending country. Hume's (1973) estimate of an annual flow of remittances from migrants in Europe of $2 500 million has been widely quoted but is certainly an under-valuation for much money finds its way back not through banks and official channels but via letters and friends. Remittances are very significant for the emigration countries. In 1970 they accounted for an amount equivalent to 55 per cent of total exports of merchandise in Portugal; in Greece the proportion was 54 per cent, in Turkey 46 per cent, in Yugoslavia 30 per cent and in Spain 20 per cent (Seers 1979). Thousands of southern European villages have remittances as their main source of income, in some cases accounting for over half or even three-quarters of the communities' cash resources. Rarely, however, is this money used to promote the development of the regions concerned: most of it goes on maintaining members of the family left behind, improving housing and importing consumer durables. Since most consumer durables are imported from industrial Europe, the money goes straight back whence it came.

Economic and social characteristics of migrants in European cities

The distribution of migrants exhibits even more distinct spatial characteristics at the other end of the migratory chain. With one or two exceptions, such as Spanish labourers working in French vineyards and Yugoslavs working in Austrian ski resorts, migrants cluster in urban and industrial regions, their distribution determined by the types of work made available to them. In France, 40 per cent of migrants live in and around Paris, and most of the rest are in the major industrial areas of Lyons, Marseilles and the north (Ogden 1985a). In West Germany, *Gastarbeiter* are more widespread, reflecting the more diffuse spatial structure of the West German urban and industrial network. There is a relative concentration in the south, especially in Baden-Württemburg which in 1973 had 570 000 migrants in a population of 3.5 million. Also important were Südbayern and Hessen, both with over 250 000, and the populous Nordrhein-Westfalen with 680 000. Between them these four out of Germany's nine *Landesarbeitsamtsbezirken* (regional labour markets) contained three-quarters of the Federal Republic's migrants. The largest single clusters of foreign workers were in the main cities, especially Munich (with 156 900 *Gastarbeiter*), Stuttgart (130 200), Frankfurt (122 300), West Berlin (82 500), Hamburg (69 500) and Cologne (63 000). Stuttgart, with the Daimler and Mercedes car plants as well as a range of expanding light industries, had the largest relative concentration: 26.5 per cent of the workforce were migrants in 1973.

The above data for West Germany are from Salt (1976), who also gives examples of particular national concentrations. Italians and Yugoslavs dominate in the south, partly for reasons of proximity and partly because these regions took the earlier waves of migrants, most of whom came from these two countries, especially Italy. Turks are widely distributed but are the dominant group in the north. At the local scale, the pattern is much influenced by the preferences of individual employers who tend to hire from the same national group to simplify language and job training. The preference of the Ford Motor Company of Cologne for Turkish workers contributes greatly to the character of the migrant population of that city. The national groupings themselves may be further differentiated by regional origin so that, for example, the Sicilians, the Andalusians or the Croatians form residential groups apart from their respective co-nationals.

The distribution of migrant groups within West European cities is related closely to the types of housing to which they have access. Migrants are usually constrained to live in the cheaper, poorer-quality accommodation. Partly this is because they have low incomes and few capital resources, but an additional factor is their desire to accept cheap accommodation in order to maximize their savings and hasten their dream of returning home. As a result, migrants tend to be forced into quasi-ghettos which take three main forms.

Firstly, they may be concentrated in the low-quality, older type of tenement buildings found in the inner city. A 1970 housing survey in the Ruhr found that migrants, even though they paid 30 per cent more than Germans for rented accommodation, were twice as likely to be in pre-1945 housing and three times as likely to lack their own bath and lavatory. Also analogous to inner-city flats are the squalid *hôtels meublés* of the twilight zones of French cities; usually these are crammed full of North Africans. Second, and prevalent mainly in France, are *bidonvilles* or peripheral shanty-towns. These are now very much reduced in extent but in the 1960s existed as festering and insanitary sores around most major French cities. Hervo and Charras (1971) enumerated 225 separate *bidonvilles*, with a total population of 100 000, two-thirds of whom were Algerians and Portuguese. The third type of quasi-ghetto is the worker hostel built for *Gastarbeiter* in Germany and Switzerland. These single-sex dormitories, many of which are built within factory compounds, represent the ultimate in social segregation; their atmosphere has been well-captured in the photographs of Jean Mohr (Berger and Mohr 1975).

Patterns of migrant employment naturally differ from country to country, which makes a full account impossible, but most migrants have entered low-status, low-paying unattractive jobs shunned by the native workforce. The pattern of employment has also changed somewhat over time (Salt 1976). During the 1950s, most migrants were in agriculture, mining, construction and the service sector. Subsequently, there was a massive expansion into the industrial sector. By 1973, migrants made up 20 per cent of the industrial workforce in France, 12 per cent in Germany and 40 per cent in Switzerland. Within the industrial sector, migrants were especially prevalent in the most disagreeable and hazardous jobs, on boring production lines and in health-sapping industries like asbestos, rubber and bricks. In Europe's big car plants – Ford in Cologne, Volvo in Gothenburg and the Renault factories in France – 40–45 per cent of the labour force were migrants by 1973. As foreign workers have increasingly penetrated into other sectors of the economy, some stratification has developed with regard to the status of jobs taken by different nationalities. By the early 1970s, Italians no longer filled the more menial and unpleasant jobs. They had moved on to the lighter and more pleasant factory and service-sector jobs, whilst jobs like refuse collecting and street sweeping were left largely to Turks in West Germany and to Algerians in France. There are, however, considerable differences in patterns of employment between nationalities which are not related to status. In France, for instance, 58 per cent of Portuguese and 37 per cent of Algerians

worked in the building sector in 1970: but only 26 per cent of Moroccans, many of whom, along with the Poles, worked in mining. Yugoslavs, on the other hand, had a *penchant* for the automobile industry (Castles and Kosack 1985).

Although migrants form a kind of sub-proletariat or *Unterschichtung* beneath and unrelated to the social structure of the receiving country (Hoffmann-Nowotny 1978), it is clear that the migrant stratum itself is differentiated with respect to job types and housing. Italians do not sweep the streets, neither do they live in *bidonvilles*; they are the aristocrats of the brawn drain. The Spaniards are not far behind. At the bottom of the migrant hierarchy are the Turks and the Maghrebins; the Portuguese, Yugoslavs and Greeks form a middle layer. Rose (1969), in an interesting but methodologically suspect study, develops this idea further, pointing out correlations between socio-economic status, cultural background and degree of 'acceptability'. In France, for instance, the more acceptable Italians and Spaniards come from a cultural, religious and linguistic background that is not dissimilar to the French; not so the Turks and North Africans with their totally different languages and religion.

Much has been written of the social and cultural problems of migrant workers (Castles and Kosack 1985; Hammar 1985). Such issues may not be very 'geographical' but they are vitally, shamedly important. Space permits only a crude listing of some of these problems: they include general lack of integration, linguistic isolation, culture conflict, sexual frustration, separation from kin, discrimination, poor access to social services, a high rate of industrial accidents, poor health and many more.

International migration after the oil crisis

The oil crisis marked a turning point in the history of post-war European migratory movements (Lebon and Falchi 1980). Although this statement is broadly true, it needs to be qualified in two senses.

First, it can be demonstrated that moves aimed at stemming if not inverting migration flows had been taken well before late 1973. The UK, France and the Netherlands had taken steps to limit inflows from ex-colonial territories as early as the 1950s and 1960s. Switzerland attempted to stabilize its foreign workforce in 1963 and, in the 1970s, in the light of vigorous political debate associated with referenda on immigration controls, immigration legislation was considerably tightened. Denmark temporarily suspended immigration of foreign workers in 1970 and Norway narrowed the availability of its work permits in 1971. In 1972,

Table 4.1 Annual labour migration for selected European countries, 1973–85 (all figures in thousands)

	1973	1974	1975	1976	1977	1978	1979	1980	1981	1982	1983	1984	1985
(A) Inflows to receiving countries													
Workers:													
West Germany (1)	319.1	46.3	21.9	24.1	29.7	19.5	37.9	82.6	43.9	25.9	24.4	27.5	33.4
France (2)	143.5	53.4	15.8	17.3	14.2	10.0	9.2	9.5	25.7	89.2	9.0	5.9	5.5
Belgium (3)	5.9	6.1	4.1	4.2	4.7	3.9	3.4	3.8	3.5	2.3	1.8	1.7	1.9
Switzerland (4)	49.7	31.3	18.0	15.6	19.7	21.9	25.5	32.3	35.3	33.0	24.4	27.5	33.4
Austria (5)	263.4	189.8	115.7	97.2	116.9	81.1	83.1	95.4	81.9	57.2	52.7	55.2	60.3
Gross immigration:													
Netherlands (6)	73.7	95.1	55.2	48.9	49.9	55.6	72.2	79.8	50.4	40.9	36.4	37.3	46.3
Sweden (7)	24.9	31.9	30.1	39.7	38.7	31.7	32.4	34.4	27.4	25.1	22.3	26.1	27.9
(B) Outflows from sending countries													
Workers:													
Spain (8)	96.1	50.7	20.6	12.1	11.3	12.0	12.5	14.5	15.9	18.5	22.0	21.4	18.2
Greece (9)	12.0	11.0	10.0	3.0	8.0	6.5							
Yugoslavia (10)	73.5	20.0	15.0	10.0	4.9	3.5	35.0	30.0	30.0	22.0	16.0	15.0	19.5
Turkey (11)	136.0	20.0	4.0	11.0	19.1	18.9	23.6	28.4	58.8	49.4	52.5	45.8	47.4
Gross emigration:													
Finland (12)	6.7	9.6	12.1	15.7	18.2	11.9	12.5	12.0	6.9	4.6	4.6	5.1	5.5
Italy (13)	123.3	112.0	92.7	97.2	87.7	85.4	89.0	84.9	80.5	98.2	85.1	77.3	66.7
Portugal (14)	120.0	70.3	44.9	33.2	28.8	30.3	20.6	18.0	16.5	10.2	6.9	6.6	7.2

Source: SOPEMI Annual Reports, 1973–86, OECD Directorate for Social Affairs, Manpower and Education, Paris
Remarks

(1) Permanent workers excluding EC nationals
(2) Permanent workers excluding EC nationals; 1981 and 1982 figures comprise exceptional regularizations
(3) Wage earners excluding EC nationals
(4) Workers employed permanently or yearly
(5) Work permits issued
(6) Based on aliens' files at communes' registers
(7) Estimates for all immigrants

(8) Assisted emigration to Europe
(9) All destinations; Greek emigration statistics ceased in 1978
(10) Based on data from Yugoslav Employment Bureau; after 1979 modified by host country data
(11) All destinations
(12) To Nordic countries only
(13) All destinations
(14) Emigrants registered by Secretary for State for Emigration

West Germany strengthened its legislation against illegal immigrants, including the abolition of worker entry on tourist visas. The West Germans were also concerned about the build-up of ethnic concentrations in certain regions and attempted to prevent further immigrant settlement in areas where the foreign work-force was above 12 per cent (Salt 1981).

The second qualification concerns the assumption that economic factors were the overriding motive behind the ban on further recruitment. The racial factor was very important too. Looking back, it is possible to discern that anti-immigrant tension and the increasing power and ambitions of the migrants them-selves were leading to a crisis (Slater 1979). The tension exploded in a series of ugly racial incidents in France in 1973, mostly directed against Algerians. Other serious race riots occurred in the Netherlands,

as a result of which a ceiling was imposed on the number of foreigners allowed to work in Rotterdam. West Germany's stop to the recruitment of *Gastar-beiter* occurred in November 1973: the fuel crisis was the official explanation, but it was as much to do with a seething undercurrent of racial friction and an anxiety over growing numbers of foreign labourers.

From the point of view of the statistical monitoring of post-recession migratory movements, the year 1973 also saw the establishment of the SOPEMI continuous reporting service on migration (*Système d'Observation Permanente des Migrations*). Although SOPEMI acknowledges that its national suppliers of migration data lack consistency and that its sources on return flows are especially fragmentary, the post-1973 picture is clear in its essential features. With the exception of Italy, protected by EC free movement laws, all southern European countries experienced a drastic cut in emigration across the 1974 threshold. Return movements accelerated, although massive waves of return migration have not occurred.

Table 4.1 presents a synthesis of the available SOPEMI data on annual migration from sending countries and to host countries for the period 1973–85. The lack of comparability of the national data sets should again be stressed; see the 'Remarks' section in Table 4.1. While all sending countries except Finland experienced a reduction of flows during the mid-1970s, the host countries can be divided into two groups: those in which the foreign workforce diminished rather sharply between 1974 and December 1978 – Austria (−20.5 per cent), West Germany (−19.8 per cent), Switzerland (−17.5 per cent) and France (−9.2 per cent); and those in which some continued increase is discernible – the Netherlands (+20.2 per cent), Sweden (+12.2 per cent) and Belgium (+10.2 per cent). Böhning (1979) calculates a total return to Mediterranean countries of about 1.5 million migrants during 1974–78, the bulk of whom returned during the first two post-recession years.

By the early and mid-1980s the pattern of flows had become generally more stable. After the severe post-1973 recession cutbacks many countries, both sending and receiving, saw their respective out and inflows rise somewhat to reach a new 'steady state', albeit at a much lower level than the 1960s and early 1970s. Where exceptional departures from this new equilibrium pattern occur, specific circumstances have operated, as in the 'regularization' of illegal immigrants' status in France in the census year of 1982.

It is worth paying special attention to the West German figures for immigration and returns, not only because they are more tenable than most other countries' statistics, but also because they show interesting trends in very recent years. Table 4.2 records immigration and return migration of foreigners from 1967 to 1984. After the temporary negative balance of the recession year 1967, immigration grew rapidly to nearly a million a year during 1969–70, coupled with low levels of return. The next inversion of the trend came in 1974 and lasted for four years. This was a period when returning migrants leaving West Germany exceeded new entrants, the stimuli being the laying-off of many migrant workers and the reduced job opportunities for new entrants. In 1975 the annual return flow reached its post-war peak of just over 600 000. During 1978–81 a new four-year cycle emerged, one of renewed net outflow. Declining return over these years could be interpreted partly as a function of the ending of the chaotic mass return effects of the recession. In the slightly longer term, many immigrants

Table 4.2 Migration into and out of West Germany, 1967–84 (all figures in thousands)

Year	Inflow	Outflow	Balance
1967	330.3	527.9	−197.6
1968	589.6	332.6	+257.0
1969	909.6	368.7	+540.9
1970	976.2	434.7	+541.5
1971	870.7	500.3	+370.4
1972	787.2	514.5	+272.7
1973	869.1	526.8	+342.3
1974	538.6	580.4	− 41.8
1975	366.1	600.1	−234.0
1976	387.3	515.4	−128.1
1977	422.8	452.1	− 29.3
1978	456.1	405.8	+ 50.3
1979	545.2	366.0	+179.2
1980	631.4	385.8	+245.6
1981	501.1	415.5	+ 85.6
1982	312.7	433.3	−120.6
1983	273.2	424.9	−151.7
1984	331.1	545.1	−214.0

Sources: Statistisches Jahrbuch für die Bundesrepublik Deutschland, various issues; recent data from SOPEMI.

decided to stay rather than return. With increasing restrictions on free entry, especially for Turks (the majority immigrant group in West Germany), the decision to go home appeared irrevocable and so a growing section of labour migrants have preferred to stay on, even in times of hardship and unemployment. Secondly, the rallying of the West German economy in the late 1970s permitted the resumption of a healthier migratory balance. A third reason for the resumption of a positive balance during 1978–81 was the relaxation of restrictions on family members joining male workers: hence an increasing proportion of the inflow during the late 1970s and early 1980s is made up of wives and young children. Fourthly, West Germany's liberal asylum policy encouraged many political refugees, both genuine and spurious, to seek a safe haven in the Federal Republic. Most came from Asia and entered via the Berlin 'loophole'. The lax control over such asylum seekers has since been tightened somewhat. Finally, the growth in the migration of high-level professional managerial and technical manpower contributed to the expanded inflow. This is also borne out by the disaggregated country of origin data which show increasing numbers of Belgians, French and Dutch moving into West Germany. Then in 1982 the balance turned negative once again, with escalating net and gross outflows resulting from renewed job cuts consequent upon the second oil crisis.

In one country, return migration in the 1970s had an added dimension. Following Portugal's revolution of 1974 and the decolonization of its African territories, nearly 1 million *retornados* or colonial settlers returned (Lewis and Williams 1981). Most arrived from Angola in late 1975. Their absorption posed special problems for the Portuguese economy, both because of their number, equivalent to a tenth of the Portuguese population, and because most arrived with few possessions and little or no money. By the late 1970s, most of the *retornados* seemed to have been successfully integrated. They tended to settle in the north-east, where many had come from originally, and around Lisbon, their arrival point from Africa. As a fairly entrepreneurial group, many have made good use of government funds made available to them. They have some parallels in this respect with other European ex-colonial refugees such as the French *pieds noirs* retreating from Algeria in the early 1960s, the Belgian refugees from the Congo and British settlers (including Asians) driven out of East Africa.

Impact of return migration on sending countries

During the 1960s, one of the chief benefits of labour migration to industrial Europe was thought to be the formation of returning cadres of skilled workers who could aid the development of countries like Greece and Italy. Twenty years and a lot of empirical research later, the debate is put in very different terms. Firstly, southern European 'temporary' migrants are now universally recognized as having among them a much larger proportion of permanent emigrants than was thought likely in the 1950s and 1960s. Although most emigrants abroad hold fast to the ideal of return, for many this becomes a myth: as the return is continuously postponed, they are steadily turning themselves into permanent expatriates. This is probably even more true of Britain's coloured immigrants, as Anwar (1979) has shown in a study of Pakistanis in Rochdale. Second, it is clear that whilst emigration involves a positive selection of the young and the vigorous, return migration entails a negative selection from among the emigrant community, sending back those who have not adapted, who are not upwardly mobile and who suffer problems of physical and mental health. Cerase (1974), writing of returns to Italy, has popularized this kind of return as the 'return of failure' and the 'return of conservatism', and Baučić (1973) has documented the double-selection filter in Croatia where the combination of an outflow of

dominantly innovative, educated and industrially-trained migrants and a backflow of untrained 'rejects' with poor education levels actually caused the illiteracy rate in this region to rise from 4.5 per cent in 1961 to 6.8 per cent in 1971.

At the village level, the behaviour of the returning migrant appears to follow a consistent pattern right across southern Europe from Portugal to Turkey (King 1979). The first ambition, indeed for many the *raison d'être* of the whole migration process, is to improve the housing environment. This usually implies building a new house rather than improving the old. In rural Portugal, the *casa francesa* is the symbol of success of returning migrants; in appearance, the new dwellings resemble the French suburban houses built by the same migrants during their 'other existence' as emigrant construction workers (Bretell 1979).

The second main characteristic of return migration, at least in rural areas, is the mushrooming of small, remittance-financed businesses, termed *Bazarkapitalismus* by Kade and Schiller (1969). Typical enterprises are shops, bars, hairdressers, cobblers, carpenters, car-repair workshops and taxis. Being one's own boss appears to confer prestige, but these self-employed enterprises rarely flourish in villages continually denuded by depopulation. Opportunities for larger-scale industrial investment are limited, as are restaurants and hotels since most migrant villages are well off the tourist beat. Few returnees go back to farming or invest productively in agriculture. They may buy small plots of land for security, speculation or just to potter about in, but their impact on the local agricultural economy – except to inflate land prices – is nil. As former farmhands or general rural labourers, their experience of farm management is limited and their emigration will not have furthered this at all. In any case, a return to working the land is not the migrants' ambition: they emigrated in order to *escape* being peasants and farm labourers.

Much less is known of returnees who go back to live in urban areas. In Greece it is clear that many emigrants who originated from rural districts do not return there but resettle in regional towns or in Athens. After their experiences abroad, their preference is for an urban life style and they perceive better returns for their accumulated capital in urban property than they could get by investing it in the rural economy (Unger 1986). Migrants who are fortunate enough to be able to return to an area undergoing some tourist development have even better chances, for here there are many possibilities to invest their savings in small hotels, restaurants, snack bars and other services. Evidence from many parts of southern Europe confirms the leading role that returnees often play in the evolving tourist economy of coastal and island regions (King et al 1984; Manganara 1977; Mendosa 1982).

Recent trends: towards a European melting-pot?

The migrant labour issue is now seen in terms of stocks rather than flows. No longer are migrants overtly viewed as a kind of cyclical shock-absorber, although this does not mean that some renewed migration might not occur if Western Europe's economic horizons were to brighten. Turkey had 1 million workers on the waiting list for recruitment to West Germany when the 1970s recession first occurred, and the pent-up potential has probably increased since then.

Return migration will continue to play a significant part in the European international migration scene. Numbers of returnees have fallen somewhat since the mass returns of the 1970s, but a steady stream will be maintained by the essentially temporary character of much post-war labour migration and by those who wish to return home upon retirement. France and West Germany have tried to hasten immigrants' departure by financially aiding the return home. The French scheme of 'assisted voluntary repatriation' was introduced in 1975, initially for unemployed migrants resident in France for less than five years, but later extended to employed and longer-established immigrants. The incentive was a free ticket to their home country and a grant of 10 000 francs – the famous 'million centimes'. By 1981, when incoming President François Mitterrand rescinded the return policy, 93 000 individuals had taken advantage of the return bonus, a small reduction in France's immigrant population of 4.4 million (Ogden 1985a). The German return policy is more recent, although it should be remembered that the *Konjunkturpuffer* ideology always implied a rapid return and denied, at least in theory, the possibility of much permanent settlement. It was not until 1983, following urban riots, escalating racial tension and rising unemployment, that the West German parliament approved legislation granting lump sums to those immigrants who became unemployed through company closure or bankruptcy. The 'buy them out' policy offered each prospective repatriat 10 500 Marks (£2 500 approximately), together with 1 500 Marks for each child, plus refund of social-security payments (Salt 1985a, b). Following the French experience, the likelihood is that most of those who take the money and go are merely those who were planning to return anyway.

More important than a declining trend in return migration is what is happening to the migrant stock.

The main feature of change here is the appearance on the labour market of wives and children of migrant workers, thus considerably altering the structure of the minority labour supply. Processes of integration are beginning, helped by a very definite shift in host country policy towards assimilation, respect for ethnic background and family reunion. However, progress is patchy. Salt (1985a) asks whether the difficult-to-integrate and racially-abused second-generation Turkish children in West Germany are 'young Turks or little Germans'. He maintains (1985b) that the immigrant children are a social time bomb ticking away. In 1981, France and West Germany each had around 1 million foreign children under the age of 16. Generally poorly educated by the host country's standards, these young people are being poured on to a labour market already burdened by high rates of unemployment; their chances of finding satisfying jobs are extremely poor. On the other hand, in some of the earlier-established migrant communities, such as the Italians in France and Belgium, the third generation is now being born, a generation that generally has few ties to its ancestral homeland and may not even speak the language. By the late 1970s, the proportion of mixed marriages reached 1 in 10 in France and 1 in 13 in Belgium (Lebon and Falchi 1980). International labour migration, for all its negative aspects, is beginning to play a role in European integration and in ethnic melting.

Finally, before we turn to internal migration, two further types of international labour migration should be mentioned. The first of these is the migration of high-level professional and technical manpower between the industrialized countries. This is a long-established flow whose relative importance has been enhanced by the freezing of 'brawn' migration in 1974. Higher salaries, experience and career advancement appear to be some of the motives for this kind of migration, but few detailed studies have been made (Salt 1981, 1984). Some of these migrants move internationally but within the same firm or organization, given the extent of multinational enterprise in Western Europe.

The second form of migration is even less well documented. This is the move into former emigration countries such as Italy and Greece of substantial numbers of clandestine migrants from the Third World. Any visitor to Rome, for instance, will be struck by the visible throng of migrants from Ethiopia, Somalia, North Africa, India and other Third World countries. Nearly all are illegal immigrants and they live under conditions which are, if anything, worse than those encountered by Italians in industrial Europe in the 1950s and 1960s. Italy's experience as an emigration country counts for nothing as far as these migrants are concerned; they perform the most menial tasks in Italy's capital for wages that are often a fraction of the legal minimum. Mostly, they work in hotels and restaurants. There are probably at least 500 000 in Italy and somewhat smaller numbers in Greece, Spain and Portugal (King 1984). As the chain of migrant exploitation stretches outwards, the whole hideous cycle begins anew.

Trends in internal migration

The international migrations considered so far in this chapter must be set alongside the more profound if less dramatic internal movements that have occurred within individual countries. At least in the West European context, internal migration is a much more complex phenomenon than international labour migration for it encompasses a whole range of types and scales of movement. Identification of these patterns by the geographer or the demographer depends very much on the data frameworks used. Inter-regional tabulations based on data available at province or county level conceal more local-scale moves between villages and towns or within conurbations. Whilst rural–urban migration has been historically the most important form of migration in Western Europe, we should not ignore urban–rural movements, of growing importance in the 1970s and 1980s, as well as inter-urban, intra-urban and rural–rural migration. All these patterns exist in Western Europe; the problem is one of finding the requisite data and, if that can be done, of devising appropriate statistical and cartographic modes for their proper portrayal.

Rural–urban migration

As the most universal form of spatial relocation in Western Europe, at least until recently, rural–urban migration deserves special attention. It is, however, as Clout (1976) points out, an elusive phenomenon, for it depends on definitions of 'rural' and 'urban' and is frequently confused with rural depopulation and with the decline of the agricultural workforce, processes considered in more detail in Chapter 8. For many countries, rural–urban flows are impossible to disaggregate from available inter-regional migration statistics which incorporate rural–urban movements to varying degrees depending on the nature of the regions involved. In highly-urbanized countries such as the UK and West Germany, the majority of inter-regional movement is composed of inter-urban flows. In rapidly-urbanizing countries like Spain, Portugal and Greece, on the other hand, most inter-regional

movement consists of rural migrants moving to expanding towns, notably capital cities. It should also be remembered that much of Europe's post-war *international* migration has been rural to urban.

The rural–urban drift in Western Europe is centuries old, accelerating and then decelerating according to various economic and cultural trends. One of the earliest waves of rural–urban migration took place in medieval Italy as Renaissance urban and industrial growth drew in workers from the surrounding countryside to powerful city-states like Venice and Florence. Later it was the Industrial Revolution which sucked in population to north European coalfields and to growing towns specializing in products like iron, textiles and pottery, although Parish (1973) has stressed that significant rural–urban migrations had become established in many countries before the onset of the Industrial Revolution.

Since 1945 virtually all rural regions of Western Europe have experienced outmigration. In areas of particularly severe migratory loss, more than half the population has departed. The myriad of migratory filaments which tie together villages and towns, near and far, can never be properly mapped for they are so complex. Perhaps more useful are broader generalizations such as those of Merlin (1971a), who studied the rural–urban mobility of the French population between the censuses of 1954 and 1962. Merlin's typology of rural–urban migration identified four groups of regions. First, there was a group of highly-urbanized regions such as Paris, Nord and Lorraine which had high rates of rural outmigration to cities within the regions concerned. Second, there were regions, such as those located in the Paris Basin, which had high rates of outmigration but to places, such as Paris, beyond the regional boundaries. Third, there were the agricultural regions of the west and south-west (Bretagne, Aquitaine, Limousin, etc.) which had moderate rates of outflow but which nevertheless failed to retain most of this movement. Finally, two regions, Alsace and Pays de la Loire, had moderate rates of rural outmigration and retained most of these migrants in regional towns.

The patterns of the intensity of outmigration from rural areas are quite hard to pin down. At a macro-regional scale, outmigration is most marked from the agricultural periphery of Western Europe. But local studies show that young people living in countryside areas which are close to towns depart more readily than their counterparts in remote areas where facilities may actually be poorer and employment possibilities more narrow. At the same time, there is also a clear indication that the smaller the settlement, the greater its chance of rapid loss through migration, for larger villages, with their wider range of social facilities and economic opportunities, have a better base for retaining their populations (Clout 1976).

Migration from rural areas has important impacts on both the departure and reception areas. These are somewhat analogous to the effects of international migration. The dramatic increase in the pace of rural–urban migration in southern European countries since the war has provoked exceptional strains on urban areas like Barcelona, Milan and Athens. Rural migrants to cities like these not only undergo a difficult adjustment to city life, they also suffer many objective difficulties such as cramped and insanitary housing, discrimination and poor access to public services (see Ch. 8). Nowhere is this seen clearer than in Italy where the post-war Italian 'miracle' brought millions of rural people pouring into northern industrial cities that infrastructurally and socially were quite unprepared (Bethemont and Pelletier 1983). If the mayor of Turin complained that his had become a 'southern' city, others profited from the influx of south Italian workers, not least the Fiat empire which dominates the city's economy and unscrupulous landlords who packed the migrants into inner-city garrets (Fofi 1970). In other southern European cities, illegal squatter settlements appeared: *bidonvilles* for the internal migrants. These peripheral slums, not unlike the shanty-towns of Third World cities, have been studied in detail in Istanbul (Karpat 1976) but are also widespread around Athens and Thessaloniki in Greece. In fact, about half of Greater Athens' population growth has been ascribed to rural migrants settling in peripheral squatter housing (Romanos 1969).

Main patterns of inter-regional migration

Fielding (1975) has accomplished pioneering work in constructing maps of internal migration rates for the 1960s on a common scale, minimizing the distorting effects of the absence of a uniform data base. The overall picture (Fig. 4.3) largely speaks for itself so only a few descriptive and interpretative remarks will be made. There is a major, if somewhat attenuated, area of migration balance and gain in the central industrial belt of Western Europe; further areas of net gain, some of them quite dramatic, are to be found around the Mediterranean coasts of eastern Spain, southern France and northern Italy. These are surrounded by a dominantly rural periphery of net migration loss. The areas with highest net gains include favoured retirement areas such as south-west England and the Côte-d'Azur and some rapidly-expanding capital cities like Copenhagen, Oslo and Madrid. Other areas of positive migration are newer industrial areas such as the southern Paris Basin, Munich, western Switzerland, Barcelona and Valencia-Alicante. The regions of biggest migration loss are mostly remote upland areas of forestry, pasture and poor-quality farming: interior Spain and Portugal, southern Italy, northern Scandinavia, Scotland and western Ireland. Less dramatic losses are found in the older industrial areas which pock-mark the central industrial axis – Lorraine, the Belgian Limburg and the French Nord – and in some of the less remote rural regions such as western France, Alsace and the southern Po Plain.

Three features which Fig. 4.3 does *not* show are worth noting. By illustrating net migration as an annual rate per thousand resident population, absolute numbers and the volume of gross flows are missed. This is crucial in the case of London and the south-east which appears to have a migratory 'low profile' on Fig. 4.3 and yet is known to have a very high rate of gross mobility, dominating the spatial pattern of inter-regional flows in England. Second, there is no idea of the return migration component, either in the dominant flow or in the subsidiary stream, where it is likely to be more important. Unfortunately, studies of internal return migration are frequently small scale, inconclusive and unable to demonstrate dramatic effects on sending areas (Nicholson 1975; Townsend 1980a). Third, there is no indication of the regional patterning of the flows themselves in terms of significant pairs or clusters of origins and destinations. Net flow maps do exist for some of the larger European countries and very clear trends emerge, particularly for the 1960s (Federici and Golini 1972; Wood 1976). For France, the flows are to Paris and the Mediterranean littoral from the centre and from the eastern and western peripheries. For Italy, the streams are from the south and the islands of Sicily and Sardinia to Rome and the industrial north-west (Lombardy and Piedmont). British flows focus on the London region. For West Germany the net flows are relatively weak but are generally to the south. Spanish flows are more complicated, with four main areas of attraction: Madrid, Barcelona, Valencia-Alicante and the Basque country. During the 1950s, Madrid and Barcelona accounted for 80 per cent of the net immigrants, a proportion which fell to 66 per cent in the 1960s, due largely to the relative decline in the attractive power of Madrid. During the 1970s and 1980s, it has been the Mediterranean provinces which have been the main focus of growth. Valencia and Madrid attract migrants mainly from adjacent provinces but Viscaya and Barcelona have been able to attract from a wider area. Most notable is Barcelona's ability to 'capture'

Annual migration
rate per thousand
population

+ 28·0
+ 17·0
+ 6·0
+ 2·0
− 2·0
− 7·0
− 17·5
− 36·0

★ No data

0   500
         km

Fig. 4.3
Net internal migration in Western Europe during the 1960s
(after Fielding 1975).

most of the Andalusian migrants, a feature dating from the 1920s when large numbers of southerners worked on the Barcelona Fair and the Metro (Bradshaw 1972, 1985).

Interpreting his own maps, Fielding (1975) groups Western European countries into three internal migration types. Firstly, there is a group of less-developed, mostly peripheral countries which have marked spatial contrasts and a very wide range of positive and negative migration rates (Fig. 4.3). Areas of severe depopulation are territorially dominant but these are partly compensated by nodes of rapid urbanization based either on industrialization or tourism. Spain and Portugal provide the best examples of this pattern, but this group also comprises Ireland, Italy, Austria and parts of France. Second, there are countries in which an agglomeration process has coexisted with more localized decentralization of industry and population. Examples here are Sweden, Norway, Denmark, Switzerland and to a lesser extent France, whose transitional status is due to the deceleration of its rural exodus and to its development of some of the features of regional industrial decline characteristic of the third group. In this group, comprising the UK, West Germany, France, Belgium and the Netherlands, internal migration was dominated by the twin processes of metropolitan decentralization and losses from declining industrial regions, with rural depopulation largely exhausted at an earlier period.

The case of France

France is the most representative European country from the point of view of internal migration for it contains elements of all three categories mentioned above: it still has a large residuum of rural population; it has experienced massive metropolitan and resort-oriented growth; and there has been some decentralization of population to regional nodes and to ex-urban rural hinterlands. With France's strong traditions in demography and population geography, many detailed and rigorous studies are available which trace the evolution of internal migration in the period since 1945 (Courgeau 1978; Courgeau and Lefebvre 1982; Limouzin 1980; Merlin 1971a; Pourcher 1970). Neither has French internal migration been neglected by English scholars, some of whom have concentrated on particular regions of outmigration such as Normandy (White 1980), the Auvergne (Clout 1974a) and the Ardèche (Ogden 1980).

The early post-war period was dominated by migration from rural areas to the dominant city-region of Paris. This was a trend traceable at least to the mid-nineteenth century since when France has lost 12 million rural dwellers, many *départements* shedding over 50 per cent of their rural populations between 1851 and 1968. Paris, meantime, more than tripled its population, fed by a steady stream of migrants from all parts of the provinces, from all age groups and from all social classes. During the 1950s and early 1960s, an average of 100 000 migrants came to Paris each year; migration ties then were especially strong with the belt extending west to Brittany. The internal migration process was not, however, a simple link between rural periphery and urban metropolis. Only 41 per cent arrived in Paris direct from their village of origin; most had 'step migrated' with one or two stops en route to the capital.

A 1961 survey of more than 6 000 migrants in Paris (Pourcher 1970) showed that 60 per cent came to the French capital because of work reasons: to find a job, to improve prospects for promotion or to obtain a higher income. These results contradict the oft-repeated opinion that rural migrants move to big cities to find better living conditions and social facilities – the 'bright lights' argument. For manual workers, farmers and service personnel, Paris offers, through its vast range of urban jobs, the decent standard of income that cannot be guaranteed in rural areas. For higher-status managers, professionals and civil servants, coming to Paris sets the seal on a successful career. Not only does the move to Paris enable the migrant immediate advancement, it also creates the conditions for the furtherance of upward mobility in the future. Up to the early 1960s it could be said that Paris was the only really major pole of attraction for 'economic migrants' in France (Pourcher 1970). But the disadvantages of such a monolithic magnet became all too well known: they included housing shortages, pressure on services, choking traffic, social problems, psychological tension. . .

The problems were equally serious – though of a very different type – for the rural areas of outmigration. Ogden (1980) has described what happens to rural *communes* sapped by prolonged migration. A sample of *communes* in the Ardèche (eastern Massif Central) recorded a collective loss of population of nearly 60 per cent between 1861 and 1975. The selectivity of the out-movement causes imbalance in the residual population which becomes disproportionately old and female, deprived of innovators and social leaders. Schools, shops and other services close down. This downward rural spiral is not, of course, peculiar to France; it can be found in most countries of Western Europe. Traditional peasant society, with its local dialects, customs, crafts, and also hardships, collapses. More localized mobility patterns among the residual population focus around marriage links. Only

20 per cent of couples in the Ardèche consist of partners born in the same *commune*, and increasingly marriage links are long distance as an expression of established migration trends and occupational diversification. This refutes the notion that rural population loss took place against a backcloth of immobility in the residual society. In fact, in France as a whole, more than 1.5 million people moved between rural *communes* between 1962 and 1968.

During the late 1960s the predominantly rural–urban pattern described above changed. The 1968 and 1975 censuses showed that the pace of internal mobility was maintained with 10 per cent of the French population changing its residence each year. But the big cities, especially Paris, no longer attracted as many immigrants, and rural losses lessened. A process of population redistribution had started in which the two-way flows between origins and destinations were more balanced. Now, the rural–urban imbalances created in the past are being redressed and in many areas rural *repopulation* is in evidence. This trend is confirmed by recently published results of the 1982 census (Ogden 1985b). Fel (1974) suggests that the rural reservoir for migration has emptied so that populations are starting to stabilize at a level where there is a balance between agricultural resources and their human exploiters. This equilibrium explanation is only part of the story for it ignores dynamic influences emanating from over-crowded cities which people are leaving, often in search of a more peaceful rural life style.

The evidence for the reversal in internal migration trends can be presented in two forms: by region and by size of settlement. The regional picture is given in Fig. 4.4. This shows the pattern of losses and gains for the four intercensal periods 1954–62, 1962–68, 1968–75 and 1975–82; in each case the net migration rate is standardized by the population of the region concerned. It is clear that the general high rate of internal migration noted above is highly differentiated regionally. The main region of gain initially, Paris, became a region of migratory loss by 1968–75. Conversely, many regions of initial migratory loss started to gain, some as early as 1962–68, many more by 1968–75 and 1975–82. In the cases of Brittany and Corsica, the switch from heavy losses to quite strong gains has been dramatic (Dean 1986). Overall, it is Paris and the north-east where migratory attractiveness declines most; and the south, south-east and west where the pulling power increases most. The particularly notable thing about the most recent intercensal period is the general decline in inter-regional mobility.

The second mode of analysis is by settlement size. Figure 4.5 shows the net annual migration rates for the

three intercensal periods according to the various size categories of *communes*. Moving from 1954–62 to 1968–75, the curves pivot clockwise around a point near the small towns (5 000 to 20 000). Net immigration to urban *communes* declines through time; the more urbanized the *commune*, the more marked the decline. In fact, there has been a decline in immigration since 1962 in 95 per cent of French towns with over 50 000 inhabitants. At the same time, net emigration rates have declined for rural *communes*, and in the larger rural *commune* classes net outmigration has given way to net immigration. Now it is the rural *communes* that are growing more quickly than their urban counterparts – the first time in more than a century that this has happened (Ogden 1985b).

In terms of time, the balance was tipped for the rural *communes* around the mid-1960s. Initially, the *communes* most affected were those found on the outskirts of major towns. Later other *communes* were affected, deep in the countryside. Here the net immigration was often relayed out by the intermediary functions of small towns attracting industries. In the case of remote *communes*, the initiative of local entrepreneurs and *commune* mayors often played a crucial role (Limouzin 1980). Increasing numbers of elderly people move to the country on retirement. For some, this involves a return to the area of origin; for others, it involves a move dictated by scenic and climatic attractiveness, perhaps influenced by holiday experiences. The migration stream out of Paris has a marked bi-modal age pattern with the over-60 retirees and the 30s mid-career migrants, mostly middle- and upper-class professionals: the higher the socio-economic status, the greater the feeling of attraction to rural areas.

Thus the established, almost clichéd conception of France as divided between centralizing and largely Parisian urbanization on the one hand and rural depopulation on the other needs fundamental revision. As Ogden (1985b) points out, this is not so much a 'new age of the peasantry' as a new state where decentralization of population allows marked demographic growth in regions, like Brittany, the Alps and even parts of the Massif Central, which have previously known only a century or more of rural exodus.

The extent to which the French experience in internal migration and counter-urbanization is replicated in other West European countries has been examined by Fielding (1986). By the 1970s, only Spain failed to show clear symptoms of the end of urbanization (Greece was not included in Fielding's analysis). Even more interest attaches to trends in the

Fig. 4.4
Evolution of net internal migration in France (after
Courgeau 1978 and Ogden 1985b).

1980s, however. Here the evidence is limited to the
eight countries with annual registry data (Belgium,
Denmark, Italy, Netherlands, Norway, Sweden,
Switzerland, West Germany). Generally it seems that
the tempo of internal migration has slowed markedly
in recent years, and for most countries there is now
only a weak relationship between net migration and
population density or settlement size. Only West
Germany and Italy show continuing evidence of
counter-urbanization into the mid-1980s; for the rest

it appears that the clear-cut counter-urbanization of
the 1970s has come to an end.

Inter-urban migration

Earlier sections of this chapter and the French case-
study material indicate the decreasing relevance of
rural–urban migration in Western Europe, not only
as a process but also as a concept. Instead, inter-
regional migration, particularly in the more urbanized,

Fig. 4.5
France: net intercensal migration rates, by size of
commune (partly after Bourgeois-Pichat 1981).

industrialized countries of northern Europe, is increasingly dominated by inter-urban movements. Net flows
are irrelevant and misleading in this type of migration
which is characterized by high rates of *exchange*
between urban areas (Wood 1976). Also important,
of course, is intra-urban residential relocation, the
greater part of which takes place in and around the
larger conurbations; it has a very different social and
economic significance to inter-regional migration, not
least because it is normally independent of employment change.

A theoretical rationale for the growth in importance
of inter-urban migration has been provided in a
visionary paper by Richmond (1969), who placed
changing types of internal migration in the context of
three broad stages of socio-economic evolution: the
traditional, the industrial and the post-industrial.

Traditional society was agrarian, quasi-feudal, with
non-mechanical modes of transportation and a tight
network of communities (*Gemeinschaft*); the form of
population movement was rural–rural with coercive
push factors dominant. The move to industrial society,
which was a more associative, class-based, mechanical
Gesellschaft, was accompanied by rural–urban migration operated by dominantly pull factors. Finally,
the second half of the twentieth century, in north-west
Europe and North America, is called by Richmond
Verbindungsnetzschaft – a social system in which
interaction takes place rapidly through a multitude of
communications systems which increasingly make
distance irrelevant. In this post-industrial phase,
migration is predominantly inter-urban, two-way and,
for certain categories of personnel, *is the norm*. Like
other forms of occupational and social mobility,
spatial mobility has become a functional imperative in
advanced post-industrial societies; its role is not only
to allocate human resources in a more economically
productive way, but also to provide choices and
opportunities for individuals.

The most promising explanations of inter-urban
movements involve life-cycle stages and career
patterns. Once more, there is a clear parallel with the
international migration of high-level manpower
between urban–industrial regions of Europe noted
earlier. In general, mobility is greatest in the early
years of single adult and married life. In England and
Wales, mobility is often initiated by the move of the
educationally better qualified away from home to
institutes of higher education. Educational background is also related to career paths. The available
evidence clearly indicates that long-distance inter-
urban migration tends to take place most intensively
among higher-income professional and managerial
workers. The mechanism of 'spiralism' is classically
invoked to explain this feature, since the motivations
of these groups are towards promotion and higher
salaries (Wood 1976). Manual workers, on the other
hand, are much more sedentary: stronger home ties,
poorly-developed career structures, relatively low
incomes and the virtually ubiquitous existence of
unskilled and semi-skilled manual work provide little
incentive to move. Much less clear, however, are the
migratory propensities of intermediate status occupations such as skilled manual workers, technical
workers and the junior white-collar grades.

Direct evidence for the existence of inter-urban
migration in Europe is largely confined to the case of
England and Wales, following on from the definition
of 100 Standard Metropolitan Labour Areas (SMLAs)
which cover only a fraction of the country's area but
contain three-quarters of the population. The main

elements of a complex pattern can be summarized as follows (Flowerdew and Salt 1979; Wood 1976). The pattern of inter-urban movement is, to use Richmond's term, 'multi-way', with large flows producing rather small net balances between SMLA pairs. Even areas of high net inmigration have considerable gross outflows – the pattern characteristic of rapidly-growing SMLAs around London such as Luton, High Wycombe and Guildford. Other high net gains are recorded for 'retirement' SMLAs such as Bournemouth, Blackpool and Southport and for New Towns or designated growth centres such as Basildon and Basingstoke. Most of the SMLAs experiencing a net migratory loss are either in the north of England or are the largest SMLAs such as London and Birmingham. The geographical pattern of migration flows, especially those south of the Severn–Wash line, is dominated by moves to and from London, a result entirely to be expected in view of the capital's labour market area. By contrast, peripheral SMLAs such as Rhondda, Wigan and Sunderland have relatively few links. Significant regional clusters of flows surround large SMLAs like Birmingham, Manchester, Liverpool, Leeds and Newcastle. These centres seem to perform a dual role, acting as foci for exchange of workers with neighbouring SMLAs and also as nodes for inter-regional streams.

Inter-regional migration policy

Most European governments have adopted some kind of internal migration policy, mainly to even out spatial imbalances in job opportunities but also, in the UK, France and the Netherlands especially, to decant population from major concentrations such as London, Paris and Randstad. Migration policy may be examined at two levels. One focuses on the individual migrant or potential migrant and may be regarded as the attempt to make people 'respond more sharply to stimulants that may well improve their socio-economic position' (Klaasen and Drewe 1973). The second view is 'organization-centred', the organization being either the community as a whole acting through national or regional government, or a private institution such as a large multi-locational firm. At an official level, migration policy is often linked with regional policy. The best example in Europe is Sweden whose comprehensive mobility policy, meshed closely with regional employment planning, has affected 6 per cent of the working population.

Finally, the case of the UK may be briefly reviewed for the variety of policies which have been used. Here there are three strands of government migration policy (Johnson and Salt 1981). First, the restriction of the growth of built-up areas of London and other major cities has led to a policy of population decentralization with residential growth steered to satellite towns, many of which are New Towns. During the period 1966–71, the twenty-eight British New Towns received 12 per cent of the net and 8 per cent of the gross movement of migrants leaving the conurbations. The second strand is the policy of trying to reduce outmigration from depressed areas by encouraging new employment growth in the so-called Assisted Areas – a policy, briefly, of 'work to the workers'. The migratory effects of this policy are difficult to judge because nobody knows how many migrants would have left the Assisted Areas without the regional incentives policy, but it has been estimated that the outflow of migrants could have been twice as high (Brown 1972).

Labour transfer schemes are the third element of policy. These date from the Industrial Transference Scheme initiated in 1928 and continued in the post-war period with the 1946 Resettlement Scheme, the 1962 Resettlement Transfer Scheme and the Employment Transfer Scheme (1972). The spatial pattern of these assisted moves shows clear net losses in the Assisted Areas and a concentration of gains in the London and south-eastern regions. Assisted movers were predominantly young and male; about three-quarters were unemployed before transfer.

Unfortunately, the three policies do not work harmoniously. The New Towns have been taking workers and their families out of the conurbations while, at the same time, the Employment Transfer Scheme has brought population in. Transfer schemes have been criticized for exacerbating congestion in certain prosperous metropolitan areas and at the same time contributing to the further decline of depressed areas. Disturbingly high proportions of assisted migrants quickly return to their home areas; wastage rates of 25 per cent appear to be the norm. Other groups of needy people, such as the unemployed who live outside the Assisted Areas, have slipped through the net of migration assistance. Housing difficulties are often a constraint on assisted labour migration. Not all these criticisms are entirely valid, but it is clear that the UK, like most other West European countries, has no well-defined and effective migration policy.

Further Reading

Berger J, Mohr J 1975 *A Seventh Man: the story of a migrant worker in Europe*. Penguin, London

Castles A, Kosack G 1985 *Immigrant Workers and Class Structure in Western Europe*. Oxford University Press, London

Hammar T (ed) 1985 *European Immigration Policy: a comparative study*. Cambridge University Press, Cambridge

Krane R E (ed) 1979 *International Labor Migration in Europe*. Praeger, New York

Ogden P E (ed) 1983 *Migrants in Modern France: four studies*. Occasional Paper 23, Department of Geography, Queen Mary College, London

Salt J, Clout H (eds) 1976 *Migration in Post-war Europe: geographical essays*. Oxford University Press, London

5

Energy

The evolution of energy demand

The importance of energy in the economies of Western Europe was abruptly demonstrated by the 1973 oil crisis, and it is appropriate that any examination of this sector should give prominence to the post-crisis era. Yet it would be wrong to view this period in isolation. Understanding the impact of the OPEC-induced upheaval requires a knowledge of major trends, and the causal factors behind them, in the preceding decades. In addition, our interpretation of post-crisis developments must recognize that, in a number of important instances, they have been founded on initiatives taken before the crisis struck. Momentous though it was, 1973 was essentially a turning point rather than a starting point. The present chapter therefore examines energy issues in this broad temporal context, focusing particularly on attempts to contribute to the economic development of Western European nations by planning their fuel industries. In doing so it concentrates on energy supply questions, but at the outset it is necessary to sketch the other side of the equation, the evolving scale and geography of energy demand.

Energy consumption in Western Europe has risen beyond all expectations in the post-war period. In the 1950s the proportional increase was one-third; in the 1960s it rose to two-thirds; and only under the influence of the crisis did it fall back to little more than one-tenth in the 1970s. Some of this upswing can be attributed to population growth, but by no means all: per capita energy consumption in the mid-1980s was twice as great as thirty years before. The primary impetus behind the growth came from the industrial sector, which at its peak – in the early 1970s – accounted for almost half Western Europe's energy consumption. But industry's dominance has been undermined since the 1973 oil crisis as major energy-consuming industries have contracted, as surviving

Table 5.1 Structure of European Community energy demand

	1979	1981	1986
Industry	35.1	33.8	30.3
Transport	22.5	24.6	27.7
Residential and other consumers	42.4	41.6	42.0
	100	100	100

Source: Commission of the European Communities 1988 *Basic Statistics of the Community.* Eurostat, Luxembourg

activities have used energy more efficiently and as non-industrial consumers have prospered. By the mid-1980s, manufacturing in the EC accounted for less than a third of total demand, compared with 42 per cent absorbed by private and service-sector customers (Table 5.1). This sectoral division of demand is, of course, the summation of consumption patterns at the national level, and the precise balance between industrial and other consumers varies considerably throughout Western Europe (Fig. 5.1). Above all, this reflects the diversity of development paths followed by individual countries. For example, Luxembourg's industrial consumption is exceptionally high simply because of the steel industry's unusually prominent position in the economy. Denmark and the Republic of Ireland, in contrast, share common ground in their relatively recent movement from agriculture to light industrialization, a trend betrayed by industry's low share of total energy consumption.

Chiefly because national energy consumption is dictated by population size and the scale and nature of the economies – variables which evolve only slowly – the geography of total energy demand (Fig. 5.1) is likewise slow to change. Even so, long-term shifts can be identified, as can be demonstrated by correlating

Fig. 5.1
Total energy demand, 1984.

Table 5.2 Per capita energy consumption, 1984 (tonnes of oil equivalent)

Luxembourg	7.7	Denmark	3.1
West Germany	5.2	France	2.7
Norway	4.5	Switzerland	2.6
Netherlands	4.0	Rep. of Ireland	2.2
Belgium	3.4	Italy	2.1
Finland	3.4	Greece	1.5
United Kingdom	3.3	Spain	1.5
Sweden	3.2	Portugal	0.9

Source: United Nations 1986 *Energy Statistics Yearbook 1984.* United Nations, New York

national energy consumption figures for 1951 with those for 1961, 1971, 1978 and 1984. The resulting coefficients decline from +0.981 to +0.907 to +0.867 and finally to +0.843. The geography of this adjustment in the pre-crisis era is identified when demand growth is expressed in per capita terms. In the West European core, two major countries – France and West Germany – experienced demand increases corresponding closely with the West European average. The UK, Belgium and Luxembourg, countries which had unusually high per capita consumption figures at the outset, recorded growth rates well below the average. And on the northern and southern peripheries the typical pattern was for growth to exceed the average, especially in southern Europe. The net effect of these contrasting trends, which continued with modifications into the 1980s, was to reduce – but by no means eliminate – the peaks and troughs of the energy demand 'surface' (Table 5.2).

These, then, are three major features of post-war energy demand: impressive growth up to the first oil crisis, perceptible change in the geography of energy consumption and, coupled with this change, the emergence of a less accidented demand surface. On their own, these features might well have made the problem of adjusting energy supply to demand a relatively easy one to solve. But efforts to achieve this adjustment have been handicapped by a fourth demand characteristic: major shifts in consumers' fuel preferences. In addition, OPEC's use of oil for

political ends has complicated the supply problem by exposing the dangers of external dependence. In seeking to reduce these dangers, a number of countries have discovered that inexperience can be a substantial obstacle to the satisfactory transition to new energy sources. As we shall see, these factors have enveloped the supply side of the energy sector in uncertainty, strengthening the argument for rational planning yet simultaneously acting as major constraints on effective management.

Oil versus coal in the cheap energy era

The first phase of coal industry planning has been thoroughly documented and need not be reconsidered in detail (Gordon 1970). Briefly, Western Europe was still 85 per cent dependent on coal in the early 1950s and, almost without exception, the industry's planners saw coal as the unchallenged fuel of the future. Energy demand was strong and planning for maximum production became the norm. Only the newly-established European Coal and Steel Community (ECSC), which had no direct control over production, warned that the era of European energy self-sufficiency was over and that coal's future depended on ensuring that it could face rigorous competition. The experience of countries without coal industries bore out the ECSC's conclusion – in at least eight energy-deficient countries imported liquid fuels had already captured a third or more of the market – and the reality of the threat from oil was forced on coal producers in the late 1950s and early 1960s when coal demand failed to recover from a minor economic recession. Thereafter, almost every market shrank rapidly as oil displaced coal and captured the lion's share of demand growth (Fig. 5.2). By 1970, coal's share of European Community demand was down to 27 per cent and, instead of leading the industry into a retrenched yet defensible position, the ECSC was obliged to assist

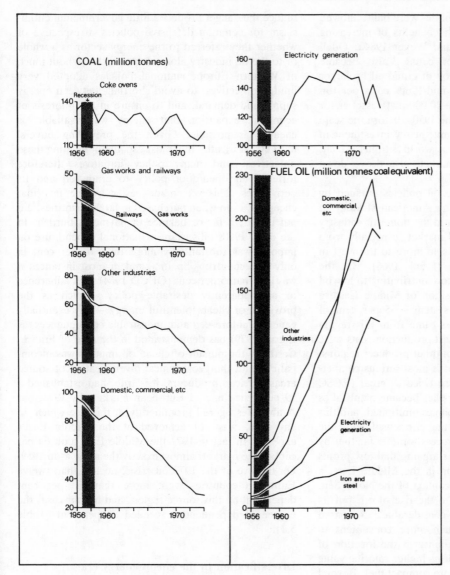

Fig. 5.2
Use of coal and fuel oil in
Western Europe up to the
first oil crisis.

governments by acting as a fire brigade dealing with the regional and social consequences of collapse (Collins 1975). Moreover, the situation would have been even worse if one substantial coal market, electricity generation, had not been artificially expanded in coal-producing countries by the development of preferential policies – between 1959 and 1964, power-station coal consumption in Western Europe rose from 110 to 150 million tonnes. Even so, from then on the growth of even this relatively sheltered market was captured by oil.

Why were coal industry planners so conspicuously unsuccessful in combating the advance of oil? As is well known, at its simplest the problem was that, as

the 1960s progressed, refiners were increasingly able to market fuel oil at prices well below the cost of coal (ECSC 1964; Ray 1976). In Hamburg, for example, the price advantage of 43 DM per tonne in 1960 had risen to 162 DM in 1972. But this was only the basic arithmetic, behind which lay a battery of factors working to oil's advantage.

One was the oil industry's low labour requirements; these enabled it to contain the effects of rising wages while wage inflation forced up the cost of coal. A second was the rapid expansion of the European refinning industry, from 50 million tonnes capacity in 1950 to 863 million in 1973. Simultaneously, this minimized reliance on expensive imported refined products and, because larger and larger refineries were built, allowed Western Europe to enjoy the benefits of increasing economies of scale (Molle and Wever 1984a; Odell 1986). These economies, of course, also became significant in the transportation of crude oil by larger and faster tankers – by the mid-1960s costs per ton mile were twice as great for a 20 000 dwt vessel as for one of 70 000 dwt; while in the 1950s, before the scale factor became highly significant, heavy investment in new tankers had produced a world surplus which, through the large charter market, also drove down transport costs.

Other factors included the oil policies pursued by the USA and the USSR. The American strategy of controlling imports to safeguard the domestic industry diverted oil on to the world market, especially from Venezuela, while the USSR sold more to the west in exchange for hard currency (Frank 1966). But the most fundamental supply factor contributing to low oil prices was the dominant position of Middle Eastern producers in the European system – 65 per cent of Western Europe's oil supplies came from this region by the early 1960s. Middle East production costs were substantially less than those of other producer regions: in Venezuela, the Middle East's most serious competitor in this respect, they were twice as great (ECSC 1964). Also, Middle East supplies became plentiful as producer countries and companies multiplied, and this led companies to discount selling prices well below the official posted levels. This process went so far that by the mid-1960s the OECD was arguing that low profits posed a threat to exploration in the Middle East, a warning now familiar in the context of the North Sea.

Cost factors were crucial to the rise of oil, but its qualitative appeal was also considerable. Compared with coal, fuel oil was much more convenient to handle, allowed greater flexibility in the location of storage areas and, because of its higher calorific value tonne for tonne, was a far more compact fuel. Beyond this, the precision of refining operations ensured consistent fuel quality, while advances in the design of oil-fired equipment led to increasingly efficient consumption coupled with precise temperature control. Additionally, efficient combustion meant lower pollution levels, a significant factor in countries seeking to control air pollution by legislation.

Governmental response

At the international level the strategic dangers of heavy reliance on the Middle East were stressed by the ECSC (1964), by the OECD (1964) and by the Commission of the European Communities (1968). But repeated pleas for international cooperation to reduce the danger produced little governmental enthusiasm for common defensive policies, irrespective of whether they referred to the energy sector as a whole or to the oil industry alone. Instead, throughout much of Western Europe national policies adopted very limited objectives: to avoid shortfalls between energy supply and demand, and to ensure in the interests of economic expansion that energy was available as cheaply as possible. Given the prevailing buyers' market, oil was the fuel most capable of meeting these objectives, and many policy initiatives therefore fostered an open-door policy to crude oil and its derivatives. This was made easier by the fact that cheap oil, even when purchased in large quantities, did not impose a major balance of payments burden. In the early 1960s oil's share of national expenditure on imports was substantially more than 10 per cent in only one country – Spain – and in most instances it was less than 5 per cent (OECD 1964). Yet adherence to an apparently desirable policy – such as the provision of cheap, plentiful energy – may eventually generate unforeseen and undesirable consequences, as Lucas (1979) has demonstrated in the case of France. Certainly the pursuit of cheap oil imports was incompatible with the geographical diversification of source areas. African producers, it is true, had established a 29 per cent share of European markets by 1972, but Arab states figured prominently in this rise which, in any case, was not achieved at the Middle East's expense. In fact in 1972 the Middle East took 64 per cent of the market, almost exactly the same as in 1959. On the eve of the 1973 oil crisis, no less than twelve European countries were more than 60 per cent dependent on this source region, and in four cases the degree of dependence exceeded 80 per cent (Table 5.3).

Diversification in the cheap energy era

Although the main theme before 1973 was imported oil's advance at the expense of coal, the argument that governments were indifferent to the potential problems of dependence on the Middle East should not be overstated. Well before the stimulus of the oil crisis, attention was given to a wide range of possibilities for developing more secure resources.

Dutch gas and the North Sea

Many European countries already possessed small oilfields, a fact which encouraged governments to license more widespread exploration. The significance of this work lies not in its immediate impact on the oil market (indigenous production in the late 1960s was

Table 5.3 Oil consumption and sources, 1972

Source regions for West European consumption

	(mill. t.)	(%)
Africa	190.8	29
North America	0.0	0
Caribbean	17.1	3
Middle East	418.7	64
Communist bloc	24.0	4
Others	1.4	0
	652.0	100

National dependence on Middle East

	Total oil consumption (mill. t.)	Middle East dependence (%)	Oil as % of total energy consumption
Belgium	36.2	78	55
Denmark	9.7	81	94
France	117.8	66	68
West Germany Republic of	104.6	41	53
Ireland	3.4	62	65
Italy	118.7	67	76
Netherlands	67.6	73	34
United Kingdom	107.2	68	45
Austria	5.7	65	54
Finland	9.2	32	75
Norway	6.4	82	51
Portugal	4.3	88	83
Sweden	11.2	44	81
Switzerland	4.8	35	82
Greece	7.2	85	68
Spain	38.7	67	65

Source: United Nations 1976 World Energy Supplies, 1950–1974. United Nations, New York

a mere 20 million tonnes) but in the chance discovery of one of the world's largest natural gas deposits at Slochteren in the northern Netherlands in 1959. With initial proven reserves put at 1 100 billion m^3, the consequences of this discovery could not be confined to the Netherlands. Wider exploration received a powerful boost and, in particular, the location and geological characteristics of the Slochteren deposit turned attention in a new direction – towards the North Sea.

Investigations here quickly confirmed the existence of two potentially productive zones, the northern and southern basins. Because at this stage countries encircling the North Sea had not all ratified the 1958

Geneva Convention on the Continental Shelf, precise territorial claims could not be established immediately; but ratification was completed in 1964, and exploration rapidly gathered momentum. Initially attention focused on the southern basin, between the UK's Yorkshire–Lincolnshire coast and the Dutch Wadden Islands, where exploration and exploitation were helped by relatively shallow water. Then in 1969 the discovery of the Ekofisk field in Norwegian territory stimulated interest in the northern basin, and by the 1973 oil crisis a sharp contrast had been identified between the resources available in the two areas (Bailey 1977; Ion 1977). Natural gas predominated in the south, but in the north oil deposits were typically associated with greater or lesser volumes of gas. What was also apparent was that the benefits of this new diverse resource region were very unevenly distributed among countries with North Sea rights. The northern basin, extending along a narrow north–south axis for 700 km, came almost entirely under the jurisdiction of the UK and Norway, while sovereignty over productive parts of the southern basin lay with the UK and, to a lesser extent, the Netherlands. Fortunate though they were, however, the countries which benefited significantly from this major wave of exploration also faced the challenge of devising policies for rational exploitation. We shall return to their varied responses in a later section.

Alternatives for electricity generation

Electricity generation was a major growth industry in this period, with output increasing more than fivefold between 1950 and 1973. By the early 1970s, oil accounted for half Western Europe's conventional thermal power production and was poised to lever coal out of its last major stable market. Yet the choice of energy inputs was not simply that of coal or oil, and many countries were able to pursue alternative strategies which would retard industry's rapidly-growing dependence on oil.

One such strategy was increased use of lignite or brown coal, a fuel of low calorific value, but an attractive one when capital-intensive opencast mining is possible. The Republic of Ireland and Greece, two countries particularly poor in energy resources, both expanded their output of this fuel in the 1960s, but the country best placed to exploit it was West Germany. Here output rose from 96 million tonnes in 1960 to 118 million in 1973. In terms of import substitution, this was equivalent to approximately 23 million tonnes of oil, compared with actual oil imports of 113 million tonnes in 1973. Within West Germany the dominant source area was, and remains, the Rhenish brown

Table 5.4 Hydro-electric power development, 1950–74

	Output (bill. kWh)			
	1950	1960	1970	1974
Western Europe	110.4	229.5	337.3	385.1
EC	49.5	105.8	125.9	123.5

	HEP as % of all electricity generation	
	1950	1974
Western Europe	43	27
EC	26	12
France	49	32
West Germany	19	6
Italy	92	28
Austria	79	67
Finland	88	47
Norway	100	100
Sweden	95	76
Portugal	46	74
Switzerland	98	77
Spain	74	38

Source: United Nations 1976 *World Energy Supplies, 1950–1974*. United Nations, New York

Table 5.5 Early development of the nuclear power industry

	Initial production	Nuclear power as % of total electricity generation, 1974
Belgium	1962	0.4
Finland	1977	0.0
France	1958	7.8
West Germany	1961	3.9
Italy	1963	2.3
Netherlands	1968	5.9
United Kingdom	1956	12.3
Sweden	1964	2.7
Switzerland	1969	18.0
Spain	1968	8.9
EC		6.4
Total Western Europe		5.7

Sources: United Nations 1976 *World Energy Supplies, 1950–1974*. United Nations, New York; United Nations 1981 *Yearbook of Energy Statistics, 1980*. United Nations, New York

coalfield, where electricity generation is vertically integrated with mining, and where advanced opencast technology may eventually allow exploitation up to 1 000 metres deep (Ray and Uhlmann 1979; Ion 1977).

Hydroelectric power was an option open to many more countries and, from Scandinavia to Iberia, was exploited on a rapidly increasing scale. Thus Western Europe's production more than doubled in the 1950s and rose again by two-thirds before the oil crisis. This development must be placed in perspective: despite the absolute expansion, HEP's share of total electricity generation slipped from 35 per cent in 1960 to 23 per cent in 1973. Yet in the early 1970s Norway, Sweden, Switzerland, Austria and Portugal all obtained the large majority of their electricity from this source, while in Finland, Spain, France and Italy it remained far from insignificant (Table 5.4). For these countries, past investment was shortly to provide its most valuable economic return as inflation and balance-of-payments problems intensified under the pressure of escalating oil prices.

The final major alternative for electricity generation lay in the development of nuclear power. As with oil, this strategy necessitated external dependence with respect to supplies, but the dangers were perceived to be far less, primarily because relationships with the

main producer countries – Canada, the USA, South Africa and Australia – were stable. In terms of economic advantages, nuclear power appeared similar to HEP. High investment costs would be offset, it was predicted, by low operating costs – ECSC calculations indicated that nuclear power stations would produce electricity for roughly half the price that coal-fired plant would achieve (ECSC 1964). This encouraged widespread interest in nuclear investment, but by the oil crisis nuclear energy's contribution to Western Europe's total electricity consumption was less than 6 per cent. Only two countries – the UK and Switzerland – generated more than a tenth of their electricity in this way (Table 5.5). These achievements fell well short of the protagonists' hopes.

At this stage, delays in the expansion of nuclear power were not primarily a reflection of environmentalists' hostility to the industry (Collingridge 1984a). Opposition was gaining momentum, but political and technical factors were much more influential. Most countries were unwilling to cooperate on reactor development and construction, even in the European Community, which had established Euratom for these and similar purposes (Pearson 1981). Within the industry itself, power struggles were significant, particularly over the problem of which reactor system should be adopted. In France, for example, *Electricité de France* fought a protracted battle with the *Commission à l'Energie Atomique* and was eventually successful in ending the gas graphite reactor programme imposed by the *Commission* (Lucas 1979). More generally, many delays were caused by the difficulties of transposing high technology from the research environment to the commercial world, and these difficulties were compounded when – as in Britain and France – decisions were made to abandon one system in favour of another. Finally, increasing economies of scale in conventional generators raised average thermal efficiency to approximately 30 per cent and, although this was far from ideal, the savings made contrasted sharply with the growing financial burden caused by policy arguments and technical delays in the nuclear branch of the industry (Reid, Allen and Harris 1973).

Oil crisis and the European response

The history of oil price dynamics is well known and need not be covered in great detail (Bailey 1977; Odell 1986). As oil prices sank in the 1960s, the trend was increasingly interpreted in centre–periphery terms by the unindustrialized producers. Within OPEC, which had been formed in 1960, a more united attitude emerged and prices were roughly doubled in 1970–73. But the first real shock came in 1973–74 when Arab unity was hardened by the Arab–Israeli Yom Kippur war: an oil embargo was placed on the Netherlands in retaliation for her pro-Israeli stance; supplies to the West in general seemed suddenly insecure; and the price of crude oil was virtually tripled. A period of quiescence followed, but was abruptly ended by the start of the Iran–Iraq conflict, with OPEC prices doubling once more in 1979–80. In real terms, this raised the price of Saudi Arabian crude to six times the 1973 level (Odell 1981). The effect of this second oil crisis was to give a major boost to economic restructuring in Western Europe which lasted throughout the 1980s.

What is particularly interesting is that this impact was sustained even though OPEC proved unable to maintain prices at early 1980s levels. This failure partly reflected a decline in demand in industrialized countries, but it was also a consequence of dissent within OPEC. Dissension led several producers to raise output above agreed quota levels, and even major production cutbacks by Saudi Arabia could not prevent the emergence of a crude-oil surplus. Oil prices at first fell steadily. Oil imported to Europe in 1981 averaged $36.5 a barrel, compared with $29 a barrel in 1984, but the value of oil then crashed in 1985/86 as Saudi Arabia rejected its balancing role and OPEC cooperation broke down. In what has sometimes been called the third oil crisis – one which

primarily hit LDC producers – European oil import prices fell to approximately $13 a barrel, recovered to $18 in 1987 and then began to fall once more to $16.

It is important to appreciate that the severity of this decline was closely connected with a geopolitical miscalculation by OPEC countries. These argued that if their output rose, non-OPEC producers would compensate by reducing production to sustain prices and, therefore, tax revenues. This did not happen, and in Europe the UK was particularly resolute in maintaining output.

Industrialized countries in general welcomed the anti-inflationary effects of cheaper oil, and even some producer countries were prepared to trade lower-revenue income for these benefits.

Reactions

While one immediate effect of the 1973 upheaval was to provoke numerous national energy reviews, it also prompted many OECD countries to take the first significant step towards international cooperation in energy sector development – the formation of the International Energy Agency (IEA) in 1974. This organization quickly produced agreement on an oil-sharing scheme to be activated in future crises (IEA 1980a), but more importantly it has subsequently been deeply involved in monitoring and in attempting to guide the energy sector. As the only major Western European country that has not joined the IEA is France, these activities are highly relevant to the present discussion.

The attempt at guidance has taken place within the framework of twelve principles for energy policy and a further fourteen principles for action on coal (IEA 1980a). The central element in the design is reduced dependence on oil imports, with substitution by coal, natural gas and nuclear power providing the chief medium-term insurance against energy shortfalls. In addition, member countries are strongly encouraged firstly to improve the sector's efficiency by pursuing wide-ranging conservation policies and, secondly, to concentrate on the long-term development of renewable energy sources, such as solar, wind, biomass and geothermal power. Emphasis is placed on the need to price energy realistically to promote interest in conservation and renewable power schemes, while intensive research, development and demonstration (RD and D) are considered essential for the emergence and adoption of new technologies capable of effective competition with oil (IEA 1980b; UN Economic Commission for Europe 1983). Although some of this RD and D expenditure can be expected to come from industry, governments have been left in no doubt that

Table 5.6 Oil import dependency in Western Europe

	Oil imports (mtoe)	Oil imports as % of primary energy consumption
1973	716.2	59.4
1979	598.7	46.5
1980	514.9	41.5
1981	441.8	36.6
1982	383.0	32.4
1983	342.2	29.0
1984	337.7	28.1
1985	311.6	25.2
1986	346.9	27.9

Source: British Petroleum (annually) *Statistical Review of the World Energy Economy*. British Petroleum, London

their leadership may be crucial to success.

Several indicators of progress towards these goals can be identified. As a later section demonstrates with respect to oil and gas resources, unrealistically cheap energy has been abandoned as a policy platform. There has also been a substantial reduction in oil imports and in their contribution to primary energy consumption (Table 5.6). Indeed, this reduction in imported oil dependency has progressed much further than seemed possible during the second oil crisis. In 1980, for example, the IEA predicted that European oil imports would be approximately 500 million tonnes in 1985 and would account for almost 40 per cent of primary energy. In reality, the figures were 311 million tonnes and 25 per cent. In addition, a number of outstanding conservation programmes have been devised, those in Denmark and Sweden being particularly advanced (Schipper 1983, 1987), while almost all European IEA countries have increased in real terms their RD and D expenditure. This exceeded $2 billion a year by the turn of the decade, with relatively equal attention being given to conservation projects, new coal technologies, alternative energy sources and support technologies for the electricity industry.

Despite these favourable signs the IEA's success to date must be considered partial. Outstanding conservation policies in Denmark and Sweden only highlight the inadequacy of steps taken in much of the remainder of Western Europe. Reduced oil imports are partly a consequence of restructuring efforts, but they also reflect recessional influences and increased European oil production. There are indications that cheap oil has recently stimulated imports (Table 5.6), and declining prices have not encouraged governments to maintain the expansion of RD and D expenditure into alternative energy sources. The IEA's (1980a)

judgement that in the RD and D context 'There is no country that cannot and should not do more' remains valid a decade later. This conclusion is underlined by the fact that the lion's share of diversification investment in the 1980s has been absorbed by a single controversial energy source – nuclear power. Between 1982 and 1986, the European Investment Bank, which primarily responds to investment demand in EC countries, allocated 56 per cent of its power production loans to nuclear projects. In contrast, geothermal energy and alternative energy sources accounted for only 3 per cent of investment, while combined heat and power projects absorbed even less (Table 5.7). Even if nuclear power is excluded from the calculations on the grounds that its capital intensity ensures that it dominates investment, the proportions allocated to new forms of energy generation remain modest relative to the remainder of the sector.

Although progress in the development of entirely new energy sources has been unimpressive, the fact that more mainstream forms of energy production have received high levels of investment indicates that energy planning activity has been intense at the national level and within the individual energy industries (IEA 1984). Reappraisals have to some extent led to the reversal of past strategies – for example, as we shall see in a later section, with respect to consumption. But recent years have also been marked by a strengthened commitment to the process of diversification which was already in progress before the oil crisis. Above all, this has meant increased determination to derive maximum benefit from newly-discovered oil and gas resources, coupled with renewed pressure for the development of nuclear power. As the following discussion of these major themes demonstrates, however, widespread appreciation of the economic and strategic value of secure supplies has not brought about a golden age for energy planning. Indeed, in many respects governments and planners have experienced a rougher ride since 1973 than at any time in the post-war period.

New indigenous resources – the exploitation challenge

Before considering the problems of oil and gas exploitation, the background to their development must be sketched. The evolving geography of their extraction has been examined in detail by Odell (1986) and is summarized by Fig. 5.3, in which they are shown according to a common measure – million tonnes of oil equivalent (mtoe).

By the time of the oil crisis, Dutch gas production was already well advanced. Output had reached

Table 5.7 European Investment Bank allocations to energy production projects, 1982–86

	All projects		Projects excluding nuclear power	
	(million ECUs)	(%)	(million ECUs)	(%)
Nuclear power	3 249.4	56.4	—	—
Conventional thermal power stations	500.6	8.7	500.6	19.9
Hydroelectric power stations	673.5	11.7	673.5	26.8
Geothermal energy and alternative energy sources	175.1	3.0	175.1	7.0
Heat and power generating plant	112.8	2.0	112.8	4.5
Development of oil and gas deposits	972.5	16.9	972.5	38.8
Solid fuel extraction	75.9	1.3	75.9	3.0
Total	5 759.8	100	2 510.4	100

Source: European Investment Bank 1987 *Annual Report, 1986.* European Investment Bank, Luxembourg

60 mtoe a year, 70 per cent of the peak it would eventually achieve towards the end of the decade. Gas from the British sector of the southern North Sea was also flowing strongly by this time – 1973 production was 25 mtoe – and, as in the Netherlands, it was tracing a smooth upward output curve. In Norwegian waters, and in the British sector of the northern basin, later exploration and longer lead times meant that product flows were minimal before the mid-1970s. But northern basin yields then rose markedly, although with different results on either side of the median line. Norwegian production was more than 60 mtoe in the mid-1980s, almost half of this being accounted for by gas. British northern basin production consists primarily of oil and has been expanded more rapidly. Output exceeded 100 mtoe in the early 1980s and has now stabilized at approximately 134 mtoe. Today, therefore, output from this area is greater than from any other part of the North Sea or adjacent areas.

This rapid exploitation of the North Sea since 1975 has depended partly on the discovery of giant fields, such as Statfjord, Brent and Forties. The operators' initial estimates of recoverable oil reserves in these three fields alone totalled 900 million tonnes. But these giants are not typical. In the British sector, for example, more than half the oilfields currently in production had initial reserve estimates of less than 50 million tonnes, and 85 per cent were thought to contain less than 100 million tonnes. In the difficult operating conditions found in the North Sea, the diseconomies associated with exploiting relatively small fields can be substantial. For this reason, it might be anticipated that falling prices have recently hindered exploitation of, and exploration for, additional deposits. At first sight the evidence suggests

that this has in fact occurred throughout most of the 1980s. In the British sector, for example, company investment in field development fell by 31 per cent between 1981 and 1986 (Department of Energy 1987). However, it will be shown later in this chapter that a distinction should be drawn between exploration and exploitation activity before and after the 1985/86 oil price crash.

For those fields which are in production, size has also influenced the mode of transport to land, although this should not be overstressed. Some small fields, such as Argyll (reserves 6.5 million tonnes) and Montrose (12 million tonnes), load directly into tankers, but so do the Beryl A and Statfjord fields (66 and 412 million tonnes respectively). The majority of active fields are, however, linked with the Shetlands and the mainland by the now extensive pipeline system, one major advantage of which is its ability to operate irrespective of weather conditions (Fig. 5.3).

A search for additional reserves has been pursued outside the main producing areas, although recently this activity has been affected by the downward price trend. In UK waters, little has been discovered outside the main northern basin, although the Morecambe Bay deposit off the Lancashire coast, which contains 100 mtoe of gas condensate, is an exception to this rule. Norwegian waters are more promising – exploration to date has been less comprehensive than in the British sector and as yet has been largely limited to the area south of 62°N. The Danish sector, too, is under-explored, one reason being that until recently all rights were vested with a single consortium which felt no urgency to invest. Evidence from nearby sectors, however, suggests that there may be nothing of outstanding interest in Danish waters. West

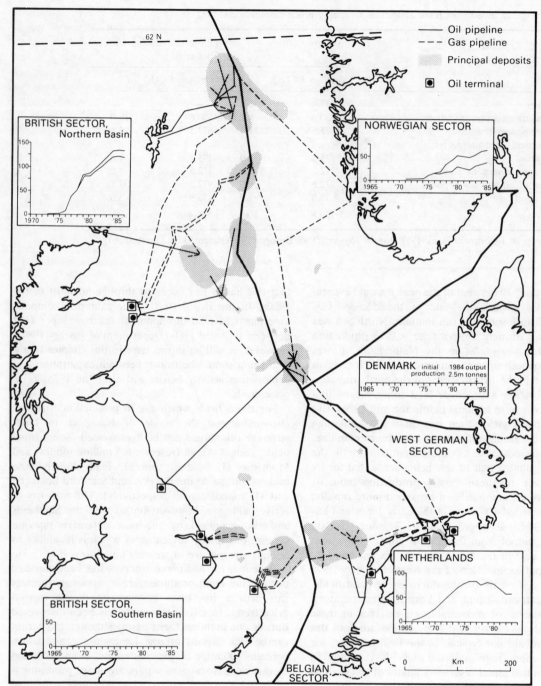

Fig. 5.3
North Sea oil and gas. (Output is measured in millions of
tonnes of oil equivalent. For the northern basin in the
British sector, and for the Norwegian sector, the lower
output curve represents oil; the upper curve represents oil
and gas.)

German discoveries have been minimal and, although numerous Dutch gasfields have been proven on land and north-west of Den Helder, 70 per cent of the country's reserves still lie in and around the Slochteren deposit. Meanwhile, the exploration wave has spread to the Mediterranean and is concentrating initially on Italy where, before the advent of Dutch gas, several of Europe's more important gasfields were to be found. Most Italian discoveries have been in the Adriatic, but the Ionian Sea off Calabria is also promising, as is the Sicilian offshore zone. In 1986 Italy borrowed over half the finance made available by the European Investment Bank for the development of oil and gas, the large majority of the loans being employed in offshore projects.

The vast programme of exploration and production that has been undertaken to date has necessarily involved the oil companies in an intensive learning process. This is particularly true of technological aspects of the industry, and the experience of operating in the North Sea's extreme weather and sea conditions is already proving beneficial in other parts of the world. But the governments and energy ministries of the countries concerned have also had to learn rapidly in order to erode the oil companies' natural advantage of past experience, to establish rational exploitation programmes and to ensure that society derives an adequate financial return from the new resources. The production curves in Fig. 5.3 may suggest that this governmental learning process has proceeded smoothly but, if so, they are highly deceptive. In reality, the obstacles to, and the disagreements about, effective control have been too numerous to consider individually. Thus we must focus on a selection of major themes.

Dutch natural gas – exploitation, pricing and income

Partly because of state participation with the original discoverers, Shell and Esso, and partly because of the tax structure imposed on the industry, since the late 1970s natural gas has provided more than a tenth of the Dutch government's income. In 1985, before the energy price collapse, the proportion was almost a fifth. Although this may imply the pursuit of a well-implemented exploitation strategy, much of the evidence suggests that the policy adopted in the era of cheap oil severely impeded the maximization of returns in the high-cost energy era. Moreover, the strategy eventually adopted to solve this problem hit government income hard when the energy price collapse occurred.

The initial policy was one of rapid development to exploit the resource before nuclear energy came into its own. From the mid-1960s a price structure which undercut competing fuels, coupled with the exceptional cleanliness and efficiency of natural gas, ensured that the consumption curve rose steeply. By the early 1970s the fuel had captured 60 per cent of the domestic heating market and was supplying approximately half the energy inputs to industry, electricity generation and horticulture. Naturally, a great deal of this remarkable progress was made at the expense of coal and, indeed, of oil: between 1965 and 1972, industrial oil consumption fell by 45 per cent and oil's share of the total energy market declined from two-thirds to a half (Pinder 1976). This trend was officially encouraged because of its import-substitution effect on the balance of payments, but in this connection a further major impact was anticipated from gas exports, which were in fact a central element in the policy of obtaining swift returns. Although they only began in 1963, by 1970 36 per cent of production was sold abroad.

Gas demand continued its remarkable growth in the early 1970s, but the oil crisis and the Arab oil embargo caused an urgent review of energy policy, the outcome being an almost complete reversal of the exploitation strategy. According to guidelines adopted in 1976, consumption was to be reduced to the minimum level consistent with contract obligations, no new export contracts were to be concluded and existing contracts were not to be renewed. If domestic demand ran ahead of production, as was anticipated by 1985, the shortfall was to be covered by oil and gas imports rather than by higher output, despite the balance of payments penalty. After a second policy review in 1979, the emphasis on conservation was reinforced by declaring the Slochteren deposit a strategic reserve, the depletion of which should be retarded (OECD 1980b).

Price rises aimed at conservation, coupled with intensifying recession, produced a 15 per cent fall in home demand between 1975 and 1980. But exports behaved differently, achieving a fivefold increase during the decade. West German consumption rose particularly quickly, to account for half the exports, while Belgium and France each purchased a fifth and Italy a tenth. Altogether, 60 per cent of the gas extracted in 1980 was exported. Although this rapid increase occurred partly because foreign consumers used their contractual rights to obtain secure supplies following the oil crisis, an additional major factor was that export prices became increasingly attractive. This was chiefly because, even though contract terms had been reviewed in the aftermath of the oil crisis, they remained too inflexible to allow the Netherlands to control foreign demand through the price mechanism. In fact the contracts were particularly deficient in two respects: gas price increases triggered by rising oil prices could take up to a year to come into effect, and price indexation was inadequately linked to the cost of oil. By 1980, therefore, exported gas was underpriced by 30 per cent. Even without new contracts, the Netherlands was committed to supplying 550 billion m³ of natural gas to her neighbours by the mid-1990s, an amount equivalent to 447 million tonnes of oil. Thus the most immediate problem became the need for contract revision to minimize foreign-exchange losses.

Discussions opened in 1979, but the fourteen major purchasing companies understandably showed little enthusiasm for renegotiation. Lack of progress quickly made the problem a major political issue, the most trenchant view being that quick results should be achieved by invoking a law of 1974 and halting supplies. Ultimately, however, the issue was tackled more subtly by the appointment of a retired diplomat, well known throughout the European Community, as the country's official negotiator. Armed with the threat of cessation of supplies, by late 1980 this emissary had successfully concluded substantial contract revisions. These included the rapid upward adjustment of gas prices to rises in the price of oil, and a phased increase which raised the average price of gas at the Dutch border by 20 per cent. In this way, export earnings were improved by up to 2 billion guilders a year, compared with an original target of 3 billion guilders. But the formula which allowed gas prices to rise in line with those of oil also required gas charges to be lowered if the value of oil fell. When oil prices collapsed, therefore, the consequences for the national exchequer were dramatic. Income from exports is estimated to have fallen by 67 per cent between 1985 and 1987, while government revenue from domestic and export sales fell by 54 per cent. This has necessitated urgent reappraisal of government expenditure, one of the main targets being economies in the extensive Dutch welfare state. (In the mid-1980s, total social-security costs accounted for a third of the national income.) There have, it is true, been benefits. Disposable income in private households has risen as gas prices have fallen, and production cost reductions have helped export industries. Yet in an economy as open as that of the Netherlands, higher disposable incomes primarily stimulate imports, and low gas prices make it increasingly difficult to sustain energy conservation as a significant national policy.

Controlling oil and gas development – the British experience

The relationship between private enterprise and the state has aroused more political controversy in the UK than in any other part of the North Sea petroleum province. As in the remainder of the province, private enterprise was essential to initiate exploration and development, and more than sixty companies now have a financial stake in British sector resources. The private enterprise view has been that this diversity is in itself a protection against capitalist manipulation. More than half the companies have an interest in only one field, and half the financial holdings in individual fields are of 20 per cent or less. The policy initiated by the Labour Party, however, was to counterbalance private interests – particularly multinational capital – by extensive state participation (Department of Energy 1974). Thus the British National Oil Company (BNOC) was created in 1976 to negotiate a majority (51 per cent) holding in existing private sector production and to exercise the option of majority participation in all future commercial developments. Yet in 1982 the Conservative government, having separated the production and trading functions of BNOC, sold a majority holding in Britoil, the company created to take over BNOC's production activities. One justification for this step was that, although BNOC had not purchased a majority holding in any field (Department of Energy 1982), it had become the target of heavy criticism from the remainder of the industry. This argued that the nationalized company curtailed competition, reduced investment by creating uncertainty in the private sector and occupied a favoured position by being both a quasi-independent producer and a government agency. But, in addition, the Britoil sale was devised to further two major government policies, privatization of nationalized activities and the realization of assets to reduce the Public Sector Borrowing Requirement (Webb 1985). The issue raised by the sale is whether the proceeds, together with the results of allowing the private sector greater freedom, will in the long run offset the loss of earnings from a nationalized BNOC and the supposed benefits of state control. Light was shed on this issue towards the end of 1987 when British Petroleum and the Atlantic Richfield Corporation both showed interest in purchasing Britoil. British Petroleum eventually made a takeover bid which valued the company at £2.27 billion, almost four times the £548 million raised for the Exchequer by the original sale five years earlier.

Contrasted political attitudes have also been intertwined with the pricing strategy for British gas. Anti-inflation policies pursued by the Labour governments in the 1970s prevented household gas prices rising as rapidly as those of oil, with the result that by 1980 gas was being sold to domestic consumers for less than half its true value. The consequent rapid increase in consumption led to winter supply shortages, discounts were offered to companies willing to sign interruptible contracts and new customers were only accepted if they had a legal right to supplies. Revenue losses and the disincentive to conservation caused by low prices led the Conservative government elected in 1979 to impose closely phased price increases, doubling the cost of household supplies in two years. This rapidly raised profits, allowing the imposition of a substantial windfall profit tax. But consumption proved so insensitive to price increases that little was done to bring demand in line with supply.

One policy response has been to increase supplies by imposing strict controls on the flaring of 'waste' gas considered by companies to be an uneconomic by-product of oil production in the northern basin. As late as 1982, the amount flared off was equal to 11 per cent of British gas production, but by then the new controls were operating and the practice was rapidly diminishing. If present trends continue, flaring will be negligible in the 1990s. The gas saved is either re-injected for later extraction or is piped ashore via extensions to the pipeline network. Gas landed from the northern basin rose by 4.7 mtoe between 1982 and 1986. The second policy response has been to encourage increased production from the main gas-producing area, the southern basin. Several new fields have been brought into production and improved extraction methods have been employed on older gasfields. This has reversed a production decline which developed in the late 1970s as output from the established fields fell through depletion.

Gas demand has been so buoyant, however, that these measures have done no more than prevent a deterioration of the demand/supply gap. The outcome has been that this gap has had to be bridged throughout the 1980s by substantial imports from Norway. These have fluctuated from year to year but have normally accounted for between 20 and 25 per cent of total gas consumption (Stern 1986). One footnote that may be added is that the strong demand for natural gas in the UK assisted the sale of the British Gas monopoly in 1986 as part of the government's privatization programme.

Governments of both persuasions have been careful to ensure that the selling price of North Sea oil reflects its world market value. Two factors have prevented a repetition of the Dutch and British mistakes of selling gas cheaply. Firstly, exploitation began in the era of high prices so that there was no policy legacy from the cheap energy years to be overcome. Secondly, the nature of the oil, which has a low sulphur content and is best suited to the production of light distillates, meant that in the early years of production it was not well matched with British demand and with British refinery technologies. At the outset, therefore, the efficient use of the resource demanded that large quantities of oil should be exported at market prices to pay for more suitable imports from traditional suppliers. Sixty-five per cent of production was exported in 1985, mainly to Western European markets.

Successive governments have also agreed on the necessity for a strong tax regime, the result being a long-running conflict between industry and the state over the relationship between taxation policy and resource development. From a government's viewpoint, the first problem is to determine the level of taxation the industry will bear without lowering exploration, investment or production below desirable levels. The second problem is to impose it. The tax regime adopted after the 1973 price rises was intended to divert 70 per cent of companies' net revenues to the Exchequer, and it has been argued that the industry has understated resources and has held back on investment in an attempt to force more liberal treatment (Odell and Rosing 1976). But the industry's view is that numerous adjustments to the tax regime reduced the developers' share of marginal income from 40 to 10 per cent between 1974 and 1982. After allowing for oil price rises and general inflation, this meant a 50 per cent reduction in real income per barrel. This, it is argued, contributed substantially to a 20 or 30 per cent shortfall between production forecasts and achievement, and it is also claimed that the harsher treatment encouraged a rapid decline in investment, which gave rise to widespread talk of an investment strike (Department of Energy 1976, 1982).

Recent taxation changes and incentives intended to stimulate investment are detailed in the Department of Energy's annual publication on the *Development of the Oil and Gas Resources of the UK*. Indicators of company attitude provided by this report suggest that the North Sea investment did become more attractive in the 1980s, even though oil prices began to decline very early in the decade (Table 5.8). A decrease in the number of development wells drilled in 1982/83, which was a reaction to the initial price falls, was followed by a substantial rise in drilling in 1984 and 1985. Exploration and appraisal activity rose steadily

Table 5.8 Drilling activity in UK waters

	Exploration wells started	Appraisal wells started	Development wells started	Mobile rig activity (rig years)
1978	37	25	96	18.1
1979	34	15	102	16.1
1980	32	22	122	20.6
1981	48	26	137	24.6
1982	68	43	118	30.1
1983	77	51	95	34.2
1984	106	76	108	49.1
1985	93	64	133	51.7
1986	73	40	85	35.3

Source: Department of Energy 1987 *Development of the Oil and Gas Resources of the UK.* HMSO, London

between 1981 and 1984; and mobile drilling rig usage increased each year up to 1985. What is also evident, however, is that the 1985/86 price collapse was too severe for increased drilling activity to be maintained. Although drilling cutbacks are unlikely to have a sharp impact on output, production has peaked and it may be that in the new price regime companies will be unwilling to invest to offset the natural output decrease that is shortly anticipated as oil fields are depleted.

Norwegian strategy and the national economy

In theory, several factors reduce the argument for rapid development of Norway's oil and gas. HEP is attractively priced; the small-scale economy has a very low demand for oil – only 8 or 9 million tonnes a year; and it has long been argued that the swift build-up of the industry and the injection of large revenues into the economy pose a threat to society and the manufacturing sector. Moreover, constraints of physical geography cannot be ignored. The Norwegian Trough, running parallel to the coast, has hindered pipeline construction to the mainland, while topography on the mainland continues to pose problems for pipeline development. Against this background, Norway has long professed a commitment to a 'moderate' pace of development, which apparently distinguishes her depletion policy from the early rapid exploitation strategies pursued by both the Netherlands and Britain (Ion 1977; Noreng 1980).

Moderation, however, is a term requiring definition, and the intention to curtail production must not be overemphasized. Indeed, the cynical might conclude that, with respect to the presentation of policy, Norway has attempted to have her cake and eat it. By 1980, oil and gas output was six times greater than domestic oil consumption and by 1985 it was nine times greater than demand. In reality, a strategy of establishing the industry as Norway's primary exporter has been pursued and, with the construction of pipelines to the UK and West Germany (Fig. 5.3), has been achieved with ease. In 1975, oil and gas exports totalled only 9 per cent of all export earnings; by 1981 the figure was 30 per cent and by 1985 it had soared to 49 per cent. In this way, Norway became the largest net exporter of oil and gas in the OECD.

Successful though Norway's experience may appear to have been, it has become clear that the general economic policy that has been built on oil-sector expansion has created major structural problems (OECD 1987a). In the late 1970s the country embarked on a wide-ranging and costly anti-recession policy which included, among other things, heavy subsidization of employment in non-oil activities. By the mid-1980s, between 6 and 7 per cent of all labour costs were being met in this way, and in several activities the level of subsidization was much higher (Table 5.9). This was particularly true of agriculture, fishing, shipbuilding and state-owned industry. One apparently advantageous effect of this policy was to reduce unemployment to remarkably low levels. Between 1984 and 1987, unemployment fell from only 3 per cent to less than 2 per cent. But the very welcome social benefit of low unemployment was in itself an indicator that necessary labour rationalization was being discouraged by the subsidization policy. Productivity failed to rise and low unemployment caused inflationary wage pressures. The result was that Norwegian producers rapidly became less competitive and, therefore, more addicted to government policy support. Manufacturing output, for example, failed to grow between 1975 and 1985 whereas, in industrialized countries in general, expansion averaged 25 per cent.

A further problem has been that, as the competitive prospects of the non-oil sector have declined, support

Table 5.9 Government subsidization in the Norwegian economy

	Subsidies as % of average labour costs per man year			
	1973	1980	1983	1985
Agriculture	21	59	67	64
Forestry	7	15	16	13
Fishing	16	44	35	36
Manufacturing	3	6	9	8
of which:				
Shipbuilding	0	52	73	117
State-owned companies	16	17	41	34
Service sector	0	0	0	0
All businesses	2	3	7	6

Source: OECD 1987 *OECD Economic Surveys: Norway.* Organization for Economic Cooperation and Development, Paris

in the form of orders from the oil industry has increased. Fifty to sixty per cent of the industry's orders are placed with Norwegian producers; a third of all turnover in large metal, machinery and equipment companies is generated by the oil sector; and shipbuilding's dependence on oil-related business rose from 7 per cent in 1978 to 40 per cent in the mid-1980s. At first sight – like exceptionally low unemployment – this support appears essentially advantageous. But its effect, coupled with stagnation in many non-oil activities, has been to make the oil industry an increasingly dominant growth pole in the Norwegian economy. Given the instability of oil prices, the desirability of this is highly questionable. As yet, the impact of post-1985 oil prices is not evident in official statistics, but oil industry demand fluctuates in sympathy with the cost of oil and a substantial recession in equipment orders can be anticipated. If this were to continue into the 1990s, the consequences for the Norwegian economy would be serious. So far as policy is concerned, therefore, revitalization of the non-oil sector has become an urgent necessity in order to reduce over-reliance on an energy industry that is essentially controlled by global, rather than national, forces.

Nuclear power in the post-crisis era

Since the 1973 oil crisis the nuclear power industry's growth record has been far from insignificant (Table 5.10). France and Belgium generate almost two-thirds of their electricity in nuclear power stations; in West Germany, Finland, Sweden and Switzerland, the

proportion is more than 30 per cent; and, overall, the nuclear power industry has increased its share of European electricity production from 6 to 26 per cent.

It is necessary to appreciate, however, that much of this growth has resulted from the commissioning of stations which were already under construction or planned when the crisis struck and, as Maull (1980) has stressed, the revised capacity targets set in the immediate post-crisis period have not been met. One reason for this failure is that the revised programmes adopted in the mid-1970s were wildly optimistic. In the European Community, for example, a fivefold capacity increase was proposed by 1980 and a further tripling by 1985. Relatively slow progress also reflects the continuing influence of the technical arguments and delays so familiar in the 1960s; Pearson (1981) has demonstrated the importance of this factor in the British case. In most of Western Europe, however, the argument was not about the merits and demerits of competing nuclear technologies, but about the desirability of any form of nuclear power.

The environmental confrontation

The nature of this sometimes violent debate is well known and need not be examined here (Lucas 1979; Maull 1980; Pilat 1980; OECD 1979a). What is significant is that, while the protest movement's precise impact cannot be established, there is no doubt that it has exerted a major influence on the industry's international growth performance.

In several countries anti-nuclear campaigns have prevented governments from embarking on nuclear programmes or substantially expanding existing toeholds in the industry. Both Denmark and the Republic of Ireland have drawn back from earlier proposals; in Austria, the Zwentendorf station on the Danube stands complete but uncommissioned; it is probable that widespread opposition to the Netherlands' two nuclear stations will at least prevent continuation of the expansion programme (de Vries and Dijk 1985); and Belgium is unlikely to embark on additional nuclear plants. Furthermore, the anti-nuclear movement has achieved considerable success by inflicting delays on the more ambitious programmes of other countries, particularly West Germany and Italy. By the mid-1980s, West Germany's nuclear capacity was only 25 per cent of the original 1990 target, while in Italy only 5 per cent of the planned capacity had been completed. These delays have worked in the opposition's favour by forcing higher safety standards and substantial increases in capital costs. In order to speed progress by reassuring the public that fears of nuclear power are unfounded,

Table 5.10 Nuclear power in the post-crisis period

	Nuclear power as % of total electricity generation			Nuclear output 1985	European Investment Bank loans, 1984–86
	1974	1980	1985	(mill. kWh)	(mill. u.a.)
Belgium	0.4	23.3	60.3	32 692	110.3
Finland	0.0	17.3	48.0	17 782	—
France	7.8	23.6	64.9	213 087	147.1
West Germany	3.9	11.3	31.1	119 461	204.0
Italy	2.3	1.2	3.8	6 717	303.8
Netherlands	5.9	6.5	6.1	3 674	—
United Kingdom	12.3	13.0	19.3	53 767	990.3
Sweden	2.7	22.0	44.0 (a)	50 995	—
Switzerland	18.0	28.3	39.6 (a)	17 396	—
Spain	8.9	4.9	22.1	26 768	—
EC	6.4	12.6	30.6	456 166	1 755.5
Total Western Europe	5.7	11.6	26.5 (a)	542 339	1 755.5

(a) 1984 data

Sources: United Nations 1976 *World Energy Supplies, 1950–1974*; United Nations 1981 *Yearbook of World Energy Statistics, 1980*; European Investment Bank 1980 *Information*, no. 26; European Investment Bank *Annual Reports*; Commission of the European Communities 1987 *Basic Statistics of the Community*

numerous safety modifications have been made to basic designs. This has involved additional material costs, but the main penalty has been longer construction periods, causing increased labour costs and escalating interest charges on unproductive capital. These cost factors are now so substantial that at least 30 per cent of the capital cost of Britain's pressurized water reactor at Sizewell can be attributed to safety measures.

Four other facets of the nuclear debate must be noted. Firstly, despite British emphasis on remote locations, the opposition movement has been strengthened because many nuclear power stations are close to major population centres (Openshaw 1982). For example, in Belgium the Tihange station on the Meuse lies only 20 km upstream and upwind from Liège; Spain's Lemoniz development is adjacent to Bilbao; and in France the siting policy has frequently preferred locations near the load to reduce transmission costs and losses (Lucas 1979). Similarly, the fact that at many sites an accident could lead to transfrontier pollution has been a strengthening factor – dense populations could be threatened by events only kilometres away yet beyond their country's jurisdiction. This argument was powerfully reinforced in 1986, when a major escape of radioactive material from the Chernobyl power station near Kiev spread within days to affect the whole of Western Europe. We shall return to this disaster, and the general problem of

transfrontier pollution, in Chapter 6.

Second, although opponents may be in a majority at the local level, this is not invariably the case, and at the national level it is not normally so. The Austrian nuclear programme, it is true, was halted by a referendum; and, after Chernobyl, the Swedes voted for eventual decommissioning of existing nuclear plants. But in Switzerland a referendum has rejected abandoning this source of power, and in national elections around Europe anti-nuclear candidates have rarely polled more than 5 per cent of the total vote. The movement is, therefore, essentially a minority force which has chiefly operated outside parliamentary systems yet has exerted considerable influence on the evolution of energy policy.

Third, the opposition has not always been successful, especially in the case of France. Here the attack has been particularly powerful and prolonged, yet there has been little sign of compromise on the basic policy (Lucas 1979, 1985; Collingridge 1984b). It is true that in the early 1980s the programme was scaled down, but this primarily reflected slower demand growth, rather than effectiveness on the part of the environmental lobby. By the early 1990s, more than forty French nuclear power stations will be operating, and their contribution to total electricity generation will exceed 70 per cent. By then the industry will satisfy more than 30 per cent of *all* French energy consumption, compared with 27 per cent in 1985. One reason for this relatively smooth progress is that *Electricité de France* and the monopoly construction firm, *Fromatome*, have made the building programme a highly standardized affair, but its implementation is dependent upon resolute government support and, indeed, a willingness to use force to put down opposition. Despite recent socialist hesitation, this strong government stance is in turn dependent on the official commitment of all political parties to the transition to nuclear power, and it is assisted by a licensing system which severely restricts opportunities for effective public participation in the decision-making process. Moreover, as the nuclear construction industry has grown, its contribution to the economy as a whole has become widely appreciated – all the major trade unions have joined the political parties in stressing the importance of a growth industry employing more than 125 000 people.

Fourth, while the nuclear debate is primarily conducted at the national level, it also has an important international dimension. The most widely-recognized aspect of this is the international protest movement, and the fact that there is supranational pressure for the industry's development is frequently overlooked. The most avid international support has come from the European Commission, although its earlier argument that 'The pursuit of vigorous [nuclear power] programmes is an essential element in an economic policy for Europe' has been tempered by the view that, following Chernobyl, nuclear power development 'is clearly only possible if the public is reassured as regards safety' (Commission of the European Communities 1981a, 1987a). The European Investment Bank is the institution that is most heavily committed to supporting the Commission's encouragement of nuclear power. Between 1982 and 1986 the industry absorbed more than half the Bank's loans, the principal beneficiary being the UK (Tables 5.7 and 5.10). So far, probably because they operate through governments and have no direct responsibility to an electorate, the Commission and the Bank have not come under heavy attack from the protest movement. Whether this relatively comfortable situation can be maintained in the post-Chernobyl era is a matter of conjecture, but the Commission's more moderate stance may well reflect a desire to avoid external criticism.

Coal – a glowing future?

One popular assumption in the immediate post-crisis period was that the new circumstances heralded the resurrection of the coal industry, but attitudes varied in the industry itself. In France the wave of optimism found little support, the programme which emerged being one of continued contraction, admittedly at a slower rate, to a production plateau of 10 million tonnes in the late 1980s. Similarly, Belgium saw no scope for re-expansion, but adopted the goal of halting the production decline at the 7 million tonne level. Greece and Spain, on the other hand, embarked almost immediately on more intensive exploitation of lignite and low-grade coal deposits, while Western Europe's major coal producers also adopted optimistic scenarios for the remainder of the century. West Germany planned to halt contraction and then re-expand capacity by up to a quarter, while the NCB proposed an ambitious two-phase investment programme to increase output by between 25 and 50 per cent (Greene and Gallagher 1980; Manners 1981; North and Spooner 1977, 1978; Spooner 1981).

Little difficulty has been experienced in expanding lignite production, but – because of this fuel's low calorific value – output is equivalent to no more than 37 million tonnes of oil a year (Table 5.11). What is also notable is that lignite mining in West Germany – Western Europe's largest producer – fell in the 1980s as the energy market eased. Production growth has therefore been achieved primarily through the industry's development in two energy-deficient southern European countries, Greece and Spain.

So far as hard coal is concerned, consumption in the 1980s has fluctuated, and this at first sight suggests that producers have at last stemmed the tide of decline that characterized the pre-1973 era (Table 5.12). As Table 5.11 demonstrates, however, the end of dramatically declining demand has not led to stabilization of the supply side of the industry. Since the 1973 oil crisis, coal output has continued to decrease in all producer countries except Spain (where it has expanded) and Belgium (where it has stabilized at a lower level than anticipated). In Western Europe as a whole, output contracted by almost a quarter between 1973 and 1985. The reality is, therefore, that more stable demand has benefited low-cost overseas producers rather than Western Europe's indigenous coal industry. Imports have fluctuated in sympathy with consumption and have doubled since the early 1970s (Table 5.12). Before the first oil crisis, imports supplied less than a fifth of the coal burned; by the 1990s the proportion is likely to exceed 40 per cent.

Bleak though the picture is for the indigenous coal industry, the situation would be much worse but for the fact that one branch of the coal market – electricity generation – has grown substantially as governments have renewed earlier efforts to reduce the power industry's oil consumption (Schaller and Motamen 1985). In the UK, for example, the CEGB's

Table 5.11 Post-1973 lignite and coal production trends

Lignite	Production, 1973 (mill. t.)	Production, 1980 (mill. t.)	Production, 1985 (mill. t.)	Change, 1973–80 (%)	Change, 1980–85 (%)
Austria	3.6	2.9	3.1	−19	+7
France	2.8	2.6	1.8	−7	−31
West Germany	118.7	129.9	120.7	+9	−7
Greece	13.3	23.2	35.9	+74	+55
Italy	1.2	1.4	1.9	+17	+36
Spain	3.0	15.5	23.6	+417	+52
Total	142.6	175.5	187.0	23	+7

Coal	Production, 1973 (mill. t.)	Production, 1980 (mill. t.)	Production, 1985 (mill. t.)	Change, 1973–80 (%)	Change, 1980–85 (%)
United Kingdom	130.2	128.2	90.8	−2	−29(a)
West Germany	103.7	94.5	88.8	−9	−6
France	25.7	18.1	15.1	−30	−17
Belgium	8.8	6.3	6.2	−28	−2
Spain	10.0	12.6	16.1	+26	+28
Total	278.4	259.7	217.0	−7	−16

(a) Output affected by industrial dispute.

Sources: Commission of the European Communities 1982 *Energy Statistics Yearbook, 1980*. Statistical Office of the European Communities, Luxembourg; OECD 1987 *Energy Statistics, 1970–85*. Organization for Economic Co-operation and Development, Paris

latest generation of oil-fired power stations was loaded very lightly after the 1979/80 oil price rise until a prolonged miners' strike forced them into full production. In West Germany, several laws have been implemented to phase out the use of oil and natural gas in power stations. Welcome though the growth of power station demand has been, however, the consequence is that three-quarters of Western Europe's indigenous coal industry is now reliant on a single market. Moreover, for four reasons, the future of this market is uncertain. Firstly, the cost of fuel oil – the main conventional fuel which competes with coal for electricity generation – has fallen substantially in the wake of the 1985/86 oil price crash. Secondly – as has been shown above – despite the influence of environmentalists, many nuclear power stations have been commissioned in the 1980s, and others are due for completion. If there is surplus capacity, these can be operated at the expense of coal-fired plant. Thirdly, even if the pace of nuclear power expansion lessens in the aftermath of Chernobyl, it is by no means certain that substitute power stations will burn indigenous fuel. In the UK, for example, there are plans to construct by Southampton Water the first major power station to be dependent on imported

coal. Fourthly, if political willingness to maintain the indigenous coal industry weakens, existing power stations could switch from indigenous to imported coal. Returning to the Southampton Water example, one proposal is that the coal terminal should have the capacity to supply large inland plants. This highlights the increasing competition between European mining and overseas products.

Coal for Europe or European coal?

Although it is clear that the European coal industry's prospects have not been revolutionized, it may yet hope to recapture lost ground as a result of world-wide efforts to convince consumers that the fuel's reputation for being dirty, inefficient and inconvenient is false. These efforts, to which European interests are major contributors (Ray and Uhlmann 1979), entail extensive research into new consumption technologies, coupled with an aggressive attitude to advertising coal's attractions. Some lines of investigation, such as fluidized-bed combustion, which is likely to improve efficiency and reduce pollution, are highly promising and should appeal to many industrial users as well as the electricity industry. Others, including coal gasifi-

Table 5.12 Post-1973 coal consumption and import trends

	1973	1980	1983	1985
Consumption (mill. t.)				
European Community	324.4	330.0	315.8	319.1
Western Europe	330.0	338.1	321.4	328.6
Imports (mill. t.)				
European Community	52.8	99.0	82.5	110.7
Western Europe	58.2	106.7	89.3	121.0
Imports as % of consumption				
European Community	16	30	26	35
Western Europe	18	32	28	37

Source: OECD 1987 *Energy Statistics, 1970–85.*
Organization for Economic Cooperation and
Development, Paris

cation and liquefaction, are in relatively early development stages and, if they are economically viable at all, are unlikely to exert a substantial influence on the market before the end of this century. Here it may be noted that the return to lower oil prices has handicapped research and development of gasification and liquefaction processes because consumers' potential savings from oil substitution have been greatly reduced.

Even if these research and marketing efforts prove highly successful, European producers will still be faced with the stark reality of price competition (Gordon 1987). Cost analyses produced by the European Community show that the imported product can now be marketed in European ports for less than $50 a tonne, no more than half or three-quarters of the cost of European coal. Given this continuing large price differential, it is widely accepted that a high proportion of any demand increase which occurs up to the end of the century will be met by overseas suppliers. This has long been the view of the European Commission (1980), which has predicted that imports will satisfy 80 per cent of additional demand by the year 2000. What must be emphasized, however, is that existing – as well as new – demand is a potential target for imported coal. The evidence in Tables 5.11 and 5.12 is that indigenous coal producers are poorly placed to defend their current markets. There is little to suggest that output from most producer countries will not continue to decline, to the benefit of the imported product.

A final point is that, because the industry is usually far from benign at the point of production, the future balance between European production and imports may be influenced by environmental, as well as cost, considerations. Opencast mining destroys landscapes,

flora and fauna; and it may also cause social dislocation, as in the Rhenish brown coalfield, where whole villages have been compulsorily relocated. Deep mining is less devastating, yet totally new collieries almost always entail the colonization of previously rural areas. In the past the impact of mining on the countryside was usually accepted, but surface workings, colliery spoil, dust emission, industrial traffic and incoming population are now commonly regarded as threats to the environment and the local community (Department of the Environment 1981a). Against this background it is increasingly argued that future demand estimates are insufficiently reliable to justify new large-scale developments when, if required, coal could be purchased from stable and politically-sympathetic countries. This was the issue raised during the public inquiry into the NCB's Vale of Belvoir proposals and, although the opposition's victory was not total, it is clear that the industry failed to establish that national benefits would decisively outweigh local environmental and social costs (Department of the Environment 1981b; Manners 1981).

Natural gas, external dependence and the security of supplies

While increased dependence on imported coal can be anticipated, this trend is firmly established with respect to natural gas. Demand for this clean, highly efficient fuel rose so rapidly after 1970 that many supply companies and governments were obliged to look beyond the Netherlands to satisfy their countries' needs (Boucher and Smeers 1985, 1987). Initially there was considerable interest among coastal states in liquefied natural gas (LNG), especially from Algeria. But despite limited construction of liquefied natural gas terminals, such as that at Zeebrugge, the basic import policy has switched to reliance on long-distance pipelines. These greatly reduce risk – liquefied natural gas is a highly dangerous commodity – and they are able to transport gas in large quantities. Pipelines now enable Western Europe's consumers to draw on four major suppliers – the Netherlands, Norway, the USSR and Algeria (Fig. 5.4). Of these, the Netherlands has decreased in importance in the 1980s as a more conservationist policy has been pursued, while purchases from the USSR and Algeria have grown impressively.

In Western Europe these developments have been actively encouraged at the international level on the grounds that they will substantially reduce oil demand and will therefore benefit the security of energy supplies. Imports from the four main suppliers account for well over half the gas consumed in most importing

Fig. 5.4
Natural gas, 1985: (a) consumption (million tonnes of oil equivalent) and percentage imported; (b) exports.

countries (Fig. 5.4) and, in Western Europe as a whole, gas imports are equivalent to almost 100 million tonnes of oil a year. Without these supplies, oil imports would therefore be substantially higher. The positive official attitude to the growth of the international natural gas trade is again seen most clearly in the stance of the European Commission and in the

activities of the European Investment Bank. Between 1973 and 1981 the Bank loaned almost 1 600 million ecu for Community oil and gas development projects, almost half of this being for import diversification through projects such as the Trans-Austria (TAG) link with the USSR and, most important of all, the Algeria–Italy pipeline (European Investment Bank 1980: 5–9; Annual Report, 1981). In the period 1984–86 the Bank invested 1 400 million ecu in oil and gas development and – although the gas supply network was much nearer completion than in the 1970s – the proportion allocated to pipelines was still almost a third (European Investment Bank 1987, Annual Report).

This strategy has caused little controversy in Western Europe, but highly adverse reaction in the USA underlines the closeness of the relationship between energy planning and geopolitics (Adamson 1985; Manne, Roland and Stephan 1986). The American view is that because almost half the gas comes from potentially hostile sources – the USSR and Algeria – there is an unnecessary threat to security. As an alternative to one Siberian pipeline project, the US administration unsuccessfully canvassed a scheme which would entail substantially higher gas exports from the Netherlands during the present decade and from Norway in the 1990s. In addition, an embargo on the use of American technology on the Siberian project, which was ostensibly a protest against Soviet repression in Poland, reflected geopolitical objections to Western Europe's growing dependence on Russian gas. Given these opposed views within the western alliance, it is important to examine more closely the political threat to supplies.

Several factors point to the conclusion that the apparent threat to the security of supplies is exaggerated. One powerful disincentive for the USSR to threaten the West by halting exports is that gas sales provide badly needed hard currency for the Soviet economy. Also, although the popularity of this fuel has rapidly increased in Western Europe, its share of total energy consumption is still limited. Except for the Netherlands, no country is more than 30 per cent reliant on gas, and in many cases the proportion is 20 per cent or less. A third point is that Western Europe's internal pipeline system is now so highly developed that in times of crisis indigenous gas could rapidly be substituted for curtailed imports from the USSR or North Africa. And, finally, although Norway and the Netherlands are disinclined to increase substantially their regular gas exports, they have acknowledged their ability to guarantee European supplies in times of crisis. It is highly unlikely that in an emergency these countries would not come to the assistance of their neighbours, and indigenous gas resources can therefore be seen as an international asset providing much-needed insurance against politically-motivated manipulation of this major branch of the energy sector.

Retrospect and prospect

While the geography of energy demand has evolved at a gradually decelerating pace, the geography of supply has changed beyond recognition through market forces and, to a degree, the planning process. From a state of heavy self-reliance in the early postwar period, Western Europe became fully integrated into the world energy system in the 1960s. At the same time a number of strategies for indigenous resource development were adopted, but it required the 1973 oil crisis to achieve general acknowledgement of the need to reshape the geography of supply to improve national and – to a lesser extent – international security.

Impressive progress in this direction has been made, firstly, through a sharp reduction in oil imports and Middle Eastern dependence (Table 5.6) and, secondly, through the compensating development of Western Europe's oil and gas resources (Fig. 5.3). But these departures should not be allowed to create the impression that the days of external dependence are over. Instead, this phenomenon is assuming a modified form through large-scale purchases of natural gas and increasingly substantial coal imports. As has been indicated, it is arguable that these imports are much less strategically dangerous for Western Europe than was the earlier dominance by the Middle East. Coal is readily available from politically friendly countries, and European gas reserves provide important insurance against unilateral action by either the USSR or Algeria. Yet it is still the case that, in Western Europe in general, the energy gap is better described as a gulf. Despite higher energy production and only modest demand growth, consumption in the mid-1980s was almost twice as great as indigenous production (Table 5.13). Moreover, the availability of North Sea oil has contributed to the fact that nearly half the energy inputs still come from oil and its derivatives. New energy sources have received very little impetus, and the only source of energy that has increased its share of consumption is primary electricity, an achievement resulting from expansion of the most controversial source of power – the nuclear programme.

With respect to energy planning, as much of the discussion in this chapter shows, the record is littered with examples of governments and agencies struggling, and often failing, to meet goals. Evidence underlining

the difficulties of guiding this vital, yet volatile, sector is abundant. To a great extent, this reflects the continuing power of oil prices, the control of which lies firmly outside Europe. Inexperience of managing new energy sources has also been important, as the Norwegian energy saga graphically demonstrates. But two other neglected factors that have increased the problems of planning are the political fragmentation of Western Europe and the multi-faceted character of the energy sector itself. Political fragmentation has militated against international coordination, even in the European Community. This has left the planning process in the hands of a multiplicity of agencies, many of which have been responsible for relatively narrow sections of the energy sector within individual countries. Although these agencies are increasingly subject to the overall control of government departments, each has its own viewpoint and interests to protect, with the result that their conflicting claims inevitably impede progress towards rational planning. This observation, coupled with the broad outlines of post-war energy trends, suggests that the history of intervention in Western Europe's energy sector can be understood best by relating it to the 'mixed scanning' theory of planning (Etzioni 1967). This argues that external crises periodically force authorities to make fundamental reappraisals of planning goals – in the energy context the coal and oil crises of the late 1950s and 1970s are obvious outstanding examples. But between these episodes, 'incremental' planning holds sway as agencies feel their way step by step, focusing on their own narrow fields of responsibility and generally avoiding the search for policy alternatives which might prove unpalatable.

Looking to the future, there is little to suggest that Western Europe will substantially narrow its energy gap (Guilmot, McGlue, Valette and Waeterloos 1986). Indigenous coal output is likely to fall, while North Sea output is officially expected to dwindle rapidly in the early decades of the next century. If the North Sea and adjacent areas follow the pattern of petroliferous areas in other parts of the world, where initial resource predictions have proved to be substantial underestimates, the timing of this decline will of course be delayed (Odell and Rosing 1976; Odell 1986). But the scale of any increase in economically exploitable oil and gas resources is highly uncertain, as is the future of most other aspects of the energy sector. How likely is it that the era of rapid demand growth will return now that oil prices have fallen? Can coal mining restructuring enable a substantial indigenous industry to be maintained in the next century? Is the argument that Europe has safely restructured its external dependence complacent? Can

Table 5.13 Western Europe's energy in the 1980s

	Production		Consumption		Balance	
	(1980)	(1985)	(1980)	(1985)	(1980)	(1985)
Total (mtoe)	545	644	1 072	1 120	−527	−476

	1980	1985	Change
Consumption by energy type (%): Solid fuels	25	21	−4
Liquid fuels	52	47	−5
Gases	18	17	−1
Primary electricity	5	15	+10
	100	100	

1985
(% of total oil imports)

Dependence on Middle Eastern and North African oil:	
Italy	44
France	34
West Germany	30
Netherlands	37
Spain	50
United Kingdom	23
Belgium	25

Sources: OECD 1987 Energy Statistics, 1970–85. Organization for Economic Co-operation and Development, Paris; United Nations 1986 Yearbook of World Energy Statistics, 1984. United Nations, New York

new forms of energy play a significant role in the early decades of the next century? What will be the ultimate future of nuclear power, and how will conflicts between energy and the environment be resolved? These, and many other questions, are the issues confronting the energy planners and governments of today. The future remains unsure.

Note

Many series of energy statistics are available. The most useful for the European Community energy market is the Commission's Energy Statistics Yearbook, although its publication is inclined to be slow. All Western European countries are covered by the OECD's Energy Balances of OECD Countries and Energy Statistics. The OECD's Oil and Gas Statistics also provide useful detail on consumption and trade. The United Nations' World Energy Supplies takes a historical perspective and is now updated by the Yearbook of Energy Statistics. Annual Bulletins of Electrical Energy Statistics for Europe and Gas Statistics for Europe are also published by the United Nations

and enable particularly detailed investigations of these increasingly important energy industries to be undertaken. Finally, many papers in the journals Energy Policy and Energy Economics provide extensive data and analysis of the European scene, as does the periodical Petroleum Economist.

Further Reading

Boucher J, Smeers Y 1987 Economic forces in the European gas market – a 1985 perspective. Energy Economics 9: 2–16

International Energy Agency 1984 Energy Policies and Programmes of IEA countries. OECD, Paris

Lucas N J D 1985 Western European Energy Policies. Clarendon Press, Oxford

Manne A S, Roland K, Stephan G 1986 Security of supply in the Western European market for natural gas. Energy Policy 14: 52–64

Maull H 1980 Europe and World Energy. Butterworths, London

Odell P R 1986 Oil and World Power 8th edn. Penguin, Harmondsworth

Taylor E, Davey W G 1984 Energy in Western Europe. Energy Policy 12: 409–24

6

Industry

Forgotten growth?

It is increasingly easy to overlook the contribution of the post-war industrial upswing to the present-day scale, structure and geography of Western Europe's industrial systems. By the mid-1950s the recovery from wartime devastation was complete, and in most countries the growth process was clearly established. Between 1955 and 1963 output in Western Europe as a whole rose by 54 per cent, and on the eve of the oil crisis production was virtually two and a half times greater than in the mid-1950s. Moreover, although the Norwegian and Luxembourg economies experienced a series of pronounced cyclical setbacks because of their heavy reliance on shipbuilding and the steel industry, this experience was exceptional. In most countries the growth curve after the early 1950s was remarkably smooth, the most marked hesitations prior to the oil crisis being episodes of relatively slow growth in the late 1950s, around 1967 and in the early 1970s.

Naturally enough, individual industries contributed to this expansionary impulse in varying degrees (Table 6.1). Textiles and clothing, two important nineteenth-century growth industries, fared badly – output in both increased by less than 40 per cent between 1960 and 1974 – but these were exceptional cases. Basic metals and the food, drink and tobacco industries achieved moderately rapid growth, while output from the burgeoning chemicals industry more than trebled. The most typical growth industries were, however, those which roughly doubled their production over the fifteen-year period. These included a broad cross-section of the manufacturing sector: from metal products (a catch-all category including many producer and consumer goods) to furniture manufacturing, paper products and publishing.

Despite variations between industries, manufacturing's performance as a whole was far better than

Table 6.1 Industrial output, 1960–75

	Growth Index, 1974 (1960 = 100)	Share of Western European output, 1975 (%)
Chemicals, petroleum products, rubber and coal products	325	14.8
Wood, furniture, etc.	215	4.4
Metal products	207	38.2
Non-metallic mineral products	203	4.6
Paper, printing and publishing	192	6.8
Basic metals	177	7.6
Food, drink and tobacco products	177	12.9
Clothing industries	139	4.5
Textiles	138	5.1
Other industries	203	1.1

Sources: United Nations 1977 and 1981 *Statistical Yearbook 1976* and *1979/80*. United Nations, New York

many governments – still haunted by the spectre of the 1930s Depression – had dared to anticipate. So great was the upward thrust that, at least in central and northern parts of Western Europe, labour shortages began to afflict the manufacturing sector, even though population growth and the contraction of agriculture simultaneously increased labour supplies. It is true that these shortages were also a reflection of the rapid expansion of the service sector, but the latter's progress was heavily dependent on industry as a creator of wealth and, therefore, of demand. One important

Fig. 6.1
Manufacturing trends: (a) output change; (b) employment change.

indicator of the strength of labour demand in the more successful economies was the attraction of migrant workers in large numbers to satisfy both the manufacturing and service sectors. This process operated at a variety of scales, its earliest expression being the

flow of Italian workers into the West German, French, Belgian and Swiss economies (King 1976). But as Italy expanded economically and Italian labour became less readily available, other countries on the edge of and beyond Western Europe's southern periphery were quickly integrated into the international labour supply system (see Ch. 4). 'Guestworkers' from Spain, Portugal, Greece, Algeria, Morocco, Yugoslavia and Turkey flowed into the main industrial economies, except the UK. By the time of the oil crisis, when the industrial growth process was abruptly interrupted, West Germany was host to nearly 2.5 million foreign workers, 60 per cent of whom worked in manufacturing. A similar number worked in France, where Algeria and Iberia were main source regions, but in proportional terms the country most heavily affected was Switzerland. Here 600 000 guestworkers comprised almost a third of the labour force. Although international labour migration was a striking example of centre–periphery processes in operation, its spontaneity should not be exaggerated. As Salt (1976) has shown, the rapid build-up of the guestworker phenomenon was engineered by the major host countries, all of which established highly-developed systems to remove natural obstacles to migration to radically different language and cultural areas.

Despite the polarization of labour from south to north, the most important differences in national manufacturing growth rates before the mid-1970s were not those distinguishing an advantaged core from a disadvantaged southern periphery. As Fig. 6.1 reveals, in reality the distribution of growth was much more complex and simultaneously resulted in divergence from and convergence towards a more even industrial development 'surface'. So far as divergence was concerned, one major feature of the geography of industrial expansion was the average and below-average performance of the economies in the northern periphery. But divergence was also increased because countries in Western Europe's industrial core recorded growth rates that were far from identical. While substantial successes were achieved in the Netherlands, West Germany and France – where growth was significantly higher than the norm – Belgium's performance was not outstanding, and in the UK and Luxembourg industrial output rose by little more than 50 per cent. Convergence, on the other hand, was brought about by unusually rapid expansion in the southern periphery as Portugal, Spain, Greece and Italy all more than trebled their industrial production. In absolute terms this trend was most significant in Italy and Spain, which came to rank fourth and fifth in Europe's manufacturing league table and account

Table 6.2 Manufacturing employment in Western Europe's core and periphery

	1975 (%)	1985–86 (%)
Southern periphery (Italy, Spain, Portugal, Greece)	19.9	27.2
Industrial core	68.9	62.2
of which: Netherlands, West Germany, France	*43.6*	*42.1*
Belgium, Luxembourg, UK	*25.3*	*20.1*
North-western periphery (Finland, Norway, Sweden, Denmark, Ireland)	6.4	6.4
Other countries (Austria, Switzerland)	4.8	4.2
	100	100

Source: International Labor Office 1986 *Yearbook of Labor Statistics*. International Labour Office, Geneva

for 85 per cent of the southern periphery's industrial employment. Impressive though it appears, however, the relative advance of the Mediterranean zone must be placed in perspective. As we have seen, at least in Portugal, Spain and Greece, industrial expansion was insufficient to stem the flow of guestworkers to stronger European economies. Moreover, in the mid-1970s seven out of ten industrial workers were still to be found in Western Europe's traditional industrial core, compared with one-fifth in the southern periphery (Table 6.2).

Multinational firms and Western Europe's industrial system

Many factors contributed to the buoyancy of industrialization before the oil crisis but, despite intensive investigation, their individual significance remains a matter of contention (Aldcroft 1978; Boltho 1982; Postan 1977). One factor which proved particularly interesting for the geographer, however, was the speed with which multinational firms developed and penetrated Western Europe's industrial system. This theme has generated an extensive literature, partly devoted to the phenomenon of multinational expansion in its own right but also, and increasingly, concerned with the penalties associated with the internationalization of capital (Blackbourn 1982; Dicken

1986a; Franko 1976; Hayter 1982; Hamilton 1976, 1978; Savery 1984; Taylor and Thrift 1986).

Although multinationals grew most rapidly in the 1960s, the foundations were laid decades earlier. By the inter-war period, two basic processes for multinational development were taking root in Western Europe. The first involved the transatlantic transfer of capital by US companies; largely because of language and cultural affinities, this investment flow was strongly biased towards Britain, although this predisposition must not be exaggerated. In the car industry, for example, Ford established factories at Manchester (1911), Berlin (1925), Dagenham (1931) and Cologne (1932). Similarly, General Motors' acquisition of the British Vauxhall company in 1925 was followed in 1928 by the takeover of the German firm Opel. The second process entailed the growth of indigenous European firms to multinational status (Hartner and Jones 1986). The Philips combine provides an outstanding early example. By the 1920s this firm had developed an extensive sales network in Europe but continued to confine production to the Netherlands. Then, to combat the trade barriers erected as part of the Depression's rising tide of protectionism, the firm's basic strategy switched to production in the major market areas. This reorientation was so successful that, by 1939, 60 per cent of the labour force worked outside the Netherlands (Pinder 1976).

Both processes blossomed in the post-war period, the rate of penetration being fastest in the oligopolistic basic and final-consumption industries, such as oil and petrochemicals, electronics, cars and household durables. However, it has been the expansion of US multinationals that has attracted most attention from – and has generated most controversy among – geographers and economists. By the early 1970s, US investment in Western Europe was four times as great as European investment in the USA and, on an annual basis, a third of all US foreign investment was being channelled into the Western European economies.

Locational preference and spatial disequilibrium

As Hamilton (1976, 1978) has emphasized, this major capital flow was far from evenly distributed geographically. At one end of the scale, the most popular target economy was the UK. Here US investment had reached $127 per capita by 1970, a degree of penetration again reflecting, as in the pre-war years, the absence of language barriers and the cultural 'proximity' of the two countries. But the per capita figures for Belgium and the Netherlands ($75 and $67) were also substantial, most probably because of the attractions of core locations in the EC and – especially in the Belgian case – because of government enthusiasm for foreign investment (Thoman 1973; Riley 1976). Conversely, France, with per capita investment of $37, and Italy (only $14) were relatively unpopular targets for US investment. In the French case this may well have reflected anti-US feelings prevalent in the Gaullist era; certainly Young and Hood (1980) have established that US investors perceive France to be a difficult operational environment. Italy, meanwhile, was disadvantaged by her peripherality to the main European markets and – not least – by the strong socialist bias of her turbulent political system.

Important though they were, the spatial preferences shown by American corporations were by no means identical to those of Western Europe's indigenous multinational firms, with the result that the latters' locational strategies tended to mute the major international contrasts noted above. As a succession of OECD and EC investigations have demonstrated, and as surveys by Blackbourn (1982) and Dicken (1986a and b) have revealed, data on multinationals' penetration of individual countries are dated and far from comprehensive. But the indications are that by the mid-1970s foreign-controlled firms accounted for between 20 and 30 per cent of industrial production in all the leading European economies (Table 6.3), a proportion that would rise if purchases from dependent national companies were included. In contrast, the degree of penetration achieved in many smaller economies – especially in the periphery – was 10 per cent or less. Allowance must of course be made for aberrant cases: in the periphery, the Republic of Ireland pursued a very effective policy to attract foreign investment. Yet the overall pattern indicates that the rise of the multinationals intensified rather than ameliorated core–periphery contrasts at the Western European scale.

Opinions concerning the propensity of multinational investment to exacerbate disequilibrium at the intranational scale are divided. Problem regions have been highly active in the competition to attract foreign investment, and Yannopoulos and Dunning (1976) have reasoned that the effect of this investment on inter-regional disequilibrium cannot be predicted. Conversely, however, Blackbourn (1978) argues that multinationals must be regarded as a spatially destabilizing force. Once again, resolution of the issue is hindered by a lack of reliable data, but from an examination of general location patterns it seems probable that US investment has been biased towards leader regions and that the attitudes adopted by European multinationals only partially redressed the balance (Hamilton 1976, 1978). Young and Hood (1980)

Table 6.3 Multinational corporations' penetration of national economies

	Foreign investment's share* of manufacturing output by value (%)	Survey date
Austria	23	1976
Denmark	9	1976
Finland	3	1977
France	28	1975
West Germany	22	1976
Italy	24	1977
Norway	10	1977
Portugal	10	1975
Spain	11	1971
Sweden	7	1976
United Kingdom	21	1977

* Based on firms at least 50 per cent owned by foreign investors.

Source: OECD 1981 *International Investment and Multinational Enterprises: recent international direct investment trends*. Organization for Economic Cooperation and Development, Paris

accept that multinationals have often made a significant contribution to employment growth in problem regions, yet their conclusion is that, despite the subsidies available, the less favoured areas have experienced slower than average growth in foreign investment. Similarly, Blackbourn (1982) argues that a location in the economic core is likely unless political influences lead the multinational corporation to prefer a peripheral region.

The multinationals – self-interested parasites?

Although the problem regions have been anxious to generate employment growth and promote the restructuring of their economies, it is important to consider whether multinational capital's tendency to avoid these regions has been entirely disadvantageous. Criticism of even relatively restricted foreign investment flows began to be voiced before the present recession struck, and concern has intensified as economic conditions have deteriorated (Bassett 1984; Blackbourn 1982; Dokopolou 1986a, 1986b; Hayter 1982; McDermott 1979). Initially, the critical standpoint was that in various ways multinational capital is parasitic. Profits, for example, are likely to be remitted to a company's home country, rather than being reinvested to generate further growth in the host economy. Similarly, although they use local labour, firms may depress multiplier effects by choosing to purchase materials and components elsewhere – sometimes from independent producers but often from other branches of the corporation. Before the recession it was argued that multinationals could disrupt the labour market by inflating wage rates and attracting workers from local firms. And it has also been observed that investments frequently exploit the product life-cycle concept: research, development and other high-level activities are commonly retained as headquarters' functions while decentralization to branches takes the form of established products or components. Thus host areas may become technologically subservient to other regions or countries. This subservience will cause employment to be biased towards low-level functions, so that labour demand is unlikely to match the broad cross-section of educational attainment. But the implications of the product life-cycle go beyond this because of the probability that – even in strong economic conditions – the future of branch plant products will be scrutinized as innovation, technology and changing demand require headquarters' decision-makers to re-examine their final product mix. The spatial structures of multinational activities dictate that the crucial decision-making based on this re-examination is largely external to the host region and, in most instances, to the host country. As Western Europe's economy has deteriorated, realization of the dangers of external control has sharpened, and concern for regional economies has been placed in the much wider context of national economic welfare. Finally, it has been argued that, by dominating a locality or region, the branch plants of major corporations depress the formation of small firms that are necessary to the long-term health of local economies. This may occur, for example, because branch plants may absorb potential entrepreneurs, or because they do not require numerous local linkages for their survival.

Objections to multinational investment must not be accepted uncritically (Dicken 1986b). Young and Hood (1980) noted in a study of US investment in Scotland that, at the local level, research and development functions may not be totally absent, as is commonly supposed. Also, corporations may decentralize aspects of decision-making and, as multinational investment has reached maturity, there has been a greater tendency to re-invest profits in the host country. Once again, recent reliable data are infrequent, but the OECD (1981) has estimated that 60 per cent of investment by US firms resulted from internal cash flow in the late 1970s. The same OECD report also questioned the assumption that slackening

Table 6.4 Shifts in the relative importance of US and European multinational capital

	Source of capital		
	USA (%)	EC (%)	Other areas (%)
*Belgium**			
1959–68	65	23	12
1969–73	35	42	23
1979	29	56	15
France			
1971	31	52	17
1978	15	61	24
West Germany			
1970	46	22	32
1979	37	36	27
Netherlands			
1968–70	49	34	17
1974–76	34	18	48
1977–79	4	56	40
Sweden			
1976	18	30	52
1979	22	39	39
United Kingdom			
1974	48	9	43
1979	55	15	30

* Excludes further investment in existing projects.

Source: OECD 1981 *International Investment and Multinational Enterprises: recent international direct investment trends*. Organization for Economic Cooperation and Development, Paris

economic growth would trigger a flight of capital from Western Europe. Although the evidence available was partial, and although US investment generally declined in the 1970s (Table 6.4), the indications were that the onset of recession had a more serious impact on indigenous investors than on multinationals. Evidence that the impact of multinational disinvestment can be exaggerated has also been provided by Townsend and Peck (1986) in an investigation of the role of foreign investment in the UK's recession. An analysis of 1 633 instances of job loss suggested that foreign corporations' 'patterns of disinvestment broadly reflected those of UK-based private corporations when adjusted for initial concentrations in certain regions'. Moreover, chiefly because of higher initial productivity in foreign-owned plants, job losses per thousand workers were on average 25 per cent lower than in British plants. Townsend and Peck (1985, 1986) and Peck and Townsend (1984) also emphasize, however, that restructuring by large corporations – national as well as international – has been a central feature of UK deindustrialization. Corporations have, of course, had many opportunities to restructure throughout Europe as well as in the UK. Indeed, the existence of the EC – in which the large majority of Western Europe's multinational capital is concentrated – has provided a major market within which this rationalization can proceed. Wabe (1986) offers an analysis of the regional impact of deindustrialization in the EC. We shall return to the question of restructuring, and the strategies employed to achieve it, later in this chapter.

Industrialization, pollution and hazards

Post-war industrial expansion brought prosperity to Europe, but some forms of industrialization entailed environmental impacts that have become major issues since the mid-1970s (Commission of the European Communities 1976, 1987b; OECD 1979b, 1984). Particularly important were increased energy demand, coupled with the greater scale of industrialization and the emergence of new types of waste product, especially from the chemicals industry. Simultaneously, the public's perception of environmental degradation increased as education, pressure groups and – perhaps most important of all – television brought about widespread awareness of the environment's vulnerability.

Despite the introduction of more stringent legislation and improved technology, air pollution remains a principal offender and is frequently associated with basic industries such as oil refining, chemical manufacturing and the production of steel and other metals. One dimension of this problem is the substantial impact on local populations, as Pinder (1981) has shown in the case of Rotterdam. But increasing concern is now being voiced at the supposed effects of international air pollution, especially by sulphur dioxide and, to a lesser extent, nitrogen oxide and hydrogen chloride (Commission on Energy and the Environment 1981; Environmental Resources Ltd 1983; OECD 1977). These, it is argued, originate in Europe's principal industrial zones but are carried by winds to relatively lightly industrialized regions, such as Scandinavia, where they are washed out of the atmosphere as 'acid rain'. When this falls on acidic ground it cannot be neutralized, and it is contended that ecological damage to rivers, lakes and forests then ensues.

Though the causal link with environmental damage has not been proved conclusively, the evidence is substantial. Sulphur emissions are commonplace and

have in some instances become worse as development has proceeded. Power stations in the UK, for example, are responsible for about half the sulphur discharged because, as the Health and Safety Executive (1981) has underlined, control technology 'was not suitable for application to large power stations built since 1945, and from these sulphur dioxide is all discharged from suitably designed tall chimneys'. The result is that modern 2 000 MW oil-fired power stations are often licensed to emit up to 650 tonnes of waste products *a day*, the dominant constituents being sulphur dioxide and sulphur particles. Although some environmentalists have overstated the case, this type of pollution is certainly carried long distances. Estimates by the OECD have concluded that 88 per cent of the sulphur deposited in Norway and 80 per cent of that falling on Sweden is 'imported' (OECD 1977). Yet, despite the existence of the Geneva Convention on Long-range Transboundary Air Pollution, in practice the industrialized countries have had little incentive to invest to protect remote environments outside their boundaries. Consequently, questioning the causal link between emission and environmental impact has been a standard substitute for remedial action (Commission on Energy and the Environment 1981). However, international pressure for reform has been maintained and has been reinforced by the realization that acid rain is implicated in the degradation of many valued forest environments within the industrial countries themselves. By the mid-1980s, countries were increasingly accepting the need for tighter emission standards (OECD 1983, 1984), perhaps the most impressive convert to the cause of emission control being West Germany. The heaviest investment programmes aim at the reduction of power station pollutants. In the UK, modifications are planned at the CEGB's largest power stations, and the installation of emission 'scrubbers' has already begun in West Germany. Here some of the earliest projects are in the lignite-burning power stations near Aachen where the sulphur content of fuel is particularly high. What must be recognized, however, is that progress will not be dramatic. Investment costs and technical considerations mean that improvement programmes will at best be completed by the end of the century.

Water pollution, chiefly in the form of chemical waste, also possesses a long-distance dimension, the effects of which are again difficult to reduce because improvement often necessitates international agreement and active cooperation (Walter 1975; Taylor, Diprose and Duffy 1986). In the West European context, progress towards these goals has been made via the Oslo Convention for the Prevention of Marine Pollution, the London Convention on the Dumping of

Wastes at Sea, the Barcelona Convention on the Protection of the Mediterranean Sea and the International Commission of the Rhine against Pollution (see Ch. 11). Yet industrial wastes still reach the marine environment either by direct dumping at sea or via rivers and outfall pipes. Dumping is now controlled by national licensing systems and, because waste products must pass through ports on the way to the dumping grounds, the practice is relatively easy to police. It is most important for France, Belgium, the Netherlands, West Germany and the Republic of Ireland, and the official claim is that most of the waste disposed of in this way has a low toxicity level and contains low levels of persistent materials (Ministry of Agriculture, Fisheries and Food 1982: Sheet 4.10). The pattern of discharge via rivers and outfall pipes is much more complex, involves far more pollution sources and, chiefly for this reason, is associated with many more unknown factors. The problem is severe in southern Europe where it is exacerbated by the enclosed nature of the Mediterranean and limited tidal movements. Action such as the Community-supported programme to improve the Bay of Naples has scarcely scratched the surface of the task. Around the North Sea, the available data suggest that direct discharge is most important for the UK and Scandinavia, economies that do not rely heavily on dumping at sea. But the conclusion that the continental seaboard from France through to West Germany is relatively benign in this respect must be treated with caution because of the absense of reliable data for major estuaries.

This is underlined by recent experience in Rotterdam, where consultants have established that 100 000 tonnes of oil-contaminated residues and 275 000 tonnes of chemical waste disappear each year. It is believed that much of this waste is collected by 'floating dustmen' and then dumped illegally, often in local waters. New national legislation has enabled stricter regulations to be applied in an attempt to control this problem, but these will do nothing to ameliorate a second environmental issue that is the legacy of generations of heavy industrialization in Rotterdam's hinterland. Silt dredged from the port has in the past been used to raise land for building purposes. Tests have now shown, however, that this silt is often badly contaminated with heavy metals, to the extent that it is unfit for use in residential building programmes. Since dredging must continue, safer methods of silt disposal have had to be devised. These include the construction of an offshore storage basin that will be sealed to prevent the seepage of pollutants into the surrounding sea. While it is arguable that problems such as these are particularly acute in Rotterdam because of the port's scale, their emerg-ence inevitably raises questions about other ports and estuarine areas.

The problem of water pollution also illustrates the difficulties of achieving successful international cooperation in environmental protection, an issue considered in detailed case studies by Guruswamy, Papps and Storey (1983), Haigh (1986) and Taylor, Diprose and Duffy (1986). A long-standing example of procrastination over international pollution is provided by the dispute between the Netherlands and France over the discharge into the Rhine of waste salts from potash processing in Alsace. These discharges significantly increase the treatment costs of downstream water consumers who rely on the river. In the mid-1970s, the French were releasing 7 million tonnes of salts into the Rhine each year, 40 per cent of its total salt load. A French undertaking to reduce discharges drastically was obtained in 1976 under the Bonn Convention for the Protection of the Rhine from Chlorides, and a preferred alternative method of disposal was identified – the injection of waste into safe geological strata. Six years later no progress had been made, largely because France had not ratified the terms of the agreement. Eventually, in June 1986 – only six months before emission reductions were due to be completed – France announced that she had decided against disposal by injection. The way out of this impasse has yet to be identified. Even when agreements do produce action on the part of polluters, however, the effects may not be those originally anticipated. Stricter regulations governing discharges into West German rivers aimed to ensure that treatment would take place either on site or at specialized land-based treatment plants. Often this has occurred, but tighter controls have also led to toxic waste shipments down the Rhine. These shipments are normally dumped in the North Sea or, in some cases, are incinerated at sea by special vessels. The environmental organization Greenpeace has fought a protracted campaign against these practices but, since governments license these forms of disposal, it has had limited success. Both these examples illustrate the difficulty of implementing the fundamental principle, strongly championed by the European Commission, that the polluter should pay for the reduction of waste to a harmless state, preferably at its source (Commission of the European Communities 1976, 1987b; Ellington and Burke 1981).

The European Community and pollution control

The leading organization working towards international cooperation in pollution control has been the European Community. March 1987 to March 1988 was designated the Community's Year of the Environment, but this was only one high-profile episode in a programme of activity initiated in the early 1970s. Two Action Programmes adopted in 1973 and 1977 aimed to stimulate remedial efforts to control existing industrial pollution. A third Action Programme launched in 1983 underlined the benefits to be gained by preventive action to limit the environmental impacts of new projects. The major measure introduced in this context has been a Community directive (1985) requiring that major infrastructural and industrial projects undergo a form of environmental impact assessment. A fourth Programme, intended to run until 1991, re-emphasizes the importance of prevention and ambitiously urges that environmental interests should be taken into account by all economic and social policies (Commission of the European Communities 1987b).

One positive form of action that has been taken is the mobilization of European institutions to encourage environmental protection investment. The European Regional Development Fund granted 300 million ecu for environmental protection projects between 1975 and 1986. In the same period, the European Investment Bank loaned 1 300 million ecu for similar schemes. Yet the scale of the problem is such that the assisted projects are in many ways demonstration schemes pointing the way for much more widespread action.

Also, while the Community makes great play of its environmental protection activities, and while its supranational status makes it a unique vehicle for the attack on international pollution, its record to date has been criticized (Klatte 1986; Kromarek 1986). Even if it is accepted that uniform emission standards throughout the Community are not desirable (Taylor, Diprose and Duffy 1986), permissible pollution levels still vary unsatisfactorily between member countries. The Commission's powers are poorly defined, and the publication of directives is not equivalent to their effective implementation. It is widely believed that the European Commission is much more deeply committed to protection measures than is the Council of Ministers. And the financing of environment policy is poorly organized. At present the principal prospect that more effective Community action can be achieved lies in the provisions of the Single European Act, the draft of which was adopted in December 1985. This Act is essentially concerned with integration issues (Lodge 1986) and it contains a specific section extending the Commission's powers to enforce, coordinate and integrate environmental regulations at the international level (Kromarek 1986). But even this measure has been criticized for weakness by the European Parlia-

ment, and it will be several years before conclusions on its effectiveness can be drawn.

Hazards

As well as generating pollution problems, some forms of industrialization that have achieved rapid growth have brought in their wake considerable potential hazards (Health and Safety Executive 1979). For example, because of the volatility of the products handled, oil refineries and petrochemical installations inevitably entail the danger of explosion. This is so despite their emphasis on fail-safe systems and automation, as was strikingly shown when an explosion and fire destroyed the Nypro (UK) chemical complex at Flixborough, Lincolnshire. Even though the works occupied a greenfield site, and even though the incident took place outside normal working hours, twenty-eight out of the thirty-two workers present were killed and 2 000 distant buildings were damaged (Department of the Environment 1975). But hazard risks are not confined to blast and fire resulting from explosions. Another potential danger is the release of dangerous substances as a result of an explosion or of a less spectacular plant failure. As with blast hazard, the immediate problem is likely to be restricted to a limited area. This occurred in 1976, for example, when dioxin – a poison 10 000 times more toxic than cyanide – was released from the Hoffman-La Roche plant at Seveso in northern Italy (Ellington and Burke 1981). Yet there is clearly scope for wind-borne hazardous emissions to be spread more widely. Although this long-range dimension is not a major problem in the chemicals industry (because escapes are usually diluted naturally by air movements) the risks have long been apparent to the anti-nuclear power lobby. That this concern is not misplaced was graphically demonstrated on 26 April 1986 when an explosion and fire at the Chernobyl power station in the Ukraine released into the atmosphere up to half a one-Megawatt reactor's contents (Lopriano 1986). Within three days the radioactive cloud from this disaster had reached Sweden, Denmark and West Germany, and in eight days the whole of the continent – and 300 million people – were affected (Fig. 6.2). Because of the long-term nature of radiation damage, the likely consequences of this accident – higher cancer rates and mortality – will not be apparent for years. The reactor itself has been contained in a concrete shell, and work is continuing to deal with contaminated soil from the area. Meanwhile it is not known when, or if, the 100 000 people evacuated in a 30 km radius of the site will be allowed to return. Defenders of nuclear

29 April 1986

30 April 1986

1 May 1986

3 May 1986

Fig. 6.2
The Chernobyl nuclear cloud,
29 April to 3 May 1986.

power argue that higher safety standards in Western Europe make a comparable accident extremely improbable (Nuclear Energy Agency 1986). Critics point out that the cause of the accident was human error – to be specific, unauthorized operator experiments at the plant. They also argue that this Europe-wide hazard was created by a reactor that was not particularly large and that a similar accident in Western Europe might be of larger magnitude and would almost certainly affect areas of higher population density. As was noted in Chapter 5, the spatial relationships between nuclear power stations, major population centres and national frontiers are such that even a restricted release of radiation could well have a major impact outside the country of origin.

In addition to illustrating the problem of local impact, the Seveso incident demonstrates that accidents involving dangerous chemicals can have other serious international implications if control in the aftermath is insufficiently rigorous (OECD 1985a). In this instance a contract for the destruction of residual dioxin, combined with 2 tonnes of inert material and

sealed in forty-one drums, was placed with a West German firm, Hannesman. The consignment was known to have left Italy in 1982, but it then disappeared amid rumours that it had not been destroyed. In May 1983, after the director of a French waste disposal firm – Spelidec – had spent two months in detention, the drums were discovered in a disused abattoir near St Quentin in northern France. Only then was Hoffman–La Roche forced to undertake the safe incineration of the dioxin-contaminated material.

Local communities vary greatly in their perception of potential industrial hazards. Many have shown very little concern, but in some instances the reaction has been intense, one outstanding example being that of Canvey Island on the north side of the Thames estuary. Here the concentration of oil refining, petro-chemical production and liquefied natural gas handling, all in close proximity to major residential areas, has brought about strenuous local protests that have forced official action (Health and Safety Executive 1978a, 1978b, 1981). Although it is now claimed officially that the resulting research, plant closures and stricter controls have reduced potential hazards to 5 per cent of estimates made in the mid-1970s, the issue remains live. In Rotterdam, similar safety concerns, coupled with intense awareness of air pollution and the environmental implications of growth, have imposed major restrictions on the development options of port and industry (Pinder 1981; Rijnmond Public Authority 1983). By the early 1970s, several years before the impact of recession brought expansionist policies into question, environmental opposition with substantial support among the local population had led to the defeat of grandiose plans to double the scale of the world's largest port. And a scheme for a steelworks near Rotterdam, with an annual capacity of up to 10 million tonnes, was likewise halted by the guerilla tactics of an impressively diverse local protest movement.

Canvey Island and Rotterdam are, of course, extreme examples. It is also true that, at least with respect to fatalities, the actual occurrence of major hazard incidents has been infrequent relative to the growth of potentially hazardous activities. This has been demonstrated in the late 1970s by the UK's Health and Safety Executive during an investigation of four types of major hazard which could occur in the energy and chemicals industry (Table 6.5). The Executive's conclusions were confirmed statistically by the Rijnmond Public Authority (1983). Nonetheless, the threat or experience of industrial pollution and hazard in Western Europe have triggered innumerable campaigns to protect communities and the environment. These protests have been so numerous and, very often, so successful that theories of spatial and economic development require adaptation to incorporate the environmental movement.

Hazards, pollution and industrial location theory

Since the Second World War the European economies have witnessed the introduction of many items of legislation intended to ameliorate the impact of industrial projects on the surrounding environment. Planning legislation, for example, has controlled the siting of industrial activity; it is now commonplace for regulations intended to moderate a project's visual and aural intrusion to be applied; and, although pollution continues to be a problem, official attitudes to emissions into the atmosphere and surface water are far more strict than in the immediate post-war period. The impetus for these changes has frequently come from interest groups in society as a whole, groups such as the town and country planning profession, the medical and public health professions and, increasingly, voluntary organizations concerned with environ-

Table 6.5 Major industrial hazard incidents involving fatalities in Western Europe

Location/nature	Date	Fatalities
Flammable gas/ vapour emissions		
Ludwigshafen	1948	207
San Carlos	1965	21
Rotterdam	1968	2
Amsterdam	1971	8
Flixborough	1974	28
Beek (Netherlands)	1975	14
Antwerp	1975	6
Reactive substance emissions		
Oppan (West Germany)	1921	561
Brest	1947	21
Antwerp	1964	4
Chlorine emissions		
St Auban	1926	19
Rauma (Finland)	1947	19
Mjodolen (Norway)	1940	3
Walsum (West Germany)	1952	7
Ammonia emissions		
Lievin (France)	1968	6
Landskrona (Sweden)	1976	2

Source: Health and Safety Executive 1979 *Advisory Committee on Major Hazards, Second Report.* HMSO, London

mental degradation. These have identified problems and, although their efforts have often failed, in many other cases they have successfully campaigned for legislation to curb the impact of offending development. Such groups have acted on behalf of society, and we may therefore argue that legislation introduced as a result of the democratic process of pressure, counter-pressure and parliamentary debate summarizes society's tolerance to development. The legislation can, in fact, be conceptualized as a ceiling or 'society tolerance limit' below which proposed industrial developments must stay if they are to be accepted (Fig. 6.3). Within a country, this society tolerance limit is likely to form a relatively even spatial surface, simply because it is defined by national legislation, although the fact that regulations allow planning decision-makers a measure of discretion ensures that some inter-regional warping is likely to occur. Beyond this we may hypothesize that throughout Western Europe the surface rises and falls abruptly as the transition is made from one legislative regime to another.

The concept of society tolerance limits does not, however, take full account of the recent role of en-

a

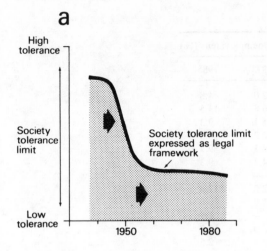

High
tolerance

Society
tolerance
limit

Society tolerance limit
expressed as legal
framework

Low
tolerance

1950   1980

b

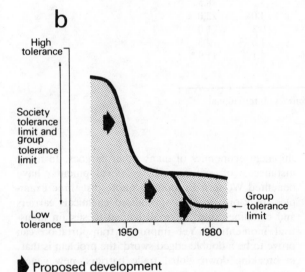

High
tolerance

Society
tolerance
limit and
group
tolerance
limit

Group
tolerance
limit

Low
tolerance

1950   1980

▶ Proposed development

Fig. 6.3
The concept of tolerance limits to development.

vironmental pressure groups in the development
decision-making process. Indeed, a very pronounced
feature of the period since the late 1960s has been that
many groups have become active primarily *because*
tolerance limits set by the legislation in force have
been perceived to be inadequate. On specific issues,
therefore, these groups have attempted to lower the
tolerance surface around endangered localities, in
some instances to ameliorate the impact of existing
industries, and in others to ensure that proposed
developments are either excluded completely or are
only allowed to proceed in a greatly modified form.
But the goal of lowering the society tolerance surface

is not achieved simply by opposing the undesirable
implications of industrialization: it can only be
attained by the successful exertion of influence on
those with decision-making power.

Strategies for achieving this influence have taken
many forms, but two broad approaches (which are not
mutually exclusive) can be identified. In the first,
advantage is taken of the fact that, as a statutory
requirement, most of Western Europe's planning
systems now incorporate some form of public participation. Within this framework it is open to protesters
to argue the case for a restrictive application of legislation, and in many instances they do so. But as Lucas
(1979) has emphasized in his study of the French anti-
nuclear movement, what is presented as a participation exercise may offer objectors little or no direct
contact with decision-makers. Similarly in the UK,
there is growing dissatisfaction with a public inquiry
system which may make participation in major issues
a highly expensive exercise, with no guarantee that a
conclusion favourable to the opposition will be upheld
by the relevant government minister.

The second approach is quite different and may be
adopted either because participation procedures are
non-existent or weak, or because the statutory system
is perceived to restrict the opposition by employing
quasi-judicial investigative methods to form a barrier
between objectors and decision-makers. This alternative is direct confrontation with industry and/or
political decision-makers, confrontation intended to be
so intense that the former will withdraw to less hostile
investment environments and the latter will perceive
clear political advantages in opposing development.

When schemes are blocked through either route the
effect is to bring into operation a new and lower group
tolerance surface (Fig. 6.3). This may represent attitudes within the local community or the interests of
vociferous groups external to the locality in question.
But the consequent lowering of the tolerance surface
cannot be considered permanent. Permanence can
only come through legislative modifications (which will
spread the new lower surface through the national
space) or through the introduction of new local regulations or plans. Unless this happens it is quite possible that the group surface will evaporate as time
elapses, circumstances change and issues die down.

From growth into crisis

Although environmentalism remains an important
influence on industrialization, since the mid-1970s its
progress has been matched by a resurgence of concern
for Western Europe's industrial future. In this connection it is important to recognize that, despite re-

Table 6.6 Manufacturing employment and unemployment, 1975–85

	Manufacturing employment		Unemployment (%)	
	1985 ('000)	Index (1975 = 100)	1975	1985
Austria	563.6	88	2.0	4.8
Belgium	764.5*	74	6.8	13.5
Denmark	515.3	96	5.1	9.3
Finland	497.0	96	2.2	6.3
France	4 742.1	86	4.1	9.7
West Germany	7 607.0	89	4.7	9.3
Greece	982.0	115	—	5.1
Republic of Ireland	189.2	93	12.2	17.4
Italy	4 101.0	79	5.9	10.6
Luxembourg	37.0	77	—	1.7
Netherlands	961.0	86	5.0	12.7
Norway	354.0	90	2.3	2.5
Portugal	926.1	112	4.5	8.5
Spain	2 120.9	71	4.0	22.0
Switzerland	710.7	99	0.3	1.0
Sweden	533.0	80	1.6	2.8
United Kingdom	5 519.0	74	4.1	11.9

* 1984

Source: International Labor Office 1986 Yearbook of Labor Statistics. International
    Labor Office, Geneva

cessions following the two oil prices shocks, *industrial output* trends have not been entirely adverse. In most countries, production recoveries have been made, but this contrasts with *industrial employment*, which continues to decline (Table 6.6). It is this decline, coupled with the associated phenomenon of large-scale unemployment, that has underlined for individuals and governments the reality of the crisis to be faced.

Superficially, the re-emergence of the pre-war unemployment spectre might suggest that the problems of the 1980s can be explained simply in terms of recession triggered by the energy price shocks of the 1970s. Important though it is, however, the recession is a relatively late arrival superimposed on the consequences of other major forces that have been gathering strength since at least the early 1960s. Just as much as the onset of deep recession, these forces demonstrate that it is essential to view Western Europe in its global context if today's industrial malaise is to be understood.

One of these long-term factors has been the improvement of maritime transportation and the associated development of ports (Pinder and Hoyle 1981). Here the fundamental point is that the technologies which created the crude oil supertanker have been adapted to revolutionize the transport and trans-

shipment economics of many other cargoes. In many instances, of course, these developments have benefited Western Europe: to quote just three examples, bulk-ore carriers, specialized chemicals carriers and container ships have all helped to sustain industrial momentum. Yet improved transportation can prove to be a double-edged sword: the problem is that, in breaking down global trade barriers, new generations of specialized ships have made Western Europe an attractive market for producers around the world. Without the ocean-going car transporter, Western Europe would export fewer vehicles but would also be less exposed to the rigours of global competition.

Beyond this, however, competition has intensified as a result of the new international division of labour. This is the spread of manufacturing, at the global scale, to countries offering advantageous production conditions. As Fröbel, Heinrichs and Kreye (1977, 1980); Blackaby (1979); Torre and Bacchetta (1980); Dicken (1986a); and Steed (1978a, 1978b) have demonstrated, this decentralization from the global industrial cores of Western Europe and North America is closely associated with the availability of cheap labour, especially in the Third World. But the rise of Japan, where engineering wage rates are typically three or four times higher than in countries such as Brazil or South Korea, shows that high-cost labour areas can compete effectively by exploiting productivity. Also, it is important to recognize that the global shifts are in many ways a reflection of the power of decision-makers in the late twentieth century. One aspect of this factor is that the organizational structure of multinational companies has made them ideal vehicles for transferring production from advanced to developing economies (Taylor and Thrift 1986). A second is that, in aiming for import substitution and/or export orientation (Pollock 1981), government policies in many industrializing countries have significantly sharpened international competition in a wide range of industries, from textiles and clothing to shipbuilding and steel.

Three industries – oil refining, petrochemical production and car manufacturing – have been selected to illustrate the impact of these new forces on Western Europe's industrial system. The first spotlights the consequences of recession, defined as a slump in anticipated demand. The second illustrates the transition from recession-generated crisis to one based on the pressures of global competition. The third provides a case study of adjustment forced from the outset by intense competition between major world manufacturing power blocs. All three demonstrate that – far from being confined to traditional industries – major difficulties confront many of the most successful post-war activities on which Western Europe's recent prosperity has been heavily dependent.

Oil refining

Western Europe's post-war economic take-off stimulated – and was in turn stimulated by – the spectacular expansion of oil refining. Refinery capacity in 1976 – the peak year – was almost 1 050 million tonnes, compared with 230 million tonnes in 1960. Most of the growth was concentrated in the European core (Fig. 6.4), although a significant number of projects were implanted at coastal locations in the Mediterranean periphery, the planning theory being that in a variety of ways these would act as catalysts for local economic development. But soon after the 1973 oil price shock it became apparent that the industry's policy of growth must be abandoned (Bacchetta 1978), and after 1979–80 – when the second price shock hit the European economies – the crisis in refining became intense (Molle and Wever, 1984a, 1984b). In Western Europe as a whole, refinery utilization rates fell from 69 per cent in 1979 to 58 per cent in 1981. By then, the capacity surplus was equivalent to more than 30 average refineries, and most of the industry was making substantial operating losses on its basic refining activities. One estimate (*Petroleum Economist*, August 1981) was that these losses averaged $18 tonne, but in some areas they were considerably worse. For example, in West Germany, where the indigenous capacity surplus was exacerbated by product dumping from other European countries, losses in 1981–82 were probably at least $50 a tonne. Similarly, losses in the French refining industry were in the region of $3 billion in 1981.

Understandably, investment in new refineries for major expansion schemes virtually ceased in this new economic climate and, as yet, there is no sign of a recovery in construction (Table 6.7). But, in addition to reducing construction, fundamental changes in the extent and nature of the refiners' West European operations have been imperative to return the industry to a sound financial footing (Pinder and Husain 1987a).

The most obvious restructuring strategy pursued in the 1980s has been the rapid reduction of surplus capacity. Between 1979 and January 1987, the industry's capacity was lowered by 31 per cent (Fig. 6.4b). This was achieved in two ways. Firstly, no less than 46 refineries were closed in this period. As Table 6.8 demonstrates, relatively large undertakings were not immune from this closure process. The largest shutdown to date has been the Ravenna refinery (annual capacity 12.3 million tonnes) owned by the Italian company SAROM. But, in general, companies have opted to close small refineries; in 1979 the average capacity of all refineries was 6.5 million tonnes, while the average size of closed refineries was only 4.2 million tonnes. This partly reflected the fact that small refineries were often vulnerable because they failed to achieve sufficient economies of scale. But many were also prime targets for closure because the technologies they employed were insufficiently advanced (Pinder and Husain 1987a, 1987b). We shall return to the role of technology in the industry's survival strategy below.

Secondly, in addition to closing refineries, companies reduced unwanted capacity by adopting a far less obvious strategy known as downrating. This entails maintaining refineries in production, but substantially reducing their capacity by taking out of commission surplus refining units. In sharp contrast to closures, this strategy was chiefly applied to relatively large refineries which could be contracted without severe reductions of scale economies in the refining process. The average size of refineries downrated was 10.6 million tonnes before contraction and 8.1 million tonnes afterwards. Altogether, the downrating strategy was responsible for 47 per cent of Western Europe's total capacity reduction in this period, the remaining 53 per cent being accounted for by closures. The

Fig. 6.4
Oil refining: (a) refinery
capacities at peak year
(1976); (b) capacity and
throughput, 1980 and 1987.

effects of this disinvestment on refinery utilization rates is apparent in Fig. 6.4b. In most countries, and especially those with major branches of the industry, throughput as a proportion of total capacity has risen significantly. In 1985 the utilization rate for the industry as a whole was 72 per cent, not far short of the 80 per cent target adopted generally in the industry.

Impressive though it was, disinvestment was not the only strategy open to the refiners in their attempts to improve the industry's economics. In the early 1980s one of the industry's major handicaps was that over-production of relatively heavy and low-value products (such as high-sulphur fuel oil) was particularly serious, primarily because of the limitations of traditional distillation technology. But the application of more versatile cracking processes to the heavier fractions allows lighter products to be obtained, and the fact that refineries already equipped with these technologies remained profitable triggered a major investment

wave. By the mid-1980s more than 30 projects expanding the capacity of conversion facilities had been completed in the core and the southern periphery. As a result, fuel oil's share of total refinery output fell from 34 per cent in 1979 to 23 per cent in 1985.

Although the pace has slackened, investment is still continuing and a variety of technologies is being employed (Fig. 6.5). Vielvoye (1985) has argued that investment will need to be maintained until the end of the century to counteract falling demand for relatively heavy refinery products. What must be recognized, however, is that current investment is taking place after the oil price collapse of 1985–86. Consequently the profits to be made from the conversion of heavy products are now less attractive. In June 1985 the margin between gasoline and fuel oil prices was almost $12 a tonne, but by July 1987 the difference had narrowed by two-thirds. One result of this may be that companies will opt for relatively cheap thermal conversion technologies rather than the more effective – yet costly – advanced 'cracking' techniques. Indeed, even before oil prices fell, the most popular solution to the problem of surplus heavy products was the speedy introduction of well-tried thermal conversion processes (Pinder and Husain 1987a). Crisis did not encourage most companies to risk high-cost advanced technology investment strategies.

Three further points relating to oil refining restructuring are appropriate. Firstly, disinvestment by traditional European refiners has provided opportunities for inward investment from outside Europe. The prime example is the foothold gained by the Kuwait Petroleum Corporation by purchasing Gulf Oil's marketing network and its refineries in Rotterdam and Denmark. Secondly, however, most closures and cutbacks have had more serious implications for the localities affected. Closures clearly entail the loss of employment, even though the industry's capital intensity means that typical redundancies (300–400) are less

severe than is often the case when deindustrialization occurs. In addition, the business tax base of local authorities may be severely hit, while reduced oil imports have obvious implications for port revenues. The effects on ports have been very uneven, but it is not uncommon for oil traffic to have decreased by 50 per cent or more (Table 6.9). Where decline has been severe, most ports have been very unsuccessful in generating alternative traffic. Refinery closures also pose a physical planning problem more normally associated with old industrial areas in major conurbations. Given the lack of demand from industry, how can redundant sites of perhaps 2 km² be recycled for the good of the economy and the community? Satisfactory solutions to this problem have scarcely begun to be formulated.

Thirdly, although the crisis in Western Europe's refining industry can largely be attributed to the recession, the indications are that the global spread of refining capacity will become an additional compli-

Table 6.7 New refineries and refinery expansion programmes

	Total capacity 1987 (mill. t.)	Refineries planned, 1986		Expansion schemes, 1986	
		No.	Capacity (mill. t.)	No.	Capacity (mill. t.)
Western Europe	663	0	0.0	2	3.1
Africa	102	2	12.3	3	8.2
Middle East (a)	235	2	14.1	7	24.8
Far East (b)	512	2	11.9	6	8.0
North America	837	0	0.0	6	9.9
Caribbean and South America (c)	348	2	10.3	12	28.4
Communist World	861	3	9.4	0	3.1
Total	3 558	11	58.0	36	85.5

(a) Including Egypt
(b) Including Australasia
(c) Including Mexico
Sources: *Oil and Gas Journal* 1986 **17**: 75–9; *Oil and Gas Journal* 1986 **51**: 78–103

cating factor by increasing significantly the volume of high-grade products traded internationally. This would set the scene for a further price squeeze that the European refiners now fear. The threat of imports is greatest from Middle Eastern and North African countries. Even though declining oil revenues forced Saudi Arabia to cancel a number of projects in the mid-1980s, the Middle East and Africa accounted for 41 per cent of world capacity expansion in progress in 1986 (Table 6.7). In 1985, Western Europe imported 30 million tonnes of products, 20 per cent more than anticipated by the European Commission. By 1990, imports are expected to reach at least 40 million tonnes and this, too, may be an underestimate. Although this inflow is modest relative to the European industry's total output, increased supply can only magnify the difficulties of re-establishing healthy profit margins. This underlines the fact that, although Western European refiners acted decisively to contain the crisis in their industry, there is no prospect of a return to the economic climate considered normal in the pre-crisis era.

Petrochemicals

In many ways Western Europe is the cradle of the petrochemicals industry. It is the home of four of the world's five largest chemical concerns – Bayer, BASF, Hoechst and ICI – while the two largest indigenous oil companies (Royal Dutch Shell and BP) both have extensive petrochemical interests. In addition, the sector's post-war growth naturally stimulated the entry of many other firms, indigenous and foreign. Yet plentiful capacity, and price cutting as producers strove to

maintain their market shares as the recession deepened, manoeuvred the industry towards financial crisis. Against the background of rapidly rising crude oil prices, in the West German market the price of polystyrene rose by only 75 per cent between 1973 and 1982, while that of polypropylene actually declined. Because of their bias towards high-volume, standard products, the effects were felt particularly badly by oil companies: BP lost nearly $1 000 million on chemicals between 1980 and 1982. But European chemical companies in general saw relatively healthy returns diminish rapidly in the early 1980s. And the European companies' overall performance would have deteriorated even more rapidly if losses in high-volume products had not been offset by better returns on foreign activities and high-technology chemicals.

The strategies adopted by petrochemical producers in response to crisis have been similar, but not identical, to those employed by oil refiners (OECD 1985b). Capacity cutbacks, involving closures and downrating, have been frequent. Early examples included decisions by BP and ICI to close seven plastics installations in the UK, and by BASF in West Germany and DSM in the Netherlands to curtail polyethylene capacity by 20 per cent. A recent example is that of the ICI and Enichem partnership which, in 1986–7, closed plant capable of producing 300 000 tonnes of PVC a year. The aim of this contraction was to halve PVC over-capacity in Europe. Investment has also been central to the recovery strategy. Although the number of construction projects significant at the world scale has slumped in the crisis period (Table 6.10), many revamping schemes have been undertaken in existing installations

Table 6.8 Refinery size and closure, 1979–87

Capacity (mill. t.)	All refineries (%)	Closures, 1979–87 (%)
> 15.0	6	0
10.1–15.0	11	4
5.1–10.0	34	33
<5.0	49	63
	100	100

Total closures = 46 (29 per cent)

Source: Southampton University Oil Refinery Database

and others are in progress or planned. These schemes are primarily cost-cutting exercises, designed to achieve higher plant efficiency. Specific goals are the more economical use of raw materials, flexibility allowing plants to switch to cheaper raw materials and improvements in the design and control of production processes. Progress in this latter area has been particularly closely related to the development of advanced

Table 6.9 Oil imports in a sample of European ports (million tonnes)

	1973	1979	1986	Change (%) 1973–86
Rotterdam	142.0	120.0	71.0	−50
Le Havre	63.1	55.1	26. 6	−58
Milford Haven	30.2	23.5	12.4	−59
Wilhelmshaven	24.9	27.9	16.1	−35
Liverpool	13.4	2.2	1.6	−88
Medway Ports	9.9	7.1	0.0	−100
Bordeaux	7.5	6.3	0.2	−97
Antwerp	8.5	3.3	6.3	−26
La Coruna	3.4	3.8	5.5	+61

Sources: Port statistical series and direct communications

computer software to facilitate design, process control and operator training (Pathe 1986).

Unlike the refining industry, however, the petro-chemicals sector has actively pursued a third survival strategy – ownership restructuring. This has taken several forms. In Italy, a government-orchestrated

Fig. 6.5 Major refinery conversion projects and planned completion dates.

Table 6.10 Petrochemical projects under construction and planned

	Under construction		Planned
	1982	1986	1986
Austria	2	1	
Belgium	4	1	
Finland	–	–	2
France	1	1	
West Germany	10	2	2
Greece	4	2	
Italy	1	1	
Netherlands	5	3	1
Norway	1	–	
Portugal	6	1	
Spain	6	6	
Sweden	1	–	
UK	3	2	
Total Western Europe	44	20	5

Sources: Oil and Gas Journal, Worldwide Construction Reports 1982 **43**: 115–26 and 1986 **17**: 80–5

rescue plan reorganized the industry under ENI and Montedison. Mergers of interests have been undertaken, such as the PVC production partnership between ICI and Enichem noted above. This joint venture has created the European Vinyls Corporation. Similarly, BP and Atochem (a subsidiary of Elf) have merged their polypropylene production interests in France. But the most impressive aspect of ownership reorganization has occurred as firms have manoeuvred to specialize in their strengths and dispose of weak elements in their product ranges. In the UK, an outstanding example of this strategy was provided by a major exchange of assets between BP and ICI. The effect was that BP withdrew from the PVC market while ICI ceased production of low-density polyethylene (LDPE). Outside the UK, ICI has sold much of its LDPE business to Atochem but has bought Atochem's interest in ethylene oxide derivatives. In the Netherlands, meanwhile, Shell has purchased the Hoechst polystyrene plant; and in West Germany, BP has acquired marketing control of Bayer's polyethylene output. In this way BP has become the second-largest marketer of polyethylene in Western Europe. From these examples it is evident that the petrochemicals industry has been forced into a state of flux that would have been inconceivable before the oil price shocks.

As in the refining industry, restructuring was initially triggered by declining demand. But in the 1980s the petrochemicals industry has faced increasing global competition much more severe than that as yet experienced by oil refining. This challenge chiefly reflects the expansion of Middle Eastern petrochemical capacity and, above all, the completion of twelve substantial petrochemical plants in Saudi Arabia. Although this country aims at all world markets, sales in Europe have proved particularly attractive. Within a year of large-scale shipments starting in 1985, Saudi Arabia was the largest marketer of every chemical it sold in Western Europe. This dramatic rise was a consequence of low production costs and an absence in Europe of effective tariff barriers. Developing countries such as Saudi Arabia enjoyed modest duty-free quotas for sales in Europe and tariffs applying to sales above these quotas were low. In contrast, the US allowed no duty-free quotas and applied tariffs which controlled the import of many products, even from neighbouring Mexico and Canada. In 1986 the European Community countries reacted by imposing tariffs on many imported petrochemicals, effectively raising their cost by 13 per cent. Yet the signs are that this has not halted the influx.

While this is another indication of Saudi Arabia's low production costs, it is also a consequence of the reorganization of capital in the world petrochemical industry in the 1980s. Here the key point is that Saudi Arabian expansion has been partly achieved through joint ventures with existing major companies. For example, the Kemya plant is a partnership between the Saudi Sabic company and the Exxon Corporation. Similarly, Mobil and Yanpet have joined forces to operate a plant on the Red Sea coast. Joint ventures have facilitated penetration of the European market in two ways. One is that the major companies' marketing experience has been available for the recruitment of industrial consumers. Thus Mobil established a marketing company in Brussels and built a network of customers before its venture with Yanpet came on stream. The other is that companies have in some instances cut back European production in favour of imports from their overseas ventures. A case in point is that of Exxon's subsidiary Essochem Europe, which has shut down an ethylene cracker at Cologne and sold another in Sweden; as an alterative, ethylene-based products now come from the Sabic/Exxon Kemya plant. Integration with the world production system has therefore made a significant contribution to the pressures faced by the Western European branch of the industry.

The West European car industry in its global context

The development of the car industry has been interpreted by governments and economic planners in terms of growth-pole theory (Perroux 1955; Pinder 1983), and there is ample justification for this view. The end process, final assembly, is essentially a 'propulsive' activity which not only creates a large, well-paid labour force, but also animates a host of component firms and producers of basic inputs such as steels, alloys, rubber and machine tools. In some traditional foci of the industry (the West Midlands, the Paris region and industrial northern Italy are good examples), many of these linked activities have clustered in geographic space around the assembly firms. But from the macro-economic planner's point of view a more significant characteristic is that the propulsive assembly firms and their linked activities have formed powerful groupings in 'economic space' – in other words, they have become aspatial poles of development penetrating national economies and assisting their progress to higher development levels. In the EC, which has generated the overwhelming majority of Western Europe's car production, the consequences of penetration by this single growth pole were clear by the early 1980s. Car assembly employed almost 2 million workers; in linked activities the dependent labour force was almost twice as great; and the industry absorbed 20 per cent of the Community's steel and machine-tool production (Commission of the European Communities 1981b).

By the early 1980s, the industry had – at first sight at least – survived the onset of recession and rising competition reasonably well. Car exports still earned the Community as much as they did for Japan, while net export earnings on the car trade covered 20 per cent of the oil import bill. Even so, at the global scale, shifts in the balance of power between major sectors of the industry revealed all too clearly that the role of European car production as a propulsive force in the economic system was severely threatened (Table 6.11). Between 1970 and 1980 car usage in Western Europe rose at roughly the world average rate, yet output increased by only 1 per cent. During the same period the general trend was for the major production regions to achieve substantial gains in exports, the outstanding exception to the rule being the EC where they fell by 23 per cent. This represented an absolute decline of nearly 600 000 cars a year, caused mainly by the collapse of sales in North America and the Pacific region (Table 6.12). Meanwhile, imports to the Community rose eightfold in the 1970s, from 149 000 to 1 362 000. This accounted for 30 per cent of the rise in imports in the world as a whole.

One factor contributing to this reversal was the growth of Western European car production outside the Community, and especially in Spain. Here an

Table 6.11 Europe's declining role in the world car industry, 1970–80 (% change)

	EC	USA	Japan	Rest of world	Total
Passenger cars in use	+61	+36	+194	+127	+68
Production	+1	+7	+122	+102	+35
Exports	−23	+148	+426	+56	+77
Imports	+810	+41	+161	+85	+90

Source: Commission of the European Communities 1981 *Bulletin of the European Communities Supplement 2/81*

aggressive expansion policy, heavily reliant on foreign investment by EC and US companies, rapidly raised production to 900 000 cars a year by the early 1980s. This development was encouraged by a Spanish import tariff barrier of 37 per cent and by an import tariff of only 4 per cent to the European Community. The majority of Community import growth, however, was based on the competitiveness of the Japanese branch of the industry – 60 per cent of the growth was captured by Japanese producers. From a mere 45 000 cars in 1970, imports from Japan rose to 743 000 in 1980 (Fig. 6.6).

Comparative advantage – Europe versus Japan

By 1985 the European Community's trade deficit with Japan had reached 18 110 million ecu, 22 per cent of which was attributable to Japanese vehicle imports. By this time, almost 900 000 Japanese cars were entering the Community each year. This amounted to 45 per cent of all car imports to the Community of Ten. (If the figures are adjusted to reflect the Community's expansion from ten to twelve members, the Japanese share of imports to the EC rises to virtually three-quarters.) Moreover, this penetration was achieved despite two obstacles. The first was strong and effective protectionist measures taken by France and, above all, Italy to exclude Japanese imports. Without these measures, Japanese sales in Europe would by now be several hundred thousand higher each year. Secondly, large-scale imports were achieved despite a major deterioration of the exchange rates for European currencies against the yen. In 1986 the European Currency Unit (ecu) was valued at only 166 yen compared with 370 in 1975.

As is well known, much of Japan's success can be attributed to productivity advantages. Although the efficiency of European car plants varied enormously

Table 6.12 The European Community's car exports to major world markets

Destination	Export volume ('000)			
	1970	1980	1985	Adjusted 1985 data (see note)
Non-EC Europe	647.5	729.1	894.9	658.1
Africa (excluding Nigeria and South Africa)	104.3	82.3	123.1	175.5
Middle East	74.6	141.8	142.2	NC
Far East (excluding South Korea and Taiwan)	70.7	59.0	66.5	87.5
Oceania, Australia and New Zealand	119.9	25.6	42.2	NC
North America	993.9	501.0	591.0	NC
South America (excluding Brazil, Argentina, Mexico, Venezuela)	39.8	40.5	43.7	61.9

Note: Adjustments to 1985 data entail (1) recalculation of non-EC sales to allow for Community expansion to 12 members and (2) inclusion of countries previously excluded from African, Far Eastern and South American data.

Sources: Commission of the European Communities 1981 *Bulletin of the European Communities Supplement 2/81*; 1986 *External Trade – Analytical Tables*

in the 1980s, productivity in a Japanese assembly plant was typically three times better than the best European practice and up to six times better than in the UK (Commission of the European Communities 1981b). Above all, this reflected the ability of Japanese producers, developing in the recent past, to limit the size of their workforces by substituting automation technology for labour. But cost control has also been linked to the question of wage rates. Although these rose rapidly in 1976–78, they subsequently stabilized and are now less than half the prevailing West German rate, which is the highest in Europe.

Despite the Japanese industry's success in penetrating the European car market, however, it has had to contend with the effects of recession on sales and, increasingly, with more competitive European products. This has led to the adoption of two strategies to maintain growth in the European market. The first has been to exploit cost advantages by reducing profit margins (Jones 1981). The second, which has been particularly important in the 1980s, has been to concentrate on quality as an attraction to the customer. Many models eclipse their 1970s forerunners in terms of comfort and road-holding, and the challenge to European producers has been intensified by installing as standard equipment traditional 'extras' such as radios, electric windows and sun roofs.

Impressive though they are, Japan's advantages and strategies do not by themselves explain in full the contrasting fortunes experienced by these two major branches of the industry. They fail, in fact, to highlight the full framework of constraints within which Western Europe's industry must operate. To a degree these constraints arise from labour relations. The

impact on productivity of the UK's highly complex union system is legendary and, at least until recently, in Western Europe in general the unionization of labour has often acted as a brake on the reduction of manning levels. Similarly, employment protection legislation – highly desirable though it is for the individual – has raised the potential cost of rationalization programmes. These constraints are the offspring of societal attitudes, but other highly significant limitations can be traced back to the political geography of Western Europe. The most important effect of this factor has been to retard reorganization at the European scale. Trans boundary mergers of national car industries have been shunned and reorganization by US manufacturers has by no means eradicated their early preference for simultaneous operations in several European host economies. Political fragmentation has therefore perpetuated organizational fragmentation, with consequent losses in economies of scale. This does not imply that the industry has fossilized, yet mergers have chiefly taken place within rather than between countries, and individual firms still command relatively restricted market shares. Five leading firms account for three-quarters of Western Europe's output, whereas only two supply the same proportion in both the USA and Japan.

A second, associated, limitation caused by fragmentation is that research and development is relatively inefficient. This problem, it is true, is of limited significance for US firms in Europe since their operations are part of a world system within which innovations can be readily transmitted. Indeed, research and development experience in Europe has been central to US manufacturers' attempts to switch to

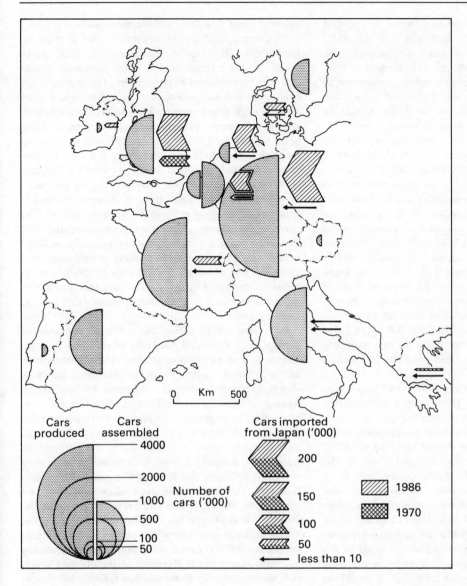

Cars
produced

Cars
assembled

Cars imported
from Japan ('000)

- 4000

- 2000

- 1000

Number of
cars ('000)

- 500

- 100
- 50

200

150

100

50

less than 10

1986

1970

0   Km   500

Fig. 6.6
The European car industry
and Japanese competition.

new, more fuel-efficient, product ranges at home. European manufacturers, however, inevitably tend to duplicate efforts in this field beyond the point at which the pursuit of alternative approaches to specific problems is desirable.

Thirdly – and this point is considered by the European Commission to be more important than the loss of economies of scale at the final assembly stage – fragmentation contributes to serious diseconomies and lack of standardization in the components industry. One indicator of this lies in the number of component manufacturers supported by the final assembly market. Comprehensive monitoring of the number of component firms is difficult to achieve because of the

industry's complexity, but in the early 1980s components manufacturers were five times more numerous in Western Europe than in Japan. European firms were also significantly smaller than their Japanese counterparts: the proportion employing less than 100 workers was approximately 40 per cent in West Germany and 60 per cent in France, compared with 15 per cent in Japan.

The evolving economic environment and European responses

The problem of competition would be serious enough, even if the environment in which the Western European car industry must operate were to remain constant. However, this environment is highly fluid and several factors may increase substantially the difficulties to be faced. Although at present they pose little threat in the European market, producers in Latin America, South Korea, India and Africa are providing stiffer competition around the world. In Eastern Europe the industry is reaching a new level of maturity and technological sophistication, with the result that exports to Western Europe (only 160 000 vehicles in 1979) reached 223 000 in 1985. In addition, the US branch of the industry, hit by severe crisis in the early 1980s, has implemented a series of projects intended to improve fundamentally production efficiency, as well as the mismatch between product ranges and market demand. In embarking on these projects, the primary aim of the US industry was to defend itself against Japanese rather than European producers. Yet the implications for Western Europe are nonetheless substantial: highly-efficient competition increases the difficulties of reviving exports to the USA, which fell by more than 400 000 in the 1970s (Table 6.12). Also, US manufacturers may compete more effectively with European products in markets around the world.

Against this background, the European Commission has urged the industry to pursue rapid restructuring within the overall context of free competition. It is impossible and, in the interests of productivity, undesirable to avoid the loss of several hundred thousand jobs, plus those lost during reorganization in the components industry. If the industry adopts a constructive, cooperative stance, employment decline may be achieved by orchestrated rationalization rather than uncoordinated *ad hoc* closures, but labour shedding must be associated with the aggressive use of technology. Technology is in fact at the heart of the Commission's view that the car industry is not only capable of survival, but can continue to fulfil its growth-pole function by propelling the West European industrial sector towards a new structure and level of development. The fundamental argument advanced by the Commission is that the need to optimize production costs to combat foreign competition, combined with the technological improvements called for by the deteriorating energy situation, have provided the car industry with the opportunity to become a basic driving force behind the growth of high-technology industries (Commission of the European Communities 1981b). Seizing this opportunity, it is maintained, will generate new forms of high-grade employment, encourage the spread of automation to other industries and protect Western Europe from external control in this vital technological field.

This scenario is highly ambitious, and it must be remembered that the Commission has little direct power. At the international level the principal weapon that can be deployed is persuasion. The industry has been exhorted to revolutionize its technological basis and intensify active cooperation in long-term research and development programmes. Governments have been encouraged to be more liberal in funding research. And there has also been pressure to harmonize national legislation relating to vehicles. Progress in this sphere, it is argued, will increase the prospects of establishing a more uniform European market which will encourage economies of scale. Beyond this, correctly-formulated legislation should ensure that European manufacturers are not automatically excluded from major global markets on safety or environmental grounds. But although legislation has the power to influence the product, how efficiently that product is produced remains the ultimate responsibility of the industry itself.

It is now evident that the pace of constructive change has accelerated markedly in response to these economic and political pressures. Various responses to the growing challenge can be identified, the most widely publicized being the decisions by two of the weaker companies – Rover and Alfa-Romeo – to attempt to strengthen their market foothold by joint ventures with Japanese producers. Less well known, but of considerable significance, is the attempt to transform essentially European firms into international corporations along the lines of the major US manufacturers. This strategy has been adopted primarily by firms in the West German and French branches of the industry. Volkswagen has taken over Chrysler's operations in Brazil and Argentina, and has two US plants producing 500 000 cars a year. Similarly, Renault has assembly plants in the Republic of Ireland and Spain, produces engines in Portugal, has taken a holding in Volvo and is using a stake in American Motors as a platform for manufacturing in the USA. In addition, within Western Europe a number of initiatives have been taken to increase scale economies in the production of engines and other components. There is, for example, a network of production agreements between Peugeot, Renault, Volvo, Fiat and Alfa-Romeo, while a Joint Research Committee has been established by Renault, PSA, Rover, Fiat, Volkswagen and Volvo. A major initiative taken by this Committee is collaborative work to define the required characteristics of electronic components, a step which should establish a truly European market in this field.

Despite the growth of collaboration, however, the greatest progress has been achieved by restructuring undertaken within firms. This has naturally entailed a swing to automated production, coupled with labour shedding in old plants and low manning levels on new production lines. Thus Renault's plant at Palencia, northern Spain, has an annual output of 100 000 vehicles but only 3 300 employees. The company's Seville plant has a workforce of 1 600 yet manufactures 500 000 gearboxes a year. But, in addition to embracing new production technologies, European producers have responded to the global challenge by emulating the Japanese strategy of quality improvement. In this context, one goal has been greater mechanical reliability – long since a strong point of Japanese products. The second goal has been the introduction of new models matching imports in terms of performance, equipment and comfort.

Evidence that European restructuring efforts are bearing fruit is now emerging. Three indicators are particularly important. Firstly, European production, after stagnating in the 1970s, grew by almost 10 per cent between 1980 and 1986. This was comparable to Japan's production increase in this period (11 per cent). Secondly, output expansion was achieved in almost all producer countries, the only major exception being France (Table 6.13). Thirdly, exports also revived after 1980 and by 1985 were worth 20.1 billion ecu. This was equivalent to almost a third of Western Europe's oil import bill. Three markets – non-Community Europe, North America and Africa – accounted for 92 per cent of this improvement (Table 6.12). What is also significant is that export performance has been partly attributable to a strategy of specialization in products that are not primarily targets of the Japanese. Outstanding in this respect are exports by Jaguar, BMW, Mercedes and Porsche to the US. More generally, cars of over 1 500 cc capacity accounted for 97 per cent of sales in North America, 83 per cent in the Far East and 62 per cent in non-Community Europe. In contrast, only 40 per cent of Japanese sales in the Community were in this size category. Market specialization has become increasingly important to Community producers in their attempts to combat competition.

Conclusion

An increasingly popular framework on which to set the remarkable dynamism of the Western European industrial system is provided by Nicolai Kondratieff's theory of long waves in economic life (Freeman 1984). This hypothesizes that innovations form the basis for

Table 6.13 West European car production, 1980–86

	1980 ('000)	1986 ('000)	% change
Austria	7	6	−14
Belgium	214	231	+8
France	3 488	3 010	−14
West Germany	3 521	4 313	+23
Italy	1 445	1 662	+15
Netherlands	81	119	+47
Spain	1 029	1 266	+23
Sweden	235	353	+50
UK	924	1 016	+10
Total	10 944	11 976	+9

Sources: Commission of the European Communities 1981 *Basic Statistics*; 1987 *Eurostatistics: data for short-term economic analysis*

extended phases of economic expansion which carry economies to new scales of development and levels of sophistication, but then lose impetus and give way to down-wave periods. In these, direction is lost and uncertainty prevails. Western Europe's impressive post-war industrial growth, the foundations of which lay in technological discoveries made in the pre-war and wartime periods, can clearly be related to this concept. Similarly, the economic deterioration since the late 1970s bears all the hallmarks of a down wave.

Yet this economic interpretation avoids substantial geographical issues that have emerged in this discussion. Although the expansionist era was in macro-economic terms an unprecedented success, it was associated with unbalanced growth at both the national and international scales. The rise of new forms of industrial organization – especially multinational firms – raised the questions of external dependence and control. Improved legislation by no means eradicated local or long-range industrial pollution. And, almost unanalysed until it had reached an advanced stage, the industrial sector was exposed to greatly intensified competition as the effects of the long wave spread from global core economies to the industrializing periphery.

All these problems have been carried forward into the down wave, a period in which resources to solve them are becoming increasingly scarce, partly because of the growing desire of governments to curb public expenditure. While resources are limited, however, new policy priorities aiming to initiate a new Kondratieff upswing can be identified. For example, strategies designed to encourage the foundation and expansion of small firms were originally formulated by the EC (Pinder 1986), but in the 1980s they have burgeoned at the national level (Haskins, Gibb and Hubert 1986). As computer technologies advance, the spotlight is focusing on the need to raise awareness in all industries of the potential benefits of computer-assisted manufacturing (Commission of the European Communities 1985; Woods 1987). Assessments of such initiatives will be priorities in the 1990s. In the meantime, evidence presented in this chapter indicates that the West European industrial scene is by no means all doom and gloom. Recessional pressures have been intense and global competition remains severe, yet – as the oil refining and car industries demonstrate – far-reaching company restructuring strategies can do much to restore some industries' competitive prospects. As the end of the century approaches, therefore, Western Europe's industrial economy appears far less at risk than in the early 1980s. There is, however, a danger of assuming that successful industrial restructuring will ensure that manufacturing once more becomes the major source of employment growth within the economy. A much more likely scenario is that, as automation proceeds, industrial survival will be achieved through the continued substitution of capital for labour. In much the same way that industry replaced agriculture as the dominant generator of employment, it is to the service sector that we should look for large-scale job creation in the coming decades.

Further reading

Aldcroft D H 1978 *The European Economy, 1914–70*. Croom Helm, London

Commission of the European Communities 1985 Advanced manufacturing equipment in the Community. *Bulletin of the European Communities, Supplement* **6/85**

Dicken P 1986 *Global Shift: industrial change in a turbulent world*. Harper and Row, London

Environmental Resources Ltd 1983 *Acid Rain: a review of the phenomenon in the EEC and Europe*. Graham and Trotman, London

Freeman C (ed) 1984 *Long Waves in the World Economy*. Frances Pinter, London

Fröbel F, Heinrichs J, Kreye O 1980 *The New International Division of Labour*. Cambridge University Press and Maison des Sciences de l'Homme, Paris

Haigh N 1986 *European Community Environmental Policy, Volume 1, Water and Waste in Four Countries*. Graham and Trotman, London

Pinder D A 1983 *Regional Economic Development and Policy: theory and practice in the European Community*. Allen and Unwin, London

Savery J 1984 *French Multinationals*. Frances Pinter, London

Taylor D, Diprose G, Duffy M 1986 EC environmental policy and the control of water pollution: the implementation of Directive 76/464 in perspective. *Journal of Common Market Studies* **24**: 225–46

Wabe J S 1986 The regional impact of deindustrialization in the European Community. *Regional Studies* **20**: 23–36

Woods S 1987 *Western Europe: technology and the future*. Croom Helm, London

7

The service sector

The tertiary transition

It is abundantly clear that each of the economies of Western Europe is now established in the post-industrial era, despite the enduring imprint of manufacturing activities old and new and the fact that the greater share of the land surface is still devoted to agriculture. Indeed, it is sometimes remarked that the so-called industrialized economies should be renamed service economies. Varying forms of service activity have always existed but their range and importance in Western Europe has increased markedly since mid-century as levels of development and personal well-being have been enhanced, even when economic crisis and rising unemployment since 1973 are taken into account. As central place theory informs us, low-order 'traditional' services, such as retailing, distribution, schooling, basic health care and local administration are spread widely through the settlement hierarchy, while top-level, specialized and innovative activities cluster in a small number of highly-developed, information-rich metropolitan centres, notably national capitals and 'world cities' (Hall 1984). It is at these focal points that international finance and banking, marketing, advertising and the media are particularly prominent. Departing from theory, the promotion of tourism in many coastal, mountainous and culturally-rich environments has greatly boosted the significance of service facilities for visitors in many Mediterranean and Alpine areas (see Ch. 10).

With respect to both employment and financial importance, the production of food and manufactured goods has been overtaken by the generation and delivery of services to support the production of goods and to enhance the quality of life. Three-fifths of the gross value added in the eighteen economies derives from services, which employ a comparable share of the total workforce. Over the last two decades, the absolute number of jobs in both the primary and secondary sectors has contracted sharply in Western Europe as a result of rationalization in farming, forestry, mining and traditional manufacturing and because of the challenging interaction of an array of social, political, financial and organizational processes that are summarized conventionally by the harsh term 'de-industrialization' (Goddard and Champion 1983). By contrast, the number of employees in service activities in the eighteen countries rose from 58 630 000 to 78 690 000 between 1971 and the start of 1986, by which time tertiary employment was substantially greater than the primary (11 506 000) and secondary (45 957 000) sectors combined. This transition from the production of goods to the delivery of services has implications for every man, woman and child in Western Europe. It permeates all aspects of human well-being, affecting economic dynamism, employment opportunities, educational requirements, class and gender relations, regional disparities and a host of other characteristics relating to the quality of life. Once-vibrant activities have become 'sunset industries' and service-related 'sunrise' employment has brought new opportunities to some localities but has denied them in others. The economic geography of Western Europe is being painfully refashioned and so too is its social geography, as old skills are no longer valued and new ones are required in an age of computing and information technology (Marstrand 1984). Indeed, the services revolution has infiltrated the total geography of our eighteen nations so thoroughly and forcefully that it is simply taken for granted.

'Service employment' and its synonym the 'tertiary sector' represent a poorly-defined, catch-all category which lumps together most activities that do not directly involve producing farm crops, extracting minerals or manufacturing commodities. Services therefore range from international banking to tourism, from government and administration to entertain-

Table 7.1 Origin of Gross Domestic Product, by sector, 1985 (%)

	Goods	Market services	Non-market services		Goods	Market services	Non-market services
Austria	44	41	15	Italy	46	40	14
Belgium	36	49	15	Netherlands	39	47	15
Denmark	34	43	24	Norway	46	40	14
Finland	46	37	17	Portugal	48	41	12
France	41	45	14	Spain	47	43	10
W. Germany	45	41	14	Sweden	39	36	26
Greece	48	42	10	UK	42	42	16

ment, and from health care and education to distribution and retailing. Some service jobs are emphatically in the private sector, others depend on the state; some are filled predominantly by men (e.g. transport), others involve mainly female staff (e.g. domestic and hotel services); some are immensely well-paid, others place their workers well below the poverty line (Seabrook 1985). City financiers, civil servants, opera singers, bus drivers, kitchen staff, hotel porters, dustmen and lavatory cleaners are all service employees! Thus the tertiary sector stretches from the most comfortable and well-rewarded members of society to the most exploited 'guestworkers' suffering the crudest discrimination.

Trying to classify this great variety of activities has become something of a craft industry among social scientists in recent years. A fundamental distinction between 'market' (or private) services and 'non-market' (state-organized) services is clear enough and effectively separates central and local government and state education and health services from the enormous array of privately-funded retailing, leisure and financial operations (Table 7.1). Likewise, another distinction between 'producer' (or intermediate) and 'consumer' (or final) services provides a helpful although complex classification. In the case of producer services (such as wholesaling, business or planning consultancy, public relations and market research), the output is used exclusively by other industries, whereas consumer services (including retailing, passenger transport, building societies and leisure functions) deal directly with the public (Daniels 1982, 1985). Some researchers have distinguished 'quaternary' activities which embrace a high-order component among the broad array of services. Typical quaternary activities would include the legal professions, accountancy, management consultancy, banking, insurance, central and local government, higher education and research (Goddard 1975).

The number of service workers throughout Western Europe rose by 344 per cent between 1971 and 1986, but markedly different rates of growth were in evidence between nations, regions and individual localities. For example, increases were below average in West Germany (+19 per cent), Belgium (+24 per cent) and the UK (+25 per cent), but were particularly dramatic in several Mediterranean countries (e.g. Portugal +81 per cent, Italy +66 per cent) and northern nations (e.g. Norway +79 per cent, Luxembourg +59 per cent). Variations in census definition between countries may account for a fraction of these differences but the real explanation lies, first, with the level of economic development in each country prior to the onset of the energy crisis and, second, with the national mix of service activities, each of which displayed its own distinct growth trend. For example, long-urbanized, services-rich economies, such as those of West Germany, the Benelux countries and the UK, displayed slower rates of growth than those of the services-poor developing economies of the Mediterranean where office employment and tourism-related jobs were increasing rapidly from a notably low base line.

According to United Nations' statistics, not far short of half (47 per cent) of all service jobs in Western Europe involve 'community, social, personal and other services' which are strongly represented in the Nordic welfare states of Denmark (55 per cent) and Sweden (57 per cent) (Fig. 7.1). Employment in 'trade, restaurants and hotels' covers almost one-third (31 per cent) of the total, being very significant in tiny Luxembourg and in popular tourist destinations (Spain, Switzerland, Italy). The remaining 22 per cent of service jobs are divided equally between 'transport, storage and communications' (well represented in Greece, Iceland, Norway, Finland and Austria) and 'finance, insurance, real estate and business services' (which are particularly significant in France, the Neth-

Norway
1·3

Finland
1·4

Sweden
2·8

Denmark
1·7

Ireland
0·6

Netherlands
3·4

U.K.
15·6

Belgium
2·4

W.Germany
13·4

Luxembourg
0·1

Switzerland
1·8

Austria
1·7

France
12·6

Portugal
1·7

Spain
5·3

Italy
11·3

Greece
1·6

■ Community, social and
personal services

▨ Finance, insurance,
real estate, business

▨ Transport, storage,
communications

□ Trade, restaurants,
hotels

1·7 Total millions

0 ————— 500 Km

Fig. 7.1
Tertiary employment by
category (%), c. 1984.

erlands, Denmark, the UK and in Switzerland, which has the rare distinction of having more bank branches than dentists).

These four groups of service have developed in very different ways since 1975. Taking Western Europe as a whole, the fastest rates of growth involved the financial and business sector which expanded substantially in almost every country. However, an important distinction must be drawn between the high-earning power employees in big business operating in national capitals and 'world cities' (notably London and Paris) and the more modest implications of additional main street banks and building societies in provincial towns (Daniels 1983; Green and Howells 1987). The financial group was followed quite closely by rapid job creation in community, social, personal and other services, especially in the Nordic states. On average, jobs in trade, restaurants and hotels increased only modestly across Western Europe, but stronger growth occurred in Mediterranean (Italy, Portugal, Spain) and Alpine (Austria) nations that were exploiting their

tourist facilities vigorously. Finally, total employment in transport, storage and communications has risen only slightly since 1975, with increases in some countries being offset by losses in others.

At a finer scale of analysis, a distinction must be drawn between countries that have traditionally concentrated high-order finances, services and administration in their capital cities only (e.g. France, Spain and the UK) and those that have supported them in a more deconcentrated fashion (Reitel 1976). The best example is undoubtedly the array of ministries and administrations in each state (*Land*) of the Federal Republic of West Germany. Recent measures to devolve some political responsibilities to the regions of France and especially to Spain may tone down the tertiary supremacy of their capital cities. With 70 per cent or more of their gross value added being derived from service activities, sixteen regions (Fig. 7.2) form the emphatically services-rich parts of the EC. Roughly half of these areas house major administrative and/or financial functions in the form of

Fig. 7.2
Proportion of gross value added derived from services (1983).

national capitals (e.g. Copenhagen, Madrid, Rome) or 'world cities' (e.g. London, Paris, Brussels, Rand-stad Holland) (Burtenshaw, Bateman and Ashworth 1981). In addition, the tiny city-state of Hamburg, with top-level commercial, shipping and publishing activities, also falls into this class. Such core areas are the leading nodes of West European capitalism and form the most affluent components of their national territories and – in some cases – of the whole of the EC. The remaining services-rich regions are strongly geared to tourism (including Provence, Corsica, the Canary Islands and the Balearic Islands). Unlike the first group of regions, these Mediterranean holiday playgrounds are particularly vulnerable to economic fluctuations elsewhere in Western Europe. Extra accommodation is constructed when demand is buoyant, but when bookings slump cut-throat 'bargains' have to be offered to avoid hotels standing empty or planes operating below capacity. Out-of-season unemployment is endemic, and domestic and catering staff are notoriously poorly paid, since the financial margin is drawn exceedingly tight. A job in the service sector is by no means always rewarded with a pot of gold, nor for many people is there even a glimpse of the rainbow.

Geographical expressions

The geography of Western Europe has been reshaped at both the regional and local level as a direct result of the services revolution. The economic potential of many core regions has been reinforced but, in addition, new opportunities have been realized in provincial areas, thanks to the development of tourism, the relocation of office work and the creation of completely new service functions. Detailed land-use plans have been transformed not only in long-established central business districts but also in greenfield sites whose accessibility and economic significance have been enhanced by the massive increase in private motoring that has affected sizeable sections of all West European societies over the past quarter century. These themes are interwoven in the discussion on many pages of this book (e.g. Ch. 8 on Urban Development and Ch. 10 on Recreation and Conservation); a small but significant sample has been selected for particular attention at this point.

Offices
The office is the vital ingredient and the most powerful

symbol of the services revolution, with additional office space being provided in a host of ways (Cowan 1969; Daniels 1975, 1979). Changing the function and internal arrangement of existing warehouses, factories, shops or residences forms the simplest solution which may, indeed, be the only one possible in an urban conservation area (Damesick 1979; De Smidt and Wever 1984). But in many business districts, not only individual buildings but whole blocks have been demolished and replaced with modern office premises. Complete redevelopment offers the chance of providing exactly the floorspace and facilities that a business client may require. It also offers the developer the opportunity of maximizing the financial return from his investment. In this way the detailed fabric of central districts of London, Brussels and almost every large city in Western Europe has been subject to piecemeal transformation and the installation of high-rise office blocks in place of low-rise buildings (Bateman 1981). (By virtue of a ban on construction of skyscrapers, the heart of Paris is an exception to this rule.) The risks involved in such operations are considerable, with the slump in demand for floorspace during the mid-1970s leaving extensive areas and even whole office buildings unoccupied for months and, in some notorious instances, for years on end.

A more radical response to the demand for modern office accommodation has been the construction of completely new business districts some distance from the traditional CBD. The Part-Dieu district in the eastern suburbs of Lyons and Hamburg's City-Nord are interesting provincial developments which were designed to provide good facilities for major firms. However, the most striking example in the whole of Western Europe is the creation of 1 550 000 m^2 of offices in a suite of controversial towers at La Défense in the suburbs of Paris, some 9 km north-west of Notre-Dame. Over the past thirty years, 70 000 jobs have been installed in the offices, shops and other service activities of La Défense. Its success has further distorted socio-economic imbalances in greater Paris, where the de-industrialization of eastern working-class districts contrasts with the growth of tertiary employment in more emphatically middle-class neighbourhoods on the west. A major challenge for Parisian planners and politicians is to stimulate new employment opportunities in offices, leisure activities, research institutes and high-tech industries on the eastern side of the city (Tuppen and Bateman 1987). The scheme for constructing a massive office complex at Canary Wharf in London's docklands has a similar strategic aim of installing jobs and new opportunities in an area of serious economic decline (Lenon 1987).

The utility of relocating offices away from congested and expensive national capitals in order to stimulate additional employment in the provinces has been appreciated by planners in several West European countries and special laws have been passed and agencies set up to this effect. The most comprehensive schemes involved the work of the Location of Offices Bureau between 1963 and 1978 which encouraged firms to decentralize their activities and their workforce to cheaper premises in provincial cities or in outer parts of south-east England (Marshall 1985). Routine, paper-shuffling operations in government, banking, insurance and many other activities were relocated in quantity, taking full advantage of postal, telephone and telecommunications services to maintain links with clients. Roughly comparable policies shifted a number of routine functions from Paris to the French provinces, but success was greater with government departments than with commercial firms. Likewise, some government agencies have been shifted from Stockholm and from Randstad Holland (Öberg and Oscarsson 1987; De Smidt 1985).

By contrast, top-level office functions (in both the public and private sectors) and many of a particularly innovative nature have remained firmly established in Western Europe's capitals. Conventional wisdom maintains that such cities provide the only environments where top-level managers and directors can have face-to-face contacts with their counterparts in finance houses, banking and government (Donnay 1985). A second strand of reasoning argues that the status of a 'world city' – and the nation it symbolizes – would be reduced if high-order functions moved away. The rather ambivalent attitude of the French government to decentralizing office activities may be explained in this way.

The introduction of new technology in the form of telephones and visual telecommunications has revolutionized practices on London's stock market and has done away with some time-hallowed face-to-face contacts, but the attractiveness of the City of London for financial dealing seems to remain as strong as ever. Deregulation of trading has accelerated demand for new, spacious offices that can house large computing facilities within the 'square mile' and its immediate environs and, perhaps, as far eastwards as London's docklands. Modern telephone systems have transformed many aspects of office activity and have certainly reduced some locational constraints; however, it is unlikely that advanced telecommunications will remove the friction of distance and provide complete spatial freedom, thereby producing a measure of economic convergence between metropolitan cores and provincial peripheries (Gillespie and Goddard 1986).

Fig. 7.3
Main science parks in Belgium, France, West Germany and the UK.

For unlike the ubiquitous telephone service, really advanced systems of electronic communication will be market-led and will probably serve only areas of established economic advantage and the routeways between them (Dupuy 1981). It is most unlikely that investment will be forthcoming to equip peripheral areas or 'sunset' industrial zones.

Innovative developments

During the past couple of decades, many important new trends have added to the complex impact of the services revolution on the geography of Western Europe. Three examples relating to research, leisure and retailing provide a view of these innovative developments.

The first involves the creation of science or technology 'parks' where research and development are undertaken, important services are generated and perhaps also a range of high-tech industries are to be found. Inspired by the success of Silicon Valley in California and Boston's Route 128 in New England, developments of this kind have been perceived as a panacea to many economic and social ills and have been attributed with remarkable powers of job creation and income generation (Hall and Markusen

1985). An information-rich environment, usually adjacent to a dynamic university or other establishment undertaking vibrant and useful research, is accepted as a prerequisite for a successful science park. An 'attractive environment', expressed in landscape, climate, mountains or cultural activities, forms a secondary but still important contributory factor. There is, in fact, considerable diversity of approach, with various initiatives emerging from universities, city councils and regional planning organizations. In the UK, the Cambridge science park opened in 1973 and now has over 1 300 employees (Fig. 7.3). It has been emulated by a dozen other universities or development agencies, but with relatively modest results. Although not a science park in the narrow sense of the term, the real British success story involves the M4 corridor to the west of London, with good access to government research institutions, universities, an international airport and the national motorway network.

The science park idea germinated early in Belgium, with four universities having created them by 1974; by contrast, developments have come much later in the Netherlands. The quality of research in universities and other institutions, coupled with the attractions of the Alpine environment, have given rise to a 'Silicon Bavaria' phenomenon, with 40 per cent of West Germany's computer software suppliers located around the city of Munich. West German technology centres have been established to stimulate the growth of 'future' activities in a wide range of locations including areas of industrial decline (e.g. the steel towns of Dortmund and Saarbrucken), already prosperous cities (e.g. Bonn, Heidelberg and Stuttgart), and West Berlin which receives substantial financial support from the federal authorities and where there are close links with the technical university. French science parks at Grenoble (3 600 jobs) and Nancy (800 jobs) and the constellation of high-tech activities in the Bièvre valley to the south-west of Paris, each benefit from established university expertise. However, the large development at Valbonne-Sophia Antipolis is an entirely new creation that originated in the early 1970s following government decisions to focus a range of 'future' activities on the Côte d'Azur. The state invested heavily to establish the infrastructure of Sophia Antipolis, where it relocated the prestigious Ecole des Mines, other research institutions and the Air France international reservations centre which required innovative telecommunications systems. Now 4 000 people are employed on the technology park and more than half are specialists who have moved from other regions to work in the attractive environment of the south of France. Local people work mainly in low-qualified positions and private investors have been somewhat reluctant to follow the example of the public sector. Innovation transfers mainly involve links with Paris and with international agencies; indeed, the impact of Sophia Antipolis on the regional economy has been rather small. The hard truth is that it takes much more than a university, some land and some sunshine to produce a Silicon Valley!

A second new development reflects the fact that the great majority of West Europeans have more free time and greater amounts of money to devote to non-essential items than ever before. Providing facilities for leisure-time use has indeed become a major 'industry' with important spin-offs for catering and the hotel trade and with very real appeal to visitors from overseas, many of whom are no longer satisfied with the round of castles, cathedrals and coasts but seek innovative attractions which entertain or educate and sometimes manage to do both. For example, the top ten sites frequented by visitors in the UK during 1986 included a number of modern attractions and theme parks as well as castles, zoos and gardens (Table 7.2). At present, De Efteling in the Netherlands is Western Europe's largest theme park which attracts about 2 300 000 visitors each year, but in March 1987 a contract was signed for Euro-Disneyland to be constructed on 1 785 ha of farmland within the perimeter of Marne-la-Vallée new town to the east of Paris. Access will be by *métro* and by motorway, with opening scheduled for 1992, when roughly 20 000 jobs will be created. If the promoters' estimates prove correct, the theme park will attract about 10 000 visitors each year, of whom half will come from beyond France. A second phase will involve the construction of hotels, shops and offices on the margins of Euro-Disneyland. Theme parks also provide an imaginative way of restoring derelict land with the 'World of the Smurfs' (northern Lorraine) and 'Wonder-World' (Corby, East Midlands) both being developed on the sites of former steelworks. Plans are under way for the vast shell that once housed London's Battersea power station to be occupied by a unique indoor theme park. In a rather different style, it is notable that the suite of *grands projets* currently being completed in Paris embraces an important array of cultural attractions (e.g. the controversial extension of the Grand Louvre museum, the creation of the museum of the nineteenth century in the Orsay station building, the museum of science and industry at La Villette, the institute of the Arab world, and the Bastille opera house). In addition, exhibition complexes and

Table 7.2 Top ten sites visited in the UK, 1986*

Madame Tussaud's	2 391 000
Alton Towers	2 250 000
Tower of London	2 020 000
Magnum Centre	1 326 000
London Zoo	1 190 000
Kew Gardens	1 147 000
Thorpe Park	1 060 000
Drayton Manor Park	962 000
Jorvik Viking Centre	868 000
Edinburgh Castle	832 000

* Number of visitors where there is an admission charge.

congress centres offer other promising mechanisms for creating service-sector employment and attracting income; indeed, it may well be that the congress hall is one of the most important tertiary facilities in the urban environment (Labasse 1984; Law 1986).

A third major development involves the retailing revolution which has favoured the construction of hypermarkets, superstores and commercial centres (often with a department store and a range of shops and banks) at sites that are well served by main roads or motorways and where there is abundant space for parking (Fig. 7.4) (Metton 1982). Each country in Western Europe has its own traditions regarding opening hours, retail chains and individual operators (Beaujeu-Garnier and Delobez 1979; Bird and With-

Fig. 7.4
Major shopping centres and hypermarkets in the Paris region, 1981 (after Metton 1982).

erick 1986). Likewise, planning regulations with respect to shopping outlets vary both locally and nationally. Therefore it is hardly surprising that the retailing revolution has operated with differing speed, intensity and form from country to country. Even now, the trend is less developed in the UK than in France and several other nations; however, the largest shopping complex in Western Europe has been constructed on what was formerly a power station's waterlogged ash dump alongside the River Tyne at Gateshead. The site forms part of the Tyne and Wear enterprise zone and has a potential clientele of 1 300 000 within 30 minutes drive. The completed MetroCentre boasts over 200 000 m^2 of floorspace which is occupied by shops, department stores,· restaurants and support facilities. Despite national variations, there is no doubt that with high rates of car ownership, more families having freezers, and increasing numbers of women in full- or part-time employment outside the home, shopping for many households has been transformed from a daily ritual to a weekly, fortnightly or monthly bonanza. The competition can be deadly for conventional main-street shopkeepers who see a sizeable proportion of their clientele being attracted to hypermarkets, retail warehouses and do-it-yourself superstores (Jones 1984). In France the situation became so controversial that city-centre traders engineered special legislation in 1973 to dampen down the proliferation of large peri-urban shopping facilities (Dawson 1979, 1980). However, the clock cannot be turned back and for very many car-owning West Europeans, convenience shopping means an occasional trip out of town. City centres can only hope to recapture trade by ensuring a range of attractive outlets (pedestrian streets or precincts, good department stores or indoor shopping complexes, and boutiques) and by providing adequate cheap parking space. But even a glittering, purpose-built shopping centre in the heart of a city is not without its problems. It can easily become a place where young unemployed people congregate and may acquire the reputation of being slightly dangerous. Its car parks can become places of petty theft and crime, so more security guards are needed. And, of course, its very existence 'steals' activity and trade from old-fashioned shopping streets which all too rapidly display boarded-up windows, charity shops and declining pubs and cafés. In the evening the outer doors of the new shopping complex are locked, since it is 'defensible' private property and not a public thoroughfare. Increasingly the life and death of city centres and shopping streets is being decided in the boardrooms of urban development corporations and major retailing companies.

Transport and trade

Road and rail

With 157 300 km of functioning railway line, 28 000 km of inland waterway, 32 500 km of motorway, 332 600 km of main road, a host of oil and gas pipelines, numerous air and ferry services, and a variety of major ports and airports, the densely-peopled nations of Western Europe display the most complex network of connectivity of any comparably-sized section of the Earth's surface (Table 7.3; Fig. 7.5a). Indeed, that distinction is far from new; it was valid in earlier centuries although the range of components was strikingly different. The pattern has evolved substantially since mid-century and important changes have occurred with respect to both volume and mode of transportation. Undoubtedly the most significant has been the growth of private motoring which has endowed individuals and families with completely new forms of spatial choice and travel convenience but has also generated serious problems for all kinds of public transport.

In 1985 there were 117 million private cars on the roads of Western Europe (more than three times the 1960 total) and over 14 million commercial vehicles. As well as the privilege of personal mobility, mass car ownership involves serious problems of congestion, pollution and consumption of land for new highways and parking facilities. No fewer than 51 600 people were killed and 1 630 000 injured on the roads of the Twelve in 1984, but mercifully these figures represent sizeable reductions since the mid-1970s. Construction of new motorways, highways and by-passes continues apace although with somewhat less vigour than before the energy crisis. Nonetheless, motorways are still rare in many regions although high densities serve West Germany, the Benelux countries and parts of northern Italy. But all motorways were planned by individual nations which placed the requirements of their core areas at the top of their agenda and paid less attention to the needs of peripheral areas adjacent to neighbouring countries. The EC has long argued the need to plug the gaps and has advanced loans through the EIB to assist construction of Alpine motorways (Brenner Pass and Val d'Aosta) and the links between Paris and Brussels, Lorraine and the Saar, and between France and Italy along the Mediterranean.

Over the past twenty years, Western Europe's railways have lost passengers to air services and to the use of private cars, and increasing volumes of freight have been transferred to movement by lorries. Railway authorities have reacted in differing ways to these critical changes. Most have successively rationalized

Table 7.3 Major ports and airports in Western Europe, 1984

Port	Cargo (million t)	Airport	Passengers (million)	Freight (thous. t)
Rotterdam	224.4	London*	43.1	684
Marseilles	86.6	Paris*	31.4	712
Antwerp	80.3	Frankfurt	19.0	732
Le Havre	53.5	Rome	13.5	177
Hamburg	50.6	Amsterdam	10.9	440
Genoa	42.2	Madrid	10.6	164
London	41.7	Copenhagen	9.7	177
Tees-Hartlepool	33.5	Palma	9.3	25
Milford Haven	30.6	Zurich	9.1	205
Dunkirk	30.2	Milan	7.8	102

* More than one airport.

their networks and the services operated on them, closing little-used stations and passenger services and retaining some lines simply for the movement of freight. Investment has been concentrated on improving track and rolling stock on a limited number of major axes. The Beeching Report (1963) on Britain's railways was a well-known analysis of this kind. The most recent (1987) example is a review of traffic flows and financial turnover on Swedish railways. This made grim reading, with market forces identifying the predictable logic of retaining only a few trunk lines and closing all passenger services in the northern two-thirds of the country. By contrast, other authorities – such as those in Italy – have accepted the necessity for heavy and sustained subsidy on the basis of the social role that the railway plays in local as well as inter-city travel. A third reaction has been for railway authorities to rise to the challenge posed by road and air transport by introducing innovative and greatly accelerated services along a small number of carefully selected routes. The rationale for this kind of policy has been boosted by growing concern over the amount of land being taken for motorways and airport extensions and by the telling fact that trains are far more efficient energy consumers than either cars or planes for inter-city journeys on the West European scale.

French and West German railway authorities have each introduced its own type of high-speed train using existing tracks. In addition, a couple of new sections of line have been built in West Germany in order to shorten the north/south route between Hamburg and Munich and to link Mannheim and Stuttgart. Their construction has been particularly desirable since West German railways simply inherited part of the much larger pre-war German network which focused

emphatically on Berlin and was not particularly well provided with north/south links. By far the most impressive progress has been achieved in France with the opening in 1981 of a TGV (*train à grande vitesse*) service on the heavily-used route between Paris and Lyons (Fig. 7.5b). The rail distance between the two cities was trimmed from 510 to 425 km by slicing a special track with neither tunnels nor level-crossings through the Paris Basin and the hills of western Burgundy, whose gradients can be negotiated successfully by the powerful TGV locomotives. Travelling time from city centre to city centre has been cut from 3 hr 50 min to 2 hr, which compares very favourably with total travel time by plane. Equally important are the improved services which fast TGV trains provide beyond Lyons with, for example, Geneva being only 3 hr 20 min and Marseilles 4 hr 20 min away from Paris. In planning their TGVs, the French deliberately democratized the service, allowing second-class passengers to travel on the fastest trains for the first time in a generation. Many passengers have been wooed back to using the train and some postal services between Paris and the south of France are now carried by TGV rather than by plane. The rule of thumb that says that air travel will attract a majority of travellers between two cities if the competing centre-to-centre rail journey takes 4 hours or more is having to be rethought.

TGV Sud-Est is a clear success story, but it is just the first part of a much larger plan. Some 285 km of new track are being built for the TGV Atlantique which, by 1989–90, will provide even faster services than those operating between Paris and Lyons, bringing Nantes and Rennes just 2 hr travelling time from the capital and Bordeaux only 3 hr away. Already the TGV has adopted an emphatically inter-

(a)

navigable waterways
(<1500t)
deep waterways (>1500t)

30 million tons
10 million tons
5 million tons
1 million tons

London
Rotterdam
Bremen   Hamburg
Le Havre
Antwerp
Genoa
Marseilles
Alicante

0   500 Km

Fig. 7.5
Transport systems: (a) ports
and navigable waterways;
(b) railways (after DATAR,
Paris).

national dimension with the Paris–Berne service being
inaugurated in spring 1987. Just a few months earlier,
the transport ministries of France, Belgium, West
Germany, the Netherlands and the UK had accepted
a Franco-German draft report on the desirability of
a high-speed inter-city network. Some observers interpreted the Paris–Berne service as a vital breakthrough
in a French plan to ensure that the TGV becomes the
standard for high-speed train travel throughout
Western Europe. Additional TGV services for
northern and eastern France have been proposed but
not yet agreed since the logic of making extensions
into neighbouring countries stirs up a complex set of
problems. By virtue of political and cultural divisions
within Belgium, it would be desirable for future high-
speed links to serve major cities in both Flanders and
Wallonia. It would also be expedient to serve
Amsterdam, but this northern extension might not
prove viable if West German passengers could use an
improved service through Belgium. Transport minis-

ters in five West European nations continue to debate
this vital but controversial issue; and, of course, the
idea of a TGV service reaching the Channel ports
would only make sense with the completion of a
Channel tunnel.

The Channel tunnel

A number of major improvements to Western
Europe's motorways and rail services have been
achieved in recent years but a few significant links are
still missing. Bridges have been proposed to span the
Straits of Messina (between the Italian mainland and
Sicily) and the Great Belt and the Sound (between the
Danish islands and southern Sweden), but by far the
most notable omission is some form of fixed link
between northern France and south-eastern England.
A Channel tunnel was first proposed in 1751 and the
twenty-sixth scheme (this time for a publicly-financed
tunnel) was abandoned by an incoming British Labour

(b)

main railway lines
TGV
projected TGV

0   500 Km

government for reasons of cost. But since that time the volume of cross-Channel traffic has increased substantially, with many more cars and coaches using ferries and hovercraft for holiday travel and for freight movements which have been facilitated by container-ization and technical improvements (but also risks!) in roll-on roll-off ferries (Vickerman 1986, 1987). In January 1986, a Socialist president and a Conservative prime minister announced the agreement of their governments to a proposal from a Franco-British consortium for a privately-financed 37 km long rail tunnel to run between Calais and Dover and to be completed by 1993. Cars and lorries are to be loaded on to special trains that will shuttle through the tunnel. Long-distance passenger trains will operate directly between the two capital cities.

The principal benefits of the fixed link will be a reduction in the time – if not the money – costs of travel and the encouragement for more journeys for passengers and freight. The main financial costs are

to do with construction and operation, but there are profound social and environmental implications as well. After so many dashed hopes in past decades, the present scheme is not attracting investment as readily as had been hoped and has given rise to profound opposition in some quarters in Britain. Environmental groups in Kent oppose the further desecration of 'the garden of England' by terminals, marshalling yards, new roads and predictably overcrowded motorways. Motorists do not see much point in a project that simply gives them the choice of loading on to a ferry or a train. Local politicians fear that construction workers may not be recruited locally and that after 1993 many ferry services will be forced to close, with consequent loss of jobs, especially in Folkestone and Ramsgate. MPs from northern England fear that the tunnel will simply increase the nation's north/south divide. Academic analyses suggest that eastern Kent may benefit during the construction phase from an accumulation of goods, capital, people and services, but that the long-term local effect may involve large job losses and poor prospects for further industrial or commercial development (Gibb 1986). By contrast, and as northern MPs fear, the economy of inner Kent and south-eastern England as a whole may benefit from its enhanced accessibility. French attitudes to the tunnel project are far more optimistic, since northern France is not part of 'the home counties' but is an industrial and former mining region with a disturbing history of employment decline. It is, by definition, closer than south-east England to major continental markets and is in receipt of substantial regional development aid from Paris and from the EC. There is abundant land for terminals, improved rail and motorway links, and the local population has made important strides in enhancing the skills of its labour force for employment in high-tech and other new economic activities. It would seem, in fact, that northern France has everything to gain (Chisholm 1986; Bruyelle 1987). Just as the Channel tunnel proposal has proved highly controversial, so the idea of establishing a fixed link between Denmark and Sweden has given rise to great differences of opinion. Would a road and rail bridge across the Sound from Copenhagen to Malmö be appropriate, or would that seriously damage the environment and hence a rail tunnel between Helsingor (Denmark) and Helsingborg (Sweden) be preferable? The debate continues.

A common transport policy?

Western Europe's transport network has experienced numerous technical improvements in recent years but it still comprises a set of quite distinctive national systems. Transport policy was given a chapter of its own in the Rome Treaties and the EC has been trying to organize a common market for land transport ever since 1957 and for air and sea transport since 1973. Many agreements have been reached on individual items but the overall result has been modest. This state of affairs has been condemned by the European Parliament, and in 1983 the European Commission identified the following policy targets: to improve integration of national transport policies; to create a better climate of competition between and within different forms of transport; to enhance efficiency and productivity by eliminating bottlenecks and bureaucratic constraints; and to support major infrastructure projects of Community-wide importance. In an attempt to avoid marine accidents, safety standards have been laid down for vessels at sea and entering port. In addition, numerous schemes to promote road safety have been implemented and finances allocated to many parts of the Community to improve many kinds of transport infrastructure, including roads and railways in Greece, the Tyne–Wear metro railway in the UK, and ferries operating in the Irish Sea. The need to integrate the Spanish economy more closely with those of her neighbours in the EC has emphasized the need to improve trans-Pyrenean rail links (including a fast service between Barcelona and Perpignan) and to accelerate the expansion of the Spanish motorway system.

Only in the last ten years has the EC become active in the realm of air transport, which directly employs 300 000 in the Twelve and a further 200 000 ancillary staff. The EC is playing an important role to encourage the liberalization of routes and the cutting of passenger fares by involving a range of competing companies rather than the traditional 'duopoly' arrangement whereby two national airlines each command roughly half of the traffic between any two countries. Full 'deregulation' on the American pattern is not possible since the twelve nations regard their national airlines as status symbols of their respective governments rather than simply as commercial carriers of passengers and freight. For this reason, the transport ministers have been remarkably reluctant to facilitate competition and price cutting on a wide scale; however, they have set 1992 as the deadline for action. Bilateral 'open skies' agreements between the UK and the Netherlands and a relaxation of pricing rules for flying between the UK and the Republic of Ireland have already given rise to some remarkably cheap flights. Special deals have also been arranged for a range of services between the UK and six other West European countries but, after having led the fight for greater competition, Britain back-tracked prior to the privatization of British Airways. Such loss of enthusiasm was to the dismay of liberalizing neighbours, most notably the Dutch. Unfortunately, the chance of permitting wider price reduction in the Community was blocked in July 1987 on the eve of the institutional reforms associated with the Single European Act by a Spanish veto that was triggered by the sensitive status of Gibraltar airport, which is regarded under EC law as a British regional facility. Eight years of hard negotiation were wrecked temporarily and the question of cheaper flights had to return to the drawing board and to the European Parliament.

Trade

From the world perspective, the eighteen small countries of Western Europe are rich, markedly industrial and emphatically urban. These characteristics derive in part from domestic resource endowment but have also been shaped and intensified across the centuries

Table 7.4 Imports and exports for the EC, EFTA and Western Europe, by commodity class, 1985 (%)*

	Foodstuffs	Mineral fuels	Raw materials	Machinery	Others
Imports					
EC 12	10.9	20.6	7.4	24.4	36.7
EFTA	6.1	14.7	5.3	30.1	43.8
W. Europe	10.2	19.8	7.1	25.2	37.7
Exports					
EC 12	10.1	9.1	3.6	32.7	44.6
EFTA	3.4	11.5	6.3	27.2	51.6
W. Europe	9.1	9.4	4.0	31.9	45.6

* Commodities according to the Standard International Trade Classification: food, beverages and tobacco; mineral fuels, lubricants and related materials; crude materials, oils and fats; machinery and equipment; others.

on the basis of trade. Some nations established vast colonial empires to supply raw materials and absorb manufactured products; others involved themselves in transporting other nations' commodities; few were content with being engaged in purely local transactions. Since mid-century the balance of world commercial power has shifted, with decolonization and industrial development modifying the nature of the relationship between Western Europe and the states of the developing world, and new industrial and commercial superpowers emerging in eastern Asia to challenge the role of the West.

The eighteen nations of Western Europe still live by trade and together account for almost two-fifths of the total value of the world's commercial transactions, commanding a notably greater share than either the USA (14 per cent) or Japan (8 per cent). As Chapter 2 discussed, the EEC (33.2 per cent of world trade) and EFTA (5.2 per cent) evolved in quite distinct ways and are very different institutionally, although both have the central objective of stimulating and facilitating trade between their respective members. The idea of establishing a 'common market' or customs union was of course at the heart of the Treaty of Rome (1957). Three years later the Stockholm Convention gave rise to EFTA, which aimed to create free trade in industrial goods for all members (with special arrangements for farm products and fish); to assist in forming a single trade market throughout Western Europe; to promote the growth of world trade; and to encourage economic expansion and better living standards. Austria, Denmark, Norway, Portugal, Sweden, Switzerland and the UK were its founding members, with Finland becoming an associate member in 1961 and Iceland joining in 1968. Successive enlargements of the EC trimmed back the dimensions of EFTA, whose six current members have

no common policy on anything except trade, unlike the complex links that bind members of the EC one to another. Nonetheless, the EFTA nations are also associate members of the EC and free trade in industrial goods between seventeen countries became possible in 1977 and extended to the eighteenth nation when Spain entered the EC at the start of 1986. Tariff walls have been removed within the Community but a host of non-tariff complications remain, such as differing technical and other standards between member states and the existence of complicated frontier controls which can involve haulage firms in great financial loss and time-wasting as their lorries are subjected to lengthy formalities. Compared with the USA, the Community still has a long way to go before it becomes a real common market.

The structure of imports and exports by commodity classes shown in Table 7.4 summarizes the main features of commercial activity in the EC, in EFTA and across the full range of West European nations. Foodstuffs and raw materials together make up one-sixth of the total value of trade (imports plus exports) for the eighteen countries, with a roughly equal proportion being accounted for by mineral fuels (basically oil) and related materials. Machinery, equipment and an enormous range of manufactured products (listed as 'other' commodities) make up no less than 70 per cent, being relatively more significant in the total trade of EFTA than in that of the EC.

The commercial profile of each country is unique, being conditioned by the relationship between its specific resource endowment, its level of economic development and the resultant mix of activities, but several key points emerge from the complex information shown in Fig. 7.6. Food imports are less significant in the trading profile of each of the EFTA members, whereas foodstuffs account for a quarter of

Table 7.5 Imports and exports for the EC and EFTA, by value, 1985 (%)

	EC 12	USA	Japan	Rest of world
Imports to EC 12 from	53.4	7.9	3.3	35.5
Imports to EFTA from	58.2	6.3	4.5	31.0
Exports from EC 12 to	54.9	10.1	1.2	33.8
Exports from EFTA to	53.2	8.4	1.7	36.7

the value of exports from Denmark, Greece and the Republic of Ireland. Mineral fuels (especially oil) represent a particularly large component in the import bill for Finland and the Mediterranean countries (with between a quarter and a third of the cost of all imports to Greece, Italy, Portugal and Spain deriving from these commodities); by contrast, the export of mineral fuels is an impressive – if temporary – feature in the trade of three nations surrounding the North Sea oil province (amounting to 22 per cent of the value of all

exports from the UK, 24 per cent from the Netherlands and 50 per cent from Norway). The importance of timber products emphasizes the role of raw materials in Finland's trade profile, while machinery and related equipment figure very prominently in the range of exports from West Germany and Sweden.

During the past quarter century the volume and value of commercial transactions by and between West European nations have risen substantially. Thus the share of EC imports from member states increased

Fig. 7.6
Exports and imports by commodity classes, 1985 (hundred million ecu).

Table 7.6 Percentage of intra-community trade, by value, 1985 (%)*

	Belg	Denm'k	W. Ger	Greece	Spain	France	Irel'd	Italy	Neths	Port	UK
Bel/Lux.	x	1.5	26.8	0.7	1.2	27.7	0.6	8.5	20.4	0.4	12.2
Denmark	0.4	x	36.0	0.1	0.2	9.7	0.1	9.9	7.7	0.1	28.1
W. Ger.	13.5	4.7	x	2.0	3.5	21.6	0.9	17.4	17.0	1.0	18.4
Greece	0.3	0.1	35.6	x	0.2	14.8	0.1	23.8	5.6	0.1	13.3
Spain	4.9	1.3	19.2	1.0	x	30.8	0.7	13.3	6.8	4.2	18.0
France	15.4	1.4	31.0	1.2	4.9	x	0.9	20.7	8.0	1.1	15.3
Ireland	4.3	1.2	15.7	0.6	1.9	12.4	x	5.3	7.6	0.3	50.6
Italy	5.5	1.7	34.9	2.6	3.6	29.5	0.5	x	5.5	0.1	15.2
Neths	19.8	1.9	40.4	0.1	0.1	13.4	0.8	8.1	x	0.4	13.0
Portugal	6.1	3.2	23.0	0.3	5.8	20.1	0.9	7.2	9.2	x	24.0
UK	8.3	3.9	27.0	0.8	4.1	19.9	10.4	9.8	14.5	1.3	x

* Calculated on basis of import statistics.

from 40 per cent in 1962 to 53 per cent in 1985, and the proportion of exports rose from 43 per cent to 55 per cent over the same period (Table 7.5). As Tugendhat (1987) has stressed, for each of the older member states the rest of the Community is not just its principal export market and source of imports, but is overwhelmingly so. Thus the Benelux nations (and also the Republic of Ireland) are particularly strongly committed to intra-EC trade with over two-thirds of both imports and exports (measured by value) involving other EC countries. By contrast, at least four-fifths of the commercial contacts of the four southern member states involve 'the rest of the world' (particularly Mediterranean countries) and Denmark retains substantial links with its Scandinavian neighbours immediately to the north.

Not surprisingly, the six EFTA nations collectively derive the greatest share of their imports (58 per cent of value) from the EC, to which they send 53 per cent of their exports. Given their location in the heart of central Europe, it is not surprising that particularly high proportions of the trade of Austria and Switzerland involve the EC states that are their nearest neighbours. Likewise, facts of geography and history combine to maintain significant exchanges among the Nordic members of EFTA and also the distinctive commercial relationship between Finland and its vast eastern neighbour – the USSR. Focusing exclusively on the Twelve, the matrix of intra-Community trade (Table 7.6) identifies the enormous commercial weight of West Germany which commands 24 per cent of the value of all imports in the EC and 28 per cent of all exports and is the leading trading partner with no fewer than six member nations (Denmark, France, Greece, Italy, Netherlands, UK). Tradition and sheer proximity explain why 51 per cent of Irish trade within

the EC is with the UK and why 40 per cent of Dutch trade within the Community is with West Germany and a further 20 per cent with Belgium. Further south, a centuries-old commercial alliance helps account for a quarter of Portuguese commercial activity within the Community being with the UK. As with most elements of the contemporary human geography of Western Europe, one finds that complex aspects of continuity with the past underlie the drama of recent change.

Uncertainties

In some respects the distinction between the service sector and modern high-tech manufacturing has become blurred; however, as this chapter has shown, the broad shift from manufacturing to service-based employment has had profound consequences throughout Western Europe (Marquand 1980). Serious social and geographical polarization has resulted, with members of the 'services elite', such as 'yuppies' working in the City of London, enjoying remarkable financial rewards; the same cannot be said for the underclass of lowly service workers on whose labour the comfort and well-being of the high-fliers depends (Townsend 1987). Likewise, some regions have enjoyed far greater propensity than others to flourish as a result of the services revolution. By its very dynamism, diversity and seemingly inexhaustible capacity to accommodate, the tertiary sector may appear to have provided an escape route in many localities, although it must be noted that many service activities are staffed by women and young people and may comprise part-time rather than full-time jobs. The mismatch between the 'old' work lost by men in their prime and the 'new' work of the tertiary sector can be both considerable and traumatic. Day-to-day relationships in very many families are having to be rethought.

There is no doubt that plenty of potential remains for applying human ingenuity to the creation of new brands of service employment in the future, but one is forced to question whether the 'tertiary bubble' really has an infinite capacity for growth. In recent years we have become accustomed to talk of sunset industries, but already there are sunset services! As many West Europeans have been required to understand, jobs in public services (e.g. education, health care and local and national administration) are very vulnerable to changes in government financial policy. Even more worrying is the harsh truth that any future decline in international financial dealings and in West European economic vitality in general would produce a widespread reduction in spending power that would send massive shock waves throughout the full array of market services. The ultimate uncertainty remains the ever-fluctuating relationship between the number of new jobs created by modern technology and the volume of old ones destroyed as a result of it.

Further reading

Bateman M 1985 *Office Development: a geographical analysis*. Croom Helm, London

Beaujeu-Garnier J, Delobez A 1979 *Geography of Marketing*. Longman, London

Daniels P W 1985 *Service Industries: a geographical appraisal*. Methuen, London

Dawson J A (ed.) 1980 *Retail Geography*. Croom Helm, London

Hall P G, Markusen A 1985 *Silicon Landscapes*, Allen and Unwin, London

8

Urban development

Old cities: new problems

Past and present

The countries of Western Europe are richly endowed with urban settlements whose diversity derives from important differences in planning practice as well as variations in culture and provides a powerful source of fascination for residents and visitors alike (Lichtenberger 1970; Burtenshaw, Bateman and Ashworth 1981). Most towns and cities originated as classical or medieval foundations which were enlarged subsequently for a complicated set of political and economic reasons, most notably during successive waves of industrialization that transformed parts of north-west Europe during the nineteenth and early twentieth centuries but had little impact in southern Europe until after 1950. The physical expansion of towns and cities has formed the main manifestation of urbanization in recent decades, although an important array of completely new towns has also been built in the UK and more recently in France (Merlin 1971b; Goursolas 1980). Ravages of war and the implementation of slum clearance and modernization schemes in inner-city areas have erased many historic townscapes; however, most cities still contain important collections of old buildings. Now the dual task of conserving and rehabilitating them is receiving sympathetic attention in many countries, for a combination of aesthetic, social and political reasons. As Paul White (1984) insists, 'diversity' is the best word to characterize the housing situation of Western Europe, which ranges from the shanties of Lisbon to the neat middle-class suburbs of Zurich, and from the massive post-war housing estates (*grands ensembles*) around Paris to the tall, carefully conserved seventeenth-century houses of old Amsterdam.

National definitions of 'urban' settlements are remarkably idiosyncratic but it is clear that most residents in the eighteen countries of Western Europe live in towns and cities, with the latest international collation of statistics (*c.* 1980) identifying no fewer than 131 cities of more than 250 000 inhabitants apiece (Fig. 8.1). Two world cities in highly-centralized countries dominate the list (Paris, 8 707 000; London, 6 696 000) and are followed by three rapidly-growing capitals in southern Europe (Athens, 3 300 000; Madrid, 3 200 000; Rome, 2 914 000) and there is a further score of cities with between 1 and 2 million residents apiece (Table 8.1) (Wagstaff 1968).

Myths and realities

Historically, major towns and especially capital cities have tended to display a remarkable propensity to flourish as centres of innovation and generators of employment and wealth, so much so that self-sustaining growth appeared to be almost one of their intrinsic characteristics. There were, of course, exceptions to the rule, such as the city of Vienna which stagnated following the dismemberment of the Austro-Hungarian empire after the First World War. Nonetheless, the majority of regional development programmes in recent decades have accepted unquestioningly the assumption that official policies could be devised and implemented to steer new employment and housing to ailing provinces or to greenfield sites without causing irreparable damage to the total habitat, economy or society of metropolitan areas.

Unfortunately, such confidence has proved to be increasingly misplaced since the optimistic days of the 1960s. Large cities throughout Western Europe have tended to lose at least some of their traditional strengths, and new human problems have arisen which undermine much of the buoyancy that such places habitually displayed. The root causes of these difficulties are complex in the extreme, reflecting the declining health of national and regional economies since the early 1970s, the changing social structure and human aspirations of city dwellers, and the growing

1,000 000
500 000
200 000

Fig. 8.1
Major urban settlements in
Western Europe, *c.* 1984.

realization that the built environment of the city is the product of political decisions which may be challenged and even overturned. Strikes and riots have, of course, occurred in urban areas in the past but their proliferation in recent years points in a particularly clear way to the problems of urban life and helps paint a scenario for the final years of the present century that is very different from that conceived by past generations of city administrators and regional planners. In short, the urban geography of Western Europe in the late 1980s is more problematical and emphatically more controversial than that of the 1960s (Burtenshaw 1985; Klaasen 1987).

Deconcentration

The wide view

In recent years, the continuing 'growth' of cities has tended to take on more dispersed forms, with new

housing being installed in peripheral estates (sometimes beyond the city's administrative limits) and in more distant 'rururban' localities which offer pleasant residential environments and from which daily commuting is possible by private or public transport (Lichtenberger 1976). In the heart of the city, slum-clearance schemes and urban-renewal programmes have swept away old housing areas and have contributed to a decline of the local residential population. Such deconcentration or 'counter-urbanization' has been in evidence in the USA for at least a couple of decades and it is arguable that it simply represents another phase in the complex set of processes labelled as 'urbanization' (Berry 1976, 1978; Fielding 1982).

In any case, deconcentration is by no means a new phenomenon in Western Europe, with the 'City' of London having recorded its peak residential population as early as the mid-nineteenth century and the introduction of cheap season tickets on Belgium's railways in 1869 allowing workers to commute to major

Table 8.1 Top twenty cities in Western Europe, *c.* 1984 (millions)

Paris	8.707	Stockholm	1.387
London	6.696	Copenhagen	1.379
Athens	3.300	Oporto	1.360
Madrid	3.188	Munich	1.292
Rome	2.914	Naples	1.221
West Berlin	1.889	Lyons	1.221
Lisbon	1.812	Turin	1.152
Barcelona	1.755	Marseilles	1.111
Milan	1.666	Rotterdam	1.025
Hamburg	1.637	Brussels	1.020

Note: The figures derive from various United Nations publications and are the closest available to 1984. They may well underestimate conditions in rapidly-growing cities in Mediterranean Europe.

cities from 'suburban' towns and villages dispersed in many parts of that country (Clout 1978; Kormoss 1976). Comprehensive research in Sweden has shown that population growth during the 1960s was dispersing away from major cities in favour of medium-sized towns, lower down the urban hierarchy, and there were plenty of additional examples of individual cities elsewhere in Western Europe 'turning themselves inside out' during that decade (Falk 1978a, b; Matthiessen 1980). Such evidence raised very real fears that what had been assumed to be North American problems of downtown decay and exurban sprawl were destined to occur on this side of the Atlantic as well.

In a major piece of comparative research, Hall and Hay (1980) showed that as early as 1950 some 86 per cent of Western Europe's 270.5 million inhabitants were living in metropolitan areas, while twenty years later the proportion of a substantially greater total (316.2 million) had risen to 88 per cent. Seventeen 'megapolitan' growth zones emerged clearly from the statistics for the 1950s and 1960s, including important axial urbanization along the Rhine, in the Rhône–Saône valleys, and in Provence. However, none of these zones was located in the outer peripheral regions of Western Europe; only one was focused on a giant city (namely Paris); and the early impact of deconcentration meant that the urban cores of London and the Randstad cities did not form part of the megapolitan zones adjacent to them. Likewise, the fastest rates of population growth in the countries of north-west Europe were being recorded in medium-sized cities, rather than in very large cities or in the 'old' industrial conurbations (Cheshire, Carbonaro and Hay 1986).

By contrast, the most dramatic rates of population growth in southern Europe did involve major cities (e.g. Barcelona, Bilbao, Madrid, Valencia, Milan, Rome and Turin) which expanded in response to powerful rural–urban migration that produced enormous losses in the countrysides of the Meseta and the Mezzogiorno (Wynn and Smith 1978). By the mid-1970s it was becoming evident that urbanization was operating in different ways in various parts of Western Europe, with a number of city regions in the UK and north-western parts of the European mainland undergoing absolute or relative decline in their cores, while growth continued in their hinterlands; conversely, in southern Europe people and jobs were still becoming more concentrated in urban core areas. Since the mid-1970s the trend towards inner-city decline has become even more pronounced and has recently started to have an impact in Mediterranean cities, notably in Italy (Dematteis 1982; Pacione 1987).

In tighter focus

A complementary analysis of population trends in over 150 functional urban regions in Western Europe confirmed the North American experience that centralization, and subsequent decentralization of both population and employment, is the process which characterizes the evolution of urban systems through time (Drewett 1979). Rates of population growth in European urban cores declined progressively between 1950 and 1975, although the precise process of change varied from country to country and from city to city. At a national scale, the major cities of Denmark, France, Netherlands, Sweden and Switzerland switched from initial modest growth to decline by the latter years (Wilkes 1983). In Belgium and the UK the trend was negative through the whole quarter century, with the rate of decline accelerating with the passage of time; by contrast, city populations continued to grow in Austria and Italy but rates of increase decelerated over the years.

Of course, national trends such as these convey only part of the story, since each functional urban region evolved in its own particular way, but it is possible to state first, that by the 1970s, relative centralization of population was occurring around only a score of major cities in Italy, southern France and other parts of southern Europe; and secondly, each major urban core in the UK and virtually every one in Benelux, West Germany, the Alpine states and northern France was displaying population decline. The traditional, taken-for-granted scenario of growth in the inner city had become sharply at odds with the facts of life across much of Western Europe (Uhrich 1987).

Publication of results of the 1981 British census

provided clear confirmation of that statement (Robert and Randolph 1983). Between 1971 and 1981 the population of England rose by a mere 0.4 per cent; Scotland had a loss of 2.1 per cent, while Wales increased its total by 2.2 per cent. Every large city in the land lost population, with the largest absolute losses being from inner London (a decline of 535 150 people, −17.7 per cent), outer London (−221 150, −5.0 per cent) and Glasgow (−219 150, −22.3 per cent). Losses of between 90 000 and 100 000 were experienced in Liverpool (−16.4 per cent), Manchester (−17.4 per cent) and Birmingham (−8.3 per cent) (Fig. 8.2). The greatest proportional loss for any local authority was 26 per cent from the London Borough of Kensington and Chelsea, the most densely-populated borough in England. In fact, each inner London borough lost over 10 per cent of its residents, with Lambeth containing 62 000 fewer residents in 1981 than a decade earlier (Ingram 1983). Relative growth occurred in the outer fringes of all metropolitan areas and especially in the less urbanized counties of eastern England, the south-west and the Anglo-Welsh borderland.

Expansion and renewal

Making good

Just as the distribution of Western Europe's urban population has been transformed over the past three or four decades, so the spatial structure and physical appearance of her major city regions has undergone profound change (Hajdu 1979). In the second half of the 1940s and throughout the 1950s, great efforts were made to reconstruct the war-torn centres of Antwerp, Hamburg, London, Rotterdam and literally hundreds of other towns and cities. Mass housing was constructed for the homeless according to the guidelines of hastily prepared plans. Money and materials were in short supply and the greater share of these building programmes remained firmly in the hands of public authorities. In some cities, such as Caen and Le Havre, the urban patterns were changed fundamentally as ownership plots were consolidated and large new blocks with wide intervening streets were laid out. On the European mainland the tradition of multi-storey living was continued and apartment houses were the usual result both in inner-city districts and on the city margins. By contrast, new terraces of family houses proliferated across many local-authority estates on the margins of large towns in Great Britain (Rose 1974). In a minority of war-damaged cities, a diligent effort was made to respect old property boundaries and building forms, and this was certainly

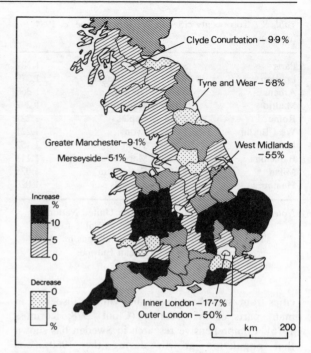

Fig. 8.2
Population change in Great Britain, 1971–81 (%).

the case in the old cores of many German cities (Hajdu 1978). For example, the completely destroyed Hoherstrasse in Cologne was rebuilt on its old pattern as a narrow, crooked street with a strong historic character, and important sections of old Frankfurt were reconstructed to convey their traditional appearance; however, subsequent commercial pressure has changed adjacent skylines beyond recognition.

By the second half of the 1950s, wartime losses had largely been made good and the need to plan future urban growth came to the fore. The large volume of post-war marriages and the resultant baby-boom meant that many couples with young children had no immediate alternative to living with parents or other relatives but were in urgent need of homes of their own. Important rural–urban migration on the European mainland intensified housing demand in cities while some countries, most notably France, needed to catch up on very low rates of home construction during the 1930s. The multiplication of new housing schemes raised the dual threat of chaotic conversion of land to urban uses and of inadequate provision of transport, schools, local shops and other necessary services on the new estates. Such was certainly the reality in the early years of the *grands ensembles* that mushroomed around Paris at this time, and similar difficulties were encountered in many other countries as well (Fuerst 1974).

Master plans

Physical planning appeared to offer the solution for coping with these problems and a crop of master plans, laden with axes of expansion, growth nodes, transport corridors, new towns and even green belts, duly appeared. Every master plan varied in detail, according to the site of its central city and the administrative, political and cultural contexts within which it was fashioned (Hall 1967, 1977). For example, around Stockholm the construction of large estates of suburban apartments, such as Farsta and Vällingby, was coordinated with the building of an underground railway system that had been started in 1945 and exceeded 100 km in 1980. Each group of estates was provided with a commercial precinct, within which movement by pedestrians and vehicles was kept separate, and large parking facilities were installed to cope with the rising tide of private car ownership. Thus, the new suburb of Skärholmen, to the southwest of Stockholm, was completed in 1968 and was equipped with shopping facilities to service a clientele of 300 000, as well as being provided with the largest car park in Scandinavia (Goldfield 1979). The last socalled 'underground suburbs' within Stockholm municipality were constructed during the 1970s, but similar models have been employed in surrounding local authorities which are served by extensions of the underground, suburban surface railways and the network of motorways installed in the late 1960s and 1970s to facilitate journey-to-work movements throughout Stockholm's metropolitan region. Such estates of apartment blocks fringed many Continental cities as master plans were implemented, but in Britain they tended to be built as a result of slum-clearance schemes in inner-city locations, with pairs or terraces of single-family houses being the usual formula on the margins of cities (Duclaud-Williams 1978; Pacione 1979).

Master plans had to be modified in response to subsequent changes in demography, economic health and political conditions with, for example, the 1965 *Schéma directeur* for the Paris region undergoing revision in 1969, 1975 and the early 1980s (Moseley 1980; Flockton 1982). In addition, these master plans were implemented with varying degrees of success in response to the fact that the concept of physical planning tended to be accepted more readily in the countries of north-west Europe than in the Mediterranean south, where piecemeal, chaotic urban sprawl forged ahead in defiance of official plans.

Urban sprawl

By way of example, the city of Rome grew very rapidly in the 1960s and early 1970s, with recent migrants finding accommodation wherever they could: in crowded tenements, caves and the hastily-built shacks and houses in the *borgate* which mushroomed haphazardly around the old city regardless of the 1962 development plan (Ferrarotti 1972). Some 800 000 people live in the *borgate* and they are organizing themselves to demand proper municipal services: paved streets, public transport, schools, health facilities and, in some localities, even the most basic of necessities like electricity and drains. Not surprisingly, the costs of providing such facilities after suburbanization has occurred are astronomical. Now the administration is trying desperately to compel developers and private individuals to respect official plans so that this kind of chaos may be avoided in the future.

Since the mid-1950s, Lisbon and Porto have been beset by comparable problems which have resulted from the recruitment of large numbers of workers from the countryside for Portugal's rapidly-expanding industries (Williams 1981). Illegal housing settlements (*bairros clandestinos*) sprang up and were further swelled by the arrival of repatriates from Angola and Mozambique. The *bairros* varied in quality from quite respectable houses to miserable shanties but all shared in the distinction of being poorly serviced and existing in contravention of land-use plans. The authorities have cleared the worst peripheral slums, although greater emphasis of late has been placed on providing services. Similarly, the *barracas* around Barcelona, Madrid and other Spanish cities have sprawled alongside railways and across wasteland, hillslopes and patches of public land (Naylon 1981b). Many of their shanties lacked electricity, water and mains drainage and during the 1970s numerous residents' action groups came into being to influence the authorities and ensure that such shortcomings be set right. Towards the eastern end of the Mediterranean the recent sprawl of greater Athens (3 300 000) exhibits comparable features. The city continues to grow by 100 000 new residents each year, but one in every five of its dwellings has been constructed without planning permission. Arguably Athens has few slums but about half of all dwellings depend on cesspools until the construction of a new sewerage system is finished.

Downtown transformation

Priorities and ambitions

Each master plan was ambitious and expansionist, emphasizing the allocation of new housing to peripheral locations but paying much less attention to changing economic and social conditions in the city core and the inner suburbs (Michael 1979). Each programme took it for granted that city centres would continue to flourish, thereby drawing people and jobs to them and generating ever-growing quantities of wealth that would be available for wise allocation elsewhere. To enable central areas to perform these roles even more vigorously in the buoyant economic climate of the 1960s, a number of modernization programmes were announced for clearing parts of the central areas of many west European cities to enable the installation of office accommodation on a massive scale, with shopping facilities, cultural equipment and new apartments occasionally being included. At this time, rising rates of car ownership afforded greater flexibility in journey-to-work behaviour than ever before in Western Europe, but car ownership remained less widespread than in North America where decentralization and suburbanization of employment were forging ahead very rapidly. In Western Europe, many people continued to rely on public transport for travelling to work and railway lines and bus routes remained strongly focused on central areas. Unlike the demise of many downtown areas in North American cities in the 1960s, city centres in Western Europe continued to flourish as seats of government, administration and commerce, still requiring a large and growing labour force to service them.

Indeed, some cities took on a range of additional functions following the course of national and international events. Brussels, Luxembourg and Strasbourg acquired new roles following the creation of the EEC and other supranational organizations. At the same time, Paris and several other capital cities were being vigorously promoted by their national governments as 'ideal' locations for Europe-wide headquarters of multinational corporations which were increasing their power dramatically. In addition, administrative and commercial offices dealing with routine matters were being established in many provincial cities as part of official policies for decentralizing paperwork as Western Europe's economies became emphatically 'post-industrial' (Tuppen 1977).

The office booms that characterized many of Europe's cities in the 1960s were designed to satisfy the ambitions of city politicians and the requirements of businessmen at one and the same time. Planners and administrators were keen to 'modernize' their cities and sanctioned the use of public funds for provision of new roads and other infrastructural features. Nonetheless, each of these schemes also depended heavily on massive injections of capital from finance houses, pension funds and big business in general. Thus the Stockholm city plan of 1962 advo-

cated the wholesale demolition of the city's Central Business District (CBD), with a quarter of the cleared area being proposed for new thoroughfares and walkways, a quarter for multi-level parking, and the remaining half for new commercial buildings (Sidenbladh 1965; Hall 1979). The plan was not implemented in its original form but the CBD was duly demolished and rebuilt with high-rise office blocks, shopping precincts, an impressive 'culture house' and a vast lower-level concourse which is filled with animation during the day but acquires a much more sinister appearance at night.

Waves of destruction

The collective impact of programmes such as these was to unleash a new wave of destruction in many city centres in the name of 'slum clearance' or 'urban renewal' which swept across many of the old dwellings that had provided cheap accommodation and many of the workshops which had offered local sources of employment. Whole communities could be destroyed in a matter of months or even weeks! Some residents were rehoused in public-authority houses or apartments on suburban housing estates, others simply sought cheap accommodation wherever it was to be found, while those with sufficient capital behind them purchased property in more desirable parts of the city, undertaking new journey-to-work movements by public transport or by car.

Many inner-city firms were already beset by functional inefficiencies stemming from trying to operate in old, cramped but usually cheap workshops which were only accessible along narrow city streets. Often such firms were small and had little capital behind them; many simply went out of business when urban-renewal schemes got underway since they were not able to cover the relocation costs that would be involved in moving to alternative and almost inevitably more expensive accommodation out in the suburbs. The office blocks and shops that rose where humble workshops had once stood could not provide replacement work for those who had lost their industrial jobs, just as the new expensive apartments that rose from the ruins of modest tenements could not provide replacement housing for those of limited means. In some neighbourhoods, communities were dispersed; in others they were substantially diluted as middle-class newcomers moved into new expensive apartments or invaded and restored what remained of the old housing stock in adjacent areas, thereby placing it beyond the reach of the working-class population.

Popular protests and gentrification

Such transformation of inner areas in many cities during the buoyant years of the 1960s soon gave rise to strong opposition. Conservationists lamented the planned erosion of historic townscapes and opposed schemes that would involve further demolition. They advocated careful restoration of existing properties rather than total destruction and construction of new buildings. Such arguments could, of course, easily open the way for 'gentrification' unless action were taken by municipalities to subsidize rents in rehabilitated housing and thereby ensure that established residents could continue to afford to live there. At the same time, citizens' action groups criticized the destruction of traditional working-class communities and the loss of long-established forms of local employment (Pickvance 1976). The effective control of many city centres by the forces of international capital aroused deep-rooted local hostilities, as did the social transformation of some inner-city areas which paralleled the construction of luxury apartments and the gentrification of old housing stock that escaped demolition (Castells 1978, 1983).

This kind of opposition became forceful throughout Western Europe during the critical years of the late 1960s and has continued to be expressed in various forms ever since. Economic recession, energy crisis, high rates of inflation and devastating unemployment dampened the demand for new office space for perhaps a decade after the mid-1970s and certainly reduced the supply of public capital for inner-city modernization schemes. Redevelopment projects were slowed down or even halted and many historic sections of the built environment were thereby granted a reprieve. By the mid-1980s the demand for modern office space had picked up dramatically in London and some other major cities but was certainly not experienced in all urban centres. During the period between the affluent 1960s and the present day, profound human problems have appeared in many of Western Europe's inner-city areas, and planners have been made painfully aware of the complex economic, social and political implications of any programme that they propose (Waterhouse 1979).

The process of gentrification, whereby newly incoming middle-class households restore deteriorated urban property, especially in former working-class neighbourhoods, has continued apace in many West European cities throughout the past quarter-century (Smith and Williams 1986). Instead of settling for an outer suburban existence, these well-paid professionals and service-sector workers were rediscovering the qualities of living in truly urban neighbourhoods. Ordinary, often poorly maintained, houses were purchased cheaply by the pioneer gentrifiers who themselves undertook the restoration of their property or engaged small builders to do so. Areas that were well served by rapid-transit systems and contained homes that displayed 'period charm' were the prime targets for gentrification during the first wave. Since property values were continuing to increase, the restoration of housing continued to be a good capital investment for individual households who were duly joined by developers and building companies that moved in to renovate old tenements and to convert empty warehouses into attractive apartments.

The urban space of less obviously appealing neighbourhoods also began to be transformed with, for example, London's gentrification affecting not only Islington and Clapham but also Hackney and Balham; while Parisian gentrification extended from the evident attractions of the Marais to more distant quarters in the city's east end. As well as enhancing the quality and visual attractiveness of housing, gentrification greatly boosts its price and brings with it a new middle-class range of up-market services and shops, including delicatessens, wine bars, boutiques and the mandatory proliferation of estate agents, which take the place of ordinary retail outlets. This transformation of values associated with the invasion of the 'yuppies' effectively excludes less well-paid households from purchasing a home in a gentrified neighbourhood. The obvious and highly contentious consequence of gentrification is the displacement of the working class, a process which can be intensified so easily by well-intentioned conservation policies.

Conservation

Responsibilities

Legal powers for protecting individual buildings of architectural merit or historic interest were being acquired by government agencies and local authorities in every state of Western Europe from the latter years of the nineteenth century onwards, but only recently has attention been directed to conserving groups of houses, complete streets and neighbourhoods rather than separate buildings. Individual nations have approached this challenge in various ways and a very great deal normally depends on initiatives taken by local authorities as they set about implementing detailed land-use plans (Rodwell 1975). However, a number of types of approach may be distinguished.

Urban conservation has been a very centralized affair in France and the Netherlands. For example, Dutch legislation of 1961 provided protection not only for individual buildings and whole neighbourhoods but even surrounding stretches of landscape, while one year later the French 'Malraux Law' empowered central and local agencies to define 'safeguarded sectors' where a blend of restoration and rehabilitation would be applied to whole neighbourhoods or selected parts of them (Van Voorden 1981; Stungo 1972). Just over sixty safeguarded sectors have been designated, which represent only one-sixth of the potential identified in 1962, with only one additional area being defined after 1976. Local residents have reacted to these schemes with varying degrees of enthusiasm; indeed, many resented the likelihood of being rehoused in the outer suburbs and opposed the process of gentrification that would probably occur in the newly-safeguarded sector. In spite of opposition and reservations about the social implications of this approach, architecturally-impressive conservation has been accomplished in Avignon, Chartres, Lyons, the Marais quarter of Paris and neighbourhoods in many other cities. Further legislation was introduced in 1976 to encourage closer cooperation between state-appointed architects and local councillors in the re-modelling of safeguarded sectors. A year later, new urban-improvement programmes were started which channel financial aid to owners and tenants who wish to improve the basic amenities of their housing property (Kain 1982). These simpler rehabilitation schemes have turned away from previous preoccupations with prestigious architecture and centralized, technocratic approaches to conservation; instead, they recognize local needs for housing, employment and services and place strong emphasis on residents' involvement and community initiative. Investment is being directed to meeting human needs rather than conserving bricks and stone.

In West Germany and Switzerland, legislation for urban conservation is enacted and applied in varying ways in the component *Länder* and *cantons*. Elsewhere, enactments have been made with regard to individual cities in Austria, Belgium, Denmark and Italy, including Salzburg, Bologna, Venice and the Christianhavn district of Copenhagen, where work was started in the early 1960s and has continued under Danish 'slum clearance' legislation of 1969 which embraces modernization of houses and wider improvement of neighbourhoods (Skovgaard 1978). Finally, in the UK, local councils were empowered to establish conservation areas under legislation of 1967 and they have been stimulated to do so by local amenity groups. Further legislation in the early 1970s gave local authorities new planning-control powers over all buildings in conservation areas. Bath, Chester, York and Edinburgh's Georgian 'new town' have been subject to particularly comprehensive conservation schemes (Ford 1978).

Local initiatives

In some instances, urban conservationists have had to enlist international aid but many individual cities, such as Bruges and Bologna, have been able to achieve a great deal through their own initiative. For example, the old city of Bruges contains some 2 000 historic houses which accommodate a residential population only half as great as that at the end of the nineteenth century. The conservation programme involves rehabilitation of old buildings, installation of a new sewer system to prevent further pollution of the canals, managing a number of pedestrian axes, establishing community facilities for nine local neighbourhoods and providing special parking areas on the margins of the old city.

The conservation work being undertaken in the heart of Bologna is more intriguing since it is the product of the city's communist administration, which has been in power for many years (Appleyard 1979). It has gained a world-wide reputation for sensitive restoration of old buildings and for controlling rents in rehabilitated properties, thereby ensuring that the existing (usually working-class) residents can afford to continue living in restored housing. Those whose homes are being renovated are rehoused for a short while in a small stock of carefully-built new apartments which harmonize with the ancient surroundings of the inner city. Participation by local residents in this effective but very expensive scheme has been encouraged by the administration, which argues that 'conservation is revolution' and that the forces of capitalism threaten to destroy the historic buildings and the traditional communities of the city alike.

The Venetian dilemma

Venice has posed even more fundamental conservation problems which have required international aid; indeed, the city's very survival was threatened following a rise in local sea level in the order of 35 cm since the 1870s. Shrinkage of the polar ice cap provided the general background to the specific problem of terrain under Venice sinking by 6 mm per annum as increasing volumes of groundwater were extracted for use by residents and by the two hundred or so industrial concerns located around the Venice lagoon. Extraction of methane gas caused further problems, as did the excavation of deep channels to allow tankers to reach nearby oil refineries which belched out air pollution. This exacerbated the damage caused to Venice's ancient stonework by thick layers of pigeon droppings. Industrial pollution and sewage destroyed plant and animal life in the water of the lagoon, causing sand islands to break up and more sea water to enter the lagoon. Tidal action intensified and, together with disturbance caused by fast-moving water craft, provoked enormous damage to poorly-maintained seawalls and foundations. General dampness in buildings and fluctuating water levels in the canals became part of the Venetian way of life. Even persistent low water created problems since it failed to allow sewage to disperse, while removing lateral support from exposed foundations; high water naturally caused devastating floods.

In November 1966, high water rose 2 m above normal peak levels, wreaking havoc in ordinary homes and causing incalculable damage to fabrics, paintings, frescoes and statues in palaces and churches. International aid was sought to devise technical solutions for stabilizing land and water levels, and appeals were launched for finance to conserve damaged art treasures and crumbling buildings (Pacione 1974). Not only did 400 palaces of architectural and artistic importance need attention, but roughly half of all the buildings in the old city demanded repair. Many ground-floor apartments were found to be quite unsuitable for habitation and half of all the houses showed signs of damp. Even more serious was the fact that the residential population of old Venice was declining fast, actually falling by more than half between 1951 and 1981 to 83 000. The younger generation had chosen to move out, leaving the decaying city to the old and poor, as well as to the tourists in their hotels and the rich in their restored town houses. Since the mid-1970s, the national government has allocated considerable sums to flood protection, social housing, urban conservation and restoring the ecological balance of the lagoon. Administrative delays have meant that not all the money has been spent and many would agree that the lagoon is in a poorer condition than in 1966. Even so, 8 million visitors come to Venice each year!

Achievements

Much has undoubtedly been achieved in the realm of urban conservation in Western Europe and the designation of 1975 as European Architectural Heritage Year did a great deal to make the principle even more widely known. For example, the everyday environment of many cities has been improved by the establishment of traffic-free streets (Hajdu 1981). West Germany, the Netherlands and Denmark pioneered such schemes, which were duly emulated by other countries such as France, where the first pedestrianized street was set up in Rouen in 1970; ten years later, 200 French towns and cities had implemented their own schemes (Devavry 1977). It is disappointing that Italy, which is so rich in old towns with narrow streets flanked by historic buildings, has made few efforts in this respect. Yet in spite of much successful conservation, it must be stressed that large sections of Western Europe's historic city centres have suffered irreparable damage as modernization has been implemented with little or no regard for the total urban environment. The piecemeal destruction of Georgian Dublin is a case in point, as a large proportion of its finest urban landscapes has been swept away in order to install speculative office blocks (Kearns 1982). Some of these were rented by government departments during the 1970s but recent financial cutbacks have trimmed that demand and have left an array of unwanted office accommodation. The central city now contains a disturbing collection of derelict land and hoardings but precious few signs of new construction (Horner and Parker 1987).

Similarly in Madrid, some individual features of the townscape have been strictly conserved, but whole neighbourhoods of architectural interest have been razed to permit office blocks and car parks to be installed (Wynn 1980). Unfortunately, legislation to protect historic buildings or neighbourhoods is not enough. Environmental pollution, associated with exhaust fumes, oil-fired central heating and indeed acid rain, is causing irreparable damage to the historic built environments of traffic-clogged cities such as Athens and Rome, as well as the urban centres of north-western Europe that are readily identified with nineteenth-century industrialization.

Modernization

Controversy in Brussels

Conflicts between modernization and conservation have been experienced in every city in Western Europe during the past quarter century, but the city of Brussels provides a particularly striking example of the differences between economic and social principles and between the power of international capital and the interests of local people. The city enhanced its international status dramatically following the creation of the EC and attracted many new administrative and commercial functions during the 1960s. No fewer than 165 major American companies had selected Brussels for their European headquarters by 1968, when the city contained over half of all company head offices in Belgium (Goosens and Rudder 1976). Office activities have become strongly concentrated in the city centre where half the jobs and no less than one-eighth of all employment in Belgium are to be found (Hengchen and Melis 1980). Sizeable sections of the old city have been razed to the ground to make way for scores of new office blocks, of which the EC's Berlaymont building is the best known.

In fact, the planned destruction of Brussels goes back to 1909 when work was started on a 4 km junction between the northern and southern railway termini, which would incorporate a new central station. Over a thousand tenement blocks were demolished in several working-class districts and roughly 100 ha functioned as a vast building site until the scheme was completed in 1952. Districts surrounding the old termini gradually deteriorated and were duly selected for urban renewal in the 1960s. The emergence of Brussels' 'European' role and the fact that the World Fair was held there in 1958 triggered off a massive phase of modernization. Inner ring roads were built, new offices constructed and a start was made on an underground railway in 1965. More road schemes and massive office development were announced, including the 'Manhattan' project which envisaged the clearance of 50 ha in the northern inner city and the eviction of over 10 000 inhabitants prior to the construction of an administrative and commercial complex that was to provide over 60 000 jobs.

Such projects aroused widespread protest from the citizens, who not only opposed the destruction of so much of old Brussels but also feared that sections of the inner city would become depopulated. Already there was plenty of evidence to show that the working-class districts which remained standing in the inner city were developing as reception areas for large numbers of poorly-paid immigrant workers, especially Italians, Moroccans, Spaniards and Turks (De Lannoy 1975). Americans and EC staff emulated the middle-class Bruxellois by moving to homes in more agreeable suburbs.

In the following decade, many new office buildings were constructed in inner Brussels and further schemes were conceived for the Marolles district and a 30 ha site opposite the southern railway terminus (Culot 1974). EC institutions continued to consume office space, particularly in response to the enlargement of the Community from six to nine members in 1972. In addition, the Belgian government acquired large new offices in the capital to house its growing administrative services. However, the financial crisis of the mid-1970s and the collapse of demand for commercial office space meant that several programmes were either shelved or halted part way. Many newly-built offices in the Manhattan district remained empty, with developers suffering great financial loss.

At the same time dozens of action committees came into being to challenge the way the city was being planned and to question the way that office development and local conservation schemes both tended to work against the interests of those working-class residents who remained in the inner city. For example, buildings in conservation areas, such as the Marolles and Sablon neighbourhoods, attracted boutiques, restaurants and avant-garde cultural activities as well as providing some renovated apartments which commanded high rents that could only be paid by middle-class incomers. Action committees roundly condemned the gentrification of these and similar areas and the effective eviction of working-class residents who have been unable to meet drastic rent increases. In recent years attempts have been made to involve the local population in conservation schemes and to provide moderate-rent housing in renovated buildings, thereby attempting to ensure that the forces of urban conservation do not work entirely to the benefit of middle-class newcomers (Bateman 1985). The entry of Spain and Portugal to the EC in 1986 absorbed empty office space in Brussels and required the provision of new blocks but under a much tighter planning regime than in the anything-goes atmosphere of the 1960s and nearly 1970s.

Housing problems of an evolving society

Supplies and demands

Despite the construction of massive housing estates on the periphery of Western Europe's cities and the fact that rates of natural increase and migration from the countryside and from abroad have all declined, shortage of accommodation remains a desperate problem for many sections of urban society (Bassett and Short 1980). Virtually all post-war housing has been built to house families that would be able to raise loans to purchase private property or would qualify for housing by local authorities or by housing associations.

Many other groups in society also require accommodation, but relatively little attention has been paid to coping with their needs. West Europeans are surviving much longer and many live alone in their old age; there are many more one-parent families; more marriages end in divorce; for a host of reasons, more young adults decide to leave their parental home; and increasing numbers of people are choosing to live alone or in domestic arrangements that do not approximate to conventional two-parent families, for which almost the entire housing stock was built. The majority of newcomers to the cities of Western Europe still need cheap and compact accommodation and that point is of special urgency for the young and the jobless.

With rates of unemployment increasing, many people simply do not command sufficient resources to buy property or rent anything other than the cheapest room. Local rules vary but many people in the groups mentioned above may not qualify for a place on a public housing list. Urban-renewal schemes have swept away much cheap accommodation upon which such people relied in the past, while legislation affording measures of rent control or security of tenure may have been designed to help the tenant but also serve to make leasing out of accommodation a much less attractive proposition for landlords.

Housing difficulties have given rise to new brands of street politics in the cities of Western Europe over the past twenty years, as residents seek to compel town councillors, urban administrators and planners to tackle problems in more effective ways. For example, vociferous action groups have sprung up in many Spanish and Italian cities: to try to improve services in recently-built working-class estates around Milan and Turin; to draw attention to the appalling housing conditions in the back streets of Naples; and to demonstrate how rents have been purposely inflated in central Rome with the result that landlords keep apartments empty for months on end until sufficiently affluent tenants can be found, even though the city endures a massive accommodation crisis (McElrath 1962; Daolio 1975). Indeed, most cities have generated a wide range of neighbourhood movements which, in the case of Madrid, have objectives as diverse as securing the installation of basic facilities in shanty-towns, opposing the demolition of downtown areas for new office blocks, and seeking to improve schools and public open spaces in pleasant middle-class suburbs (Castells 1978).

Mismatch: the case of Amsterdam

The detailed operation of housing allocation varies from country to country and from city to city; however, a general mismatch between the fixed structures of the built environment and the evolving features of society is both clear and widespread. Such problems have been particularly acute in the city of Amsterdam, where new approaches to urban renewal and inner-city housing are being implemented. During the 1950s and 1960s the rapidly-growing population of the Netherlands required additional housing on a massive scale and attention was directed entirely to new estates of family dwellings located on the fringe of cities (Anderiessen 1981). However, single people, childless couples and immigrant workers were also seeking housing and were only able to find it in rented rooms in inner-city areas.

Amsterdam contains a large historic core and extensive nineteenth-century neighbourhoods where such accommodation exists, but supply is outstripped by demand and attempts at controlling rents have not been adequate. Students attending the city's universities and colleges, young workers in tertiary employment, younger and poorer members of the sizeable gay community, immigrants and repatriates from former Dutch colonies compete unequally for a dwindling housing stock which has been eroded by slum-clearance and renovation schemes and by emphatic gentrification in some districts, where housing costs have soared beyond the grasp of poorly-paid people. It is true that families with children have been moving out of inner Amsterdam and that the residential population has been declining for over two decades, but sufficient low-cost housing for incomers is simply not available and the completion rate of public housing declined appreciably in the late 1970s. For example, only 280 new units of public housing were built in the inner city in 1979 at a time when 53 000 had registered officially as needing accommodation.

Squatting

Squatting in empty buildings had been known in Amsterdam as early as 1965 and became the solution for growing numbers of Amsterdammers as housing problems became more serious and more inner-city properties were made vacant either by officials, prior to urban-renewal schemes, or by developers who were biding their time in anticipation of more lucrative deals. The city's squatters came from a wide variety of social, occupational and educational backgrounds and held a range of political views, with experience of severe housing stress often being their only common bond. They were characteristically young (usually between 20 and 35 years of age) and single, with men making up two-thirds of the total. Some had come together simply in order to obtain a roof over their heads; for others, living communally was an expression of particular social or political objectives (Cherki 1973). By 1979, it was estimated that there were between 20 000 and 70 000 squatters in Amsterdam and squatting was encountered in almost every town in the Netherlands and in major cities throughout Western Europe. For example, London contained perhaps 30 000 squatters out of an estimated national total of 50 000 (Kearns 1979).

In Amsterdam the situation became particularly tense in 1979–80 because the squatters believed that many houses were soon to be cleared by the authorities so that urban renewal could begin. They were capable of marshalling hundreds of others to keep officials out of occupied property and had enlisted a considerable amount of public sympathy, since almost every inhabitant of Amsterdam had experienced housing problems of one kind or another. Swift action by police and city officials in 1980–81 removed squatters from many properties and legislation was passed requiring owners to register empty buildings, thereby affording them protection under the civil code. Squatting was thus made an offence in the Netherlands, and Amsterdam's officials were given new powers to expropriate buildings which remained empty for more than a few months. Legislation regarding criminal trespass was tightened up in several other countries but it was also made possible for squats to be 'authorized' by property owners, thereby allowing squatters to remain in occupation until the building was required for other uses. Nevertheless, cheap inner-city accommodation remains in desperately short supply and squatting continues to be one of the contributory causes for conflict between young people and urban authorities.

Despite the fact that squatting is also illegal in German cities, the number of squats in West Berlin rose dramatically during the first half of 1981 so that one-third of the city's 600 technically 'empty' houses were occupied in this fashion. The decaying nineteenth-century houses of Kreuzberg, crushed against the border with East Berlin and sheltering a large community of Turkish 'guestworkers', have the largest concentration of squatters in the city and it was there that street violence broke out in spring 1981 as police prevented a group of young people taking over yet another empty house (Hass-Klau 1982). Planners' attempts to rehabilitate this truly 'marginal' neighbourhood met with little success until very recently (Kouvelis 1979).

In the heart of Copenhagen a vast collective squat has simply been tolerated by the authorities, with more than 1 000 squatters living in the former barracks of Christiania which stands in sharp contrast with the elegant churches, restored houses and new office blocks of neighbouring Christianshavn. Christiania conveys many conflicting images: groups of squatters and large dogs congregate beyond the stalls which offer varied merchandise and refreshments to tourists, while in the distance there is a collective bakery, workshops for recycling 'junk', and small 'eco-farms' where chickens and goats are raised and less usual forms of pot plant may be glimpsed on sunny window ledges. Murals adorn concrete walls but timber fences have been removed for use as building material or simply for firewood. The so-called 'free-city of Christiania' has existed since 1972 but opposition is growing not only in Denmark but also in Sweden and Norway where social workers complain that a share of the drugs entering their countries come via Christiania. Their governments have made strong representation to the Danes to close it down.

A flexible approach to housing policy

Squatting, admittedly, is an extreme case, but it is undeniable that the question of housing has become a major problem and a major political issue in almost every city in Western Europe. Harsh experience has shown that local needs deserve careful consideration before urban-renewal schemes or modernization programmes are initiated by city authorities and developers. Amsterdam's older neighbourhoods share numerous characteristics with other European cities (e.g. poor housing, high building densities, many poor people and inadequate cultural facilities) but some sites also suffer from the distinctive problem of having many houses whose timber-pile foundations have rotted beyond hope of replacement. In such difficult circumstances, complete demolition of buildings and subsequent reconstruction is the only possible solution. Before 1971, two fairly distinct policies were implemented in the city's older neighbourhoods: with rehabilition and reconstruction being practised in nineteenth-century residential districts. Since then, urban renewal has become a much more flexible operation in response to social conditions and the quality of buildings on each particular site.

Eleven renewal districts have been designated in the inner city and work within them demonstrates the subtlety of Amsterdam's current policies (Whysall and Benyon 1981). For example, urban renewal in the Dapperbuurt district involves total clearance and reconstruction across 38 ha to provide housing and local shopping facilities (Fig. 8.3). Community action groups have succeeded in ensuring that blocks of small apartments are constructed, as well as family dwellings, and that work is phased in such a way that local residents may be rehoused in new moderate-cost apartments in their old neighbourhood. Rehabilitation of existing housing is the dominant approach in the Spaarndammerbuurt district, although some sites will be cleared to provide open space and for the construction of cultural facilities as well as new apartments.

A mixed approach is also being employed in the Jordaan district sited between the western canals of

Fig. 8.3
Urban-renewal districts in Amsterdam.

the inner city. The neighbourhood is composed of houses constructed in the seventeenth, eighteenth and nineteenth centuries; many were in poor repair a decade or so ago but no less than a quarter have been designated as being of historic interest. An early plan for this mixed middle- and working-class neighbourhood of 20 000 people proposed considerable demolition and the installation of new traffic schemes and public open space. There was strong opposition to this project, which threatened to erode the Jordaan's character and reduce its residential accommodation by half. Current plans respect the 800 listed buildings, practise conservation and reconstruction in roughly equal proportions, and make provision for small as well as medium-sized apartments. However, it must be acknowledged that in-migration by young adults, who live in small households (often without children) and enjoy incomes well above the average for inner Amsterdam, stimulated marked gentrification of some sections of the Jordaan during the 1970s.

Malaise of the inner city

Despair

Modernization, conservation and gentrification have brought profound and highly controversial changes to many central districts in Western Europe's cities, but such innovations have been far from ubiquitous and many inner-city localities have entered into a profound malaise (Herbert and Smith 1979). Planning policies and myriad decisions taken by residents and employers have conspired to change such localities for the worse. The precise combination of problems varies from district to district but, in general terms, substantial sections of Western Europe's inner cities are characterized by substandard housing and deterioration of the built environment; many of their residents suffer multiple deprivation (Hall 1981a). Residents who have chosen to move out normally belong to professional, managerial and skilled blue-collar groups, while those who remain tend to be less skilled and less affluent members of society. They have been joined by labour migrants from abroad and, in the case of Mediterranean Europe, by people who have left the countryside in search of urban work (Van Praag 1981).

Unlike the pleasant suburbs, inner-city districts contain relatively few medium-sized, two-parent households but an abundance of old-age pensioners, single people, one-parent families and large households composed of recent immigrants. Many inner-city households depend on low or insecure sources of income, of which social security payments represent a notable share. Economic recession and rising unemployment in recent years have made the situation even worse. Poor housing, low incomes, sharply declining job opportunities and diminishing local-authority resources combine to exacerbate the deprivation experienced by many inner-city dwellers, imparting a collective sense of hopelessness and alienation (Harrison 1982; Heinritz and Lichtenberger 1986).

Violence

Such conditions do not, of course, attract private investment for creating new jobs, renovating the built environment or providing community services; by contrast, they do provide powerful causes for the outbursts of popular unrest which occurred in many west European cities in the early 1980s. Violent demonstrations over poor housing, inadequate social facilities, high rates of youth unemployment, fears of police harassment and profound disillusionment with western society occurred almost as a regular aspect of life on the streets of Amsterdam, West Berlin and Zurich in 1980 and early 1981.

In April 1981, violence broke out in Brixton (south London), but this was merely a prelude to widespread rioting which took place three months later in Brixton, Toxteth (Liverpool), Manchester and a score of other British cities. Each disturbance derived from its own specific set of tensions and frustrations, but the most serious occurred in inner-city areas which had been losing population and prosperity for decades (Lawless 1981). The people they housed were poorly paid and comprised large numbers of immigrants and their British-born children. Rates of unemployment were high, especially among young people who had grown accustomed to the notion of jobs for all, only to find that work was denied them when they came on to the labour market. Levels of dissatisfaction were highest among young immigrants and young people born in Britain of immigrant parentage.

It literally took the riots to reveal the gravity of these problems among Britain's inner-city dwellers (Hamnett 1983). Similar harsh lessons have doubtless been learned by politicians elsewhere in Western Europe and North America. Far from being endowed with eternal strength and self-sustaining vigour, the decaying inner districts of many cities have arguably emerged as Western Europe's most intractable problem areas in the 1980s. Their peaceful survival will require a mixture of economic support, social skill and political act which remains to be distilled (Home 1982). Nonetheless, some bold initiatives have been attempted.

Initiatives

Peter Hall and Paul Cheshire (1987) provide a challenging agenda for urban regeneration which, they argue, must embrace both economic and social objectives. First, urban regeneration should enhance the image of the inner city as a place to live and work by (a) improving its built environment and infrastructure of roads and public transport, and (b) developing the viable skills of local people. Second, it should incorporate measures to help offset the costs of change, especially as some of those fall on the poorer members of local society. It is likely that the city authority must operate in partnership with private developers in order to achieve these ends and to bring in new and viable activities rather than attempt to prolong the existence of moribund forms of employment and land use.

The transformation of London's Docklands from an abandoned port area to a vibrant part of the city provides a good example. The state-funded London Docklands Development Corporation (LDDC) has certainly changed the 'image' of the area (both through its publicity campaign and literally on the ground). The 'enterprise zone' on the Isle of Dogs, with its tax advantages and simplified planning procedures, has contributed to this transformation and Docklands has been perceived as an investor's bonanza (Church and Hall 1986; Church 1988). New and converted housing (very largely for sale and often at high prices), a range of modern employment opportunities, a new light railway, a business airport, a vast tertiary complex and new shopping facilities add up

to a remarkable – and in many ways successful – change (Marmot and Worthington 1986). But as house prices escalate and new jobs are occupied by incoming white-collar home-owners investing in the Docklands, one is left wondering what has been gained by ordinary, working-class local people (Townsend 1987). Have the interests of the poorer members of local society been defended? Or is that an impossible dream in a planning scenario that seeks to encourage the fastest possible transition to the economy and society of the twenty-first century?

In central Scotland, the Glasgow Eastern Area Renewal (GEAR) project has operated since the mid-1970s to effect a comprehensive social, economic and environmental regeneration of 1 400 ha from which population and industry had retreated since 1960. Objectives included promoting job creation, training for employment, overcoming social disadvantages, diversifying the social structure, and improving and maintaining the environment of buildings and open spaces. Pacione (1985) reports that important improvements have occurred in Glasgow's east end since the mid-1970s and that many of these are the outworking of the GEAR project. Housing has been improved, overcrowding reduced and buildings restored. Now there is less privately-rented accommodation but more housing provided by the local authority, housing associations and private developers. Landscaping has enhanced the visual environment. By contrast, unemployment remains high and the GEAR project has not been particularly successful in achieving its social goals (Donnison and Middleton 1987). Both 'east end' experiments reinforce the message that planning is not just about buildings and landscapes but rather about promoting the quality of life in all its aspects. We have seen, all too disturbingly, that it is much easier to change the urban environment than to improve people's lives.

The challenge of the post-war estates

A quarter of a century ago, West Europeans used to think that the inner-city crisis that was so evident in the USA would never happen in their great cities. Their hope was sadly misplaced. Nor could they have imagined that the big estates of social housing that they were building at that very time would soon become the second focus of desperation and deprivation. Hundreds of thousands of blocks of relatively low-cost housing were built on tens of thousands of estates (Castells 1983). Construction standards were often poor and features of internal and external design were questionable. Vast numbers of inner-city dwellers and migrants from the provinces and from overseas were housed in this way. Roughly the same social housing product can be found throughout Western Europe, from London or Paris to the rapidly growing sprawls around Mediterranean cities. For example, in France no less than one-fifth of all families live in *grands ensembles* and two-fifths of all households headed by immigrants. Provision of adequate schools, shops and other community facilities sometimes came as an afterthought. Even so, the estates continued to grow, with Glasgow's Easterhouse housing nearly 60 000 people at its peak, Sarcelles and Massy-Antony (near Paris) 50 000 and 40 000 respectively, Gropiusstadt (West Berlin) 45 000, and Les Minguettes (Lyons) 35 000 people (Barrère and Cassou-Mounat 1980; Tuppen 1988).

Whole estates as well as individual blocks acquired particular roles. Some were 'respectable' and reasonably well maintained; others were used by housing authorities as 'dumping grounds' for the homeless, for immigrants, for large or one-parent families, for those on social security. Many estate dwellers who could afford to move on to 'better' estates or to individual houses did just that, thereby reinforcing the socio-economic deprivation of the people and the places that they left behind. At the same time, unemployment rates were rising throughout Western Europe and the great estates became problematical in environmental as well as human terms, with internal damp and structural defects becoming widespread in very many blocks (Wynn 1984).

By the early 1980s, vandalism, crime, racial attacks, deprivation and despair characterized many post-war estates as well as the inner cities. The violence at Broadwater Farm estate (Tottenham, north London) in 1985 was particularly tragic but less devastating incidents were far from uncommon. Disturbances around Lyons in the hot summer of 1981 and around Paris in 1983 encouraged the French government to promote a national scheme for neighbourhood improvement that would support and to some extent finance 'bottom-up' projects for improving environmental, social and economic conditions on problem estates (Tuppen and Mingret 1986). Local politicians, administrators, community leaders and residents were responsible for drawing up ideas and implementing them on the ground (Clout 1987c). Over 120 schemes were launched and, not surprisingly, have had greatest success in enhancing housing, open spaces and community buildings. As part of these projects, some particularly problematic blocks of housing have been dynamited and surrounding neighbourhoods remo-

delled. The social and visual 'image' of some estates has been improved and interesting experiments have been started to involve residents in managing and maintaining their estates, to convert 'no-man's land' open spaces into private gardens and, indeed, to privatize some blocks and their local services. But whether this kind of neighbourhood intervention can ever reach the roots of social inequality, unemployment and racism remains open to debate.

Privatization of blocks of flats or sale to property companies has been implemented by some local authorities in the UK, with the London borough of Wandsworth being a prime example. The appearance, quality and monetary value of what were formerly 'problem' blocks have certainly changed, as different residents with much higher incomes (and very different political persuasions) have moved in. The negative side of this policy is that other blocks and estates have been used more emphatically as 'dumping grounds' for the deprived. Privatization and allied changes were recommended in 1986 by an independent enquiry into Glasgow's post-war housing estates, where many apartments are damp, open decks invite crime and violence, and the financially-starved housing authority has left repairs undone. The idea was for between one-quarter and one-half of Glasgow's corporation housing to be sold off to housing associations, cooperatives, development companies and private individuals.

Further reading

Burtenshaw D, Bateman M, Ashworth G J 1981 *The City in West Europe*. Wiley, Chichester

Castells M 1978 *City, Class and Power*. Macmillan, London

Castells M 1983 *The City and the Grassroots*. Arnold, London

Fielding A J 1982 Counterurbanization in Western Europe. *Progress in Planning* 17: 1–52

Harrison P 1983 *Inside the Inner City*. Penguin, Harmondsworth

Herbert D T, Smith D M (eds) 1979 *Social Problems and the City: geographical perspectives*. Oxford University Press, Oxford

Merlin P 1971 *New Towns*. Methuen, London

White P E 1984 *The West European City*. Longman, London

Wynn M (ed.) 1983 *Housing in Europe*. Croom Helm, London

Wynn M (ed.) 1984 *Planning and Urban Growth in Southern Europe*. Mansell, London

9

Agriculture and rural change

Agricultural populations

Farming represents by far the most extensive land use in Western Europe, and any view of geography which emphasizes the study of the landscape must recognize the importance of this 'rural space'. Large parts of the European rural landscape have been almost totally humanized by 2 000 years of continuous cultivation – even longer in the more spatially restricted oecumene of ancient Greece. For the rural geographer with a historical bent, Western Europe still offers a fascinating mosaic of agrarian regions whose 'personalities', particularly in France, Spain and Italy, still reflect the *genres de vie* so dear to the heart of Vidal de la Blache. With such a prolonged backdrop of settled agriculture, it is small wonder that farming systems are so complex and varied. Primeval landscapes are rare.

By the mid-1980s, land in agricultural production in Western Europe was approximately 150 million ha, or 44 per cent of the continent's land area. France and Spain, each with about 31 million ha, together contributed over two-fifths of total farmland. Yet rural areas are not monopolized by farming. As transport improvements, particularly the diffusion of the private motor car in the post-war period, allow the urban and rural world to interpenetrate more and more, so rural areas are seen as attractive environments for recreation, holidays and first and second homes. At worst, such pressures may eventually negate that very rurality that once attracted them. At best, planning future uses of Western Europe's countryside demands that a delicate balance be established between conserving valuable resources and permitting sufficient change and economic development for the living standards of country dwellers to be improved – by no means an easy task (Clout 1981b).

In 1985, 14 308 000 people were employed in farming in Western Europe – 8.6 per cent of the total workforce. This proportion has been falling rapidly in recent decades (it was 19.1 per cent in 1965, when farming employed 27 975 000). Between 1965 and 1985, every Western European country experienced a decline in the number of people employed in agriculture. Table 9.1 shows that the decline in the agricultural workforce was especially dramatic in Spain, Italy and Finland. Only Greece and Portugal retained more than a fifth of their economically active populations in farming in 1985. The figure for the UK, on the other hand, was already down to 4 per cent by 1960; this country had honed down its farm population in earlier decades. Agriculture in the UK is, however, more important than its manpower figure suggests, for British farmers produce around 55–60 per cent of the food consumed in the country, including virtually all the milk, eggs, barley, pork and poultry (Minshull 1978).

In spite of their shrinking numbers, farmers constitute an important electoral bloc within their respective countries and represent sizeable political interests in Western European affairs, particularly within the ambit of the Common Market's agricultural policy, to which we shall return later in this chapter. However, it should also be pointed out that many of the peasant farmers of Western Europe's Mediterranean countries (including France) are over 50 years of age; with this go an innate conservatism and lack of enthusiasm for change.

Rural depopulation

The remarkable loss of workers from agriculture since the war implies a dramatic reshaping of rural demography. The nature and effects of this exodus have already been described in Chapter 4, notably the selectivity of the out-movement, unbalancing the residual population and threatening the viability of rural communities. Not all those who quit farming

Table 9.1 Economically active population in agriculture, 1965–85

	Working population in agriculture (%)			Numbers in agriculture ('000)
	1965	1975	1985	1985
Austria	19.3	11.9	7.0	246
Belgium/Lux.	6.6	3.9	2.2	94
Denmark	14.4	9.2	5.9	163
Finland	23.5	15.8	9.3	232
France	17.9	11.1	6.7	1 679
W. Germany	10.8	6.6	5.1	1 491
Greece	47.2	36.6	25.9	990
Rep. of Ireland	31.4	22.4	15.4	211
Italy	24.8	15.4	9.5	2 156
Netherlands	8.7	6.2	5.0	291
Norway	15.5	10.0	7.0	143
Portugal	37.7	28.1	23.0	1 050
Spain	34.0	21.5	13.7	1 868
Sweden	11.1	6.9	4.7	198
Switzerland	9.4	7.0	5.5	178
United Kingdom	3.4	2.7	2.5	697

Source: FAO Production Yearbook 1985. Rome, 1986

necessarily leave the area, however: there is a distinction to be drawn between rural exodus and agricultural exodus.

Rural depopulation has affected not only farmers but also a diverse assortment of rural labour moving in search of industrial and tertiary sector work. This movement also has a social dimension as rural migrants seek the better recreational and social conditions of urban areas – aspirations which are, however, not always realized. A good example of this social component is the widespread movement of rural workers out of agriculture in the Po Valley, despite the fact that farm labour here is better paid than unskilled factory work (Romanos 1979). Village studies by social anthropologists have also shown that beyond the macrostructural economistic explanation of rural depopulation lie powerful cultural factors. At the local level, *who* moves out of agriculture, and out of the region, is often determined by land inheritance patterns and types of tenure (Douglass 1971).

Outmigration has had devastating economic and social consequences for the exporting rural areas. One critical effect is the draining of the young segment of the labour force, dramatically distorting the residual population and leading to what Barberis (1968) has called the feminization and senescence of the agricultural labour force. In Italy, half the farmers are now over 55 years of age – a staggering obstacle to the

technical and capital improvement of that country's farm sector. Beyond a certain threshold, depopulation makes it impossible for villages to sustain a viable existence. Schools, shops and other public services close down, and this only serves to increase the unattractiveness of rural life (Clout 1984).

Another result of depopulation is the abandonment of farmland and the consequent decline in agricultural production. Food must be imported to compensate these production losses, while for those farmers who remain, the potential for economic survival diminishes: mechanization, irrigation, weed control and other farming improvements become more expensive and problematic. The assumption that outmigration leads to farm rationalization was disproved by Pepelasis (1963) for Greece 25 years ago. He found that depopulation was causing damaging shortages of rural labour. Excessive outmigration retarded the expansion of cash-crop farming because crops like cotton and citrus have high labour demands at certain seasons.

When rural migrants leave, they do not sell their land, but hold on to it as insurance; it appears as patches of fallow in the rural landscape. In a study of farming in the south Italian region of Basilicata, Lane (1980) notes that small abandoned plots are a frequent sight. Their owners now live in Argentina, the USA or West Germany. In contrast to the situation in the 1950s when this region was chronically overpopulated and the agricultural ecosystem severely overstretched by overgrazing and the erosive ploughing of steep slopes, now the area could sustain a much more intensive agriculture, but lack of labour and technical expertise among the remaining, mostly old, farmers prevents this happening. In Mediterranean Europe, land abandonment is most serious in upland regions: as terraces crumble, further erosion takes place and topsoil, once carefully conserved, is washed away into silting valleys (Bransden 1985).

To this evidence from southern Europe can be added corroborative material from northern Europe, where rural depopulation has been in existence in many areas since the early nineteenth century. In industrial countries it was primarily the availability of urban and factory jobs which pulled workers out of farming. In one of the most detailed British studies, Saville (1957) found that rural depopulation continued unabated throughout the 1851–1951 period, and was especially marked in remoter areas and in smaller villages. Drudy (1978) then pointed out that the phenomenon was not confined to marginal agricultural regions of Britain but was present in prosperous farming regions as well. His study in north Norfolk showed a 7 per cent drop in population between 1951 and 1971, with many parishes losing a third or more of their population. In northern Europe, the chief causes of rural depopulation appear to be agricultural processes (mechanization, concentration on fewer crops, etc.) which lead to high rates of redundancy in farming and the lack of alternative employment opportunities in rural areas (Gasson 1974; Verrips 1975). Very recent trends are ambiguous: in some areas rural depopulation appears to be continuing; in others it is slowing down or even moving into a phase of rural repopulation.

Along with rural depopulation and the exodus from agriculture goes the demise of peasants and indeed farmers as a social class. This is signalled in the titles of a number of relevant books: *Peasants No More* (Lopreato 1967), *The Vanishing Peasant* (Mendras 1970) and *The European Peasantry: the final phase* (Franklin 1969). What is happening is not just a simple change of occupation: it is the upheaval of a whole way of life. This occurs even where the agricultural exodus is mollified by the growth of some alternative employment *in situ*. In some parts of Europe, such as the Alps and the Pyrenees, farmers have switched to tourism as an alternative existence; they earn more money for less work in the hotels or on the ski-lifts and, as a result, the whole ethos of farming is undermined (Greenwood 1976; Vincent 1980). In other areas, such as north-eastern Italy and Swabia, the diffusion of small-scale industry into rural areas enables family farms to survive as social units by providing off-farm work for some members of the household. In the wilder corners of Europe, like Calabria and Corsica, there is no alternative: here, whole villages have been evacuated. These ghost settlements stand in the landscape as crumbling tombstones to a society that is no more.

Recent studies, however, have proved that rural communities, far from being the static or declining entities often imagined, have always had a considerable volume of immigration as well as outmovement. The in-movement takes place for a variety of reasons, including agricultural employment, marriage, new rural industrial growth, commuting and retirement. In the 1970s there appeared signs of a 'rural revival' in many west European countries. Migratory trends took a reverse path: rural depopulation become rural repopulation, urbanization became counterurbanization (Fielding 1986). Relatively few of these new 'ruralites', however, have much direct concern with farming.

Part-time farming

After the exodus from agriculture, the second major socio-structural characteristic of west European

farming has been the expansion of part-time farming in recent decades. EC labour force survey data for seven countries show that second-job holding is widespread in agriculture, especially in the Republic of Ireland, Italy and West Germany (Alden and Saha 1978). While agriculture in the seven countries surveyed employs only 7 per cent of the working population, it accounts for 31 per cent of those holding second jobs. In West Germany the phenomenon of 'worker-peasants' has been well-established for generations, whereas in Italy and the Republic of Ireland a substantial part of the new manufacturing labour force is retaining links with family farming.

Part-time farming occurs when one or more members of a farm-based household are gainfully employed in work other than, or in addition to, farming the family's holding. The phenomenon may be examined under either the labour or the income share, although both can lead to complex problems of classification and definition given the diversity of experiences in part-time farming in Western Europe. If the farmer himself works off the farm, in a local factory for instance, the situation is straightforward. If the spouse of the farmer works off the farm, then again the situation is fairly clear since such off-farm earnings will almost certainly be pooled with farm income. However, if children residing on the farm have off-farm employment, contribute only casually to farm labour and do not pool their incomes with that of the holding, they have relatively little to do with the farm as a production unit and it is therefore doubtful as to whether this constitutes part-time farming.

Part-time farming is often assumed to be a kind of transitional phase of employment on the route from a predominantly agrarian society to a modern, industrial-based economy. In fact, it can be shown that part-time farming has deep historical and structural roots in the regional specialization of production and in the spread of domestic rural industry which occurred after the demise of the feudal system (Sivini 1976). In a more modern context, it can be seen as a functional adaptation to capitalistic development, providing a social base from which an individual can pick up a range of possible income supplements, either from local industry, services and public works, or as a temporary labour migrant elsewhere (Pugliese 1985).

At the risk of over-simplifying, two main models of part-time farming in Western Europe can be identified. The distinction is based on entrepreneurial roles and on the location of the non-agricultural work. The first category consists of farmers who have a small business operated from, and perhaps also located on, the farm. Examples are the farm and the guesthouse, the farm and the camp site, the farm and the transport business, etc. The second model consists of farmers who work outside the farm in factories. Here, to use Franklin's terminology, the farmer becomes a 'five o'clock farmer', an *Arbeiter Bauer* (worker-peasant), performing the heavy farm work with the aid of a tractor in the evenings and at the weekend (Franklin 1971). In the first model, the farmer retains entrepreneurial functions in his second, non-agricultural occupation. The worker-peasant, on the other hand, abandons his, for he accepts the orders of others within the strict discipline of the factory system.

The West German experience is well described by Franklin (1969). According to the Federal German Agricultural Census of 1960, 42 per cent of all farmers were in fact part-time farmers: 459 000 had businesses or other occupations, and 221 000 were elderly part-timers drawing additional income from rent, pensions and similar sources. Franklin forecasts that worker-peasants will eventually become workers and that the agricultural element will disappear, ultimately leading to the disposal of farm property. This may be true for West Germany but not necessarily elsewhere. Part-time farming is increasing in most west European countries and there is ample evidence of the investment of factory earnings in agricultural holdings, which is an indication of the part-time system's stability.

The worker-peasant structure also offers a cushioning effect in times of industrial slump, and helps to maintain population and services in rural areas. But it has important 'backwash' effects on local agriculture. One of these is the decline in milk cows, especially in areas where women can find off-farm employment easily. Second, part-time holdings are usually small and excessively fragmented. Relative to their size, they are frequently over-mechanized, since labour time is limited. Lastly, there is the appearance of *Sozialbrache*, portions of farmland left fallow for social rather than agronomic reasons, simply because worker-peasant families lack the time or the inclination to cultivate it (Hartke 1956). In some German districts, up to half the land may be under 'social fallow' (Franklin 1969).

Somewhat different perspectives on part-time farming are introduced by the Italian and British cases. The importance of part-time farming in Italy was brought dramatically to the fore by the publication of the 1970/71 round of censuses. According to the 1971 Population Census there were 3 195 000 employed persons working in agriculture. According to the 1970 Agricultural Census the figure was 6 518 000! Although one might be tempted to refer to the statistical scandals for which Italy is rather well-known, the difference is largely explained by the censuses' differential treatment of part-time employment in agriculture (Barberis 1977). While part-time farming in Italy cannot be divorced from that country's deep-seated agrarian problems, it is possible to view the phenomenon in quite a favourable light. Surveys in the Modena district of Emilia and in the region of Marche have revealed that part-time farms are more dynamic than full-time holdings. On average, part-time farmers were found to be younger, more educated, more mobile and more innovative; they had higher overall incomes and a stronger work and managerial ethic (Cavazzani 1976; Pieroni 1982).

Not only does part-time farming characterize marginal upland regions such as Marche, it also appears to be endemic on the rural–urban fringe. Farmers located in this area are subject to strong employment influences from the nearby town. Furthermore, inconveniences may result from vandalism, pilferage, pollution and the shortage of farm labour. The farmer may be encouraged or forced to change his land-use regime, perhaps by abandoning livestock production and switching to market gardening. Anticipation of urban expansion may lead to land speculation and de-investment in farming, producing a ragged, semi-derelict landscape at the urban periphery. Around large British cities some farmers are switching from livestock farming and horticulture to 'horsiculture', providing stabling and riding facilities for the 'suburban cavalry' – an army of mostly young female horse-riders. Also to be found particularly in Britain are two other types of part-time farmer: those who have businesses or professional jobs but want to live in the country and farm as a hobby; and those who have chosen to 'opt out' of the urban life style and are prepared to accept a more simple way of life, often with greatly reduced income (Jolliffe 1977).

For a long time there were no policies for part-time farming because it was regarded as a transitory phenomenon. Only in recent years has it begun to be recognized as a permanent structural feature of the agricultural scene. Yet policy-makers are still inhibited, because they do not know enough about it: with the exception of West Germany, no national government in Western Europe directly encourages part-time farming.

Land tenure

Agrarian structures do not necessarily coincide exactly with rural social structures or with economic modes of production in farming, but an analysis of land tenure adds an important institutional dimension to an understanding of agriculture in Western Europe.

Table 9.2 Structure of agriculture in the European Community, 1983

	Total no. of holdings ('000)	% holdings			Average agric. area per holding (ha)	% agricultural area owner-farmed
		<5 ha	5–50 ha	>50 ha		
Belgium	103	40.0	56.0	4.0	13.6	30.2
Denmark	99	3.4	83.3	13.3	28.8	82.8
France	1 130	26.3	59.9	13.8	25.5	48.4
West Germany	768	33.8	61.7	4.5	15.5	66.8
Greece	959	74.5	25.1	0.4	3.6	69.8
Rep. of Ireland	221	15.5	75.6	8.9	22.8	96.2
Italy	2 832	78.3	20.4	1.3	5.6	79.2
Luxembourg	5	23.9	56.5	19.6	28.0	56.6
Netherlands	139	32.1	64.9	3.0	14.5	61.0
United Kingdom	262	18.0	51.1	30.9	64.5	59.8
Total/Average	6 516	56.5	38.0	5.5	13.6	63.7

Sources: Agriculture Statistical Yearbook 1986. Eurostat, Luxembourg, 1986; *Structure des Exploitations, Enquête de 1983: Analyse des Résultats.* Eurostat, Luxembourg, 1987

Clout (1971) sees land tenure, farm size and farm layout as a complex web of structural constraints interposed between the farming population and the land it cultivates, holding back agricultural progress in many areas. These features tend to reflect the requirements of agriculture in the past; they undergo only slow natural change. Less than 1 per cent of Western Europe's farmland comes on to the market each year, making structural changes such as farm enlargement excruciatingly slow. This situation may change in the fairly near future given that so many of Western Europe's farmers are elderly and approaching retirement. Farming is an unusual occupation in that a large proportion of the new entrants come from within the sector. In France in the 1970s, only one-tenth of the people who took over farms were not farmers' sons or sons-in-law (Blanc 1987). Yet it is clear that a high proportion of farmers have no direct heir, either because they are childless or because they do not expect their existing heirs to succeed them on the farm. Only about one-quarter to one-third of farmers who are at least middle-aged have on-farm successors. The evidence on total successors (i.e. including heirs taking over the farm from outside) is unclear. Fennell (1982) suggests that around one-half of farms will have no direct heir. Partly, the proportion depends on the off-farm economic climate and job opportunities and, of course, on the viability of the farms themselves. Even where there is a successor there is no guarantee that the holding will be farmed full-time, or even at all.

Every West European state has a wealth of legislation affecting land ownership and land tenure but little of it is aimed at accelerating structural change.

Measures tend to favour owner-occupiers and to enchance the rights of tenants against landlords. Hired workers are fast disappearing in most countries, although they remain important in British and Iberian farming. Throughout Western Europe the sanctity of the 'family farm' is preserved with an almost religious zeal – indeed, the 'yeoman farmer' is close to the social ideology of both the Catholic and Protestant churches. Yet the practical and theoretical grounds for the superiority of the family farm are not well established.

Three main parameters may be recognized under the umbrella of land tenure: types of tenure (owner-farming, tenancy, sharecropping, large estates etc.); the distribution of ownership of farmland; and land fragmentation or the splitting of farm holdings into scattered parcels. Each constitutes a distinct and important axis of analysis and will be considered in turn. Comparative data on farm structure are good for EC countries and Table 9.2 provides a résumé of farm size and tenure data.

Types of tenure and modes of production

The matrix of land-tenure types of Western Europe can be dissected in various ways. One fundamental distinction is between family farms and large capitalistic estates. The difference here lies in the use of labour of members of the farm family; capitalistic estates rely mainly or entirely on hired workers. Another basic difference can be drawn, on the basis of the destination of the product, between peasant and commercial farming. Peasant farms, which can also be regarded as a sub-group of family farms, involve a high degree of consumption of farm produce by the farm family; relatively little may be destined for the market and then only for local outlets. Commercial farming, on the other hand, is totally market-orientated. Thirdly, tenure differences may be defined according to the legal relationship between the farmer and the land: owner-farmers, tenant farmers, share-croppers, etc. These three typologies inter-relate to produce a complex pattern of tenure types, the subtleties of which there is no space to examine here. However, some general trends are very clear, particularly for EC countries.

The most prominent feature of west European land tenure is the dominance of small owner-operated farms. The idea persists that peasant proprietorship lends backbone to the body politic; it is part of the 'man–family–business–community' ethic of rural society and reflects the social function of land as a source of work as well as of wealth. As a particularly labour-intensive form of enterprise, the peasant farm possesses a socially useful residual function that best manifests itself in times of unemployment and economic stagnation. Independence and hard work are two attributes epitomized in the peasant farmer who owns and controls his own assets. He also sets his own objectives: he can work for as long as he likes or for as little reward as he likes, for he is his own boss. Whether he can impose such behaviour on other members of the farm family is another issue, and undoubtedly gives rise to much intra-family conflict, particularly between father and son.

As an agricultural mode of production, family farming can also involve tenanted farms and rented land. There is wide variation in the importance of tenanted land in Western Europe and in the forms that tenancy can take. Within the EC the proportion of farmland that is tenanted varies from less than 4 per cent in the Republic of Ireland to 70 per cent in Belgium. Among other EC countries, France, the Netherlands, Luxembourg and the UK all have around 40–50 per cent of their land under rental. The tenancy situation is complicated, however, by the existence of mixed tenures (farms partly owned and partly rented) which are common in West Germany, France, Belgium, Austria and Spain. Farms under mixed tenure tend to be larger than average in those countries where they are important, which also tend to be the countries where tenancy is important, and smaller than average in countries such as Norway and Austria where tenancy is unimportant (Dovring 1965).

National attitudes towards tenancy vary enormously. Generally it is on the wane, not so much for economic reasons as for the exploitative disadvantages which are assumed to accompany landlordism. Events in agrarian history still wield considerable influence. The high Irish figure for owner-occupancy must be seen in the light of nineteenth-century Irish opposition to the British occupation and its attendant landlordism. Even though the benefits of tenancy are understood in Ireland today, the expansion of renting is politically unacceptable in a land where the words 'landlord' and 'tenant' are repugnant. The Danes look back with great pride on the emancipation of their copyholder peasantry in the eighteenth century; since that time, Danish agrarian thought has stressed that the farming community's best interests are served if agriculture is based on self-ownership. In southern Italy, landlord–tenant relationships, based on social class divisions of an almost feudal nature, left little doubt as to who was the beneficiary and who the oppressed: rents were extortionate and contracts insecure. Such conditions lasted well into the post-war period (King 1970). Now, however, rents are controlled and are of only nominal proportions. Tenancies are inheritable and tenants of four years' standing have pre-emption rights. Indeed, the Italian landlord–tenant system has virtually ceased to function, at least officially. Instead it is replaced by informal 'seasonal tenancies' and under-the-counter payments by landlords to outgoing tenants in order to get possession of the land.

On the other hand, in many north-west European countries tenanted farms are larger and more efficient than owner-occupied holdings. The efficiency of Dutch, Belgian and British agriculture has more than a little to do with the flexibility that a structure of rented farms permits. In France, tenancy predominates in the north which, by and large, also contains the richer agricultural land. Many of the rich farms of the Dutch polders are rented from the state. In Britain, conventional wisdom has it that the landlord–tenant arrangement has operated well, but it is really only in this country that an independent and strictly commercial landlord class exists which fulfils any management and capital-formation function (Harrison 1982).

Share-tenancy or *métayage*, where the 'rent' is paid in kind rather than cash, seems destined for imminent oblivion. Its main areas of importance are, or rather were, southern France and central Italy, although it is also to be found in parts of Iberia. In the classical Tuscan *mezzadria*, the crop was divided equally between the landlord and the share-tenant or *mezzadro* but, in practice, cases existed where the division was much more in favour of the landlord. Nevertheless, *mezzadria* holdings were larger than other peasant farms and security of tenure was assured for life and could even be inherited. The *mezzadro* not only had his land but also a farmhouse and most other capital equipment supplied by the landlord. Some economies of scale were available through the *fattoria*, the landlord's estate headquarters for his *mezzadria* tenancies. Encouraged by Mussolini, *mezzadria* expanded to embrace 22 per cent of Italian farmland by 1947, since when it has pitched into rapid decline, covering 12 per cent of land in 1961 and 3.4 per cent in 1977 (King and Took 1983)

More degraded forms of sharecropping are also fast disappearing. Typical is the south Italian *comparteci-pazione* contract, where tenants are paid in kind for little more than their labour on the landlord's land: security is limited to one year, there is no attempt to form a properly coherent holding and the entre-preneurial functions of the tenant are virtually zero. Such contracts have no part to play in modern agri-culture.

Farm labourers, unlike owners, tenants and share-croppers, have no formal tenure ties. The use of hired labour is the main distinction between capitalist and peasant farming, the former inevitably larger scale than the latter. In West Germany, for instance, 93 per cent of labour input on farms of 10–20 ha is supplied by the family, while on farms of over 50 ha, 82 per cent of the labour is hired, most of it on a full-time basis. In northern Italy the capitalist and peasant systems are sharply divided by topography. The break of slope that marks the edge of the Po Plain is also the agrarian division between two socio-economic systems: large capitalist farms run with wage labour in the plain; small peasant-owned or rented holdings in the hills and mountains (Fuller 1975).

When compared to family farms, capitalist farms nearly always have higher returns per unit of labour, better technical performance, greater specialization and more sophisticated market links. It is, therefore, rather strange to learn that hired workers are declining faster than the farming population as a whole. In six countries of the EC – the UK, the Republic of Ireland, the Netherlands, Denmark, West Germany and Luxembourg – the decline in hired workers during 1960–80 (50–80 per cent) was roughly twice as fast as for farmers (25–45 per cent). Clearly they have moved rapidly out of agriculture because of their lack of formal tenure status, low wages and the seasonality of much farm labour. Southern Italy's *braccianti* and Spain's *braceros* – unskilled labourers hired by the day – have all but vanished from the rural scene: they have been in the vanguard of the labour migrants streaming abroad. Fixed-wage workers, often skilled, are a more stable element of agriculture in certain regions, notably the UK, the Paris Basin, Languedoc and the North Italian Plain (Franklin 1971).

Distribution of land ownership

The wealth of data provided by the EC farm surveys reveal remarkable contrasts in the pattern of land ownership in different countries. Some of these data are summarized in the four middle columns of Table 9.2. In 1983, the average farm size in the Ten was 13.6 ha, but national averages ranged from 3.6 ha (Greece) to 64.5 ha (UK). Regional variation within national boundaries is also considerable for the larger countries of the EC. The average French farm size is 25.5 ha, yet most farms in the north-east are over 30 ha while most in Brittany, Aquitaine and the Midi are under 10 ha. In Italy, 78 per cent of farms are less than 5 ha and 90 per cent less than 10 ha. Such hold-ings are only viable economically if they are devoted to factory farming or market gardening. This is largely the case in the Netherlands and Belgium where farming is efficient and yet about half the holdings are below 20 ha, but not in Italy where most of the small farms are semi-subsistence peasant plots. Denmark and Ireland are notable for their predominance of medium-sized farms (Table 9.2). Spain and Portugal have polarized landholding regimes, with large farms accounting for most of the land and smallholdings accounting for most of the farm population. Farms are also mostly small in Western Europe's other major non-EC countries: Austria, Switzerland, Norway, Sweden and Finland. To take the Finnish example, in 1979, farms in the 2–10 ha class covered 59 per cent of all arable land, those over 25 ha only 9 per cent. The average Finnish farm has 11 ha of cropland and 35 ha of forest. The entire country contains only 367 farms with more than 100 ha of cropland (Cabouret 1982).

Of the three countries with highly polarized land-holding structures, two have had significant land reforms in the post-war period – Italy in 1950 and Portugal in 1974. Pressures for land redistribution in Spain have been resisted; here, structural policy concentrates instead on the consolidation of frag-mented holdings, discussed in the next section.

The Portuguese land reform was one of the more significant products of the 1974 revolution. Regionally, it was concentrated in the Alentejo, a rolling land-scape of unirrigated wheat, sheep and cork estates worked by under-paid landless labourers with a long tradition of political radicalism. Here, communist-inspired land seizures anticipated the land reform law of mid-1975. Latifundian capitalism was defined as the main target for expropriation and more than 1 million hectares were taken over in a matter of months. New 'collective production units' united the various seized estates within the framework of local administrative boundaries, substantially concentrating the land and the labour force. The collectives were given names like 'Che Guevara' and 'In Lenin's Footsteps'. The fact that the reform increased the size of the operating unit, and did not split the estates into smallholdings, is related partly to political ideology but also reflects a belief in the economic superiority of large-scale farming, at least under the Alentejo's prevailing agrarian regime. It is also suggested that the rural labourers, lacking a tradition of peasant landownership, did not want to become titleholders of their own small plots (Cabral 1978), but this view has been criticized (Routledge 1977).

When the communists lost their position of strength in the Portuguese government after November 1975, the impetus of the land reform weakened and went into reverse. Some usurped land was given back to landlords, a process often accompanied by violence in the countryside (King 1978). Support to the collectives was diluted and shifted instead to the peasant and capitalist sectors.

Portuguese land reform was, therefore, politically significant but its economic impact has been relatively modest. The 1 million hectares held by the new production units represent 33 per cent of the cultivated area in the reform region of Alentejo and 14 per cent of the national farmed area. Some 59 000 rural workers participate in the collectives; this is 35 per cent of the regional and 7 per cent of the national active rural population. Economic performance is difficult to monitor because of the withdrawal of government support. Agriculturally, the main change has been the development of livestock production. Outside the strictly economic sphere there is no doubt that Alentejo's rural workers now enjoy more employment, much better social welfare and, indeed, a complete transformation in the social relations of production (De Barros 1980).

Much less need be said of the Italian land reform which, more than thirty years after the event, appears as a dated and expensive irrelevance in the overall strategy of Italian agricultural development. Operating mainly in the latifundian areas of the Mezzogiorno, it moved in the opposite direction to the Portuguese reform, splitting up some 680 000 ha of large estates into 113 000 small peasant plots of around 2–10 ha. A large proportion of these plots were too small to support a family and were subsequently abandoned or used merely as part-time bases in the countryside. Only in certain rich irrigated areas such as the Sele Plain south of Naples and the Metaponto Plain stretching west and south of Taranto have the reform

holdings emerged as viable units (King 1973).

Many countries have measures aimed at farm enlargement and amalgamation. Legislation in France, West Germany, the Netherlands, Norway and Sweden encourages the use of land falling vacant for the enlargement of adjacent holdings. But the results of this kind of natural change are slow: it takes a decade to raise the EC's mean farm size by just 1 hectare.

The French policies for farm enlargement are well known. In 1960, twenty-nine SAFERs (*Sociétés d'Aménagement Foncier et d'Établissement Rural*) were set up; their objective was to buy land offered on the open market and use it to enlarge other farms that were too small. SAFERs can also acquire abandoned land, improve it and use it for the same end. SAFER policy has had most impact in the south of France, especially in Aquitaine and the Massif Central; in the north-east and in Brittany, high land prices have limited the scope for action (Perry 1969). The main problem SAFERs face is deciding which farms should receive land: should it go to large or to small farms? Considerable variation has occurred in the way SAFERs operate: they have, in places, been accused of nepotism (allocating land to acquaintances of board members) and of helping uneconomically small farms to persist (Hirsch and Maunder 1978). Further incentives for farm enlargement were introduced in 1962 with the creation of FASASA (*Fonds D'Action Sociale pour l'Aménagement des Structures Agraires*) – a fund to provide farmers retiring at sixty with an annuity if they vacated their land for enlargement schemes. As with the SAFERs, lack of funds has restricted the scale of the policy. Only modest increases in farm size have resulted from these policies.

The British experience has seen most vacated land bought up by the larger farms; farm amalgamation among smallholdings has been rare (Clark 1979). Where the land market is tight, farms may only be able to increase their size by piecemeal addition of blocks located at some distance from the holding, thereby increasing fragmentation. Renting additional farmland is not a policy actively encouraged anywhere in Western Europe; indeed, in Denmark, institutional landlords are forbidden. Denmark has also consistently legislated to limit the extent of landholdings. In 1978 the maximum limit on Danish farms was reduced from 100 to 75 ha, and residence by owner-farmers on their properties has been obligatory since 1973.

Fragmentation and consolidation

Land fragmentation refers to the internal spatial structure of the farm; it is the condition whereby a holding is split into many small non-contiguous plots. In France, for example, fragmentation is a legacy of the Napoleonic code of equal land inheritance; with each passing generation, land is divided up among all direct heirs. Large family sizes, common in many parts of rural Europe until recently, thus provoked rapid fragmentation. The phenomenon is also compounded by the frequent insistence of each heir on a share of each part of the patrimony: a holding of four plots divided among four heirs thus yields sixteen fragments.

The disadvantages of fragmentation are largely economic. Time is wasted by the farmer in travelling to his scattered plots and in moving his implements, animals and machinery back and forth; expenses on fencing, water supplies and buildings are greater. Some of these economic costs have an ecological basis, such as problems of soil conservation, drainage and irrigation. Other disadvantages arise in the social and administrative fields of rural life. Land planning becomes very difficult, for fragmentation increases the number of people involved in making a decision about a particular area. Cadastral authorities have difficulty in monitoring precise patterns of ownership, particularly where plots become fractioned into pocket-handkerchief size or where, as sometimes happens in Mediterranean areas, trees are owned separately from the land. Social tension is caused by disputes over ownership, access and damage. Some of these problems are well documented in Greece where property division is often marked by acrimony and even violence (Herzfeld 1980; Thompson 1963).

Fragmentation can, however, have a rational basis, as the work of ecological anthropologists in Alpine and Mediterranean regions shows. In these areas, microvariations in altitude, aspect, soil, precipitation, temperature and wind provide an ecological setting in which scattered farms are the logical outcome. Especially where farming is subsistence-oriented polyculture, the multiplicity of ecological niches provides ideal conditions for a range of crops and, moreover, spreads the risks of destruction by frost, hail or wind. In the Alps the key to farming success is the seasonal oscillation of man and beast which unites mountain pastures and forests with the valley-floor meadows (Netting 1981). Galt's (1979) study of viticulture on the Italian island of Pantellaria shows how fragmentation can be rational even in a monocultural setting. Here, possession of plots in different parts of the island causes variations in the grape crop in terms of sugar content and harvest time; grape-picking labour can thus be staggered and the risk of complete failure is minimized.

These exceptions apart, there is no doubt that frag-

mentation is a serious and widespread problem in European farming. Levels of fragmentation were, and still are, particularly high in southern European regions like Galicia, northern Portugal and Crete. In Denmark and Sweden, on the other hand, hardly any serious fragmentation exists, for these countries had their farms consolidated in the eighteenth and nineteenth centuries.

The progress of land consolidation in west European countries since the last war has been highly variable (Jacoby 1959; Lambert 1963). In Portugal, Italy and Greece almost nothing has been done. France has pioneered *remembrement*, parcel exchange, since a law of 1941 when 15 million hectares were estimated to need consolidation. Forty years later, half this target has been achieved. Most progress has been in the north and east where fragmentation was acute and yet prospects for the mechanization and improvement of agriculture good (Clout 1968). In the south and in the mountains, costs are greater, benefits probably less and peasant antipathy stronger. In these areas the future must be envisaged in terms of farm enlargement, livestock rearing, afforestation and recreation (Clout 1974b).

In contrast to the voluntaristic nature of French *remembrement*, land consolidation in West Germany, Switzerland and the Netherlands is more highly organized and integrated with regional and settlement planning. Resettlement of farm families is an expensive process, requiring new farmhouses, roads and other rural services, but is necessary to decentralize farmers from overcrowded villages to their newly consolidated holdings. In the Netherlands, important consolidation and resettlement schemes have transformed the landscape of the Rhine and Meuse valleys. The German policy of *Flurbereinigung* has also seen a shift from simple plot amalgamation to settlement relocation. Following laws in 1937 and 1953, rapid extension of consolidation took place, especially in Bavaria and Swabia where fragmentation was most severe (Mayhew 1970). However, much of this early work is now considered obsolete and must be re-done. A new Farm Consolidation Act was passed in 1976; now, consolidation embraces other aspects of rural planning such as recreation and environmental preservation. By 1980, about a third of the target still remained to be achieved. At the current rate of progress this should be attained by the end of the century – by which time the technical side of farming may have changed so much as to demand further reorganization programmes!

The country where land consolidation has made most progress in recent years is Spain. In the early post-war years much Spanish farmland was impossibly fragmented, especially in the northern half of the country. In the village of Santa Maria de Ordax in Leon province each farmer had 6–7 ha divided into 80–120 tracts dispersed over a radius of 5 km. Spain's First Agricultural Census of 1963 showed that the average number of plots per holding was 13.7. Fragmentation was particularly acute in Galicia where the average number of plots per farm was 32. It was less severe in Catalonia and the Basque provinces which have a tradition of *mayorazgo*, passing land to the eldest son, and in the south where large estates predominated. In 1957 the Spanish Secretary of State for Agriculture estimated that 8 million ha of farmland needed consolidation.

Spain's programme of land consolidation started in 1952 with the creation of the *Servicio de Concentración Parcelaria*. The programme has three main aims. Firstly, it tries to assign to each farmer a single plot equal in area and quality to the several parcels previously possessed. Second, the new holding should be sited within easy reach of the farmer's dwelling (where necessary, new country roads are built to facilitate access). Third, the titles of the new holdings are confirmed in the property register. Progress was slow throughout the 1950s (less than 50 000 ha consolidated per year), peaked in the late 1960s and early 1970s (350 000–400 000 ha annually), and then fell back in the late 1970s to around 200 000 ha per year (Guedes 1981). Most progress has been made in the central and northern provinces of Spain, Galicia and Catalonia excepted. After consolidation it is possible to practise such techniques as contour ploughing, soil improvement and irrigation; mechanization is more feasible on larger, more compact plots. Productive effects do, however, depend on the type of agriculture. In dry zones, output only increases marginally. In irrigated areas, where consolidation has the additional pay-off of facilitating better use of irrigation water, increases of the order of 70 per cent have been reported. Consolidation also encourages the replacement of peasant individualism by an appreciation of the value of collective action, and groups of consolidated smallholdings are now being farmed cooperatively. There are, however, some problems. One is the lack of legislation to prevent continuing subdivision. Another is the small size of most consolidated farms: at 5 ha on average, most are still *minifundios*. In Galicia, a difficult area, the policy is fuzzily conceived in relation to the local agrarian structures; it proceeds only slowly and on an *ad hoc* basis (O'Flanagan 1982).

While initially the cost of Spanish consolidation was low compared to French, West German and Swiss schemes, costs escalated after 1972 to roughly four times their level in the 1960s. Nevertheless, the overall statistics of the policy are illuminating and encouraging. By 1978, 5 million ha of Spanish farmland had been consolidated, leaving 3 million ha still to be treated. Nearly 1 million proprietors had been affected, their total number of parcels being reduced from 13 688 688 to 1 790 971. Mean plot size rose from 0.35 ha to 2.52 ha and the average number of plots per holding for those affected was cut from 14.6 to 1.9 (Guedes 1981).

Land use and production

From the human and social side of agriculture we pass to the economic. Statistically, rural land use has been well documented in most west European nations since the introductory work of Stamp (1965). The tradition of detailed land-use mapping has become firmly established in many countries although none can match the clarity and beauty of the British Land Use Survey sheets published at 1 : 25 000.

It is, therefore, rather strange that almost no attempt has been made at an overall treatment of Western Europe's agricultural geography. Van Valkenburg's work constitutes a partial exception but his analysis is based on a simple distinction between high and low 'standards of land use' (Van Valkenburg 1959, 1960). In the absence of a truly integrative study, this section proceeds on two bases: a broad and brief description of Western Europe's land-use structure; and a nation-based tabulation of FAO area and production data for the mid-1980s.

Climate largely dictates the latitudinal range of agricultural types. Given the importance of cereals in Europe's mid-latitude farming regimes, a series of east–west grain belts can be recognized (Fig. 9.1a). This east–west pattern is rotated along the north-west margins by the equitable influence of the North Atlantic Drift. At the meso-scale, topography interrupts this pattern, preventing crop growth in northern Europe in the Scottish and Scandinavian mountains, and introducing cooler climates in the uplands of southern Europe, notably the Spanish Meseta, the Pyrenees, the Massif Central, the Alps, the Apennines and the Pindus Mountains. Even more localized farming types result from micro-scale variations in soil and aspect. For instance, the vine, a typically Mediterranean crop, is found in scattered locations much further north, from the valley of the Loire to Koblenz on the Rhine: here, warm soils, sunny slopes and sheltered gorges enable it to flourish well outside its natural geographic habitat. In Brittany, the mildness of the Atlantic winters and the early spring allow the cultivation of early vegetables along certain valleys and sheltered coasts. Transport may also play a role:

Fig. 9.1

Agricultural features of Western Europe: (a) main crop belts; (b) patterns of yield intensity (after Van Valkenburg and Held 1952).

the cultivation of *primeurs* around Avignon is related not only to the environmental conditions of the southern Rhône valley but also to the development of fast access routes to Paris (Minshull 1978).

The influence of urban markets is more fully evident in Fig. 9.1b which, in spite of some uncertainty over the validity of the figures, can be interpreted as a macro-Thünian portrayal of Western Europe's cropping intensity, based on spatial variations in the yields of eight major European crops. A zone of high production centres on the North European Plain, the Rhine delta and south-east England. In this zone are to be found most of Western Europe's main centres of urban population. Away from this core of high intensity, yields diminish in all directions. Again, climatic factors are prominent: exposure to the west, frost to the north, continentality to the east, drought to the south. Topography too plays a role, for the core is girt by hill and mountain areas where yields are inevitably lower. Particularly to the south, differences in the technical standards and intellectual abilities of farmers are important, for it is in Iberia, southern Italy and Greece where most of the really backward areas of European agriculture are found. Of course, there *are* areas of high-intensity production in these

southern countries – such as the Po Plain (which can be regarded as a southern outlier of the North European Plain), the citrus orchards of Valencia and Sicily, and the specialized vineyards of the Douro Valley (producing port) and Jerez de la Frontiera (producing sherry) – but these are spatially less continuous than the zone of high-intensity production to the north.

Tables 9.3, 9.4 and 9.5 set out national statistics on land use, livestock and agricultural production. It should straightaway be emphasized that comparison between countries can be hazardous because the definitions of categories of land use vary. Particular problems arise over little-used agricultural land like mountain pastures and communal land. The area figures are, therefore, indicative rather than intrinsically accurate.

Climate, topography and soils are the main factors determining the national proportions of land under farming. Population density has also played a role, especially in the past. In the UK, 77.2 per cent of land is in agricultural use, despite extensive urbanization and the fact that only 2.3 per cent of the working population earn their living from farming. High proportions of land devoted to farming are also to be found in the Republic of Ireland (84.7 per cent),

Table 9.3 Main features of land use, 1984

	Total land area ('000 ha)	Arable and cropland ('000 ha)	% land	Permanent pasture ('000 ha)	% land	Forest and woodland ('000 ha)	% land
Austria	8 273	1 523	18.4	1 986	24.0	3 221	38.9
Belgium/Lux.	3 282	824	25.1	665	20.3	702	21.4
Denmark	4 237	2 627	62.0	228	5.4	493	11.6
Finland	30 547	2 335	7.6	130	0.4	23 320	76.3
France	54 563	18 812	34.5	12 385	22.7	14 603	26.8
West Germany	24 428	7 437	30.4	4 607	18.9	7 328	30.0
Greece	13 080	3 974	30.4	5 255	40.2	2 620	20.0
Rep. of Ireland	6 889	972	14.1	4 885	70.9	340	4.9
Italy	29 402	12 233	41.6	4 930	16.8	6 410	21.8
Netherlands	3 394	875	25.8	1 141	33.6	297	8.8
Norway	30 786	855	2.8	90	0.3	8 330	27.1
Portugal	9 164	3 545	38.7	530	5.8	3 641	39.7
Spain	49 940	20 540	41.1	10 640	21.3	15 625	31.3
Sweden	41 162	2 995	7.3	620	1.5	26 424	64.2
Switzerland	3 977	412	10.4	1 609	40.5	1 052	26.5
United Kingdom	24 159	6 991	28.9	11 650	48.2	2 258	9.3

Source: FAO Production Yearbook 1985. Rome, 1986

Greece (70.6 per cent) and Denmark (67.4 per cent). The harsher physical conditions in northern Europe mean that countries here have only small proportions of their land devoted to farming: Norway 3 per cent, Finland 8 per cent and Sweden 9 per cent. Forest becomes the dominant land use instead, covering more than three-quarters of the surface of Finland. In Switzerland and Austria the extent of cultivated land is also limited. In Alpine Europe and in the Republic of Ireland, permanent pasture dominates over arable. In Mediterranean countries a significant proportion of cropland is contributed by permanent crops like vines and orchards of olives and citrus fruits: this proportion is 25.4 per cent in Greece, 23.9 per cent in Italy, 24.2 per cent in Spain and 16.5 per cent in Portugal. It is also in the Mediterranean that irrigation becomes such a vital component of farming. Greece has 24 per cent of cropland irrigated, Italy 24 per cent, Portugal 18 per cent and Spain 15 per cent. Interestingly 26 per cent of Dutch farmland is irrigated – a reflection of the intensity of agriculture in the Netherlands. Elsewhere, figures are much lower: France 6 per cent, West Germany 4 per cent, the UK 2 per cent (all figures are for 1984).

A comparison of agricultural production indices for the triennium 1979/81 (1969/71 = 100) shows how Western Europe's farmers are increasing their yields. Most countries recorded indices within the range 110–22. The biggest increases were recorded by Spain

(136), Greece (132), the Republic of Ireland (132) and the Netherlands (132): a strange mixture for they comprise three of the poorest and one of the richest countries in Western Europe. The case of the Netherlands is exceptional, and yet instructive, for it illustrates the capacity of Europe's most intensive farming nation to go on achieving high productivity gains. The relevance of the irrigation figure just noted, and of the country's very high cereal yields (see column 3 in Table 9.4), should also be borne in mind. Also exceptional is Portugal – the only country to record a decline in agricultural production, with an index of 82. Governmental instability and recent changes in farm structure partly explain this slump.

Table 9.4 gives a breakdown of the main crops grown in the countries of Western Europe. Cereals dominate in terms of area, but fruit and vegetable harvests are quantitatively heavier in some countries – the Netherlands and the familiar group of Mediterranean nations. France and West Germany produce between them 45 per cent of Western Europe's cereals, with France producing twice as much as West Germany. There are considerable differences in the type of cereals grown: in Denmark, 68.4 per cent of cereal land is barley for livestock feed; wheat is important in all countries except Scandinavia and the Republic of Ireland; Norway, Sweden and Finland have around a third of their cereal land under oats; maize is the most widely-grown cereal in Portugal.

Table 9.4 Main crops, 1985

	All cereals			Of which (% area)							Pulses	Fruits	Vegetables
	'000 ha	'000 metric tons	kg/ha	Wheat	Barley	Maize	Oats	Rye	Sugar beet ('000 ha)		Pulses ('000 ha)	Fruits ('000 m.t.)	Vegetables ('000 m.t.)
Austria	1 054	5 553	5 267	30.4	31.7	19.7	7.1	8.3	43		—	755	463
Belgium/Lux.	379	2 195	5 793	50.9	34.6	3.4	7.7	1.6	120		2	370	1 172
Denmark	1 615	7 979	4 941	21.3	68.4	—	2.3	7.8	73		105	88	260
Finland	1 260	3 656	2 902	12.5	51.3	—	32.6	2.5	31		4	113	169
France	9 707	55 325	5 690	49.8	23.2	19.1	4.4	0.9	490		244	13 788	7 391
West Germany	4 888	25 925	5 304	33.2	39.9	3.7	11.9	8.7	403		23	3 517	2 198
Greece	1 482	4 431	2 990	60.6	20.9	13.7	2.9	0.6	43		54	3 885	4 429
Rep. of Ireland	390	1 891	4 846	20.5	73.6	—	5.9	—	34		—	21	289
Italy	4 810	18 049	3 753	63.0	9.7	18.9	3.8	0.2	233		205	18 749	14 677
Netherlands	183	1 130	6 516	69.9	21.3	—	6.0	2.7	131		25	444	2 820
Norway	342	1 274	3 726	11.4	50.0	—	37.7	0.3	—		—	134	217
Portugal	1 124	1 445	1 285	27.6	8.0	32.0	14.7	14.5	3		298	1 585	1 896
Spain	7 485	20 917	2 795	27.0	55.5	6.9	6.2	3.0	178		444	12 117	9 104
Sweden	1 520	5 773	3 799	18.2	44.1	—	31.1	3.0	52		46	185	295
Switzerland	184	1 053	5 734	53.3	27.7	10.3	5.4	2.7	15		—	739	340
United Kingdom	4 022	22 144	5 506	47.3	49.0	—	3.4	0.1	200		90	510	3 920

Source: FAO Production Yearbook 1985. Rome, 1986

Cereal yields also reveal an interesting hierarchy. The Netherlands leads by a considerable margin, with a mean yield over twice that of Spain and five times that of Portugal. Spain is the leading producer of pulses, while Italy heads both fruit and vegetable output. Vines, an intensive and remunerative crop, cover large areas in Spain (1 670 000 ha), Italy (1 100 000 ha) and France (1 080 000 ha), and are also significant in Portugal, Greece, West Germany, Austria and Switzerland. France and Italy are the main producers of wine (6 859 000 and 6 550 000 metric tonnes respectively in 1985), followed by Spain (3 331 000 metric tonnes). Regarding livestock (Table 9.5), France has most cattle, West Germany most pigs, the UK most sheep and Greece most goats. Livestock distribution, like that of many crops, is often highly regionalized within countries. In Italy, for example, most cattle are in the North Italian Plain and most sheep in Sardinia, Lazio and Abruzzo.

Nearly all Western European countries are experiencing substantial losses from the agricultural area, while woodland and urban areas show a persistent increase. Most of the agricultural loss is from cropland, although in the UK the decline is mainly in pasture (Best 1979, 1981). Yet the downward trend in farmed area is not paralleled by declining output. The spectre of insufficient food supplies by the end of the century is a figment of the imagination. Indeed, the opposite circumstance applies, and is a major dilemma of EC agricultural policy.

The Common Agricultural Policy (CAP)

In spite of trenchant criticism, the Common Agricultural Policy has undoubtedly acted as a potent force in the creation of the Common Market. Absorbing three-quarters of the Community budget over the years (but generally two-thirds during the 1980s), the CAP represents something of a success story when compared to relative non-achievement in the regional and industrial policy fields. Before the 1960s, each member state operated its own farm policy to ensure an adequate national food supply, the siege mentality of war and scarcity lingering on (Clout 1981b). Cost considerations took second place to an emphasis placed firmly on production. Trade policies reflected this fixation. Differing prices and support levels ensured protection against imports for each country; there was no way of getting farm produce to flow freely between members of the Six. A Community policy for prices, production levels and marketing was thought essential. Agriculture needed to be strengthened: in 1958, it employed more than a fifth of the Six's working population but it accounted for only 8 per cent of the EC's gross product.

Several stages in the rather slow evolution of the

Table 9.5 Livestock numbers, 1985 ('000 head)

	Cattle	Pigs	Sheep	Goats
Austria	2 669	4 027	220	30
Belgium/Lux.	3 210	5 339	105	6
Denmark	2 704	8 960	52	—
Finland	1 608	1 256	110	2
France	23 099	10 975	10 824	962
West Germany	15 688	23 617	1 300	36
Greece	757	1 115	7 900	4 660
Rep. of Ireland	5 835	1 020	2 690	9
Italy	9 106	9 041	9 500	1 089
Netherlands	5 248	12 383	814	34
Norway	976	693	2 415	97
Portugal	1 110	3 477	5 050	746
Spain	5 004	11 390	17 485	2 619
Sweden	1 837	2 589	426	—
Switzerland	1 926	1 988	361	80
United Kingdom	12 985	7 793	23 946	6

Source: FAO Production Yearbook 1985. Rome, 1986

CAP can be recognized (Bowler 1985). The first stage was the evolution of the principles of a farm policy as they were enshrined in the 1957 Treaty of Rome, specifically Articles 38 to 47. The key article was 39.1, which laid down the following objectives of the CAP: to increase agricultural productivity by promoting technical progress and the optimum deployment of labour; to ensure a fair standard of living for members of the agricultural community; to stabilize markets, assure the availability of supplies and ensure that supplies reach consumers at reasonable prices. Article 39.2 stipulated that, in the working out of the CAP, account was to be taken of the social structures of agriculture and of the disparities between farming regions. In Article 40 the scope of the proposed common legislation was spelled out: it was to include regulation of prices, aids for the production, marketing and storage of various products and common machinery for stabilizing imports and exports. It also provided for the establishment of common funds to finance the policy – what came to be known as the Agricultural Guidance and Guarantee Fund, or FEOGA.

The second stage started with harmonization of national marketing systems in the early 1960s and of product prices in the late 1960s. Initially, the marketing arrangements were harmonized for cereals, pigmeat and eggs in 1962; other products followed. The basic principles of policy were the establishment of a single market area, free international movement of produce within the Six, uniform external tariffs, community preference in agricultural trade and the sharing of the CAP's financial burden. Product price harmonization started with common cereal prices in 1967: their dual role as a human staple and livestock feed made cereals a key sector. In 1968, common prices were set for milk, milk products, beef, rice, sugar and olive oil; in 1970 for tobacco and wine. The support prices contained a bewildering variety of types – there were intervention, base, exclusion, indicative, minimum, reference, withdrawal and threshold prices – but all amounted to assuring farmers a guaranteed minimum income.

It soon became obvious that a product-based policy did not fit the realities of the EC's agricultural geography. Price levels and price differentials between products were not of an order to avoid surplus output and reorientate production in desired directions. There was no mechanism for relating overall supply to overall demand. Surpluses were drawn forth in cereals, milk and sugar.

The problem lay in the duality of the EC's agricultural systems between small-scale peasant farming and the commercial sector based on large holdings. Prices set in order to guarantee a reasonable income to the former were so favourable that they encouraged large production increases in the latter. It was discovered that pricing policy could not simultaneously meet farm income and farm production objectives: the 'guarantee' section of FEOGA was sabotaging the 'guidance' element. The cost of supporting the production of agricultural surpluses through intervention buying became the main stimulus to a realignment of the CAP in the late 1960s.

This ushered in the third phase, which separated price policies, which were to orientate production in the commercial sector, from a new set of structural measures designed to deal with the problems of the small-farm sector. This dual approach, initially set out in the Mansholt Plan of 1968, recognized that a successful agricultural policy could not treat all farmers equally.

The Mansholt Plan and after

This was the work of Sicco Mansholt, former Dutch Agriculture Minister and Vice-President of the EEC Commission on Agriculture. Mansholt's diagnosis of the ills of European farming could be summed up as too many farms, too many people working in farming and too much agricultural land. He proposed a three-pronged attack to rescue farming from its crisis of overproduction and structural dualism. Firstly, he wanted to see the EC's farm population down to 5 million by 1980 (it was 20 million in 1950). Second, small peasant holdings were to be replaced by larger agricultural enterprises practising modern techniques. Mansholt laid down that a suitable farm for the 1980s might comprise 80–100 ha of cereals or raise 40–80 dairy cows, 150–200 head of beef cattle, 450–600 pigs, or 100 000 head of poultry per year. These were ambitious targets given that, at the time of Mansholt's memorandum, two-thirds of the EC's farms were less than 10 ha and two-thirds of dairy farmers had less than five cows! Third, he prescribed a 7 per cent reduction in the farmed area, so that by 1980 the cultivated surface of the Six should be down to about 70 million ha. Land taken out of agriculture was to be used for recreation and afforestation. The areas affected by this geographical shrinkage of farming were not spelled out but clearly would include regions of limited potential such as the Massif Central, Provence, Corsica, Sardinia, Sicily and southern Italy.

Mansholt's memorandum engendered considerable hostility. His use of terms like 'business-oriented production units' sent shivers of apprehension through elderly farmers and farming associations devoted to the ideal of the family farm: they feared that this was a prelude to some kind of collectivization. A revised and moderated report was presented in 1970, but the basic strategy was unchanged. Mansholt's shock treatment was certainly effective in promoting discussion based on a new realization of the predicament of the Common Market's farm sector.

In 1972 the Community approved three measures which moved in the direction indicated by Mansholt, shifting the thrust of the CAP more towards structural change. These measures provided investment aids for approved farm modernization plans (Directive 72/159), gave lumps sums or annuities to retiring farmers (72/160) and promoted 'socio-economic guidance and training' for those leaving agriculture (72/161).

At about the same time, however, the CAP was unhinged by new developments reflecting the uneven development of member states. Between 1969 and 1973 most Community countries either floated, revalued or devalued their currencies in a succession of changing parities which wrought havoc with the concept of common agricultural prices. As a result, common prices became a fiction between uncommon partners. Further ructions were caused by the first round of EC enlargement in 1973.

From 1975 the CAP became geographically more sensitive. Directive 75/268 provided income aids or 'compensatory allowances' – based usually on the number of livestock units per farm – to farmers in mountain, hill and other less-favoured areas. This honoured the commitment obtained by the UK during its entry negotiations, but was of benefit to other countries too, especially to the Republic of Ireland,

France and Italy. Three main types of 'problem area' have been identified (Fig. 9.2). Firstly, there are mountain and hill areas with permanent handicaps to farming caused by altitude, slope or poor soils (Pyrenees, Auvergne, Alps, Apennines, Corsica). Areas with low population densities and severe depopulation are a second type; these include upland areas in Scotland, the Republic of Ireland, Wales, Belgium, southern Germany and Sardinia. Third, there are more restricted areas with special handicaps such as poor drainage, lack of infrastructure, the need for environmental conservation or the need to preserve a tourist potential. The 'less-favoured regions' policy does not necessarily cover all areas with low farm incomes but it does mark a very important change in the CAP. It recognizes that farmers in the areas concerned are unable to produce on competitive terms and enables discriminating assistance to be given.

Under the original 1975 classification, 31 per cent of the utilized agricultural area of the Community was listed as 'less-favoured'. In 1986 a new classification was introduced, raising the proportion to 48 per cent. This extension was partly linked to enlargement: Greece, for instance, has 78 per cent of its agricultural area designated as 'less-favoured', higher than any other Community country except Luxembourg. But partly it was also due to extension of the less-favoured surface in countries like Ireland and the UK.

In Greece, Italy, Ireland and France, the less-favoured areas generally correspond to regions where farming accounts for a large percentage of GDP. In these areas the per capita GDP and the productivity per person engaged in agriculture are relatively low, but since farming represents a significant slice of the economy in depressed regions, it is still an important factor. In the less-favoured areas of West Germany, Belgium and the UK, the problem is different. Here farming accounts for only a small proportion (2–4 per cent) of the gross regional product but the farming population is fairly numerous and their productivity is usually low (except in the UK); the decline of agriculture would have deleterious consequences for the rural social fabric and for employment, although the impact on the regional economy would be less serious.

Another significant new development, which has also furthered the spatial sensitivity of the CAP, was the 'Mediterranean package' introduced from 1978 onwards. This was intended to support specific types of improvement corresponding to the needs of Mediterranean farmers. Within the EC Nine, the Mediterranean region embraced most of Italy together with southern France. It contained 17 per cent of EC farmland, 18 per cent of farm production and 30 per cent

Mountain and hill areas

Less favoured areas in danger of depopulation

Areas affected by specific handicaps

0   km   500

Fig. 9.2
Less-favoured areas in the European Community, according to Directive 75/268.

of farmers: figures which in themselves are a summary testimony of the region's low labour productivity. Measures adopted by 1981 included irrigation in the Mezzogiorno and Corsica, the development of a farm advisory service in Italy, reafforestation and the improvement of rural infrastructures in upland areas of Italy and southern France, and support for cooperative ventures in Italy. Such schemes qualified for 25 and occasionally 50 per cent contributions from FEOGA.

A new agricultural structures policy

By the end of 1983, the time when the 1972 structural measures expired, it was necessary to take stock of the overall situation in an entirely new light. The 1970s policy measures had been conceived against the background of pre-1972 economic buoyancy when the climate for investment in agriculture was generally good and there were ample employment opportunities for those who opted to leave farming. By the early 1980s these circumstances had changed. The economic environment was characterized by low or zero growth rates and massive unemployment. The rise in agricultural incomes had slowed, while regional disparities had widened.

The diminishing impact of Directive 72/159 can be gauged from the numbers of farmers undertaking modernization by means of approved farm development plans, which peaked at 30 000 in 1978 but then fell to 15 000 in 1982. The retirement measure (Directive 72/160) had made only a limited impact on agricultural structure. Up to 1982 only 1.2 million ha, just over 1 per cent of the Community's total utilized agricultural area, had been released by retiring farmers. Furthermore, the potential structural benefits of this freed land were not realized, for it tended to become fragmented rather than consolidated and only 15 per cent of it went to farmers modernizing under Directive 72/159. Directive 72/161, for retraining, was even less successful.

The new structural policy comprises two main parts.

First, an earlier regulation (355/77) on processing and marketing structures in agriculture has been revised to encourage the use of new technology, the processing of new products and the exploitation of new market outlets. The ultimate objective of this measure, passed in 1984, is to enhance the value-added in agricultural production and to enable farmers to share in the resultant benefits. Second, a fresh package of 'efficiency' measures, designed to replace the 1972 directives, was approved in 1985. As regards on-farm investment aids, the new policy extends assistance to a wider range of farmers than before, particularly those in the lower income bracket. The conditions for qualifying for aid have been simplified and the objectives changed: the emphasis now is on reducing production costs, improving product quality and reconverting production in line with market requirements.

Inequities, lakes and mountains: some criticisms of the CAP

A cynic would maintain that the CAP is the very negation of what its name means. It is not Common because it is a source of endless bickering between member countries; it is not Agricultural because it is basically a prices and income strategy; and it is not a Policy because it reflects a miasma of interest groups, the most important of which is probably the political power of French farmers. Stuart Holland (1980) is equally direct when he argues that the CAP, which he calls the EC's 'agricultural albatross', is both economically inefficient and socially unjust. He maintains that its support prices are too high, its consumer prices are excessive, it functions as a disincentive to structural reform in agriculture and its subsidies, through price support, do not adequately distinguish relatively rich from relatively impoverished farmers.

Inequity appears to have been built in to the CAP from the start. One of the main reasons commonly given for the original Six developing the CAP was that this was a requirement by France as a *quid pro quo* for West German manufacturers' access to the French market. Thus the fact that the CAP benefits some states a lot more than others was accepted at the outset. Since it involves a transfer of income to agriculture from the rest of the economy it is clear that this will involve net transfers of income between states, mainly from food-importing nations like West Germany, the UK and Italy to food exporters such as the Republic of Ireland and Denmark.

So far so good. But then two clear *social* injustices appear. First, it is the lower-income groups which suffer relatively more through food price increases

than do the better off, because a much higher proportion of expenditure by the former goes on food. So, if food prices rise, this has the effect of making the distribution of income less equal (unless low-income families happen to be farmers, but most are the urban poor). Second, there is inequity within the agricultural sector. There is a positive correlation between public subsidies and value-added per head of the farming population. In other words, the CAP spends more money supporting the more productive and better-off farmers than it does on the poorer ones. The latter, handicapped by harsh environments, exploitative tenures and antiquated farming techniques, get a subsistence living; the former make large profits. This is a regressive policy by any criterion of social justice (Ritson 1982; Tsoukalis 1981).

The CAP's poor defence of consumer interests is understandable to the extent that the individual farmer has a much bigger stake in it than the individual consumer: a 10 per cent rise in CAP prices is likely to yield an increase in farm incomes of around 20–30 per cent and yet decrease consumers' real income by no more than 1 per cent. Consumers' arguments have in fact latched on to the paradox of food surpluses and high prices rather than the general price-raising impact of the CAP *per se*.

Surpluses have undoubtedly become the most publicized and most criticized aspect of the CAP. At worst, they are a moral outrage in a hungry world; at best, they are a clumsy method of guaranteeing farm incomes at the expense of the consumer. More than 60 per cent of the CAP's budget is used to dispose of farm surpluses. FEOGA expenditure in support of dairying rose steadily during the 1970s, eventually amounting to half of total support for farm produce; yet milk comprises less than 20 per cent of total EC agricultural output.

Some foods which are perishable have to be destroyed, chiefly fruits and vegetables; others, such as sugar, can be stored or converted to other uses. Cereals grown for human consumption can be diverted to animal feed. Some surplus wine has been converted to industrial alcohol. Export subsidies enable sale on world markets. Part of the butter mountain – estimated at one time to be equal in weight to the entire population of Austria – has been sold to the USSR at a fraction of its real production cost. New surpluses may come with enlargement. Already Greece has started a currant 'hill'. Greater problems lie in store with Spanish olive oil: the EC Twelve contains 2 million families involved in olive production.

With some products it is, in theory, relatively easy to encourage farmers to switch to other crops. With dairying, however, the situation is much more difficult because of the large numbers of farmers involved, many of whom are small and have little alternative to milk production. France is the Community's largest milk producer yet the structure of its dairy industry is fragmented and inefficient, in contrast to the situation in the UK and the Netherlands (Barton and Young 1975).

Towards the end of the 1970s, the Community's institutions began to realize that the unlimited nature of price guarantees had to be reconsidered. Expenditure on market-price support from the Guarantee section of FEOGA had grown by an annual average of 23 per cent during 1975–79. In 1977, a 'co-responsibility levy' of 1.5 per cent (later raised to 2.5 per cent) was introduced on all milk destined for some form of processing. Proceeds from the levy were to be used for the expansion of markets and the search for new outlets and improved products. However, at this stage the levy was not explicitly linked to a defined target for Community milk production; and it was not effective in checking the increase in the milk surplus.

In 1981 the notion of 'guarantee threshold' was introduced, and this is playing an important role in the operation of the CAP during the 1980s. The threshold idea is simply that producers must share in the responsibility for generating any production over and above a certain level. This policy of 'punishment' for over-production found its most obvious expression in the introduction of milk quotas for individual producers in 1984. In the first year of quotas (April 1984 to March 1985) total milk deliveries fell by 5 million tonnes to 99.4 million tonnes. Nearly all countries kept to their quota, although this was facilitated by poor weather and the allowance of balancing transfers between regions within countries. However, in the following year, apart from drastic shortfalls in Italy and Greece, all countries went over quota, and a similar situation is likely for 1986/87 (Naylor 1987).

The CAP and enlargement

The 'second round' of EC enlargement in the 1980s (Greece joining in 1981, Spain and Portugal in 1986) is likely to be of much greater significance agriculturally than the 1973 round. Enlargement from EC Nine to EC Twelve entails a 55 per cent increase in the farming population, a 57 per cent increase in the number of farms, a 49 per cent expansion of the agricultural area and a 24 per cent rise in agricultural production. While there are some differences in the agricultures of Greece, Spain and Portugal, they share the common features of a Mediterranean farming regime. They produce much the same range of commodities, many of which are also in competition with produce from Italy and southern France.

These difficulties are compounded by the nature of the price and market regimes for Mediterranean crops. The market organizations for durum wheat, rice, olive oil and tobacco are fairly effective in terms of support, but the regimes for wine, citrus fruits, dessert grapes, pears, peaches and tomatoes are much more modest. For the remaining fruit and vegetables the only support is the common tariff set against non-EC countries. Because the price and market mechanisms offer so little support for Mediterranean farming, the main Community approach in recent years has been concentrated on structural measures, especially aids for irrigation, processing, marketing and forestry. The 'Mediterranean package' also encourages farmers to cut back on viticulture and switch to other crops. A parallel but entirely separate argument is that the three countries need the integration of their existing agricultural structures into the CAP less than a reform of those structures themselves, particularly as regards fragmentation, the Spanish *latifundios* and generally primitive farming techniques.

The most serious problems of Greek agriculture are physical and structural: small, fragmented farms, wide regional disparities and a mostly hostile environment. Much of the Greek landscape is like a bony skeleton washed bare by eroding showers and desiccated by hot winds. Forty per cent of the agricultural area is in mountainous and hilly regions where possibilities for land improvement are limited. Despite this, agriculture retains greater importance than in virtually all other west European countries, employing more than a quarter of the working population and accounting for about a tenth of GDP. Greece is a net exporter of farm produce and agriculture makes up one-third of total exports. Fruit and vegetables are important, accounting for 30 per cent of the cultivated area and 58 per cent of agricultural exports. Other significant crops are tobacco, cotton, vines and olives.

Because of the relatively small size of Greek agricultural production, it is being absorbed into the EC without too much dislocation. Trading patterns for farm produce have not been affected much by Greek entry since they were already EC-orientated. On the CAP side, Greece is only likely to absorb about 3 per cent of FEOGA. However, the notion that Greek farmers will draw much benefit from the CAP is highly questionable. Their main crops are weakly supported by the CAP, whereas some of Greece's main agricultural imports – cereals and livestock products – are strongly supported and will therefore cost the Greek consumer dear (Marsh 1979).

Because Portugal, like Greece, is a small country,

its accession will not pose enormous problems for the CAP. However, unlike Greece, Portugal is a net importer of agricultural produce and the farm sector has been in disarray for many years. Self-sufficiency levels are low for many important commodities like beef, butter, cereals and rice. The main exports, whose combined value amounts to only half of agricultural imports, are wine, tomato concentrate, cork, fruit and vegetables. Crop yields and farm incomes are generally the lowest in Western Europe. According to Monke (1986), any problems the Community has in accommodating Portuguese farming are minimal in comparison to the problems EC membership will create for Portugal. The freeing of trade with the rest of the Community (particularly as Spain joins) could worsen the current trade deficit in agricultural products. As with Spain, a transition period of seven years has been agreed in order to give Portuguese farming time to adjust to the new circumstances.

Much more of a problem for the CAP, indeed for the EC in general, is the accession of Spain, whose sheer size and productive potential cannot be ignored. With an agricultural area two and a half times that of Greece and Portugal combined, Spain has considerable exportable surpluses of stoned fruit, citrus, olives and olive oil, wine and dried fruit. Spanish fruit production is equivalent to 23 per cent of that of the EC Nine. During the 1970–80 period, the area under apples, pears and peaches trebled. Spanish horticultural production costs are about half those of southern France and plans exist for a 300 000 ha increase in the irrigated area. Such facts are the background to the 'salad-war' of Roussillon fought between French farmers and lorry-loads of Spanish fruit and vegetables – a conflict that has already claimed several lives. Another fear is that Spanish entry will result in higher production by Spanish farmers tempted by high guarantee prices. Fennell (1979) believes this fear to be exaggerated; she points to sharply-rising labour costs (there is a heavy dependence on hired labour in Spanish farming), the likely rise in imported feedstuffs for the livestock sector and the geographical distance separating Spanish farmers from the EC's main urban markets.

France's worries about Spanish accession are perhaps too forcibly stated, but they are understandable. Spain has more vineyards than any other country in the world, and its competition in an arena of already fierce rivalry between France and Italy is of acute concern in Languedoc-Roussillon. Italy, less vocal than France, probably has even more to fear from Spain's accession. Other countries with serious misgivings about the EC's southern enlargement are those Mediterranean countries (Morocco, Algeria,

Tunisia, Cyprus, Israel, etc.) which at present have preferential trade agreements with the EC for their agricultural produce.

The CAP and the future

Digesting Iberia is not the only, nor indeed necessarily the most important, problem facing the CAP in the late 1980s. Nor, furthermore, is the CAP the major economic issue in a Community stricken by high unemployment and sinister social problems. Nevertheless, after more than twenty years in operation, it is becoming increasingly difficult to discern an overall strategy in the CAP – to see where policy is going and why. The CAP has undergone many adjustments to take account of new developments, with the result that the detailed provisions have become more and more involved, and less and less consistent with the policy's original objectives, which themselves were far from clear-cut and not without internal contradictions (Fennell 1985).

Recent attempts to reform the CAP have been prompted above all by the need to reduce its cost, both because it has come to represent an over-large element in the total Community budget and because much of the expenditure is regarded as a misallocation of resources. While few would argue the need for reform, it is disturbing to find that, just as the original policy has been invested with a psychological symbolism out of all proportion to its economic achievements, so the cutting of the financial cost of the CAP has become an obsession and an end in itself (Fennell 1985).

Further obstacles to reform are posed by the multiplicity of national and political interests. As the original moving force behind the CAP, the French are keenly involved in the ongoing debate. For several years after accession in 1973, Irish farmers gained handsomely under the CAP, their real income growing by 45 per cent in the period to 1978 (Sheehan 1980). Even West German farmers, who greeted the CAP with much foreboding, became staunch supporters (Tangermann 1979). Exactly the opposite happened with the Italians who joined with great expectations but found only disillusionment, due partly to their own bureaucratic inefficiencies (De Benedictis 1981).

The year of 1984 was a watershed year for the CAP (Harvey and Thomson 1985). Against a background of failed dairy policy, difficult problems in the cereals, beef and wine sectors, UK refunds and impending enlargement, it was widely forecast as a year of crisis and possible disintegration of the CAP. Yet out of adversity came progress. The Agricultural Council agreed a package which, in the words of Commissioner

Dalsager, constituted a 'milestone in the development of the CAP'. The package of measures passed was possibly the least favourable to farmers in the history of the CAP. Set in the context of the decision to keep the growth of the cost of FEOGA within the budgetary discipline of the average growth of EC revenues, the Council agreed to the extension of guarantee thresholds to a wide range of commodities and pegged product price increases to modest proportions.

In spite of a greater commitment on paper to reducing regional disparities, with the reinforced less-favoured areas measures and the integrated Mediterranean package, it is unlikely that the very marked national and regional contrasts in agricultural incomes and performance will change much in the foreseeable future. Figure 9.3 presents three indicators of the spatial contrasts in the economic geography of agriculture of the EC Ten in 1982. In each case, regional contrasts are marked and the pattern tends to repeat itself across the three maps, economic conditions being most favourable in the north-centre, worst in the south-east. If we make a slightly more detailed examination of the data and trends behind Fig. 9.3c, we find that the Netherlands, Belgium, Denmark and the UK are the countries where farm incomes are highest, and Italy and Greece are where farmers are worse off. In fact, the average Dutch farmer has an income more than five times that of the average Greek farmer. This, however, ignores intra-country variations. At the Community level, the mean income of the top quartile of farmers is 20 times that of the lowest quartile – a staggering inequality.

Nevertheless, it does appear that policy is becoming more geographically sensitive. Specific regional initiatives have emerged within the new structural policies of the early and mid-1980s. These include the de-specialization of vine growing in Languedoc-Roussillon, the development of cattle and sheep farming in Italy, specific policies for the rural west of Ireland, and integrated development programmes in the Belgian province of Luxembourg and the Lozère in central France. By 1982, regional measures absorbed 45 per cent of guidance section expenditure, compared to only 12 per cent five years earlier.

In less-favoured areas the basic question remains, however: what is to be done with farmers on marginal land whose work makes little economic sense in an

Fig. 9.3
Economic indicators of the spatial structure of European Community farming, 1982: (a) availability of agricultural land in ha/labour unit; (b) labour productivity (ecu/annual work unit); (c) agricultural income/head (EC average = 100).

industry which already produces large surpluses? For social, political and environmental reasons there is now a general desire to maintain a human presence in marginal areas where agriculture cannot be very efficient. The French are most committed to this. They point out that the question also needs to be asked as to what farmers in these areas would do if they were *not* supported. What would be the effects on the society and the landscape? The answer to this question can be found in certain regions of Italy where the picture is one of wholesale rural decay: abandoned land, crumbling villages, decimated populations. For Italy, unlike France, has been slow to draw its entitled benefits from the CAP.

Competing pressures for rural space

The predominantly agricultural community has become the exception in large parts of rural Western Europe. Although disguised by the unchanging character of the rural landscape, this process is revealed by employment statistics, the pattern of commuter flows and the steady transformation of consumption patterns, clothing and standards of living. Public and, even more, private transport have broken down the physical isolation of rural existence, while education, the television and other mass media have comprehensively eroded its cultural isolation.

Above all, rural industrialization has regenerated many countryside districts. The 'urban–rural manufacturing shift' (Keeble et al 1983) has taken industry, mainly small and medium firms, out of congested urban and metropolitan areas into more spacious surroundings, a process aided by the changing nature of Europe's industrial mix from heavy to light, technologically advanced and therefore more footloose enterprises. This 'productive decentralization', which also involves changes in the structure of industry, has been studied in many parts of Europe, but the classic area is the north Italian region of Emilia (Brusco 1982; Cooke and da Rosa Pires 1985). The 'Emilian model' blends small industries and a range of tertiary activities with a modernized, and mainly part-time, agriculture to create a prosperous equilibrium which, moreover, does not disturb the existing framework of village and small-town settlement.

Many other influences are also at work to change and repopulate the countryside (Clout 1984). The countryside has become fashionable for city dwellers who have responded to the attractions of open space, pleasant landscapes and the wholesomeness of nature. The phenomenal post-war growth in private car ownership (25 cars per thousand population in 1950, 324 in 1981) has both enabled natives of rural areas to travel to work in nearby towns, and encouraged urban dwellers to move into the countryside without changing their employment. Motives for moving into the countryside vary. Some of the new ruralites are affluent purchasers of large houses set in their own grounds; other incomers have more limited finances and are attracted by the availability of cheaper types of housing which are more pleasant than comparably priced accommodation in the city; yet others are retired people who are either returning to their villages of origin or seeking out new settings to live out their remaining years.

Further pressures on the countryside are brought by second homes and rural tourism, both of which bring people into rural areas on a temporary basis. Clout (1984) estimated a total of 3 million rural second homes in the EC in the early 1980s, with nearly half of these in France. Roughly 20 per cent of all French and Scandinavian households are possessors of a second home; in these countries, and in the UK, there are now more second homes than farms in the countryside. In some districts, second homes outnumber primary residences: this can happen where the demand for weekend cottages is particularly strong, as on the fringes of the Paris Basin, or where depopulation has been particularly intense, as in some parts of the Provençal Alps. Rural tourism generally creates more beneficial impacts in the field of rural employment than do second homes, although the pressures on the landscape and the environment may be greater, at least at certain times of the year. An upward spiral of tourist impact may be set in motion, with dispersed hiking and touring leading to larger and larger volumes of visitors, skiing, winter sports and almost year-round saturation in some Alpine areas (Kariel and Kariel 1982).

These changes bring not only on economic revolution to the countryside, but also strong sociological and even psychological impacts. Europe's current agricultural problems are rooted in the ambiguity of farming as both an economic activity and a way of life. The contrast is typified by setting alongside each other the elderly Greek peasant with 10 ha of hills and rocks, his baggy trousers a uniform of the past, and the young East Anglian farmer with 1 000 ha of fertile loam, a barnful of huge machines, and computerized accounts. This dualism will persist for some time, but is becoming more blurred. As Henri Mendras writes in *The Vanishing Peasant*, there will always be men who till the soil and manage their farms, but the farmer who is content to run a small subsistence holding in conformity with traditional routines, seldom going beyond the limited horizons of his own soil, is becoming rarer and rarer, and his peasant soul is disappearing with him (Mendras 1970).

In spite of continued support of family farming, the future of a 'modernized peasantry' is far from clear. The problems of elderly peasant farmers, of whom there are now many in their fifties, will persist for a decade or two. For electoral and humanitarian reasons they will continue to be supported; the economic consciences of hard-headed dirigists can be assuaged by regarding them as 'park-keepers' or 'custodians of the landscape' (Franklin 1969). Such a function will increasingly be accorded to other farmers located in upland and marginal environments. Part-time farmers, too, can play a decisive role in areas of low density where preservation of the landscape is important; some additional income can in many cases be drawn from the holiday trade. Yet strict parity of income with urban and industrial workers is as unlikely as it ever was.

The art of rural development in a crowded, mobile countryside involves formulating not just farming policy but a *land* policy to resolve and avoid land-use conflicts. Specifically, there is a need to formulate policies of amenity land use and environmental protection which neither conflict with themselves nor with other land-use and ownership policies. For, as Newby (1979) stresses, land is privately owned but the landscape is publicly consumed.

Further reading

Bowler I R 1985 *Agriculture under the Common Agricultural Policy: A Geography*. Manchester University Press, Manchester

Clout H D 1971 *Agriculture*. Macmillan Studies in Contemporary Europe, London

Clout H 1984 *A Rural Policy for the EEC?* Methuen, London

Dovring F 1965 *Land and Labour in Europe in the Twentieth Century*. Nijhoff, The Hague

Duchêne F, Szczepanik E, Legg W 1985 *New Limits on European Agriculture*. Croom Helm, London

Franklin S H 1969 *The European Peasantry: The Final Phase*. Methuen, London

Franklin S H 1971 *Rural Societies*. Macmillan Studies in Contemporary Europe, London

Hill B E 1984 *The Common Agricultural Policy: Past, Present and Future*. Methuen, London

Marsh J S, Swanney P 1980 *Agriculture and the European Community*. Allen and Unwin, London

Pearce J 1981 *The Common Agricultural Policy: Prospects for Change*. Routledge and Kegan Paul (Chatham House Papers, 13), London

Tracy M 1982 *Agriculture in Western Europe: Challenge and Response 1880–1980*. Granada, London

10

Recreation and conservation

Dimensions of demand

Both the demand for recreation and the scale and variety of provision have grown dramatically in Western Europe, as in all western industrial societies, in the past half century. People generally now have more leisure time, and more money than ever before to spend on it. Combined with the extensions to personal mobility conferred by the motor car and cheap air travel, these factors have enabled them to diversify their interests into a bewilderingly large number of different recreational activities. This, in turn, has led to an enormous expansion in the spatial scope of recreation: there is a growing predilection for travelling away from the immediate locality of the home, neighbourhood or town to satisfy recreational needs. There has also been a marked change of focus: rather than specific sites or locations being the main object, whole areas with a number of different attractions are often taking their place. The change of emphasis is important for it goes some considerable way to explaining the growing concern for environmental conservation. Rural and, to some extent, urban landscapes are seen as the backdrop against which much recreational activity takes place and they are being viewed increasingly as a rather static part of the cultural heritage. It is well known that people tend to harbour idealized and often sentimentalized images of far-away places, at odds with the reality of constant evolution and change; a desire to preserve what is best from the past for the enjoyment of present and future generations is an important stimulant to the burgeoning demands for the enactment of conservation measures in both town and country (Lowenthal 1968). This chapter examines the nature of the growth in demand for recreation and the effect that it has had on specific parts of Western Europe through the growth of tourism. It also analyses the nature of the response by both governments and private agencies to the calls for conservation measures and the effect that these have had on rural and urban environments.

In the past generation, a number of influences have acted in concert to expand the amount of leisure – time free from work and other obligations – most people have at their disposal (Parker 1976). It is not simply that the number of hours worked per week has been reduced, although this has contributed to the change, but more importantly that the actual organization of work in society, the general state of affluence of the majority, and the overall demographic trends have all combined to alter radically recreational aspirations and opportunities.

Holidays with pay are now the norm in industrial societies and the majority of west Europeans only work a five-day week. People therefore not only have more spare time, it tends to be organized into predictable blocks, be it at weekends or annual holidays, thus allowing for the long-term planning of more ambitious recreation projects. There has also been a marked change in the actual composition of the populations of all the west European countries, the most significant feature of which has been the general ageing that has occurred. In the region as a whole, 13 per cent of the population is above 65 years of age, compared with only 10 per cent in 1950 and 6 per cent in 1910 (Table 10.1) and, just because this age group has so much leisure time, it has a disproportionate impact on patterns of recreation and leisure.

Table 10.1 Population over 65 years of age in Western Europe in millions (%)

1910	1950	1960	1970	1986
14 (6.1%)	26 (9.3%)	32 (10.3%)	38 (13.0%)	48 (12.9%)

Other recent changes in society have also had profound effects upon recreation. The length of time spent in full-time education has steadily increased and more young people than ever before are taking higher-education training at universities or polytechnics. Among the twelve members of the European Community alone, their numbers rose from 3.9 million in 1970 to 5.3 million in 1986. It is not being argued that those in full-time education necessarily have more leisure time, but it certainly is true that young people are more likely to participate in sports and other more active recreations, and education services frequently provide them with the physical facilities to do so.

Another, more distressing, social change that has had a marked impact on the amount of leisure time for many people is unemployment. In Western Europe as a whole its rate more than doubled after the shock rise in the price of crude oil in 1973 and, in 1986, stood at 10.6 per cent of the population of working age. It would, of course, be ridiculous to imply that the first, or even the major, concern of unemployed people is to seek out new recreational opportunities, but nonetheless many of them do suddenly find that they have time to devote to hobbies and other activities that were previously denied to them.

Table 10.2 Number of private cars in use in Western Europe in millions

1950	1960	1970	1986
6.1	22.9	64.8	112.4

Important as these changes in the socio-economic structure of society are, in terms of the impact on recreation all pale beside the explosive growth in private car ownership (Table 10.2). In 1950 there were only 6.1 million cars on the roads of Western Europe compared with well over 100 million today. Put another way, one person in forty-eight owned a car in 1950, compared with one person in three in 1986. The impact of this transformation in personal circumstances for recreation was prophetically highlighted by Michael Dower in the early 1960s and his predictions have proved uncannily accurate (Dower 1965). Most people are now able to choose where they want to travel within a wide radius of their homes, without the time and spatial constraints imposed by public transport. They are also spared the inconvenience of making their way to central collecting points, such as bus and railway stations, thus encouraging them to act much more easily on impulse and significantly

increasing the amount of time spent on recreation. The major impact of widespread car ownership has been felt in the countryside, previously largely inaccessible to the mass of the population, where informal recreation is now a major land use (Simmons 1975). One of the greatest difficulties facing those trying to cater for these new recreational demands has been the fact that the planners of the 1940s and 1950s, who are still largely responsible for the framework of public access to the countryside, failed to foresee the revolutionary increase that the private car would bring to rural areas.

Despite their importance, the new developments ushered in by the improved access to transportation for the mass of the population need to be kept in perspective. For most people, the home and the immediate locality still remain the focus of their leisure-time activities. A detailed report on the leisure needs of the population of one London borough showed that, while holidays and shorter outings were considered important and desirable by people at all levels, the bulk of their recreation was locally-based and was going to remain so (Dower et al. 1981). The report urged that those in both government and private industry recognize this fact when formulating policies for investment in recreation facilities. Indeed, it went further, arguing that the lives of many significant groups, such as young married women, the elderly and ethnic minorities, were so constrained in terms of recreational choice that sports and other facilities needed to be arranged so that the particular difficulties faced by these, and other, groups could be effectively countered. These findings from London are in no way exceptional and have been corroborated by many other studies (see, for example, Glyptis 1981), for while there is some debate as to precisely which social characteristics are likely to determine the types of recreation people choose, there is no doubt about the continuing paramount importance of opportunities in, or close to, home. The systematic information available for Western Europe also indicates that while the nature of provision by local authorities is enormously varied, it is directed consistently towards those people with a better than average education and with middle to high ranking occupations. This was one of the main conclusions of an enquiry, sponsored by the Council of Europe, into recreation policy in fourteen Western European towns in thirteen countries (Mennell 1976). The picture that emerges confirms the evidence of a lack of recreational opportunities for most disadvantaged groups, already highlighted in more detailed individual studies, and indicates that the same situation is widespread throughout the region.

Tourism

Economic significance

Tourism is defined as the temporary, short-term movement of people to destinations outside the places where they normally live and work, for other than business or vocational reasons, and their activities during the stay at these destinations (Burkart and Medlik 1974). As an aspect of recreation, it has grown in line with the improvements in, and expansion of, communications that have been going on steadily since the mid-eighteenth century. The building of the turnpikes, the spread of the railway network, widespread ownership of private cars and the growth of mass air travel have all in their turn stimulated tourism to a point where it is now a significant part of every west European economy. Of the estimated 300 million international tourist arrivals world-wide in 1986, more than 50 per cent were from Western Europe.

In fact, this figure is a gross underestimate of the total amount of tourism in the region, for it only reflects international movements and takes no account of the very large volumes of domestic tourism in most west European countries. By the same token, the contribution of Western Europe to international tourism is highly emphasized when compared with other industrial nations, in particular the USA, because the very large number of relatively small states increases the number of international as opposed to domestic movements (Hudman 1978).

Within Western Europe there is very considerable variation in both the absolute and the relative net importance of tourism among the different countries (Table 10.3). In 1986, Spain earned most, followed by Italy, France, Austria, Greece, Portugal, Turkey and Switzerland. All these countries had a positive balance in excess of $US 100 million and they represent the southern margin of Western Europe. The distribution reflects an understandable desire on the part of the majority going on holiday for sun and warm seas and, in the case of winter sports, the longer winter days of the Alps in comparison with the mountains of the north in the Highlands of Scotland and Scandinavia. It is apparent from Table 10.3 that in general southern Europe's gain is northern Europe's loss in financial terms, with some countries, notably West Germany, running large deficits on their tourism accounts.

Obviously, absolute figures take no account of the differences between states in respect of either population or the overall size of the individual economies. If international tourist receipts are expressed as a proportion of total exports (Table 10.4), then a somewhat different picture emerges. Four countries, Spain,

Table 10.3 International tourist receipts less international tourist expenditure, 1986 (m US$)

Spain	10 442
Italy	7 095
France	3 197
Austria	2 722
Greece	1 338
Portugal	1 250
Turkey	916
Switzerland	862
Republic of Ireland	−24
Iceland	−35
Denmark	−354
Finland	−473
Belgium/Luxembourg	−618
UK	−765
Sweden	−1 267
Norway	−1 437
Netherlands	−2 524
West Germany	−12 838

Source: OECD 1987 *Tourism policy and international tourism in OECD member countries*. Paris

Greece, Austria and Portugal, dominate, with tourism accounting for a significant proportion of their exports. In no other country does the proportion exceed 10 per cent and for most it is less than 5 per cent. This agrees closely with the contention that the greater a state's economic potential the less will be the significance of tourism in its economy (White 1976). It also supports the thesis that tourism is well-suited to the kind of economic circumstances found in states at the periphery rather than those at the urban-industrial core of Western Europe, because the level of capital investment is relatively low, the industry is labour-intensive and financial returns are rapid (Christaller 1964). Nevertheless, such economic determinism always needs to be tempered by not losing sight of the critical importance of physical attributes, such as sun and scenery, for success, which explains why it is the southern periphery rather than the northern one that has benefited most from tourism in Western Europe.

In common with other industries that offer a rapid return on investment, tourism is intensely competitive and very susceptible to the vagaries of the economic climate. The upheaval experienced by all the western industrial nations in the wake of the doubling of oil prices in 1973 interrupted the sustained growth in tourism enjoyed throughout Western Europe in the preceding decade. Although the downturn was quite

Table 10.4 International tourist receipts, 1986, in rank order of the proportion they form of total exports

	Amount (m US$)	Proportion of total exports	1970 ranking
1. Spain	11 945	21.1	1
2. Greece	1 835	17.9	3
3. Austria	6 928	17.7	2
4. Portugal	1 583	13.5	5
5. Switzerland	4 240	8.9	6
6. Italy	9 853	8.6	7
7. Turkey	1 228	5.9	11
8. Denmark	1 759	5.8	8
9. France	9 580	5.2	9
10. Republic of Ireland	659	4.3	4
11. Iceland	42	3.2	17
UK	7 921	3.2	12=
13. Finland	597	3.0	10
Sweden	1 543	3.0	18
15. West Germany	7 826	2.6	15=
16. Norway	992	2.4	12=
17. Belgium/Luxembourg	2 269	2.1	15=
18. Netherlands	1 906	1.8	14

Source: OECD 1987 *Tourism policy and international tourism in OECD member countries*. Paris

quickly reversed, the renewed growth rates have been much more modest and the competition to attract visitors much more fierce. Superficially the rankings of the importance of national tourist industries in 1970 and 1986, shown in Table 10.4, reveal only minor alterations over the intervening years, but the shifts that have occurred have been quite fundamental. Turkey has significantly improved its position, as have most of the other countries of southern Europe, especially Greece, Italy and Portugal. At least some of the growth of tourism in these countries would appear to be at the expense of Spain, though it still heads the ranking. In 1970, tourism accounted for 33 per cent of the country's total exports, but by 1980 this proportion had fallen to 21.6 per cent. In part this reflects a general diversification that has taken place in the economy, but it also illustrates how the Spanish tourist industry has lost out to its rivals in the competition for trade.

Local impact

The impact of tourism on the receiving areas, like the previously remote Alpine valleys of Austria and Switzerland and the Mediterranean coast of Spain. is dramatic, not least because many of the more popular destinations have gone from being among the most isolated and poor areas of Europe to centres of mass tourism in the space of less than a generation (Barker 1982). The changes that occur in the local economy, the society and the landscape as the scale of tourism grows are complex and varied, but Fig. 10.1 (redrawn from Kariel 1982) provides an effective summary of the developments that occur over time. Initially, the small number of tourists coming to remote areas expect little except the opportunity to enjoy the landscape and to share vicariously in the lives of the local population. For their part, the residents see the tourists as a minor diversion from their primary task of eking a living from the land. If the tourist demand grows, this relationship begins to change, and with increasing rapidity. Tourism establishes a niche in the local economy and challenges the total dependence on agriculture; facilities – like improved and expanded accommodation – are built using private capital, followed by public investment in communications and other services. Quickly the local economy changes from being mainly dependent on agriculture to being mainly dependent on tourism and, far from accepting the visitors as an optional extra, the local community has to begin to compete through advertising and more ambitious investment in facilities for their custom. Investment on such a scale inevitably presupposes borrowing money, so that the populations of the receiving areas eventually find themselves in a position where they are as wedded to tourism as they previously were to agriculture, with the added danger of being even less in control of the means of production.

The Kariels (1982) go on to make the very important point that the changes that occur are not simply economic but fundamentally alter the whole basis of the local society. Initially, the influences on the self-sufficient, subsistence-level, agrarian society are relatively modest: knowledge of the outside world increases; more time is spent with guests and less with family and friends; working hours become more rigid; children are less involved, because they tend to help less around the home and the farm; the wife earns an increasing share of the family income independently of her husband. After a time these changes in the economic circumstances of the family are followed by changes in social structure of the community as a whole: there tends to be a decreased emphasis on religion; family size falls; levels of education improve; outmigration is slowed; the spirit of cooperation in the community is replaced by a growing sense of competition between individuals; medical care improves; there is a growing dependence on services, such as shops, outside the immediate local community.

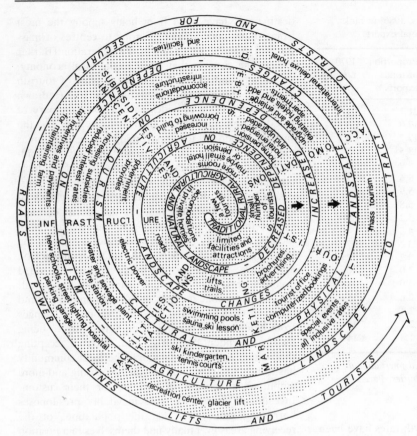

Fig. 10.1
Spiral of economic and infrastructural growth and landscape changes influenced by tourism (after Kariel 1982).

Finally, a new equilibrium is established: paid labour replaces volunteer-cooperative community work; children participate in sport; the concepts of employment and unemployment become established; employment and housing for children when they grow up is routinely found outside the confines of the family; the wife earns a growing proportion of the family income on her own account and consequently alters fundamentally her role in the family; immigration of workers occurs; there is an increased incidence of marriage breakdown; holidays are taken away from home; a revival of interest occurs in traditional customs and local language, but mainly for its curiosity value. In other words, a previously remote society has been sucked into the mainstream of the technological, urban-orientated, credit and monetary exchange society from which it was previously largely insulated. There is no intention of implying that this is in any way a disaster, or even undesirable, but tourism does impose a whole new series of constraints on the societies to which it reaches out. Also, the speed of change frequently means that local people have little

time to adapt to their new circumstances and are in danger of being overwhelmed by them.

Examples of the above transformation can be found in many of the previously more remote and backward parts of Western Europe, but nowhere are they more starkly illustrated than in Spain. Between 1959 and 1964 the country's foreign currency earnings from tourism leapt more than tenfold, from under £20 million to well over £200 million, with the numbers of foreign tourists growing from 4 to 14 million in the same period (Naylon 1967). By 1964, tourism was earning nearly as much foreign currency as all Spain's other exports put together and, although its significance has subsequently declined, it has nonetheless had a profound and irreversible effect on the economy, the society and the landscape.

Yet the effects have been highly localized and, even by 1980, 60 per cent of Spanish hotel capacity was concentrated in only seven of the country's fifty provinces. Five of these – Gerona, Barcelona, Alicante, Malaga and the Balearic Islands – were on the Mediterranean, so that the rest of Spain, except for the capital Madrid and Guipuzcoa on the Atlantic coast bordering France, was left largely untouched by the direct impact. Equally, the tourist season is also highly concentrated with nearly 50 per cent of foreign visits still occurring in the months of July, August and September. Such uneven spatial and temporal patterns raise considerable difficulties for the economy as a whole, for not only are the benefits of tourism very unevenly divided nationally, there are also long periods during the year when much of the labour force even in the tourist areas is either unemployed or underemployed.

A graphic illustration of the way in which tourism can radically alter the environments affected by it is provided by the two most southerly of the Balearic Islands, Ibiza and Formentera (Pacione 1977). Until the mid-1960s both were relatively untouched by the flocks of visitors from all over Europe who flew into Menorca and Mallorca, but in the last twenty years they have rapidly begun to catch up. Existing roads have been metalled and new ones constructed in an attempt to produce a better integrated route network and, as a result, the number of cars registered in San Antonio alone – one of ten small towns on Ibiza – rose from 960 in 1967 to 2 500 in 1975. Between 1950 and 1975 the number of hotel beds in the town rose from 500 to more than 12 000, and the local architecture has come to be dominated by multi-storey buildings, at the expense of the traditional, single-storey, stone-built houses. In the countryside, many of the scattered farmsteads have been abandoned as the inhabitants have found better-paid jobs in the towns. The decline in the size of the rural population has also encouraged the mechanization of agriculture and forced farmers to allow the more inaccessible parts of their holdings to revert to a less ordered and manicured state. Within the towns themselves, workers from mainland Spain have come on a seasonal basis to cater for the every need of the tourists and, like them, they cannot be accommodated in a traditional agricultural society. Shops and other services have had to be provided on a large scale, thus further altering the infrastructure and layout of the settlements.

Faced with such fundamental changes at all the major tourist locations, the Spanish government has had to modify its initial attitude of uncritical encouragement for expansion in the industry. In the 1950s and 1960s, when the economy was already weak, it was difficult to justify infrastructural investment in roads, water supplies, sewers and other services, especially as there was no guarantee that the expansion would continue. Now this kind of investment and measures to protect the environment are being forced on the government just to prevent the most popular

resorts on the Balearic Islands, the Costa Brava and the Costa del Sol from deteriorating to such an extent that tourists are deterred rather than attracted. In 1977, the Secretariat of State for Tourism drafted a new law to curb the environmental impact of tourist development, and also took positive action to spread demand away from the Mediterranean coast to less-developed parts of the country, thus reducing the environmental pressures in the most crowded areas and spreading the benefits of the tourist industry more widely (OECD 1980c).

The problems caused by a few popular, or even over-popular, locations and a very restricted season are common to all tourist countries and, like Spain, most have made strenuous efforts to diversify their attractions and increase the number of resorts. The greatest success in this search has undoubtedly attended the Alpine countries, which have succeeded in turning the winter inconvenience of snow and the difficulties of having to travel on skis into a multi-million dollar industry. In the winter of 1979–80, for example, foreign visitors spent $US 3 400 million in Switzerland alone; and France, West Germany, Austria and Italy also enjoyed large inflows of foreign currency (EFTA Bulletin 1981). Nearly half of the world total of 3 000 ski resorts are found in Western Europe and success is rooted in the fact that high, snow-covered mountains are found close to large and relatively affluent industrial populations (Barbier 1978). People in the region can travel quickly and relatively inexpensively from their homes to the ski resorts. It is noticeable that the more inaccessible mountains, like those of the Scandinavian countries and the Sierra Nevada in Spain, are markedly less popular as ski resorts, though in the case of Scandinavia the northerly location and consequently short winter days is certainly an added deterrent.

Skiing and all winter sports are a developer's dream, for they utilize resources of both land and people at a time when they would otherwise be severely underemployed. Most of the sports also require large quantities of equipment and specialist clothing and this has given a considerable boost to manufacturing industry in Austria, Switzerland, Norway and Sweden. Nevertheless, even such specialist equipment manufacturing can become the victim of its own success. In all four of the countries mentioned above, the market for Alpine skis has recently begun to decline, despite the continuing growth in the popularity of skiing, as manufacturers elsewhere have begun to find it worth their while to compete in the lucrative market. The obvious response of course is to diversify and all the four countries have begun to promote strongly cross-country skiing, which requires different equipment from its more popular downhill cousin. So far they appear to have tapped yet another buoyant market, but there is always the danger that it too could eventually suffer from outside competition should the market grow too large.

Nature conservation and landscape protection

National parks

Concern for the future of the natural environment and a desire not to see the rural landscape swamped by urban development and twentieth-century technology are common causes throughout the nations of Western Europe. Nevertheless, despite the unanimity that exists on the general ideals, there is great variation in the way in which the individual governments have gone about translating them into practical policies. Throughout Europe the primeval landscape, untouched by civilization, has long since disappeared, so that conservation is really about conserving semi-natural ecosystems and the remnants of the rural economies that formed them. As the experience of every country in this regard is somewhat different and the way in which they each assess the value of what remains varies, so the conservation policies themselves all have a distinctive national flavour. In the UK, for example, much of the emphasis has been on public access to open country and the need to preserve the illusion in the landscape of a pre-industrial rural scene. By way of contrast, in West Germany, where there are more than 1 100 nature reserves, the focus has been much more narrowly directed towards nature conservation. Short of detailed examination of each individual policy, however, it is often hard to say precisely what even their general aims and objectives are, because apparently synonymous designations have quite widely differing meanings in the various west European countries. The most blatant example of this is the confusion that still surrounds the term *national park*. It can mean anything from a state-owned wilderness, where public access is strictly controlled and limited so that the environment can evolve with a minimum of human interference, to privately-owned upland farmland, where access for recreation is actively encouraged and the only controls over development are planning regulations covering new buildings and mining operations.

A degree of comparability has been introduced through the efforts of the International Union for Conservation of Nature and Natural Resources (IUCN), an offshoot of the United Nations, which in the past twenty years has published three world lists of what it defines as national parks. To merit inclusion, an area must be relatively large, with one or several ecosystems not materially altered by human exploitation and occupation. It must also either be of special scientific, educational or recreational interest for its wildlife, geomorphology or general habitat, or possess a natural landscape of great beauty. In addition, the national government of the country concerned must have taken steps to protect the special features for which the area is to be designated and visitor access has to be restricted to those whose purposes are 'inspirational, educative, cultural or recreative' (IUCN 1974). In order to ease the confusion, the IUCN also requested governments not to designate as national parks any of the following:

a scientific reserve which can be entered only by special permission;

a natural reserve managed by a private institution or a lower authority without some type of recognition and control by the national government of the country;

a special reserve, such as a fauna or flora reserve, a game reserve, a bird sanctuary, or a geological or forest reserve;

an inhabited and exploited area where landscape planning and measures taken for the development of tourism have led to the setting up of recreation areas, where industrialization and urbanization are controlled and where public outdoor recreation takes priority over the conservation of ecosystems. It is further recommended that any area wrongly designated as a national park according to the above definition should be renamed as soon as possible.

Under the terms of the IUCN definition, all but the very smallest west European states have national parks (Fig. 10.2), although their number, the proportion of the total land area designated, and the national park area per capita vary widely. On most counts the Scandinavian countries emerge with the most active records (Table 10.5), with Sweden having no less than twenty-six separate national parks, 1.042 per cent of its land area designated as parkland, and 6.111 $\times$ 10^{-4} sq km of parkland per head of population. Elsewhere the picture is very variable and reflects more the enthusiasm of individual governments than the intrinsic value of the habitats and landscapes. For instance, the heavily-populated Netherlands with its almost total lack of spectacular scenery has eighteen national parks, covering 1.436 per cent of its land area, while Switzerland has but one, covering only 0.4 per cent. On the other hand, the UK has nineteen

National parks
* MAR and Ramsar sites
⑱ MAR sites in the Netherlands

Fig. 10.2
National parks (according to the IUCN definition, 1975), MAR and Ramsar sites.

designated areas, but they are all very small and encompass only 0.365 per cent of the land area, while Portugal's one national park incorporates 0.5 per cent of its territory.

The great value of such international comparisons is that it fosters a recognition of common problems and helps to promote joint and compatible solutions. This is extremely important in Western Europe where scenery and important natural habitats are no respectors of the closely-packed national boundaries. There are now a number of examples of jointly-administered national parks spanning international frontiers, such as the Hohes Venn-Eifel park on the German–Belgian border and the Maas-Schwahn-Nette park on the German–Dutch border. The scope for further similar cooperation, especially among the Alpine and the Scandinavian countries, is considerable, but so far practical political considerations have outweighed the advantages of joint action.

Wetlands and other habitats

National parks are not the only international designations sponsored by the IUCN; since 1965 it has

Table 10.5 National parks according to the IUCN definition

Country	Area of parkland (sq km)	No. of parks	% of total area in parkland	Parkland area per capita (sq km)
Sweden	5 072	26	1.042	6.111×10^{-4}
Norway	3 585	10	1.106	9.115×10^{-4}
West Germany	2 902	11	1.167	2.730×10^{-5}
Finland	2 375	6	0.705	5.125×10^{-4}
Italy	1 865	3	0.619	3.685×10^{-5}
France	1 520	8	0.278	4.430×10^{-5}
Iceland	1 310	4	1.271	6.047×10^{-3}
Austria	1 119	4	1.335	1.501×10^{-4}
UK	839	19	0.365	1.498×10^{-5}
Netherlands	591	18	1.436	4.191×10^{-5}
Spain	540	3	0.107	1.560×10^{-5}
Portugal	501	1	0.544	5.836×10^{-5}
Greece	281	5	0.213	3.310×10^{-5}
Switzerland	167	1	0.409	2.630×10^{-5}
Republic of Ireland	43	1	0.304	2.770×10^{-5}
Belgium	37	1	0.120	3.780×10^{-6}
Denmark	30	1	0.070	6.085×10^{-6}

Sources: IUCN *United Nations List of National Parks and Equivalent Reserves 1985.* Gland 1986; Nake-Mann B, Nake R 1979 *Schutzwürdige Gebiete von europäische Bedeutung.* Bonn; Wilkinson P F 1978 The global distribution of national parks and equivalent reserves. In Nelson J G, Needham R D, Mann D L *International Experience With National Parks and Related Reserves.* Waterloo, Canada, pp 603–24

published a list of temperate marshes, bogs and other wetlands in Europe and North Africa which are in need of permanent conservation and management if they are not to disappear under the pressure of agricultural improvement or other development. The sites are known as the MAR list, the name being chosen because MAR are the first three letters of the word for wetland in so many European languages (Marsch, marsh, marshland, marecage, marius, marisma). As can be seen from Fig. 9.2, there are 163 wetland sites on the list, spread among eighteen different countries, and one of the principal aims of the scheme has been to draw international attention to the dangers facing these habitats, in the hope that a convention can be agreed to ensure their long-term protection. This goal was achieved in 1971 when the *Convention on Wetlands of International Importance, especially as Waterfowl Habitat* was signed at Ramsar in Iran. However, the painful slowness with which any international agreement can be actually implemented is illustrated by the rate at which the Ramsar convention has been ratified by individual European governments. Less than half have so far done so and, even among those that have, none has extended protection to all the sites on the original MAR list.

Even within the United Nations, the IUCN does not have a monopoly of the concern for the natural environment. In 1970 UNESCO, as part of its broadly-based ecological programme, Man and the Biosphere, launched the concept of biosphere reserves. This is a world-wide programme to protect areas of land and coast, which represent important examples of biomes at a global scale. In the UK alone, nineteen sites have been so designated, although it needs to be remembered that here, as well as everywhere else, the enthusiastic activity hides a great deal of administrative duplication. For example, the Claish Moss Highland Region in western Scotland is a National Nature Reserve in the UK, is on the MAR list, has been designated under the Ramsar Convention, and is also a Biosphere Reserve.

The designations made by the IUCN and other international bodies represent only a very small proportion of the protection afforded under conservation legislation in the individual west European countries. However, as was pointed out earlier, the differing priorities and legislation mean that the practice varies in detail from country to country. In West Germany the national government, spurred on by the 1976 Federal Nature Conservation Law, has devoted much of its attention to preserving natural habitats. The emphasis is on safeguarding rare flora and fauna, rather than on the intrinsic beauty of the landscape. To some extent it is a stance that has been forced upon the authorities because of the difficulty in getting agreement on the principle of designation with the landowners. Most of the nature conservation areas are small, with some 62 per cent of the 1 139 sites being under 50 ha in extent and the total system only covering 203 176 ha, less than 1 per cent of the total land area of the country (Erz 1979). The small size of many of the areas, a common complaint elsewhere in Europe, poses great difficulties as it is almost impossible to protect them from undesirable outside influences such as pollution, trespassers and the effects of neighbouring development. Equally, since a large number of the nature conservation areas are close to centres of population, they are under constant pressure from people wishing to use them for more general recreation. This, in turn, leads to tension between the state and the largely private landowners, who resent the intrusions by the general public. They are deeply suspicious of the limitations that designation as a nature conservation area imposes on the freedom to do what they want with the land that they own. Finally, there are quite large variations between the various *Länder* in the federation in the amount of land set aside for nature conservation purposes. In part, of course, this reflects differences in the intrinsic quality of the natural environment, but much more it is evidence of the degree of commitment. The amount of land that is protected and the resources in both manpower and money devoted to managing it are vital ingredients, which ultimately determine the means of nature conservation programmes, not only in West Germany but anywhere in Western Europe.

Experience in France and the United Kingdom

In France, the most important rural conservation initiative has been the system of *parcs naturels régionaux*, made possible by the central government decree of 1 March 1967. It enabled local and regional authorities to combine to set up joint administrative machinery for running and financing such parks. There are now twenty of them spread right across the country, ranging in size from a massive 206 000 ha in the Landes area of south-west France to only 10 300 ha in the Saint Amand Raismes park on the Franco-Belgian border. The purposes of the parks are to preserve and enhance both the natural environment and the cultural heritage of the areas protected, to provide facilities for visitors and to ensure the flourishing survival of rural life and traditions (Blacksell 1976). The concept is a grand one, but the success with which it is realized in each instance depends entirely on the level of local commitment; the central

government contributes nothing directly to either the finance or the administration of this park system. Control, in most cases, is vested in a joint authority comprising the *département* and the rural *communes*, with the *département* providing the bulk of the money and the *communes* implementing most of the decisions. Obviously such a system is fine so long as it works, but if any of the constituent authorities decides not to cooperate then there is little that can be done about it. The great advantage of local, as opposed to national, control is that it ensures that the people actually living in the parks have a direct say in the way in which they are developed and managed. One of the main objections to national and international conservation strategies is that they ride roughshod over the interests of the local population; the administrative system devised for the *parcs naturels régionaux* overcomes this problem albeit at the cost of clear central direction and policy control.

The west European country with the most varied and extensive system of nature and landscape designations is the UK. Ever since the late 1940s, a comprehensive network of National Nature Reserves has gradually been designated and it now provides a measure of protection to scientifically important habitats throughout England, Northern Ireland, Scotland and Wales. At the end of 1982 there were 219 National Nature Reserves, many owned or leased by the Nature Conservancy Council on behalf of the Government (Nature Conservancy Council 1982). Others are established under Nature Reserve Agreements by which the owner and occupier retain their rights but agree, in the interests of nature conservation, to certain conditions affecting land use and management.

This kind of control over development and change is obviously the ideal if one wants to be certain that nature conservation objectives should always be paramount, but it is clearly impracticable in a densely-populated country to tie large tracts of land up for such single-purpose use. In the majority of the protected areas in the UK, the demands of nature conservation have to compete with other government objectives, notably the need to provide access to open country for recreation, as well as with the legitimate interests of the private landowners, who actually own the land and usually depend on it for their livelihood. In England, Scotland and Wales there are fifty areas set aside, because of their exceptionally fine upland scenery, in the belief that they require special protection as a part of the national heritage. The ten areas in England and Wales are actually called National Parks, although in most respects they are much closer to the French *parcs naturels régionaux* than national parks in the sense that the term is normally used; significantly, they do not appear on the IUCN list. The National Scenic Areas in Scotland are purely landscape designations, as their name implies, without any pretensions otherwise. With both the National Parks and the National Scenic Areas, however, the crucial factor affecting their public management is that not only is the majority of the land privately owned, but also that administrative responsibility is primarily with the local authorities. Apart from making the initial designation, the main concern of the national government agencies is to exert a watching brief and to channel a certain amount of finance so as to encourage the execution of the national conservation and recreation objectives for these areas.

The principle of designating land in the UK as an expression of concern about its value for the national heritage has gone well beyond the concept of the so-called National Parks. There are also forty-one Areas of Outstanding Natural Beauty covering nearly 10 per cent of the land area of England, Northern Ireland and Wales, many of them incorporating lowland farming landscapes which are otherwise unprotected. In addition, thirty-five lengths of coastline extending over 1 161 km have been dubbed Heritage Coasts, in the hope that the significance of the sea in the development of England and Wales will receive due weight in conservation policies.

As if this were not enough, the Broads in East Anglia, one of the nation's most interesting man-made landscapes, was considered so important that a special form of designation, the Broads Authority, was worked out to ensure its long-term protection. On its own, this unique solution is of only local significance, but it is symptomatic of a more general problem facing those concerned with nature and landscape conservation. In the UK and, indeed, throughout most of Western Europe, the natural landscape is only part of what needs to be preserved; of equal importance is the economic and social system that has modified and moulded the land surface. If this is to survive, it requires more than the simple isolation of the land in question that is at the heart of the concept of a nature reserve. The essential elements of the economic system have to be fixed in time as well and this involves people and the way in which they live, as well as land, flora and fauna. Managing farmland so that it retains elements of pre-industrial agricultural practice is an extremely difficult exercise and not one that any single, simple solution is ever likely to do successfully. It is, therefore, hardly surprising that in the UK so many different approaches have been adopted to what is essentially a single problem.

There is one other rather different difficulty facing those wanting to see a greater measure of protection given to the countryside for the purposes of nature conservation in the UK. Large tracts of rural land are owned and managed either directly by government, or by its agencies, such as the regional water authorities or the Forestry Commission, for specific purposes not connected with conservation. There has been increasing pressure on these bodies to broaden their limits so that their land is managed for purposes other than the primary function of water supply or timber production. It is a campaign that has met with considerable success and now, for instance, both the regional water authorities and the Forestry Commission have to include provision for public access and recreation in their management plans. The Forestry Commission administers sixteen National Forest Parks where it mixes its responsibility for tending trees with providing facilities for informal recreation. Strategies for multiple use of land such as these are the key to rural conservation in an area like Western Europe, where competition for land is always likely to be great.

Conserving the built environment

Context

Europe has an urban heritage stretching back to medieval times, and towns and cities are at the very heart of its culture. It is therefore hardly surprising that there has been a widespread propensity to view the city as an artefact and to ensure that adequate planning and other controls exist for conserving the urban fabric (Evenson 1981). Indeed, even when cities have been struck by a calamity, such as the wholesale destruction that resulted from the bombing of Germany during the Second World War, there has always been a strong tendency to reconstruct painstakingly what was there before, so as to emphasize the thread of continuity with the past, rather than introduce new shapes and novel layouts (see Ch. 8).

The seeds of organized concern about the preservation of urban areas in Europe can be traced back to the eighteenth century in some countries like France, Germany and the UK, but it is in the last fifty years that the conservation ethic has come to be so firmly embedded in the planning process. The main reason for this, of course, is the greatly increased pace of growth and change in the twentieth century. Not only have people continued to flock into urban areas, new technologies, particularly those related to transportation and building, have opened up previously undreamt of development options. On the one hand, land may now be used very much more intensively than ever before, because of the advent of steel-framed high-rise buildings rising to twenty storeys and more. Before the end of the nineteenth century, anything higher than three or four storeys was beyond the scope of mass-construction techniques. On the other hand, new forms of urban transportation, starting with the railway and progressing through trains and buses to the motor car, have dramatically extended the built-up area of cities. They have produced a much greater segregation of land uses, as people generally are more easily able to travel within the urban area, and have also created new land-use demands, in the form of railways and roads, which have had to be carved out of the existing urban fabric. Conscious of the rapid change going on all around them, citizens throughout Europe have begun to demand that not all the old be sacrificed to the demands of the new.

A second reason why conservation has recently grown in significance is the much greater strength and effectiveness of urban government. The growth of planning systems and the proliferation of regulations governing new development have enabled the desire on the part of individuals to oppose new development and change to be translated into fact. Urban conser-, vation in Western Europe has always drawn its strength from grass-roots support, with the small pressure groups formed to save particular townscapes, such as Georgian Bath or Medieval Paris, subsequently amalgamating to create a national movement like the British Civic Trust (Burtenshaw, Bateman and Ashworth 1981). To some degree the movement has also managed to transcend national boundaries. The Council of Europe has taken a number of initiatives in the past two decades to protect the built environment, the most successful being European Architectural Heritage Year in 1975. Under this scheme, forty-nine sites throughout Western Europe were selected with a view to protecting a representative selection of urban landscapes (Fig. 10.3). The list is in no way comprehensive, nor is it intended to be; the object of the whole exercise was to choose sites where the cooperation of the local authorities was assured so that an integrated approach to the conservation task could be seen to be working. This explains the inclusion of Bologna, Taranto and Verona in Italy, three towns where coordination has been successfully achieved, and the exclusion of Venice where, despite international recognition, the constituent local authorities have failed to agree on a joint plan to save the city from ever-more serious flooding.

As a policy for the future of the city, urban conservation presents a number of difficulties. One of the main reasons for the rapid cycle of demolition and reconstruction is the changing pattern of functions within the urban area, the pressure of new demands on land leading to a constant process of redistribution in the mosaic of land use. The most spectacular manifestation of this process is the suburbanization of residential development as business and commerce price it out of central locations. Unfortunately, the purpose-built buildings for one form of land use can prove less than ideal for another. Urban conservation planners have always been faced with the delicate task of accommodating new functions into the existing fabric, often in the knowledge that adapting buildings will be more expensive than complete demolition and redevelopment. Even when the financial pressures can be resisted, it is not always possible to find a demand for floorspace in a renovated neighbourhood. Conservation studies undertaken by the Ministry of Housing and Local Government in Bath, Chester and York showed that in the historic centres of these cities as much as 40 per cent of the available floor area, especially in the upper storeys, was vacant (HMSO 1969; Insall 1969; Esher 1969).

Tourism has frequently provided a convenient, though rather too easy, solution. Historic buildings, either singly or in large groups, are a considerable attraction to visitors and many can be relatively easily adapted to house the service activities, like hotels, restaurants and gift shops, which tourism demands. However, the scale of tourist demand is unlikely to be sufficient, except in a few isolated cases, to fill all the available space. In any case, much of the attraction of towns and cities is the vibrance that the concentration of activities creates and this is all but lost if buildings are preserved as in a museum.

A large part of conservation in urban areas is concerned with residential building, very often the houses of ordinary people that have become rundown and fallen into decay. In such cases, one of the consequences of renovation can be a process of gentrification, whereby low-income families are replaced by others that are better off (Hamnett and Williams 1980). Such a change is obviously a danger with any kind of improvement to the urban fabric, but is particularly likely in conservation areas because of the way in which the middle classes have dominated the conservation movement in Western Europe. Local groups, such as the Bath Preservation Trust, constantly monitor changes and campaign for conservation policies; they also invariably come to believe their own propaganda and are keen to move to the refurbished neighbourhoods. In the process, rents are driven up and the original residents tend to drift away. Conservation is not necessarily a panacea for urban problems; pursuing it too enthusiastically can turn

Fig. 10.3
Demonstration projects
selected for the European
Architectural Heritage Year,
1975.

towns into monuments to the past, where nostalgia is substituted for drive and a sense of purpose. This kind of atmosphere will be all too familiar to those who have visited Georgian Bath or Baroque Salzburg.

Government action: national and local

Throughout Western Europe there is a commitment by governments to the principles of urban conservation and to the importance of the built environment in the cultural heritage, but there is considerable variation in the legislation and policies. As a result, there is little consistency in the scale and quality of the conservation work that has taken place (see Ch. 8). In France, systematic protection of individual buildings goes back to the 1830s, and over the years some 29 000 have been nationally listed, thus affording them the protection of the central government. Since 1962, when the Malraux Act came into operation, it has also been possible to designate conservation areas ('safeguarded sectors') in towns so that whole districts may

be preserved. An initial list of 400 towns was drawn up where such conservation areas were thought to be appropriate, but only just over sixty have been approved and in only a handful of these have the actual conservation plans been agreed. The main problems have been the length of time it took to survey the areas involved and the lack of adequate finance, which has caused the scope of even agreed schemes to be repeatedly reduced. Even where work has gone ahead, as in the Marais district in central Paris, there has been considerable criticism because of the way in which many of the original residents were forced out after restoration as a result of the increased rents, and because social networks, far from being preserved, were totally disrupted (Kain 1981).

In most countries in Western Europe, urban conservation is much more in the hands of local rather than central government. The UK has the huge total of over 170 000 nationally-listed buildings, but the responsibility for their conservation is largely in the hands of local planning authorities, as is the choice of conservation areas. Some central government money is available to help with the cost of preserving particularly outstanding buildings and townscapes, like Bath, York and Chester, but the initiative for obtaining it lies almost wholly with the local authority. There is therefore considerable regional variation in the enthusiasm with which conservation policies have been pursued and it was no accident that two of the first town schemes, conservation plans for a whole settlement, were at Totnes and Ashburton, both in the county of Devon. Nevertheless, despite the rather weak central direction, the principle of urban, as of rural, conservation is probably more firmly accepted in the UK than anywhere else in Western Europe, not least because it is a policy that can be relatively easily understood and implemented by local planning authorities.

Elsewhere, urban conservation policies are similar, though with marked variations in the degree of control by the different levels of government and the extent to which the policies have been implemented. Many of the oldest and most valuable historic urban landscapes are in the Mediterranean countries where the record is generally poor. In Italy, a few towns such as Urbino and Arezzo in the Marches, Bergano in Lombardy and Bologna have been almost completely preserved, but against this must be set the fact that effective comprehensive plans for Venice, Florence, Rome and Naples have yet to be agreed (Burtenshaw, Bateman and Ashworth 1981). In Greece, it was not until the 1970s that comprehensive planning legislation came on to the statute book so, consequently, the task of conservation in the country that was one of the first centres of urban civilization has hardly begun (Papageorgiou-Venetas 1981). Nevertheless, in comparison with most other parts of the world, Western Europe is extremely fortunate in the extent to which its urban heritage is known and recorded and in the effectiveness of the policies that have been developed to conserve it.

Western Europe is unique in the diversity of cultures found within a small area and in the high level of appreciation that exists about their importance. Despite the political fragmentation, there is a strong feeling of cultural unity and a sense of belonging to a single coherent tradition. This sense of identity has been fostered by the generally high level of economic development, which has helped to foster tourism and made travel, both at home and abroad, an accepted form of recreation. Actually visiting the relics of their cultural history has made people deeply aware of both their value and their fragility and stimulated a general determination to see them conserved. The aims of recreation and conservation policies are by no means always identical and can sometimes conflict, but it is in Western Europe that the greatest synthesis has been achieved.

Further reading

Burtenshaw D, Bateman M, Ashworth G J 1981 *The City in West Europe*. Wiley, Chichester

Kain R J P (ed) 1981 *Planning for Conservation*. Mansell, London

Kariel H G, P E 1982 Socio-cultural impacts of tourism; an example from the Austrian Alps. *Geografiska Annaler (Series B)* **64**: 1–16

Mennell S 1976 *Cultural Policy in Towns*. Council of Europe, Strasbourg

Nelson J G, Needham R D, Mann D L 1978 *International Experience with National Parks and Related Reserves*. University of Waterloo, Canada

Simmons I G 1975 *Rural Recreation in the Industrial World*. Edward Arnold, London

11

The encircling seas

Marine resources

The sea has always played an important role in the life of Western Europe; there are sixteen states with coastal waters in either the Atlantic, the North Sea, the Baltic or the Mediterranean and some countries, like France, Spain, Sweden and the UK, abut more than one of these major bodies of water (Alexander 1963). Traditionally, access to the sea has been the key to participation in intercontinental trade and has been exploited by many European states since the Middle Ages. Even today, with the advent of air travel, it is a much-prized asset, providing a high degree of flexibility in international affairs.

For very much longer, the sea has also been a reliable source of food. Even in modern times, using quite primitive equipment and more or less random hunting techniques, man has usually found fish for the taking in quantities sufficient for his needs. Only in the past generation has pressure on these and other marine resources begun to mount seriously, necessitating formal agreements about the division of the oceans' bounty.

Although recent, the change has nonetheless been very rapid, as the technological advances that have transformed all aspects of twentieth-century life have been applied to exploiting the seas. Not only have fish begun to be caught with great efficiency in unparalleled quantities, thus endangering stocks, but other resources, in particular oil and natural gas, are now being exploited on a large scale. Rather than acting as a gateway to the rest of the world and providing a marginal supplement to food supplies in Western Europe, the resources of the sea are now an integral part of the industrial economy of countries such as Norway, the UK and the Netherlands, providing the bulk of their fuel supplies (see Ch. 5). Naturally, other coastal states are eager to share in this new-found wealth. They have begun to take an unprecedentedly keen interest in the boundaries and extent of their coastal waters and have inaugurated frantic explorations to ascertain whether or not they too are in a position to exploit hitherto undreamt of mineral wealth. The fact that so far most have been disappointed has done little to dampen their enthusiasm for, at a time when mineral resources of all kinds are an expensive drain on most West European industrial economies, the benefits of success are potentially enormous.

Territorial waters

From the middle of the seventeenth century there was a general acceptance that the territorial waters of coastal states should extend for 5.5 km (3 nautical miles) out to sea from the high-water mark. They were defined in this way for reasons of defence rather than economics, as the distance represented the theoretical range of cannon fire and was therefore the zone that could be defended effectively from the land. During the last century there has been mounting dissatisfaction with this definition and today the tacit agreement has all but collapsed but, in the absence of any international agency governing the exploitation of the oceans, extensions to territorial waters have been *ad hoc* and opportunist (Hodgson and Smith 1979). The USA claimed 19.3 km (12 miles) over a century ago, and all but a minority of coastal nations have now followed suit, but for most this proved only a very temporary solution, given the growing demands being made on coastal waters.

The first concerted progress towards a resolution of the problem was provided by the United Nations Convention on the Law of the Sea, which was finally signed in 1964 (Johnston 1976). It gave states the right to exploit the mineral resources of their coastal waters to a depth of 200 m (656 ft) or beyond if exploitation was technically feasible. In the furtherance of such exploitation, states were permitted to build permanent structures, such as oil wells, so long as they were not accorded the status of islands with territorial waters of their own and providing they did not pose an undue hazard for shipping. The Convention also gave states rights to sedentary species of living things on the seabed, such as shellfish and crustacea, but not to fish. The latter exclusion was very significant, for at the time it removed the major item of economic interest in coastal waters. In general the Convention has worked well, although some difficulties have emerged. In shallow, semi-enclosed seas, like the North Sea, the Baltic and the Mediterranean, the claims of neighbouring states overlap and a dividing line has had to be agreed. Also, the outer territorial limit of the shelf, as defined in the Convention, depends on the technological ability to exploit its resources, rather than any uniquely-defined boundary, which does not make for any permanent definitions in the present climate of rapid progress (Smith 1980).

Faced with such shortcomings, further negotiations were inevitable and these took place within the context of the third phase of the United Nations Convention on the Law of the Sea which began in 1973 and was finally agreed in 1982 (Blake 1987). The agenda was extremely broad, but the main concern was to agree on the establishment of a 322 km (200 mile) Exclusive Economic Zone for states with coastal waters, embracing both the resources of the seabed and the coastal waters themselves. By 1975 there was broad agreement on the principle of such a zone and most west European states have moved independently to enact appropriate legislation. Iceland first unilaterally imposed an 80.5 km (50 mile) zone from which foreign fishing boats were banned around its coasts in 1972 and then three years later extended it to 322 km. The initial reaction was one of fury and righteous indignation on the part of the UK and the other west European countries, whose fishing fleets were suddenly excluded from waters they had fished for generations, but the so-called Cod Wars that ensued were totally ineffective (Mitchell 1976). Iceland showed itself as being quite capable of enforcing its new limits and very quickly the disgruntled governments turned their attention to laying claim to similar 322 km Exclusive Economic Zones around their own coasts.

All the major west European countries have now accepted the principle of a 322 km Exclusive Economic Zone and, where possible, laid claim to the areas in question, but the extensions have raised difficult problems. In some instances the distance separating neighbouring states is much less than 644 km and an alternative definition has had to be employed. In the

majority of cases the solution has been a median line drawn equidistant from the nearest points on the base lines of the territorial waters of the countries concerned, but this was not universally acceptable. The median-line solution would have given West Germany only a very small area of the North Sea in relation to the length of its coastline and this caused a protracted dispute with Denmark and the Netherlands. The issue was eventually resolved by these two countries ceding 7 000 and 5 000 km^2 respectively of their initial territorial claims to West Germany, thus giving it the all-important north-westward extension of its sector into the more promising oil and gas exploration areas of the North Sea. Elsewhere, as between the UK and the Republic of Ireland in the Irish Sea, the median line has been accepted provisionally but is still subject to ratification (Blacksell 1979). This is significant, because the uncertainty has so far effectively precluded any exploration for oil and gas in the disputed zone (Fig. 11.1). Further complications are created by isolated islands. For instance, the Exclusive Economic Zone of the UK has been much extended by the existence of several islands around its shores, but its claim to a 322 km territory around the barren, rocky outcrop of Rockall (way out in the Atlantic and annexed for security reasons in 1955) is strongly disputed by both the Republic of Ireland and Denmark and still remains to be settled (Brown 1978).

Further difficulties have arisen with the definition and implementation of Exclusive Economic Zones as a result of the political changes that have occurred recently in Western Europe, notably the establishment and subsequent enlargement of the European Community. In 1970, when the organization still only consisted of the six original members, a Common Fisheries Policy was agreed which, among other things, gave Community fishermen equality of access to all fishing grounds in the maritime waters under the sovereignty or jurisdiction of any member state. At the time it was a relatively uncontentious decision, since the bulk of fish were caught outside the narrow territorial zone as then defined. Now, of course, the situation has altered dramatically with the newly-imposed 322 km territorial limits and the consequent pressure on domestic waters around the coasts of Western Europe from fishermen excluded from traditional fishing grounds elsewhere in the world. Within the European Community too the matter became considerably more important after 1973 when Denmark, the Republic of Ireland and the UK all joined, as Denmark and the UK both had large fishing industries. What for most member states had initially been a matter of somewhat peripheral concern was

National mineral
prospecting zones — — —
in European
Community waters

European
Community waters

Preferential fishing
zone for U.K. / Irish
fishermen

Icelandic
waters

Norwegian
waters

Faroese
waters

0   km   500

Fig. 11.1
West European territorial
waters in the North Sea and
North Atlantic.

now an issue of vital national importance. Agreement
has also been made even more difficult to achieve,
because of the uncertainty as to whether the EC or
the individual member governments should resolve the
issue of fishing rights in Community waters (Allen
1980).

When the Community was enlarged in 1973, the
principle of a Common Fisheries Policy was retained,
but in a substantially modified form. Rather than there
being unrestricted access, during a ten-year transition
period up to the end of 1982 all members were entitled
to claim a 9.6 km (6 mile) exclusive zone off their
coasts for vessels which traditionally fished in those
waters and which operated from ports in that
geographical coastal area. This zone was extended to

19.2 km (12 miles) off parts of the coasts of Denmark,
including the whole of the Faroes and Greenland,
France, the Republic of Ireland and the UK. It was
assumed that a permanent solution would be worked
out during the ten-year transition period but, inevitably, the discussions taking place within the United
Nations Conference on the Law of the Sea and the
unilateral extensions of territorial waters to 322 km
made some interim revision essential. The members
decided that, rather than attempting to enact
Community legislation, all of them would extend their
fishing limits around their North Sea and North
Atlantic coasts from 1 January 1977 to 322 km,
without prejudice to the access already agreed for the
fishermen of any member country under the terms of

the temporary Common Fisheries Policy. At the same time, the Commission promised to put forward proposals in due course for similar extensions in the Mediterranean, but so far these have not materialized.

Even with the promise of this future action over the Mediterranean, the European Commission's proposals still fell short of the needs of member states, as a number also had territorial waters in the Baltic, not to mention outside Europe around overseas dependencies. In reframing their national legislation, most wished to include all their territorial waters and not just those in the North Sea and the North Atlantic. Denmark extended its limits in the Baltic, the Kattegat and the Skagerrak, as well as claiming 322 km around Greenland and the Faroes. West Germany extended its territorial waters in the Baltic as well as in the North Sea. Both France and the UK have also claimed extended limits off the coasts of a number of overseas territories, or territories for whose external relations they are responsible. In the case of France these include Guyana, New Caledonia, French Polynesia, French Antarctica, the Wallis and Futuna Islands, the islands of Tromelin, Glorieuses, Juan de Nova, Europa and Brassas du India, Clipperton Island, Réunion and Mayotte. The UK has claimed 322 km off the coasts of Bermuda and the British Virgin Islands; and France and the UK together have made a joint claim off their condiminium of the New Hebrides (Churchill 1980).

In the seas off the shores of the EC itself the extensions of territorial waters have raised serious problems, most of them relating not so much to the principle of extension as to how to manage best the available resources so as to maximize the benefit for all the members. Given the unequal distribution of both hydrocarbons and fish stocks, friction was almost inevitable, particularly where the allocation of fisheries was concerned. The fishing industry is not necessarily dependent on nearby, shore-based facilities for its successful operation, unlike the development of oil and gas fields. Therefore the exploitation of fisheries can take place more or less independently of the particular coastal state in whose waters they happen to be located and competition for available resources is correspondingly greater. The existence of the EC has, if anything, hindered rather than helped, for it introduced a new legal dimension and imposed a very short time-scale because of the need to negotiate a revision to the original Common Fisheries Policy by the beginning of 1983.

The fishing industry

The broad continental shelf and the shallow seas around the west coast of Europe have been exploited

Table 11.1 Fish production in Western Europe, 1986 (tonnes)

Country	Catch (tonnes)	Size of catch in relation to largest national catch	Decrease/increase 1969–86 (%)
Norway	2 822 300	100	56
Denmark	1 862 100	65	280
Spain	1 250 000	44	53
UK	846 500	29	−25
Iceland	839 200	29	28
France	784 000	27	−10
Turkey	567 300	20	375
Netherlands	503 300	17	299
Italy	478 400	16	28
Faroe Isles	330 000	11	−75
West Germany	305 600	10	6
Sweden	261 300	9	−19
Portugal	246 500	8	1
Republic of Ireland	203 400	7	1 079
Belgium	48 200	1	21

Data for Greece and Finland are not available, but neither country has a large fishing fleet.
Source: OECD 1987 *Review of Fisheries in OECD Member Countries 1986*. Paris

as a fishery since time immemorial. Indeed, until the present century there was nowhere else in the world where fishing was carried on to a comparable scale, and even in 1980 some 20 per cent of the total world catch of 56 million tonnes was landed in Western Europe. As recently as 1969, however, the proportion was 31 per cent and the sharp decline reflects the growing interest in the sea as a reliable source of food in other parts of the world, rather than any absolute decline in European fisheries.

The importance of the industry to the individual countries of Western Europe varies considerably, as can be seen from Table 11.1. In general, the largest fleets and catches are found on the northern and western peripheries of the continent, with Norway, Iceland and Denmark dominating the picture. The combined population of these three countries is only 9.5 million and the large fisheries are central to their economies and obviously, therefore, of great political significance to them. All have welcomed and, in the case of Iceland, pressed for the extensions to territorial waters; they have also viewed with great suspicion the proposals for equal access to all the territorial waters of the EC. Concern about the effect that this would have was one of the main reasons for Norway withdrawing its application for membership in 1972 and Denmark lagged some months behind the other members of the EC in accepting the terms of the Common Fisheries Policy.

In order of importance, the other nations with large fisheries are Spain, the UK and France but, in terms of their economies as a whole, these are very much less important than those in the Scandinavian countries discussed above. Also, in both the UK and France the size of the fishing industries has declined sharply in recent years as access to traditional deep-water fishing grounds on both sides of the North Atlantic has been progressively barred. Elsewhere the trends are variable, though the size of the industry everywhere is small (Coull 1972).

The main fishing grounds in Western Europe are found in the shallow waters that stretch north from the coasts of France and the Low Countries across the Irish, the North and the Norwegian Seas and on over the Atlantic to the coastal waters of Iceland and Greenland (Ministry of Agriculture, Fisheries and Food 1981). A wide variety of different species are to be found, and the North Sea in particular is also important as a spawning ground. Traditionally, cod and herring have formed the bulk of the catch with smaller amounts of haddock, plaice and sole also being taken where they are locally plentiful. Almost inevitably, however, the increased scale and efficiency of fishing in the past generation has put enormous pressure on existing fish stocks, with the herring being particularly badly affected. Throughout the 1960s the catch of this fish in the North Sea alone averaged nearly 900 000 tonnes, but over-exploitation led to a rapid decline and from March 1977 until 1982 fishing for North Sea herring was prohibited entirely by mutual agreement. A similar decline caused a ban to be imposed to the west of Scotland in the Celtic Sea in 1978 and the catch for the Irish Sea was limited to 10 000 tonnes a year. The stocks of other species too have varied, though it is not clear whether this is due to over-fishing or long-term periodic changes in migration patterns. Inexplicably, the annual cod catch in the North Sea nearly doubled in the decade 1965–75 to 216 000 tonnes while, at the same time, there was an almost parallel decline in the sprat fishery.

In recent years the pressures on existing stocks of fish traditionally caught has kindled interest in other species, the most obvious example being the rise and decline of mackerel fishing. Mackerel had always been viewed rather disdainfully as a poor substitute for herring but, when stocks of the latter began to disappear in the early 1960s, mackerel suddenly started to attract international attention. From being of only local significance at the beginning of the decade, more than 1 million tonnes were landed from the North Sea alone in 1967. Catches of this size simply could not be sustained and by 1972 the stock had collapsed and with it the fishery. A similar pattern, though rather less wildly fluctuating, was seen to the west of Britain, though even here mackerel stocks have only been stabilized by instituting catch quotas and fishing seasons.

Fish processing for both human and animal consumption has also widened the range of species of interest to the fishing industry. Whiting, coley and Norway pout have all begun to be taken in large quantities in the last twenty years as a result of the growth in these less discriminating demands for fish.

All the species described above predominantly inhabit shallow coastal waters and, with the exception of mackerel, are largely non-migratory. This means that their distribution is both limited and predictable and also that access to stocks is very unequally divided. The UK, the Faroes, Iceland and Norway, surrounded as they are by shallow seas, have been particularly favoured, but the fleets from other countries have been anxious to share in their good fortune. The effects of the extensions of territorial waters have already been discussed, but the truth is that no amount of administrative manipulation can disguise the fact that there are too many fishermen chasing too few fish in the waters of northern Europe, no matter what species is being talked about. With access to coastal waters becoming more difficult everywhere in the world, European fishing fleets have begun to turn to deep-sea varieties as a substitute. In the North Atlantic, the most important of these so far has been the blue-whiting, catches of which are now believed to be well in excess of 1 million tonnes a year, but potentially a similar interest could be focused on several other species as well. The nature of the fishing industry is, therefore, changing rapidly as a result of the extended territorial waters and the increased pressure on the most easily harvested stocks. Regulation is becoming the norm in shallow coastal waters and, faced with increasing restrictions, fishermen are turning to more capital-intensive operations in the deep oceans where political restrictions are, at the moment, still virtually non-existent.

Management and regulation inside territorial waters

Western European governments have been faced with a novel and rather bewildering challenge by the sudden and mushrooming interest in the resources of their territorial waters. With little in the way of precedent to guide them from the annals of international or national law, they have each been faced with the problem of devising enforceable management policies, stringent enough to provide a sound return for their national exchequers and to guarantee the health and safety of those working in the hazardous environment of the sea, while at the same time not being so draconian as to dissuade investors from venturing risk capital.

Oil and natural gas

The most contentious and difficult problems have of course been caused by the burgeoning discoveries and exploitation of hydrocarbons in the North Sea and other coastal waters, following the massive discovery of gas in what is now known as the Groningen field on the northern coast of the Netherlands in 1959, and the first commercial off-shore find in 1965 close to the shores of eastern England at West Sole. In 1981, some 25 per cent of Western Europe's oil and virtually all its natural gas was produced within the region, the bulk of it from off-shore production sites. As invariably happens with such natural resources, however, the physical occurrence of both oil and natural gas in no way matches either the political map or the distribution of potential demand. The UK enjoys the luxury of 60 per cent of known off-shore reserves of oil and 32 per cent of the gas reserves; the figures for Norway are 35 and 53 per cent respectively. These two countries dominate the picture; for the rest, the Netherlands controls 1.8 per cent of the off-shore oil production and 9 per cent of the natural gas, while the comparable figures for Denmark are 3 and 6 per cent. Belgium, the Republic of Ireland, France and West Germany have almost nothing to show for their exploration efforts, except the small gas field off the south coast of Ireland at Kinsale Head and the pipeline linking Emden in West Germany with the Norwegian Cod gas field (Offshore Promotion Services 1980).

These variations, coupled with the very different energy demands of the countries in Western Europe, have inevitably led to somewhat different policies and priorities for the development of oil and natural gas within the region. The UK sector has been developed fastest, because of the availability of supplies combined with a large and eager domestic market. On the other hand, in the Norwegian sector the pace has been markedly slower, reflecting a determination on the part of government that the benefits of oil and gas revenues be available to Norway's 4 million citizens for as long as possible. In the Danish sector, where the finds so far have been disappointing, the circumstances have been quite different and it is probable that none of the gas fields would have been brought into production at all had it not been for the fact that in doing so the production consortium guaranteed itself further exploration rights from the government.

The most direct control over development has been by governments deciding who shall prospect and where. Two basic systems have been used to allocate prospecting rights: either the sector has been divided into blocks which have then been auctioned for specific periods, or the whole sector has been leased to a consortium. As time has progressed, the block system has come to be almost universally favoured and now only Denmark persists in treating its sector as a single entity.

There are many variations on the block principle and the size varies from sector to sector. In general, the oil companies prefer to have blocks that are as large as possible, giving them maximum freedom of action, while governments try to restrict the size so that they gain as much control as possible. Nevertheless, in seeking to maximize their influence, governments must guard against the danger of deterring the oil companies from prospecting at all.

Off Western Europe the blocks are smallest in the UK sector and the government has carefully controlled both exploration and development, exercising an ever-closer rein as time has gone on. There have so far been seven rounds of offers for prospecting rights since 1964 and it is interesting to observe how the UK strategy has changed over time. In 1964 and 1965, in the first two rounds of bidding, over 2 000 blocks were put on offer and 475 taken up, reflecting an eagerness on the part of both the government and the prospecting companies to push ahead with development as fast as possible, even though neither had any precise idea about the locations that were likely to prove fruitful. Subsequently, both the numbers of blocks put on offer and the uptake have declined sharply as knowledge about the physical extent of the deposits has become more accurate and the oil and gas companies have tailored their activity to better informed assessments of market demands and costs of extraction (Anon. 1982a).

The relationship between the public and the private sectors of the economy in the development and exploitation of oil and gas fields in the seas off the coasts of Western Europe has been both complex and dynamic. In general, governments were loath to commit public resources to the initial search but, once exploitable reserves were proven, they became increasingly interested in securing a direct stake in their development. In 1975, the Labour government in the UK established the British National Oil Corporation, a name changed later to Britoil, with a view to undertaking exploration and development on its own behalf and the company now has interests in five major oilfields. The then government also made it a condition of all new licences granted for prospecting blocks that Britoil had at least a 51 per cent share, thus ensuring direct national control over development policy. After the 1979 election and the change of political control to a Conservative administration, however, much less importance was attached to public ownership. The requirement that Britoil have a majority shareholding in new developments was abolished and in 1982 the company was sold to private investors, although with a number of safeguards to ensure that it remained predominantly in British hands. The Norwegian government has also taken steps to guarantee the state a strong stake in the development of off-shore hydrocarbon deposits, but in the Netherlands and West Germany, where the sectors have been markedly less productive, companies have maintained a much freer hand.

Fisheries

Revision of the Common Fisheries Policy, worked out by the original six members of the European Community in 1970 and supplanting the temporary, transitional arrangements agreed to ease the enlargement of the Community in 1973, has proved predictably difficult and contentious. A draft policy was published by the Commission in mid-1982 and, after six months of hard negotiation, it was accepted by nine of the ten members but Denmark, the country whose fishing industry had grown faster than any other since joining the Community, refused to accept the limitations that the policy would impose on its access to what it considered Community waters. If no agreement were forthcoming by the end of 1982, fleets from all the member countries would have had the right to fish anywhere at all in these waters, and this situation arose briefly in early 1983. By the end of January in that year, however, the Danes accepted the terms of the Common Fisheries Policy and it became fully operational.

The accession of Spain and Portugal to the EC at the beginning of 1986 imposed further strains on the policy. Spain has a larger fishing fleet than any other member state and is eager to exploit the Community's seas. Although limitations on access by its fishing fleet have been agreed for a transitional period up to 1995, there is still a threat of the Common Fisheries Policy being disrupted if permanent arrangements are not decided for Spain by that date. Portugal, which has a much smaller fleet of mainly in-shore fishing vessels, poses less of a problem (Wise 1987).

Table 11.2 Total allowable catch quotas for the main varieties of edible fish in the European Community waters (in tonnes of cod equivalent) under the terms of the Common Fisheries Policy

	tonnes	(%)
United Kingdom	464 000	(36)
Denmark	305 000	(24)
West Germany	186 000	(14)
France	162 000	(13)
Netherlands	92 000	(7)
Republic of Ireland	47 000	(4)
Belgium	25 000	(2)

Source: Anon 1982b At last a common fish policy. *The Economist* 6 Nov 1982:72

The new policy establishes a 9.6 km wide exclusive zone around all coasts, which will be treated as part of the national preserve and within which other member states will have absolutely no fishing rights. There will then be a zone between 9.6 and 19.2 km to which there will be limited access. For instance, the French will continue to be allowed to fish off south-west England, the Irish and the British will have a reciprocal arrangement in the Irish Sea, and the Danes will be able to fish in the Baltic waters off West Germany. The major problem has arisen off northern Britain where this limited-access zone has been considerably extended to protect the fishing industry in both Scotland and the Shetland Islands. Since the Danes have traditionally fished these waters, among the most productive in Western Europe, they feel somewhat unfairly treated and are determined either to see the limited-access zone reduced in size or the catches they are allowed to take from it increased (Anon 1982b).

In addition to stipulating where fishermen from each member country may fish, the policy also lays down overall catch quotas and, as can be seen from Table 11.2, the UK and Denmark between them account for some 60 per cent of the total, so that existing national interests are well catered for in the new arrangements. The purpose of these quotas is to allow some measure of Community control over the level of fishing so as to ensure the permanent conservation of fish stocks. Another feature of the policy is a three-year programme of financial aid from Community funds to the tune of £150 million to help the fishing industries in the individual member countries in adjusting to the revised provisions. Further proposals for conservation also figure prominently, including such things as limitations on the kind of net that may be used so that young fish are given some measure of protection.

Finally, there are a series of regulations governing the relationships between the Community and other Western European states as far as fisheries are concerned. These deal with matters such as catch quotas, both for Community fishermen in the waters of third states and vice versa, and the allowable level of fish imports from these countries. The latter are included not only because unrestricted imports could undermine the whole basis of the Community fishing industry, but also because there is a need to normalize relations between individual member states and some of their non-Community counterparts. This applies particularly to the UK and Iceland. The lucrative British market was all but closed to Iceland after the Cod Wars, and the introduction of the new Common Fisheries Policy offers an obvious basis for a more harmonious new start (Commission of the European Communities 1982).

The protracted negotiations and the conflicts of interest have underlined how difficult it is to agree on any joint policy among twelve independent states, each of which fears it may be compromising its own national interests. Nor is the question of access to EC waters by any means totally settled. In addition to the difficulties associated with absorbing Spain and Portugal into the Community, discussed above, access to the waters in the Mediterranean has yet to be negotiated. This will almost certainly raise formidable barriers as so many countries that are not members of the EC are involved (Kliot (1987).

Marine pollution

The growing use that is now made of the seas and the seabed in the coastal waters of Western Europe has focused attention on their long-established function as a free and unregulated rubbish dump. In the last two decades it has become increasingly evident that the growing demands on this means of waste disposal, together with the threat that massive marine pollution in the form of oil spillages could pose for the fisheries and the other economic activities in west European coastal waters, mean that some form of control is imperative.

Pollution of the sea is of course not a single problem, but rather a whole range of manifestations of the undesirable consequences of twentieth-century industrial society. Nevertheless, Johnson (1979) has identified four major facets: the discharge of effluents from land; the deliberate dumping of waste at sea; the by-products of exploiting marine and submarine resources, especially the exploitation of the seabed; and waste spillages from sea transport and navigation.

The discharge of effluents into rivers or directly into the sea takes two forms: sewage and industrial waste. Throughout the nineteenth and early twentieth centuries, as urbanization and industrialization progressed, it was the accepted way of disposing of waste in all the countries of Western Europe, and the detrimental effects on both public health and fresh-water river life were only gradually appreciated. Subsequently, great efforts have been made to clean up rivers by treating effluent, and the reduced discharges have had an incidentally beneficial effect on the coastal seas as well. The effect is, however, incidental, since it has traditionally been assumed that any effluent reaching the sea will quickly become so diluted and dissipated as to be rendered harmless and not even aesthetically unpleasant. Such an attitude is justified to the extent that there is no firm evidence of a serious public health hazard in the open seas around north-western Europe, nor apparently any long-term ill-effects on wildlife, but in the more enclosed waters of the Mediterranean and the Baltic the dangers are already obvious. In the Mediterranean basin, concern has reached such a level that the coastal states have even begun to cooperate in an attempt to reduce and hopefully eliminate discharges of both domestic and industrial effluent. There is no doubting the enormity of the challenge, but the problems involved are more organizational than technical, as evidenced by the recent history of the UK. Some 3 billion m^3 of effluent is discharged annually around the British coasts, of which two-thirds is now treated compared with virtually none a century ago. The difficulty is that the residual amount is produced by a large number of small sources scattered along the coast and the cost of further extending treatment is therefore very high.

On its own, treatment is not always a complete answer to the use of the open seas as an option for waste disposal, as in most west European countries dumping is not only allowed, but officially sanctioned. In the UK, some 7 million tonnes a year of sewage sludge are dumped in coastal waters and also a similar amount of industrial waste. The largest component of the industrial waste is colliery spoil deposited off the North Sea coast of north-east England. The scale of industrial dumping by coastal states in Western Europe varies considerably and depends less on actual demand than on the policy of individual governments. None of the other countries bordering the North Sea currently contributes more than 1 million tonnes a year, with West Germany and Belgium generating only about half that amount and Norway less than 200 000 tonnes. It needs to be emphasized, however, that none of this officially-licensed dumping includes recognized toxic wastes, which internationally-agreed conventions require to be containerized and disposed

Fig. 11.2
Tanker oil spills (of over
5 000 barrels) known to have
occurred in west European
waters since 1970.

of more than 240 km (150 miles) from land in waters more than 2 000 m (1.24 miles) deep.

Obvious, though happily so far potential rather than actual, sources of marine pollution in coastal waters are the burgeoning numbers of permanent installations for extracting oil and natural gas from the seabed. There have been several serious accidents in European waters. A blow-out of gas and oil occurred at the Bravo drilling rig on the Ekofisk oilfield in the Norwegian sector of the North Sea in April 1977. The blow-out took a week to bring under control and only resulted in the escape of 20 000 tonnes of crude oil, but it underlined the potential dangers associated with this new area of mineral exploitation and the difficulty and high cost of containing any accident. The dangers were underlined further in July 1988 when the Piper Alpha oil rig caught fire and exploded, killing over 150 workers. The fire took three weeks to bring under control.

Finally, there is the pollution generated regularly from oil tankers, transporting crude oil from all parts of the world to the unique concentration of industrial cities in Western Europe. Figure 11.2 shows that in the decade 1970–80 some thirty-seven spillages of more than 5 000 barrels of oil are known to have occurred, with a particularly heavy concentration in the English Channel and the southern part of the North Sea. Since it is thought that these large spillages account for less than 5 per cent of the total number (International Tanker Owners Federation 1980), the scale and seriousness of the threat from this source of pollution is self-evident, especially in light of the limited sanctions that national governments can exercise over shipping on the high seas.

As with all other matters relating to international waters, controlling marine pollution, as opposed to recognizing the actual and potential dangers, is a difficult task, involving several governments, all with different perceptions of the problems involved. However, the three major semi-enclosed seas abutting the coasts of Western Europe – the North Sea, the Baltic and the Mediterranean – are now all covered by multilateral agreements on the control of oil spillages. The Bonn agreement, signed by Belgium, Denmark, France, West Germany, the Netherlands, Norway, Sweden and the UK in 1969 covers the North Sea; a similar arrangement for the Baltic was signed by Denmark, Finland, East Germany, West Germany,

Poland, Sweden and the USSR in 1974; and in 1976, Cyprus, Egypt, France, Greece, Israel, Italy, Lebanon, Libya, Malta, Monaco, Morocco, Spain, Tunisia, Turkey and Yugoslavia signed a convention covering the Mediterranean. There is also an agreement signed by most of the coastal states of Western Europe aimed at controlling marine pollution from land-based sources that came into force in 1978. Significantly though Italy, whose industries contribute more than those of any other country to the pollution in the Mediterranean, has so far refused to be a party to it, underlining the fundamental weakness of any international action that depends on the goodwill of the countries involved. Indeed, while international agreement on procedures and policies may be highly desirable, effective preventative procedures are still very much the preserve of national governments. In some parts of Western Europe, bilateral arrangements, as for example the Manche Plan concluded between the UK and France in 1978 to deal with oil spillages in the English Channel, work well, but for the most part any corporate action is *ad hoc* and usually brought about by the need to respond to a particular calamity.

The recent past has seen an unprecedented proliferation in formal arrangements for bringing off-shore economic activities under some form of political control. In the main the initiative has been taken by and remains with national governments, but they have had to act against a groundswell of support for international action. Nevertheless, organizations like the EC have in general only been able to act independently insofar as individual national governments have allowed them to. A prime example is the much-vaunted Common Fisheries Policy which is mainly structured so as to protect the national fishery interests of the members of the Community, rather than any wider common goals. A similar situation, but on a much broader front, is the failure of world governments to ratify the Law of the Sea Treaty that has been under negotiation since 1973. One of the main objections is that the proposed International Seabed Mining Authority, which would be under the control of the United Nations, might adversely interfere with national programmes of exploration and recovery of minerals.

Note

The progression towards a Common Fisheries Policy was chronicled in numerous communications of the Commission of the European Communities during 1982: notably CPM (82) 338/final/5 (18.8.82); COM (82) 339/final (11.6.82); COM (82) 340/final (18.6.82); COM (82) 368/final (11.6.82); COM (82) 539/final (9.9.82).

Further reading

Allen R 1980 Fishing for a common policy. *Journal of Common Market Studies* 19: 123–39

Blacksell M 1979 Frontiers at sea. *Geographical Magazine* **51**: 521–4

Churchill R 1980 Revision of the EEC's Common Fisheries Policy. *European Law Review* **5**: 3–37 and 95–111

Hodgson R D, Smith R W (1979) Boundary issues created by extended national maritime claims. *Geographical Review* **69**: 423–33

Ministry of Agriculture, Fisheries and Food 1981 *Atlas of the Sea around the British Isles*. MAFF, London

Mitchell B 1976 Politics, fish and international resource management: the British–Icelandic Cod War. *Geographical Review* **66**: 127–39

Wise M 1984 *The Common Fisheries Policy of the European Community*. Methuen, London

12

Trends in regional development

The diversity of Western Europe

An intricate patchwork

The nations of Western Europe have shared many changes since the Second World War. Each experienced economic recovery and prolonged dynamism but then moved into a period of depression after 1973–74. Each underwent demographic revival and, although this decelerated after the mid-1960s, rural exodus and varying manifestations of urbanization served to alter the distribution of population profoundly. Each viewed the wider world through the apparatus of mass media and increasingly through tourists' eyes so that west Europeans tended to become more 'international' with regard to dress, popular music, sport and even diet and speech. Yet Western Europe remains an intricate patchwork of national and regional identities, with eighteen countries occupying a combined area only two-fifths that of the USA and each having its own currency, language (or languages) and national 'system' for getting things done.

Western Europe has been called a peninsula of Asia; it is also a realm of capes and bays and islands, of subtle variations in climate, soil quality and landscape that is quite different from the wide expanses of the greater continents. Its people display marked differences of physique, skin tone and colour of hair and eyes, but inter-regional and international migration has encouraged greater mixing than ever before. Local customs linger on but show a tendency to fade with every generation that passes. Fundamental uniqueness of place – the very substance of geography – survives but almost every nation in Western Europe has, in its own way and in its own time, introduced schemes for attempting to reduce spatial manifestations of socio-economic inequality. Some are simple, others sophisticated; some have long pedigrees, others

have appeared suddenly; some cover specific sectors, while others are much more integrated (Clout 1987a; Pinder 1983). Many are what may be thought of as 'open' or explicit regional policies, while other policies are implicit, having sectoral issues such as job creation as their focus but also having very important spatial expressions. Twenty years ago it seemed possible to believe that some of these brands of regional policy were quite successful, while others left something to be desired. Now all have been overtaken by world events and are tragically outpaced by recession, inflation and mounting unemployment (Yuill, Allen and Hull 1980; Ashcroft 1982). The 'golden age' of regional policy in the countries of Western Europe spanned the quarter-century preceding the mid-1970s; now that age is emphatically over.

Regional differences but human problems

Regional disparities are spatial generalizations, abstracted from the realities of life and work experienced by ordinary people at specific places. Contrasts in well-being and class structure are softened by the calculation of regional indicators which collapse extreme conditions into the tidier and somewhat misleading form of spatial averages. Strictly speaking, there are no such things as 'regional problems' or indeed 'problem regions' but only varying permutations of the human condition cast in different spatial settings. Although the term 'regional development' is used widely – and will certainly be employed in this chapter – it should be considered as something of a misnomer since it is ultimately human life that needs to be enhanced; regions are merely convenient packages. This point is not just a matter of pedantry; to grasp it is fundamental to any meaningful understanding of the concept of spatial differentiation.

Regional differences in economic conditions embrace a multitude of contributory factors, ranging from

Fig. 12.1
Population density.

density of population, location and array of natural resources in each territorial package, to the political power of its rulers, the entrepreneurial skills and inventiveness of its inhabitants, and the volume of capital available for productive investment (Fig. 12.1) (Allen 1979). Consideration must also be given to the relative demand for each region's products or expertise on the local market, and the efficiency of networks of communication which allow fuel, raw materials and other commodities to be brought in and manufactured goods and other outputs to be dispatched elsewhere (Brown and Burrows 1977).

Inevitably the significance of these inter-relationships at each particular place undergoes change with the passage of time. New resources and alternative forms of technology are discovered, innovative modes of communication developed and administrative boundaries remodelled, while political and commercial empires rise and fall. Resources of capital and labour are, of course, reasonably mobile and may be directed in support of areas that lag in terms of economic dynamism or fail to enjoy qualities that endowed them with greatness in the past. But adjustments of this kind are far from automatic and Western Europe is littered with localities that once flourished but have

now fallen into decline. The most striking examples are mining areas, textile towns and metallurgical districts that pioneered modern industrialization in the nineteenth century but subsequently lost their advantages because of competition from new sources of energy, raw materials and cheaper manufactured goods.

By contrast, capital cities in administratively centralized countries have flourished as dominant concentrations of labour, expertise and political and economic power. They form the largest single components of home markets, control links with the outside world and have succeeded in attracting investment capital on an impressive scale. The situation is less extreme in recently unified nations, such as Italy, or in federal states, like Switzerland or West Germany, where economic and political powers are distributed more widely. For example, the federal capital (Bonn) is literally a small town in Germany, coming nineteenth in the hierarchy of urban centres and sharing an airport with Cologne. Hamburg, Frankfurt and Munich are the largest agglomerations in the country; Dusseldorf and Frankfurt are the major commercial cities; and manufacturing, service activities and the press are distributed widely in the *Länder*.

Cores and peripheries

Capitals and many other major cities operate as normative centres in which innovations have a propensity to take place and from which opinions are diffused across wider territory (Keeble, Owens and Thompson 1982). People who live beyond them tend to be late receivers of ideas and followers of fashion, although modern systems of communication have shrunk space in ways that were inconceivable just a couple of generations ago. More peripheral locations lack the processes of agglomeration and concentration that function in core areas and enable capital and expertise to build up even further, thereby reinforcing differences between these types of region (Mény and Wright 1985; Brugger and Stuckey 1987).

Peripheral areas are fragmented in spatial, economic and organizational terms and tend to be more vulnerable to downward swings in business activity. Branch factories in the periphery are more likely to close in times of recession than are enterprises in core areas, which tend to display an ability to adapt and innovate more readily. However, in the 1980s, economic conditions have deteriorated in many of Western Europe's major cities so that the environment of many core areas differs greatly from the stereotype. After enjoying the advantages of agglomeration for decades, firms in these localities have been forced to count the cost of congestion, pollution and expensive accommodation and labour. Planned decentralization has directed jobs away from many metropolitan areas and has contributed to the economic and social problems currently experienced in inner-city districts. The employment base of metropolitan areas will be weakened even more as new technology is applied to routine office work.

The contrast between the prosperous industrialized 'centre' and the declining, largely rural 'periphery' of Western Europe was spelled out in a United Nations survey as early as 1954, and the model has been refined many times since then (Despicht 1980). Various scales of core and periphery have been identified, ranging from individual cities and their environs to the great 'Lotharingian axis' (comprising the Rhinelands, northern Italy and Paris) which differed so markedly from the Mezzogiorno and western France in the Europe of the Six (Rokkan 1980). Successive enlargements of the EC in 1973, 1981 and 1986 added south-east England to the EC's developed axis and enlarged its complicated periphery by the inclusion of the rest of the UK, the Republic of Ireland, parts of Denmark and Greece, and the whole of Portugal and Spain (King 1982). Seers' (1979) analysis of economic conditions in complete countries produced a somewhat different picture: with Spain, Portugal, the Republic of Ireland, Greece and Yugoslavia forming the periphery of Western Europe at large; Denmark, France, Benelux, West Germany, Norway, Sweden, Switzerland and Austria comprising the core; and a 'semi-periphery' of the UK, Italy and Finland being identified between them.

A regional typology

The core/periphery contrast offers a convenient starting point for discussing regional differences, but it is helpful to proceed to a more complex spatial typology, such as that advanced by Holland (1976a, b) who recognized 'over-developed', 'neutral', 'intermediate', 'depressed' and 'under-developed' regions. In addition, there are frontier regions which display quite distinctive features and problems.

1. *Over-developed regions* enjoy – or more accurately enjoyed – impressive economic dynamism but are also characterized by serious pressures on transport, housing and other types of infrastructure. Accommodating such pressures can only be achieved at high cost and after great environmental sacrifice. As has been suggested, very large shares of national population and economic life are to be found in over-developed regions. For example, the Paris region contains one-fifth of the French population and a slightly greater share of jobs on 2 per cent of national territory, while giving rise to 30 per cent of GDP. The London metropolitan region houses 23 per cent, greater Copenhagen 35 per cent, the Randstad 46 per cent, and the Rhine–Ruhr 15 per cent of their national populations (Guttesen and Nielsen 1975). Several other areas of West Germany, the industrial districts of northern Italy and arguably some cities in southern Europe also typify over-developed areas, albeit of differing magnitude and intensity of dynamism. These congested areas give rise to the most sophisticated life styles in Western Europe but also have serious social deprivation and environmental decay. In the recent past, decentralization has been seen as a remedy both for metropolitan congestion and for under-development elsewhere, but there is precious little dynamism anywhere in the 1980s and it may be argued that what does exist is desperately needed in the inner cities (Nicholson 1981).

2. *Neutral regions* are located in the readily accessible environs of over-developed areas and may be typified by outer parts of the Paris, Basin and south-east England. They function as reception zones for urban deconcentration and tend to be characterized by important population growth, expanding employment

and rising incomes. They contain many light industries and office activities which have been moved to the pleasant living and working environments that market towns and greenfield sites can offer.

3. *Depressed regions* were formerly leaders in their respective fields but have been overtaken subsequently by other areas. Rates of unemployment and outmigration are typically high and the built environment of abandoned mines, spoil heaps, workers' housing and old factories displays many features that are sadly outmoded. Classic examples are provided by coal- and iron-mining districts (such as the Ruhr, Saar, northern France, Lorraine, Wallonia, Dutch Limburg and several parts of the UK), textile areas (as in Flanders, Lancashire and west Yorkshire), and shipbuilding towns (such as those in north-east England or on the Clyde in Scotland). New examples involve areas where flourishing activities have been turned into 'sunset' industries in the course of the present recession. The West Midlands, with its collapsing engineering and vehicle industries, is a particularly tragic case. The problems of depressed regions have been further aggravated by the fact that once-healthy core areas can no longer supply employment opportunities to bale them out.

4. *Under-developed regions* are those peripheral parts of Western Europe where modern industrial capitalism failed to take root to any great extent. Jobs and incomes are still quite strongly geared to farming but many farms are too small and under-capitalized to be viable. Younger people have tended to leave the land, abandoning farming to an ageing population that is unlikely to innovate. From mid-century to the onset of economic crisis in the 1970s, large numbers of labour migrants left the low wages, underemployment and high levels of unemployment in under-developed regions to move to labour-hungry urban areas both within and beyond their national boundaries. But since 1973 this palliative has come to an end and many unemployed migrants have quit the industrial cities to return to their home areas where their presence aggravates employment problems even further. Rather than go back to the land, they often seek jobs in local market towns, but many traditional service and workshop activities are already overstaffed and their employees effectively underemployed.

The so-called black economy has come to flourish under these circumstances in the Mezzogiorno, Iberia and many other regions where men, women and schoolchildren earn a pittance in craft industries such as textiles, clothing, footwear and furniture. They have no social security, minimum wage, insurance or protection under health and safety regulations. In

some towns of southern Italy entire neighbourhoods function as clandestine workshops which disappear rapidly when word gets out that labour inspectors are about to visit (Hamilton and Just 1981). The challenge of under-developed regions is clearly not just to modernize agriculture but to create reasonable job opportunities in every other sector as well. The task is compounded by poor provision of roads, schools, hospitals and water supplies, with the latter problem being particularly serious in many Mediterranean areas, where poor soils and steep slopes hinder agricultural improvement. Remoteness from the economic core areas of Western Europe, lack of viable industrial expertise and absence of modern industrial training facilities make it all the more difficult to attract investment to peripheral regions.

5. *Intermediate regions* display employment, income and migration characteristics which reflect a mixture of conditions encountered in other types of region. For example some under-developed regions contain large, decaying urban areas which lack both the dynamism of over-developed areas and the residue of industrialization encountered in depressed areas; Naples is a case in point.

6. *Frontier regions* may be handicapped by inadequate cross-border infrastructure or by differences in income, currency and law in adjacent states. Some share general problems to which common solutions might prove advantageous; for example, many parts of the steel-making triangle of the Saar, Lorraine and southern Luxembourg face very similar difficulties that stem from the decline of their staple industry (Burtenshaw 1976). By contrast, a unique set of difficulties is experienced in the eastern fringe of West Germany and Austria which abut on to the closed frontier of the Iron Curtain.

Systems of aid

General aims

Under-developed, depressed and, to a lesser extent, frontier regions have been perceived by individual countries as meriting special treatment to promote redistribution of capital and employment. Virtually every national government defined assisted areas and devised mechanisms of regional aid in response to its unique perception of political, economic and cultural forces at work within its borders. In many cases, policies and principles proved considerably more ambiguous than the vote-catching gestures involved in making financial awards (Vanhove and Klaasen 1987).

In addition, assisted areas, mechanisms and rates of support were subject to considerable revision over the years, as the balance of political power shifted and economic circumstances changed. It would be impossible to cope with such intricacy in the present chapter, which will simply offer a basic outline.

The general aim of regional policy is to reduce spatial imbalances in economic activity and prosperity, once they have been perceived as political problems. Such perceptions derive from both moral and economic principles. It is arguable that unequal access to income and opportunity is socially unacceptable and morally unjust, and hence regional policy should be implemented as part of a broader drive for equity. In addition, it may be argued that maladaption in regional activity prevents national economies making the most efficient use of resources and thereby restricts the generation of wealth (Molle and Paelinck 1979). As a consequence of these and other arguments, the brands of regional policy implemented in Western Europe contain various strands, which include:

managing economic development to promote not only the nation as a whole but also component regions, with respect to their distinct needs, problems and potentialities;

reducing disparities between regions in terms of economic activity, welfare and prosperity;

supporting the economic and social foundations of life in the regions; and undertaking physical planning of housing, roads and other features in a coherent programme in line with national and regional aims.

Constitutional contrasts

With so many countries involved it is not surprising that Western Europe's systems of regional aid were devised under very different constitutional conditions. *Aménagement du territoire* in France exemplifies an integrated approach which was elaborated during the 1960s but had its roots in the nation's highly centralized administration and its system of national economic planning which commenced in 1947. Regional policies expanded from attempting to reduce the disparity between Paris and the provinces to providing industrial jobs in the rural west and renovating old manufacturing and mining areas in the north and north-east. Every part of the country, and hence every type of region, had its place in the grand design and was allocated a specific policy. Needless to say, the system proved more elegant and objective in theory

than in practice (Frémont 1978). After the Socialist administration came to power in 1981, a share of the responsibility for regional development was transferred to the regions themselves.

The British approach was also centralized but was far more pragmatic and sectoral in character, with a variety of policies being devised to meet a range of social and economic ends. By contrast, West Germany operates a far more decentralized system since the *Länder* are responsible for regional policy and many other economic issues. However, links were strengthened between them and the central government in the 1960s and guidelines for regional development were drawn up. Broad matters of policy and sources of finance are worked out by both federal and state authorities, but implementation of policy is left to ministers in the *Länder* (Jung 1982; Kunzmann 1981). Internal bargaining is obviously central to all brands of regional policy but is particularly critical in Belgium, where claims for assistance from the Flemish north and the Walloon south have required extremely delicate handling and compromise (De Clercq and Naert 1985).

The passage of time

Individual countries devised policies at various times in the past and adopted quite different scales for defining assisted areas. For example, extensive parts of Italy, France and, for a long time, the UK qualified to receive regional aid, in contrast with much smaller units in West Germany, Belgium and the Netherlands (Fig. 12.2). However, subsequent changes in political and economic circumstances gave rise to modifications in their territorial extent and to the type and value of assistance to which they were entitled. British schemes of regional aid began in 1934 as welfare measures in districts with high levels of unemployment. Objectives gradually broadened and policies proliferated, elaborating the map of regional assistance from the 'special areas' of the 1930s to the wide system of graded financial aid that operated in the 1970s. Nonetheless, regional policy was subject to sharp reappraisal during those decades as the balance of party political power shifted. In the summer of 1979 the Conservative government announced fundamental changes in the distribution and intensity of aid for regional job creation. In consequence, many sections of Scotland, Wales and northern England lost assisted-area status and the map was trimmed down to involve only 25 per cent of the workforce after 1982, by comparison with over 40 per cent in the mid-1970s (Townsend 1980b). Further revisions led some to write of the retreat of regional planning in the UK (Wood 1987; Damesick

Fig. 12.2
National patterns of regional
assistance, c. 1970.

Legend:

- Maximum incentive Development Area
- Modified incentive Development Area
- Existing Regional Development Area
- Industrial Reconversion or Coal Adaptation Area
- ✳ Development Pole
- ✩ Métropole d'équilibre

and Wood 1987). Early in 1988 automatic grants for industrial development in problematic regions were terminated.

Regional policies in Italy were prompted by political, economic and social problems in the Mezzogiorno at the end of the Second World War and particular attention was duly directed to that region when the 'Fund for the South' (Cassa per il Mezzogiorno) was established in 1950 to complement ministerial resources. Three phases of activity may be recognized. The first co-called pre-industrial phase extended from 1950 to 1957, when strong emphasis

was placed on land reform and improvement of infrastructures. In the following ten years, attention was directed towards encouraging modern industries by steering new branches of state-owned enterprises to southern locations which had been selected in partial deference to growth-pole theory. After 1967, policy became more concentrated spatially within the south and was aligned more closely with national planning objectives. At mid-century the Cassa had been expected to operate for a mere ten years but this was an excessively optimistic estimate of the time and investment that would be needed. In fact, the Fund continued to function until the end of 1980 with extensive backing from foreign sources, the European Investment Bank and the World Bank, as well as the Italian government. In 1984, liquidation was announced. Even before 1973–4, achievements had been limited, but economic recession inevitably stifled any great chance of success (Orlando and Antonelli 1982; Pacione 1982; King 1987a, b).

Spanish regional policy underwent profound changes after the death of Franco in 1975 and subsequent collapse of his highly centralized regime. The new constitution of 1978 granted a measure of self-government not only to the historically distinctive nationalities of Catalonia, Galicia and Euskadi (the Basque country) but also to other areas which had never displayed such a degree of separate identity (Hebbert 1982). Over a dozen sub-national units have emerged and are now negotiating their new powers. Politicians in under-developed rural regions and in depressed industrial areas alike hope that the new regime will offer the possibility of advancing their claims for economic and social progress. A new kind of regional planning is taking shape that is quite different from the functional regionalism with highly-centralized incentives and subsidies that existed under Franco but proved largely unsuccessful in steering investment and new jobs to the rural periphery. The new approach is a version of political regionalism whereby local groups organize themselves to try to improve conditions in their particular areas from the bottom up. But at this time of economic crisis, when financial resources are in short supply, it is debatable whether the poorer or smaller regions will be able to develop sufficient political muscle to attract necessary investment to improve their lot. In addition, over a dozen regionally-inspired plans may well pull in quite different directions and be to the detriment of the national interest (Hebbert 1987).

Mechanisms

Sticks and carrots

The countries of Western Europe have employed numerous techniques for encouraging economic activity in their depressed and under-developed regions. But very few have attempted to move workers to localities where jobs may be available or to implement policies of restraint in dynamic areas. For example, since the late 1940s the UK has required firms to obtain permission before creating or extending factories (above defined floor-space thresholds) in districts outside assisted areas (Law 1980). Similarly, between 1965 and 1979, permits were required before any new office or extension exceeding specified thresholds could be started in south-east England. Controls on industrial and tertiary growth were also attempted in Paris and parts of Scandinavia and latterly in the Dutch Randstad and northern Italy (Jarrett 1975; Van Hoogstraten 1985). The ultimate objective of all these measures was to restrict metropolitan growth, thereby releasing employment potential for relocation in less prosperous areas.

More usual has been the operation of financial and practical measures to promote modern industries in under-developed and depressed areas (Molle 1979). The range includes capital grants, cheap loans or guarantees for equipment, plant and machinery; construction of premises; tax relief over specified periods; aid for installing and equipping industrial estates; alleviation of certain costs (e.g. transport, energy, social-security contributions); and finance for training, retraining and housing the workforce. Promotional literature has been produced in vast quantities in order to 'sell' the environmental advantages of ailing regions and thereby attempt to change long-established psychologies and perceptions of place (Burgess 1982). Modern industries have been duly attracted and, as prestige projects, were the pride and joy of local politicians for a while. Such schemes most certainly increased regional productivity and economic output but, unfortunately, their presence did not bring true salvation to assisted areas. Most modern industries are highly mechanized and hence generate few jobs for large pools of local labour which may or may not contain skilled workers, depending on the recent economic history of each reception area. Many new factories that have been implanted in peripheral areas are highly dependent on external capital, decision-making and other production factors, while also being strongly geared to meeting external demands.

Multi-region and multi-national corporations have made extensive use of development funds to capture the best potential sites in assisted areas. However, research and development functions are retained in parent factories and laboratories located in core areas, with only less-skilled, low-paid routine operations usually being moved to under-developed or depressed areas. Links from the factories of multi-national firms are back to the home base – whichever side of the Atlantic that may be – rather than to other enterprises in the assisted area. Local raw materials are rarely used but local labour may be siphoned away from existing firms, to their overall detriment. Branch factories of multi-national enterprises prove to be highly vulnerable to closure as a result of fluctuations in the national or international economy. Despite the obvious appeal of capturing branches of modern manufacturing, wisdom of hindsight would suggest that many operations of this kind have actually reinforced long-standing structural weaknesses in assisted areas rather than reducing them, since promotion of externally-managed factories can foster a neglect of local needs, while leading to an increase in external dependence and a reduction in regional self-reliance.

Direct transfer of public investment to underdeveloped and depressed areas in the form of state-owned factories and offices can give rise to similar types of difficulty to those outlined above, with routine operations being especially susceptible to termination at times of recession or rapid technological change. Public investment to improve transport infrastructures involves payment to national or international firms which often bring in their own mobile labour force rather than taking on workers locally. Likewise, construction materials tend to be transported from outside rather than being derived from the immediate area. In any case, improved communication lines lead in two directions and may merely serve to accentuate flows of population to over-developed regions rather than promoting additional investment and job creation in less-favoured ones. Indeed, part of the temporary improvement in economic and employment conditions that was experienced in some of Western Europe's under-developed and depressed regions during the 1960s was in response to out-migration by large numbers of workers to core areas. Such outflows slackened the pressure on local job markets, while the remittances that migrants sent home allowed some improvement in living conditions for family members who stayed behind.

Growth centres

In many countries, attempts were made to counter the difficulties likely to stem from implanting individual branch factories by translating economic theories of agglomeration into spatial terms and designating growth centres at selected localities. Governments and other agencies sought to establish complexes of activities that were not only concentrated areally but between which there were functional links. Ideally, this kind of arrangement should reduce 'backwash' from under-developed regions to core areas and also encourage economic growth and the emergence of new activities locally. In addition, carefully-planned growth centres should stimulate some diffusion of dynamism and new job opportunities into their hinterlands. In brief, growth centres are attempts to reproduce artificially the kinds of functional relationships that would appear to have fostered the well-being of thriving economic regions.

Complexes of this type, admittedly of varying dimensions and with differing titles, were duly established in many countries of Western Europe during the past four decades. The best-known and perhaps most ambitious experiment was in the Mezzogiorno, but results have been disappointing. Since the 1950s, growth in domestic product in southern Italy has proved to be limited, rural depopulation and urban concentration have continued, and high unemployment and other fundamental problems remain. After having devolved some of its regional policy-making to the regions in the 1970s, Italy is currently readjusting its incentives policy and is placing more emphasis on programmes to promote agriculture, small industries, services and tourism, rather than large capital-intensive manufacturing plant (Secchi 1980).

Indeed, judgements on growth-centre policies in all parts of Western Europe must be mixed. Some intended growth centres simply failed to flourish, others emerged as focal points for regional services and new forms of employment but have been far from successful in diffusing economic growth into their hinterlands. Such partial success has, in fact, served to increase the scale of local socio-economic differences. Under such circumstances, growth centres have contributed to a shift of disparities from the inter-regional to the intra-regional level. Only in rare cases have they managed to induce an overall reduction of spatial differences in levels of living (Stöhr and Tödtling 1978).

Rise and fall

Despite their deficiencies and the fact that practice often lagged behind theory, the numerous regional policies introduced in Western Europe undoubtedly did achieve a qualified measure of success during the economically-buoyant 1960s. New factories, offices and other elements of change provided new employment in assisted areas and steered a proportion of available growth away from over-developed cores. The economic recession that followed the initial oil crisis of 1973–74 conspired to set much, if not all, of that to naught. It is true that new factories were still being opened in assisted areas during the 1970s but the overwhelming trends were for plants to close or to reduce their labour force. By the early 1980s, unemployment rates in formerly prosperous regions exceeded those that had prevailed a decade earlier in problem areas, while conditions in under-developed and depressed regions continued to deteriorate tragically (Keeble, Owens and Thompson 1981). Capital for investment by governments and businesses dwindled and, despite attempts by several countries to boost their policies in the mid-1970s, it became pain-fully clear that traditional approaches to regional development had been rendered largely powerless by the overwhelming magnitude of world events.

Under such circumstances many governments in Western Europe decided in the late 1970s or early 1980s to cut back their regional policies and their old definition of assisted areas. These were partly economy measures but, in some instances, also represented a shift towards general rather than area-specific attempts at job creation. For example, Denmark trimmed down its assisted areas in January 1979 and this move was followed by similar announce-ments in the UK in July. A year later, West Germany scaled down many of its assisted areas, partly as a savings operation but also because aid had been dispersed too widely to be really effective (Allen 1981). However, the assisted area along the East German border remained unchanged. Belgium and Italy have also contemplated cutbacks but both coun-tries need to deal with serious political problems before such reductions can occur. Furthermore, all national governments have spent less on regional aid since 1979. This move is in sharp contrast with an upward trend in expenditure in the preceding four or five years. Now the quest for general economic recovery has overtaken the kind of concern for tackling regional inequalities that emerged during the buoyant 1960s.

Several countries have modified what remains of their regional policies by lessening emphasis on poten-tially mobile manufacturing and placing greater stress on stimulating the service sector and indigenous firms which are often small in size. The UK and France pioneered this line of assistance for labour-intensive service-related schemes, and West Germany, Italy and the Republic of Ireland are directing more attention to this sector. To summarize: before the late 1970s, schemes for reducing pressure on over-developed areas by relocating activities in under-developed and depressed regions could have been shown to be making a positive contribution to national economic growth in the countries of Western Europe. The harsh fact is that such days are over and, unless the current trend of recession and unemployment can be reversed, they may never return.

The Community's quest for a regional policy

Background considerations

Over and above complicated national attempts to encourage regional development, the European Community has gradually evolved a common regional policy to apply to its expanding territory. The emerg-ence of such a policy should not be taken to imply an attempt to reduce the highly diverse regions of the member states to some kind of European uniformity. Instead, it is aimed at eliminating kinds of economic inequality that might be judged to be harmful. The case for a supranational approach may be argued on several grounds, including those of viewpoint and responsibility. First, poverty or under-development are relative concepts and what may appear to be a backward region in, say, the context of West Germany would certainly look prosperous when set against conditions in the Mezzogiorno or western Ireland. A Community approach to regional disparities should offer a broad, comparative perspective which indi-vidual states would be unlikely to take for themselves. Secondly, the very existence of the Common Market, with free movement of capital, goods and labour and the operation of various common policies, has tended to favour the more productive, central areas of the Community and has managed to deprive the periphery even more. Common regional policy has never been intended to subsume national schemes but rather to provide a forum for coordinating the strategies of member states and to allocate a limited amount of financial support. In fact, in the early 1980s, when national sources had contracted and Community spending had grown, the Community's expenditure on regional matters equalled only about one-tenth of the total sum directed by member states to their assisted areas (Klein 1981).

Despite a vast amount of discussion stressing its desirability, regional policy emerged as a latecomer among Community policies devised since the Treaty of Rome was signed in 1957. Nonetheless, limited mechanisms for tackling very specific types of spatial problem have been in existence for three decades, with the first 'European' attempt to assist certain types of depressed area going back to the creation of the European Coal and Steel Community in 1952. Loans have been duly made available to introduce new employment in areas experiencing redundancies in coal mining and steel making.

General ideas on coping with regional disparities were floated at the Messina Conference which preceded the creation of the EEC but the Treaty of Rome did not make direct mention of a common regional policy, although its preamble and several of its articles did touch on regional matters. Thus, heads of state expressed their desire to achieve the harmo-nious development of their six economies by reducing harmful differences that existed between the regions and, in particular, the backwardness of less-favoured

areas. Certainly it was intended that regional disparities and likely spatial impacts of competition, agricultural, social and transport policies should be
scrutinized. In particular, Article 130 enabled the EIB
to be set up to make loans to approved projects and
thereby help schemes to improve economic and social
conditions in backward areas. It may well have been
that the founders of the Community simply anticipated
that the general process of economic growth, that duly
operated in the 1950s and 1960s, would of itself reduce
the gap between rich and poor regions.

The 1960s formed a time of discussion and more
discussion on regional problems in the Six. A conference was held in 1961 reviewing regional policies in
the member states and in 1964 three reports were
drawn up which emphasized the desirability of all
regions contributing efficiently to the Community's
economy. They pointed to the supposed potential of
the growth centre as a mechanism for stimulating
regional dynamism, outlined the need to create new
jobs in depressed areas, and reviewed various administrative and fiscal means for encouraging regional
development in general. A year later, the need for
harmonizing objectives and coordinating regional
policies by member states and the Community was
argued. In other words, the possibility of a common
regional policy was aired.

The first economic policy programme (1966–70)
emphasized the need to improve inter-regional infrastructures, especially transport, and in 1969 there were
formal proposals for coordinating regional policies,
drawing up development programmes for problem
areas, establishing a special fund and a committee for
regional matters, and encouraging public and private
sources to invest in regional development schemes.
Two years later, national governments were urged to
pay greater attention to the 'European' dimension of
regional problems, and Community officials agreed to
consider regional difficulties when operating the EIB,
the Social Fund and the guidance component of the
Agricultural Fund.

A new imperative

By this time the matter of regional policy had acquired
extra political significance since Denmark, the
Republic of Ireland and the UK were about to enter
the Community (Jensen-Butler 1982). The largest
element of the EC budget, namely the CAP, was
thought to have little to offer the UK, but a common
regional policy should appeal to all the newcomers
since each had serious regional problems. In the final
months before enlargement, government represen-
tatives of the Six agreed to coordinate regional sub-

sidies. Henceforth there would be a system of upper
limits to financial aid, which would be fixed at 20 per
cent in subsidy equivalent for 'central' regions of the
Community but would rise to higher levels elsewhere.
In future, allocation of aid was to be more straightforward and would apply only to clearly specified areas.

As soon as enlargement took place in 1973 it proved
necessary to analyse regional disparities throughout
the Nine, and that responsibility was given to the new
commissioner for regional policy, George Thomson.
There was no possibility of undertaking a special
standardized survey; instead, Thomson and his team
had the difficult job of collating and interpreting
highly diverse sets of data, submitted quite independently by each member state. Precise definitions of
socio-economic categories, dates of data collection and
the size of spatial unit by which they were ordered
varied enormously. Some bodies of information were
incomplete or highly dubious and hence the
researchers were restricted in the number of indicators
they could use. They also had to tackle the fundamental problem of defining problem regions at the
Community scale rather than relying on the political
perceptions of each member state. The final compromise recognized such regions as those with per capita
GDP below the Community average and with one or
more of the following features:

(1) a greater share of the workforce in agriculture
than the Community average;
(2) at least 20 per cent of employment in declining
industries (e.g. coal mining and/or textile manufacture); persistently high unemployment (defined
as over 3.5 per cent and more than 20 per cent
above the appropriate national average) or annual
outmigration exceeding 1 per cent over a long
period.

The *Report on the Regional Problems in the
Enlarged Community* (known as the Thomson Report)
represented a brave first attempt to quantify regional
differences according to a specified procedure that was
applied throughout the Nine. However, a number of
critical comments must be raised. The apparently
rigorous and precise statements in the Report were
drawn from diverse and somewhat imprecise data. In
any case, information that is generalized to the
regional scale serves to conceal diverse local conditions, hence similar regional levels of income or
unemployment could well derive from very different
combinations of local values and underlying causes. In
addition, the Report tended to treat socio-economic
conditions as static features although it would have
been more meaningful to review them in an evolu-
tionary sense. Doubtless, deficiency of data was the

reason for adopting this narrow view; however, the Report did insist that future changes be monitored and the definition of problem regions reappraised.

Facts and figures

Thomson showed that in 1970, Denmark displayed the highest average per capita GDP in the Nine, with a figure almost 30 per cent over the Community average. West Germany, France, Luxembourg and Belgium were each characterized by above-average affluence, while the Netherlands (3 per cent down), the UK (12 per cent down), Italy (31 per cent down) and the Republic of Ireland (46 per cent down) came below the mean. In addition, every single region in the last three countries had a per capita GDP that was below average. Only tiny Luxembourg was entirely above the mean; each of the remaining five countries had a scatter of regions above and below the average. Greater Paris was unquestionably the richest area with an average per capita GDP that was almost double the Community average and five times that recorded in the poorest areas of the Mezzogiorno.

Agricultural employment had been retreating sharply during the 1960s and only 9.8 per cent of the Community's workforce remained in that sector in 1971. Nonetheless, many regions in the Republic of Ireland and the Mezzogiorno still had more than 30 per cent of their workers on the land and in some areas the figure exceeded 40 per cent. Western France and many remaining parts of Italy also displayed more than double the average proportion. By contrast, less than 5 per cent of employment was in agriculture in virtually all of the UK, the Ile-de-France, parts of Belgium and the German Rhinelands. Jobs in manufacturing came above the average (43.9 per cent) in most of the UK, northern France, northern Italy, the southern Netherlands, and much of Belgium and West Germany; while tertiary employment exceeded the mean (46.3 per cent) in heavily-urbanized areas and those with well-established tourism functions.

Statistics on industrial decline brought out the familiar pattern of Western Europe's coalfields together with less well-known distributions of quarrying and textile manufacture. What were judged to be high unemployment levels for the time were encountered in both agricultural and manufacturing regions in the Republic of Ireland, southern and central Italy, southern Belgium, northern Jutland, Scotland, Wales and Ulster. Heavy rates of outmigration affected much the same broad regions and also small pockets of job loss in mining districts and old industrial areas. The official collation of these indicators presented the full pattern of the Community's

Fig. 12.3
Areas qualifying for aid, according to the Thomson Report.

problem regions, which housed no less than 40 per cent of its residents (Fig. 12.3). Thomson's selection of criteria had stressed problems associated with poverty rather than affluence, but the Report did make due mention of the congestion, pollution and high costs of living that were experienced in economically 'healthy' conurbations and capital cities.

Money matters

In addition to the largely technical operation of assembling indicators and the difficult political exercise of defining critical threshold values, it was necessary to embark on even more contentious matters. Existing national schemes of regional aid had to be coordinated, the cost of the proposed European Regional Development Fund (ERDF) agreed, the appropriate share to be borne by each member country approved, and a mechanism found for levying contributions. Real transfers of money from wealthy member states to the problem regions of poorer ones would be essential if the policy were to have any chance of success. Expectations that large contributions by some states would guarantee privileged treatment when awards came to be made needed to be dispelled. In short, individual countries had to be encouraged to sacrifice a share of their national power in the cause of the European good. Not surprisingly, these pious hopes enshrined in the embryonic regional policy gave rise to massive political confrontation!

As well as defining problem regions, the Thomson Report indicated which countries were poor – by European standards – and should be net beneficiaries from the proposed ERDF, and which were rich and would therefore be called upon to be net contributors. Basking in the success of its economic miracle and with relatively few problem areas recognized by the Community, West Germany was clearly destined to be the major net contributor. It was therefore in German interests to challenge the extent of assisted areas, the basic criteria analysed by Thomson, the size of the proposed ERDF, and the relationship between contributions and receipts. By December 1973 it was clear that West Germany was determined to oppose Thomson's proposal that a Fund of *c.* £900 million be allocated by the Community during 1974–76. The Western German government advocated a much slimmer ERDF of *c.* £250 million for the same period, thereby requiring a rewrite of the regions that might hope to benefit. Moderately poor areas would be struck off Thomson's map and the absolute amount of help that very poor regions in Ireland and the Mezzogiorno could expect were trimmed down. The political situation degenerated, with West Germany refusing to contribute the large volume of resources that Thomson's recommendations required and France opposing the alternative of a skeletal Fund that would probably benefit only Italy and Ireland.

A little piggy bank

After eleven months of stalemate, the Nine agreed on 1 December 1974 to set up a relatively small ERDF of £540 million for the period 1975–78 (Talbot 1977). This amounted to little more than half the original proposal and was all the more pathetic when compared with the enormous sums being allocated at that time by individual countries to promote regional development and by multi-national corporations to set up industrial facilities in depressed and under-developed regions. Even more disturbing was the fact that such a small ERDF was launched into a world of rising inflation, mounting unemployment and ultimately profound recession. The criteria of the boom years of the middle and late 1960s that had been used by Thomson had in fact become quite inappropriate for judging the shape and scale of regional problems in the mid-1970s and were to become even more outmoded with the passage of time, as formerly buoyant cities and once healthy 'new' industrial regions fell into decline.

National definitions of problem areas were to be used, rather than Thomson's map, and the contents of the little piggy bank were to be shared among the Nine according to a quota system. Italy was entitled to 40 per cent, the UK 28 per cent, the Republic of Ireland 6 per cent (each being a net beneficiary); France 15 per cent, West Germany 6.4 per cent, the Netherlands 1.7 per cent, Belgium 1.5 per cent, Denmark 1.3 per cent, and Luxembourg 0.1 per cent (with these six countries being net contributors). This arrangement, of course, meant that regions in the Netherlands and West Germany with higher per capita GDP than the richest regions of Italy and the UK qualified for ERDF aid (Kiljunen 1980).

Community regional policy in action

Quotas and quota-free allocations

Projects for which ERDF finance were sought had first to be vetted by national authorities and details then forwarded to Brussels for evaluation and decision (Kerr 1986). Financial support for favoured schemes was transmitted to national treasuries for payment to development agencies, local authorities or firms. During the first phase of the ERDF (1975–78), grants were directed to a wide range of projects, including factory estates in Belgium, West Germany, Italy, the Netherlands and the UK, new roads to serve industrial estates in France and improvements to the antiquated telephone system in the Republic of Ireland. The Italian share of awards was devoted to the Mezzogiorno and most of the French allocation was used in the west of the country, Corsica and the Caribbean *départements*. Projects in West Berlin and Greenland received two-thirds of the grants to West Germany and Denmark respectively, while half of the sum granted to the UK went to northern England.

By this time it was clear that the economic situation of many under-developed and depressed regions was collapsing and that stronger Community action was needed. This line of argument was elaborated in a framework of guidelines passed by the European Commission in June 1977. As many had suspected, it could be shown that developed areas had enhanced their advantage to the detriment of poorer regions during the previous two decades; schemes supported by national systems of regional aid or by infant ERDF had failed to counter the trend; and the volume of capital for all kinds of regional investment had slumped in the recession. Economic restructuring was operating at the world scale and worked to the detriment of high-cost European nations in general and of weaker regions in particular.

The outcome of this debate was a modified regional policy for 1978–80. More explicit consideration was given to the regional implications of other Community policies, and fluctuations in regional well-being started to be monitored. The ERDF was increased to £1 234 million for the three-year period, with a distinction being made between a new quota-free part (5 per cent of the total) and a slightly revised quota section. Modifications in 1979 raised the share for France from 15.0 to 16.9 per cent and scaled down the quotas for six other countries by a tiny fraction. Further adjustments were made to take account of Greece's entry into the Community in 1981.

Grants from the quota section had to be used on investment projects, with 70 per cent being allocated to infrastructure schemes and the remainder to manufacturing, craft or service projects. The contribution of the ERDF was restricted to 30 per cent (or very exceptionally 40 per cent) of the cost of infrastructure schemes and to 20 per cent of other projects. Awards assisted the construction of a natural gas pipeline from North Africa to Sicily and the rest of the Mezzogiorno, irrigation and land-drainage schemes, improvements in telecommunications and railway lines, new roads and water-supply systems, as well as individual factories and hotels (Dean 1982).

In 1979, 5 per cent of the ERDF was set aside for quota-free allocation. By contrast with the quota section, the Commission had the right to suggest appropriate schemes for quota-free assistance. Money was available only for comprehensive programmes which might embrace support for feasibility or marketing surveys and research into innovative techniques as well as direct investment in job creation. This broadening of scope was important since it had become particularly difficult to attract firms into less dynamic regions. Member states wishing to seek support from the quota-free section were required to plan their programmes for several years ahead and to devise strategies for coordinating resources from national funds and private sources as well as the ERDF. Thus, five programmes had been approved by early 1982, involving the Mezzogiorno, south-west France, the border region of Northern Ireland and the Republic, a number of steel-making areas (in Belgium, Luxembourg and the UK), and shipbuilding localities in the UK. In addition, experimental 'integrated operations' were launched in Naples and Belfast to assemble Community funds and national resources to tackle a range of measures to promote economic development. These included public transport, roads and sewerage in the case of Naples, and water supply, training facilities and industrial and commercial development for Belfast (Spooner 1984; Noble 1985).

Modifications

Further guidelines for modifying regional policy were advanced in autumn 1981 and reflected the findings of the *First periodic report on the social and economic situation of regions of the Community* (1981c). This document covered the period 1970–77, namely immediately before the ERDF and during the first phase of its operation (Martins and Mawson 1980, 1982). It stressed that during those years, population growth had decelerated in the Nine, mainly due to falling birth rates. With rising rates of unemployment, migration flows tended to turn away from industrial cities and back to the periphery, while deconcentration of urban population became increasingly widespread. With the exception of some parts of Belgium, the highest rates of unemployment were found in the Republic of Ireland, the Mezzogiorno and south-west France. Nonetheless, the most rapid rates of increase in unemployment involved regions that had been regarded as strong economically and had displayed very low levels of joblessness in the 1960s.

The regional patterns of employment that Thomson had identified for the late 1960s remained clearly in evidence a decade later (Fig. 12.4). The complex human conditions underlying regional disparities were crisply summarized by indicators of per capita GDP. In the late 1970s, the whole of Italy, the Republic of Ireland and the UK generated values below the Community average, as did western France and a small scatter of areas in southern Belgium, the eastern Netherlands and northern Germany (Fig. 12.5a). As earlier enquiries had suggested, the Mezzogiorno and Republic of Ireland were by far the poorest parts of the Nine, producing indices under half the Community mean. At the other extreme, prosperity was roughly six times higher in Hamburg, Bremen, the Ile-de-France and greater Copenhagen than in Calabria and Donegal, which came right at the bottom of the regional league. In fact the gap between the richest and the poorest areas was soon to widen to 1 : 10 when Greece entered the Community (and in a few years' time was to widen even more to 1 : 12 when Portugal and Spain joined in 1986!). During the 1970s, richer regions had displayed above-average rates of growth in per capita GDP and all regions with below-average GDP had also experienced below-average rates of growth. Particularly low levels of investment worsened their already depressing positions. In

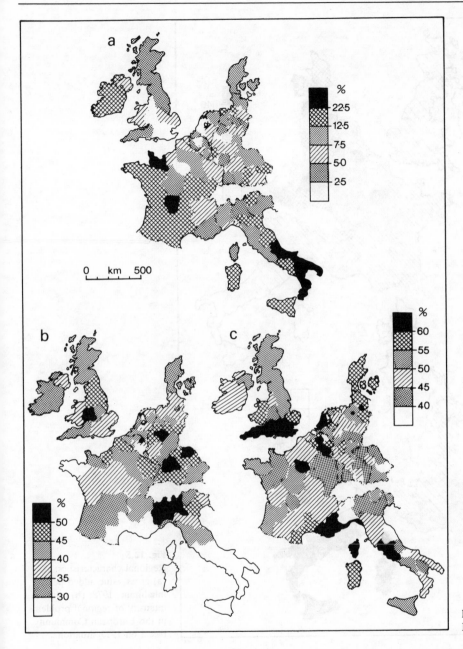

Fig. 12.4
Employment by sector, 1978.

absolute terms, every region raised its per capita GDP but in relative terms the rich grew richer and the poor poorer.

The 1981 revisions to Community regional policy paid due attention to the implications of Greek accession and introduced the following modifications. Particular stress needed to be placed on job creation and raising productivity; financial support should be focused rather more on a smaller number of particu-

larly poor regions; rather than concentrating on luring investment from the outside, greater emphasis should be given to stimulating local potential for economic growth through manpower training and marketing schemes; and regional and local authorities should be given a greater role in handling ERDF allocations. Henceforth the ERDF should function more explicitly as a development agency rather than just as a financing body. The 'sprinkler effect' of the old quota

Fig. 12.5
Regional characteristics:
(a) gross value-added per
inhabitant, 1978; (b) relative
intensity of regional problems
in the European Community,
based on 1977 situation.

system had tended to dissipate resources and the situation had not been helped by the fact that ERDF money could be used throughout the extensive assisted areas that had been designated by member countries. All this tended to make regional help from the Community somewhat haphazard. In addition, the Commission was concerned that ERDF finance had often been 'swallowed' by national treasuries for use by governments as a substitute for national funds instead of being a supplement to them.

In accordance with the 1981 revisions, the quota section of the Fund was reserved for areas suffering from serious structural problems of very low per capita GDP and particularly high long-term unemployment (Fig. 12.5b). This new 'poor man's' quota was allocated as follows: the Republic of Ireland (7.3 per cent); the Mezzogiorno (43.7 per cent); all of Greece, except Athens and Thessalonika (16.0 per cent);

Northern Ireland and parts of Scotland, Wales, north and north-west England (29.3 per cent); French overseas *départements* (2.4 per cent); and Greenland (1.3 per cent). (Greenland automatically became a part of the EC when its colonial power (Denmark) joined in 1973. In 1979 it achieved home rule and following a plebiscite it negotiated withdrawal from the EC but without discontinuing relations with Denmark. Thus Greenland left the EC in February 1985, with a handsome 'golden handshake' and a generous arrangement over fish catches in North Atlantic waters.) Conversely, Benelux, West Germany, metropolitan France and Denmark no longer qualified for assistance from the quota section.

The non-quota section was increased from 5 to 20 per cent of the total ERDF and was to be used on well-targeted schemes, especially in areas harshly affected by recent industrial decline. The idea was that neither quota nor non-quota payments would be allocated to individual developments but only to well-coordinated packages of projects or to broad-based programmes agreed between the Commission and the national governments concerned. Such programmes would span several years' activity and could include infrastructure schemes as well as investments in individual firms. This change meant that ERDF operations could be applied more consistently and be dovetailed into overall development schemes for particular regions. Further proposals for revision were put forward in 1983 with, as we shall see, a new regulation for the ERDF being launched in 1985.

The other funds

In addition to the ERDF, four older funds continued to provide Community money for tackling social and economic problems. These obviously had some effect on regional conditions:

(a) The sectoral and spatial impact of assistance from the ECSC is restricted but large loans have been awarded to modernize production and to stimulate alternative employment opportunities in areas concerned with coal- or iron-mining and steel manufacture (Collins 1975).

(b) The EIB has made important loans for regional development purposes (Pinder 1978, 1986). Irrigation and other rural projects in the Mezzogiorno and numerous transport schemes have received attention over many years, and more recently money has been directed to industrial rehabilitation.

(c) The guidance section of the European Agricultural Fund makes awards to a wide range of modernization schemes, which include farm amal-gamation, formation of cooperatives, training of workers in modern techniques, and implementation of retirement schemes for elderly farmers. Assistance is available to hill farmers and, in the late 1970s, special programmes were started to improve farming in Mediterranean areas, to drain land in western Ireland, and to support rural renovation experiments in Italy, Ireland, the Western Isles of Scotland, the Massif Central and the Belgian Ardennes.

(d) The European Social Fund supports schemes for training and retraining unemployed workers. Finance is directed mainly towards national training programmes, but local authorities and companies can also receive help, with higher rates of assistance being offered in the most seriously disadvantaged regions (Keating and Jones 1985). Given the present high rates of unemployment, the role of the Social Fund is particularly vital. (Since the start of 1986, virtually half of it has been reserved for the seven 'priority regions' of the EC where socio-economic problems are most intense.)

In addition, a New Community Instrument has been in existence since 1979 to give loans for modernizing infrastructure, developing energy resources, and boosting small and medium-sized businesses. Harsh experience has shown that Community assistance can have a greater beneficial effect if resources from the various funds are closely coordinated and, as we shall see, greater attention has been duly paid to this kind of harmonization as part of the continuing reappraisal of all Community matters that impinge on regional development.

Evaluations

Even before the ERDF came into existence, distinguished economists were arguing that its operation should be merged with or closely allied to the established funds (Cairncross 1974). That point has been repeated many times over the past fifteen years, with some insisting that the ERDF is hopelessly inadequate to have any real effect on reducing regional disparities and hence is no more than a 'cosmetic' treatment to disguise a massively serious problem. (In 1975 the Fund had accounted for 4.8 per cent of the Community budget; by 1987 it had risen to 9.1 per cent of a much larger Community budget but was still completely dwarfed by the vast price-guarantee element of the European Agricultural Fund. To put that information into perspective, we must appreciate that the total Community budget is only about 1 per cent of the combined GDP of the twelve member states.)

Some academics, such as Van Doorn (1975), simply dismissed the ERDF as a means of attempting to cope with national differences regarding contributions to and payments from the Community budget rather than a serious mechanism for tackling regional inequalities. Indeed, such a view of the ERDF as a system of budgetary redistribution has much to commend it. In a different vein, one eminent French politician likened the whole regional policy to a farce that was being staged to amuse the gallery (i.e. the new members of the Community), and there is plenty of evidence that several member states were unwilling to take it seriously. Indeed, some nations simply substracted the amount of money that they received from the ERDF from the sums that they would themselves have allocated to assist regional development.

The common regional policy, the ERDF and the older funds have undoubtedly made some contributions to job-creation schemes and infrastructural projects at particular locations; however, their overall impact in narrowing regional disparities in the Community has been less positive. Opponents argue that during the first decade of activity the modest finances of the ERDF were neither sufficiently targeted on the poorest regions nor adequately coordinated on schemes that had a reasonable chance of success. Exactly the same conclusion must be drawn from reading the Commission's own reports (1981, 1984, 1987) dealing with regional disparities and problems. These studies employed successively more sophisticated indicators to describe regional conditions but they only succeeded in demonstrating that the development gap was widening disturbingly with the passage of time. This was in response to the worsening economic climate affecting the whole of Western Europe, and the inclusion of many additional 'poor' regions in the new member states of the growing Community.

New neighbours: bigger problems

The three Mediterranean countries increased the total area and the agricultural surface of the EC by roughly a half and its population by one-fifth. As we have seen, Greece, Portugal and Spain still retain sizeable proportions of their workforce in agriculture, but their farm structures are varied, with irrigated land contrasting with hill farming (Williams 1984). Average productivity is generally modest, and exportable commodities (e.g. fruit, vegetables, wine, olive oil) face severe competition from Italy and southern France. Industrial activities are equally problematic.

Domestic firms are usually small, while a considerable number of the larger enterprises are owned by foreign capital and are therefore subject to decision-making which may have little to do with the welfare of people in Mediterranean areas. Many manufacturing activities are traditional, labour-intensive and of low productivity, while more modern firms tend to involve iron and steel, shipbuilding, textiles and clothing sectors which are already in dire straits in the Community. These industries face a difficult future and bring parts of Greece and Portugal and sections of the Spanish regions of Asturias, Catalonia and Aragon into the lengthening list of depressed industrial regions (Hudson and Lewis 1985).

Recent experience has shown that structurally-weak countries are much less able than rich ones to cope with dilemmas such as inflation, unemployment and outmoded techniques of production (Hall 1981b). Removal of trade barriers between the established Community and the new Mediterranean members has boosted competitive pressure and may well work to the detriment of existing activities in the south and to the advantage of those in the north of the Twelve (Jensen-Butler 1987). Spatial disparities have increased even further, both between strong and weak countries, and between more and less-developed regions (Secchi 1980). Already one-third of the population of Greece lives in the Athens–Piraeus conurbation, which generates more than half the GDP. Over half of all Portuguese inhabit Lisbon–Setubal and four-fifths live on one-third of the national territory which produces 90 per cent of GDP. Four provinces of Spain together accommodate 30 per cent of the national population and give rise to two-fifths of the GDP. Despite national attempts at regional development, disparities in Spain have continued to increase (Musto 1981). Faced with this vast challenge and the limited success of the existing common regional policy, it comes as no surprise that in recent years both the European Commission and the European Parliament have sought to reform the ERDF, which allocated 14 200 million ecu between 1975 and the start of 1986 but was overwhelmed by the tide of world recession.

The way forward?

An uphill struggle

In response to these criticisms, a new Regional Fund Regulation was launched at the start of 1985 which not only embraces established objectives (coordinating the regional policies of member states; introducing a regional dimension to other policies of the Community; and providing financial aid to less-favoured regions)

Table 12.1 Finance available under the ERDF (upper and lower percentage limits)

Belgium	0.61–0.82	Italy	21.62–28.79
Denmark	0.34–0.46	Luxembourg	0.04–0.06
France	7.48–9.96	Netherlands	0.68–0.91
West Germany	2.55–3.40	Portugal	10.66–14.20
Greece	8.36–10.64	Spain	17.97–23.93
Rep. of Ireland	3.82–4.61	UK	14.50–19.31

but also pays due attention to the enormity of regional disparities and the modest funds that are available. Rich governments which hold the purse strings insist that they continue to receive a share of the grants which are distributed by a system of ranges that identifies the upper and lower limits of the resources available to each member state (Table 12.1). The lower limit in each case is the minimum ERDF financing guaranteed to that member state, on condition that enough eligible requests are sent to the Commission. The variation each year in allocations between the upper and lower limits depends on the extent to which programmes and projects submitted for ERDF financing are considered significant in Community terms. In addition, three new principles are involved in the post-1985 Regional Fund.

(a) More emphasis has been placed on the 'co-financing' of programmes by the Community and individual member states, with 'programmes' being defined as coherent sets of projects within specified areas whose operation will spread over a number of years. 'Community programmes' are initiated by the European Commission, while 'national programmes of Community interest' are proposed by member states but require the approval of the Commission. The first Community programmes began to be implemented in 1987 and include STAR (promoting advanced telecommunications) and VALOREN (developing the local energy potential of less-favoured regions). Basic regulations for these programmes were adopted by the Council of Ministers late in 1986, with the regions involved being those of Greece, Portugal, the Republic of Ireland, Northern Ireland, the Mezzogiorno, Spain, Corsica and the French overseas *départements*.

(b) Extra efforts are being made to promote the indigenous development potential of problem regions rather than parachuting in manufacturing enterprises from outside. Instead of looking to external investors, the new approach gives greater support to local businesses to acquire modern technology, investigate market potential and obtain reliable capital backing.

(c) Rather than viewing the ERDF in isolation, much more effort is being made to coordinate aid from the full range of Community funds which can help promote regional development. Thus the ERDF is participating in integrated schemes and particularly the Integrated Mediterranean Programmes which pay attention to socio-economic problems encountered in Greece, southern Italy and the southernmost parts of France, each having to face the challenge of Iberian entry to the Community (Tommel 1987). The main objective of the IMPs is to coordinate EC aid from various funds and direct this to job-creation schemes in agricultural modernization and off-farm jobs, in crafts, tourism, fishing and forestry. The first IMP was launched for Crete in autumn 1986. Ecologists have voiced concern that economically-oriented IMPs may promote schemes that will cause irreparable damage to fragile Mediterranean ecosystems.

As well as these principles, the new Regulation stresses the long-repeated need to concentrate aid from the ERDF in the most problematical nations and regions. Thus in 1986, 87 per cent of ERDF finance was directed to six countries. When ERDF allocations are related to the population in the eligible areas in those countries, Greece and Portugal were treated most favourably, to be followed by the Republic of Ireland, Spain, Italy and the UK, in descending order. During that year three-quarters of ERDF money went to the Community's 'priority regions', namely the Mezzogiorno, Greece (minus Athens), Northern Ireland, most regions of Portugal and Spain, and the French overseas *départements*. These changes represent a move in the right direction, but the challenge of narrowing the 'development gap' in the Twelve remains enormous.

The widening gap

That point was hammered home by the findings of the Third Periodic Report from the Commission on the social and economic situation and development of the regions of the Community (May 1987) which for the first time incorporated detailed information on Portugal and Spain. Analysis of socio-economic trends throughout the Twelve and calculation of a new index of regional well-being (combining GDP per capita and GDP per worker, with unemployment and changes in the size of the labour force) confirmed some disturbing but not unexpected facts. Regional disparities had

indeed widened during the mid-1980s; none of the
regions of Iberia had an income level that approached
the Community average; and conditions in 'old' industrial areas (especially in the UK and Belgium) had
deteriorated. In short, the contrasts in regional well-
being could not be summarized as either north/south
or core/periphery, since Ireland formed a substantial
fragment of 'impoverished' Europe and old industrial
areas and inner-city localities posed formidable problems within traditionally-recognized 'core' regions
(Fig. 12.6).

With the adoption of the Single European Act in
1986, which strengthens the Treaty of Rome,
Community regional policy was incorporated in the
framework of the Community treaties and was
assigned the task of helping to achieve convergence
and cohesion. Put another way, all member states
undertook to conduct and coordinate their economic
policies to reduce regional disparities as they worked
towards these aims. The Community's drive to create
an internal frontier-free market by 1992 is necessary
if the EC is ever to challenge the commercial might
of Japan and the USA and will, of course, have
profound implications for uneven development in the
Twelve. This will make policies to support 'disadvantaged' regions all the more important since the experience of recent years reveals a strong preference for
high-technology, 'future' activities to cluster in localities characterized by excellent transport and
communications facilities, abundant supplies of highly-
skilled labour, and the proximity of major research
complexes and financial centres.

At the end of July 1987 the Commission published
three important recommendations for financing
Community budgets, reorganizing agricultural policies
and reforming the Community funds. It proposed a
regulation that would come into effect at the start of
1989 to coordinate the regional, social and farm funds
in a coherent pattern, with the now-familiar objective
of reducing regional disparities and lessening the backwardness of least-favoured areas. Future investments
are to be concentrated on the priority regions and may
be supplemented by EIB loans. Nested aims include:
to improve investment and productivity in deprived

Fig. 12.6
Regional characteristics in the Twelve, 1985–86: (a) GDP
per head of population at purchasing power parities, 1985;
(b) total unemployment rate, 1986; (c) synthetic index of
regional disparity according to the Third Periodic Report.

regions; to rejuvenate or replace declining industries; to combat long-term unemployment; to provide work for young people; and to encourage rural development as part of the reformed CAP. The evidence contained in the Third Periodic Report on regional conditions ensures that we appreciate the constantly changing character of regional disparity. 'Regional problems' can never be solved – they keep on being created and redefined in differing ways! The best that can be hoped is that the starkest human inequalities at the heart of regional differences may be lessened and the development 'gap' reduced in however small a way. The experience of recent decades demonstrates with harsh clarity that – in both political and economic terms – every step along the road towards that goal will be a steeply uphill struggle (Molle and Cappelin 1988).

Further reading

Clout H D (ed.) 1987 *Regional Development in Western Europe* 3rd edn. Fulton, London

Hudson R, Lewis J R (eds) 1982 *Regional Planning in Europe*. Pion, London

Keating M, Jones B (eds) 1985 *Regions in the European Community*. Oxford University Press, Oxford

Knox P L 1984 *The Geography of Western Europe*. Croom Helm, London

Pinder D 1983 *Regional Economic Development Policy: theory and practice in the European Community*. George Allen and Unwin, London

Seers D, Schaffer B, Kiljunen M L (eds) 1979 *Underdeveloped Europe: studies in core–periphery relations*. Harvester Press, Hassocks, Sussex

Seers D, Vaitsos C (eds) 1980 *Integration and Unequal Development: the experience of the EEC*. St Martin's Press, New York

And the future . . .?

It would be quite improper to try to write a formal 'conclusion' to the essays which make up this book. Western Europe in the last few decades has been seen to be a changing place, or rather a changing assemblage of places and national and regional systems, and will continue to evolve in the years ahead. The present authors started their research in the confident years of the 1960s, when positive scenarios for a dynamic future were very much in vogue. Powerful changes of direction in subsequent years have taught them – and surely all geographers – to criticize assumptions, to be ever more probing in their enquiries and to be increasingly wary of making predictions. To think of the future geography of Western Europe is to peer into the unknown; hence it is quite apposite to pose fundamental questions in the last paragraphs of this book rather than attempt to make final statements.

The European Community is now certainly a larger, very different and much more problematical institution than when it came into being in 1957; but what will happen in the rest of the century as, perhaps, another even 'less-developed' country joins? Will there be harmony and unanimity, or will the EC become a looser and even less integrated club? Will national interests and regional identity retreat, or will we continue to think of ourselves as Italians, French, Welsh or Yorkshiremen rather than as 'Europeans'? Will one or more of the existing member states of the Community choose to opt out? Moving into the wider political arena, how will relations develop between the full range of countries in Western Europe, the USA, the USSR and the nations of the Third World?

The international energy situation has changed profoundly in the past twenty years, but how will it evolve during the remainder of this century? What roles will oil and coal play, and how will the political,

economic and technical arguments in favour of nuclear energy unfold in the face of opposition from environmentalist groups (Blowers and Pepper 1987)? Will Western Europe's economies really start to recover from recession and, if so, when? De-industrialization would seem certain to continue, but to what extent will the 'new technology' of data handling make routine office work a task for computers and robots rather than for human beings? How will west Europeans cope with the future world of work, which may well mean 'non-work' for many of them during greater periods of their lives?

Rates of population growth have decelerated in the past quarter century and Western Europe has become an increasingly 'elderly' part of the world. The concept of the family and the whole realm of interpersonal relations have changed. Will these continue to evolve along the same paths as in recent years, or will there be a 'rediscovery of the family' and a return to more traditional views on human relations? Large volumes of immigration to Western Europe are no longer occurring but how will multi-cultural societies develop in the future? Will integration and assimilation become the norm, or will the distinctiveness of ethnic, social and religious minorities be respected more meaningfully?

Both rural–urban migration and counter-urbanization have been underway in recent decades with profound implications for inner-city locations and for areas beyond commonly-recognized urban fringes. Will more rural dwellers choose to stay in the countryside rather than face unemployment in the city? Will more urbanites move out to live in the countryside? Will there be sufficiently cheap energy to allow long-distance commuting to continue to expand? Will landscapes continue to be ravaged by private and collective thoughtlessness or will west Europeans become more conscious of the fragility of their environment and the scarcity of its resources? What kind of social, economic and ecological principles will guide the next generation of planners, and how will the interests of the individual and the state be reconciled to fashion the geography of Western Europe at the dawn of the twenty-first century? And to what extent will social justice be remembered in the desperate quest for economic efficiency?

Europe will be an exciting and challenging continent during the rest of this century. As we have seen, the Single European Act of 1986 incorporated a 1992 deadline for the completion of an internal market in the EC. This is fully in the spirit of the founding fathers of the Community who sought to create a 'common market' in which goods, people, services and capital would move without obstacle. Now a vigorous campaign is in progress to inform West Europeans of the great costs and inconveniences involved maintaining a dozen separate national markets (Cecchini 1988). 'Physical barriers' to commercial unity include border stoppages, customs controls and complex paperwork which plague trading firms and lorry drivers alike. Countries maintain different product standards, technical regulations and business laws, and defend nationally protected procurement markets. In addition to these 'technical barriers', differing rates of value-added tax and excise duty represent 'fiscal barriers'.

Advocates of a 'Western Europe without frontiers' envisage immense opportunities for economic growth, job creation, improved productivity, stabilization of prices, greater consumer choice, healthier competition and easier professional and business mobility after 1992. But a single market will carry threats and risks as well as promises! Competitive firms, regions and nations will benefit; their less efficient counterparts will lose out. Of course, the European home market will not materialize overnight, as if a magic wand had been waved; nor is it likely to emerge exactly to plan. National governments have given general approval to the principle of a barrier-free market but it may prove another matter when it comes to agreeing detailed deregulation measures that will have profound implications for particular interest groups (Palmer 1988). Nonetheless, there can be no doubt that the creation of a single market will be of profound significance for the human geography of the Twelve.

It will also have major ramifications for the six West European nations that are outside the EC. Many industrialists in the EFTA countries feel that competition from the EC's single internal market will pose serious problems after 1992 for nations that do not belong to the club, with obstacles to trade most probably being joined by the enforcement of new technological and industrial standards in the Common Market. Politicians and businessmen in Austria and Norway are already debating whether their nations should apply to join the EC or, like other EFTA members, simply ensure closer commercial cooperation with the Common Market during the 1990s. Over recent months the improvement of relations between the superpowers has enabled strategic tensions in Europe to be relaxed and, in turn, may make it easier for neutral members of EFTA to associate themselves more closely with their EC neighbours.

Looking to the continent as a whole, it might just be possible that growing cordiality between Moscow and Washington could be paralleled by closer links between European neighbours across the Iron Curtain. An optimist might hope that Cold War military alliances could be liquidated and, to quote John Palmer (1988), ". . . the unification of the torn halves of Europe might become more than a dream" (p. 193).

Further reading

Cecchini P 1988 *The European Challenge*. Wildwood, Aldershot

Palmer J 1988 *Trading Places*. Radius Hutchinson, London

References

Adamson D M 1985 European gas and European security. *Energy Policy* 13: 13–26

Aldcroft D H 1978 *The European Economy, 1914–1970*. Croom Helm, London

Alden J D, Saha S K 1978 An analysis of second jobholding in the EEC. *Regional Studies* 12: 639–50

Alexander L M 1963 *Offshore Geography of Northwestern Europe: the political and economic problems of delimitation and control*. Rand McNally, Chicago

Allen K (ed) 1979 *Balanced National Growth*. Lexington Books, Lexington

Allen K 1981 Some recent trends in European regional incentive policy. *Built Environment* 7: 211–21

Allen R 1980 Fishing for a common policy. *Journal of Common Market Studies* 19: 123–39

Anderiessen G 1981 Tanks in the streets: the growing conflict over housing in Amsterdam. *International Journal of Urban and Regional Research* 5: 83–95

Anon. 1981 Social changes in the OECD countries 1950–80. *OECD Observer* 107: 21–35

Anon. 1982a On or off? Western Europe's oil and gas: a survey. *The Economist* 12 June 1982

Anon. 1982b At last a common fish policy. *The Economist* 6 Nov. 1982, 72

Anwar M 1979 *The Myth of Return: Pakistanis in Britain*. Heinemann, London

Appleyard D (ed) 1979 *The Conservation of European Cities*. MIT Press, Cambridge, Mass.

Archer M S, Giner S (eds) 1971 *Contemporary Europe: class, status and power*. Routledge and Kegan Paul, London

Ardagh J 1988 *France today*. Penguin, Harmondsworth

Aron R 1964 Old nations, new Europe. *Daedalus* 93: 43–66

Ashcroft B 1982 The measurement of the impact of regional policies in Europe. *Regional Studies* 16: 287–305

Ashworth G J 1980 Language, society and the state in Belgium. *Journal of Area Studies* 1: 28–33

Avery G 1985 Guarantee thresholds and the Common Agricultural Policy. *Journal of Agricultural Economics* 36: 355–64

Bacchetta M 1978 The crisis of oil refining in the European Community. *Journal of Common Market Studies* 17: 87–119

Bailey R 1977 *Energy: the rude awakening*. McGraw-Hill, New York and London

Baillet P 1975 Une population urbanisée; les rapatriés d'Algérie. *Bulletin de l'Association de Géographes Français* 52: 269–78

Bailly A 1987a Les services et la production: pour un réexamen des secteurs économiques. *L'Espace Géographique* 16: 5–13

Bailly A 1987b Service activities and regional development: some European examples. *Environment and Planning A* 19: 653–68

Barberis C 1968 The agricultural exodus in Italy. *Sociologia Ruralis* 8: 179–88

Barberis C 1977 Tre o sette milioni di attivi agricoli? Pardossi dell'occupazione a mezzo tempo. *Rivista di Economia Agraria* 32: 571–8

Barbier B 1978 Ski et stations de sports d'hiver dans le monde. In Sinnhuber K, Jülg T (eds) *Studies in the Geography of Tourism and Recreation, vol. 1*. Ferdinand Hirt, Vienna, pp 131–46

Barker M L 1982 Traditional landscape and mass tourism in the Alps. *Geographical Review* 72: 395–415

Barrère P, Cassou-Mounat M 1980 *Les villes françaises*. Masson, Paris

Barton A P, Young S 1975 The structure of the dairy industry in the EEC. *Oxford Agrarian Studies* 4: 181–200

Bassett K 1984 Corporate structure and corporate change in a local economy: the case of Bristol. *Environment and Planning A* 16: 879–900

Bassett K, Short J 1980 *Housing and Residential Structure*. Routledge and Kegan Paul, London

Bateman M 1985 *Office Development: a geographical analysis*. Croom Helm, London

Baučić I 1973 Yugoslavia as a country of emigration. *Options Méditerranéennes* 22: 56–66

Beaujeu-Garnier J, Delobez A 1979 *Geography of Marketing*. Longman, London

Berger J, Mohr J 1975 *A Seventh Man: the story of a migrant worker in Europe*. Penguin, Harmondsworth

Berry B J L (ed) 1976 *Urbanization and Counterurbanization*. Sage, Beverly Hills and London

Berry B J L 1978 The counterurbanization process: how general? In Hansen N M (ed) *Human Settlement Systems*. Ballinger, Cambridge, Mass, pp 25–49

Best R H 1979 Land-use structure and change in the EEC. *Town Planning Review* 50: 395–411

Best R H 1981 *Land Use and Living Space*. Methuen, London

Bethemont J, Pelletier J 1983 *Italy: a geographical introduction*. Longman, London

Bird J H, Witherick M E 1986 Marks and Spencer: the geography of an image. *Geography* 71: 305–19

Blackaby F 1979 *De-industrialization*. Heinemann, London

Blackbourn A 1978 Multinational enterprises and regional development: a comment. *Regional Studies* 12: 125–7

Blackbourn A 1982 The impact of multinational corporations on the spatial organization of developed nations: a review. In Taylor M J, Thrift N J (eds) *The Geography of Multinationals*. Croom Helm, London and Canberra, pp 147–57

Blacksell M 1976 The role of *le parc naturel et régional*. *Town and Country Planning* 44: 165–70

Blacksell M 1979 Frontiers at sea. *Geographical Magazine* 51: 521–4

Blacksell M 1981 *Post-War Europe: a political geography* 2nd end. Hutchinson, London

Blacksell M 1982 Reunification and the political geography of the Federal Republic of Germany. *Geography* 67: 310–19

Blacksell M, Brown M 1983 Ten years of Ostpolitik. *Geography* 68: 260–2

Blake G (ed) 1987 *Maritime Boundaries and Ocean Resources*. Croom Helm, London

Blanc M 1987 Family and employment in agriculture: recent changes in France. *Journal of Agricultural Economics* 38: 289–301

Blowers A, Pepper D (eds) 1987 *Nuclear Power in Crisis*. Croom Helm, London

Boal F W, Douglas J N H (eds) 1982 *Integration and Division: geographical perspectives on the Northern Ireland problem*. Academic Press, London

Böhning W R 1972 *The Migration of Workers in the United Kingdom and the European Community*. Oxford University Press, Oxford

Böhning W R 1979 International migration in Western Europe: reflections on the last five years. *International Labour Review* 118: 401–14

Boltho A (ed) 1982 *The European Economy: growth and crisis*. Oxford University Press, Oxford

Bottomore T B 1971 Class structure in Western Europe. In Archer M S, Giner S (eds) *Contemporary Europe: class, status and power*. Routledge and Kegan Paul, London, pp 388–408

Boucher J, Smeers Y 1985 Gas trade in the European Communities in the 1970s. *Energy Economics* 7: 102–16

Boucher J, Smeers Y 1987 Economic forces in the European gas market – a 1985 perspective. *Energy Economics* 9: 2–16

Bourgeois-Pichat J 1981 Recent demographic change in Western Europe: an assessment. *Population and Development Review* 7: 19–40

Bowler I R 1976 The CAP and the space-economy of agriculture in the EEC. In Lee R, Ogden P E (eds) *Economy and Society in the EEC: spatial perspectives*.

Saxon House, Farnborough, pp 235–55

Bowler I R 1985 *Agriculture under the Common Agricultural Policy: A Geography*. Manchester University Press, Manchester

Bradshaw R 1972 Internal migration in Spain. *Iberian Studies* 1: 68–75

Bradshaw R 1985 Spanish migration: economic causes, grave social consequences. *Geography* 70: 175–8

Bransden S 1985 Land abandonment in Sicily. *Land Use Studies* 2: 244–6

Bretell C B 1979 *Emigrar para voltar*. a Portuguese ideology of return migration. *Papers in Anthropology* 20: 1–20

Brewin C 1987 The European Community – a union without unity of government. *Journal of Common Market Studies* 26: 1–23

Brown A J 1972 *The Framework of Regional Economics in the United Kingdom*. Cambridge University Press, Cambridge

Brown A J, Burrows E M 1977 *Regional Economic Problems*. George Allen and Unwin, London

Brown E D 1978 Rockall and the limits of national jurisdiction of the UK. *Marine Policy* 2: 181

Brugger E A, Stuckey B 1987 Regional economic structure and innovative behaviour in Switzerland. *Regional Studies* 21: 241–54

Brusco S 1982 The Emilian model: productive decentralization and social integration. *Cambridge Journal of Economics* 6: 167–84

Bruyelle P 1987 Le tunnel sous la Manche et l'aménagement régional dans la France du Nord. *Annales de Géographie* 96: 145–70

Burgess J A 1982 Selling places: environmental images for the executive. *Regional Studies* 16: 1–17

Burkart A J, Medlik S 1974 *Tourism*. Heinemann, London

Burtenshaw D 1976 *Saar-Lorraine*. Oxford University Press, Oxford

Burtenshaw D 1985 The future of the European city. *Geographical Journal* 151: 365–70

Burtenshaw D, Bateman M, Ashworth G J 1981 *The City in West Europe*. Wiley, Chichester

Cabouret M 1982 Traits permanents et tendances récentes de l'agriculture finlandaise. *Annales de Géographie* 91: 87–118

Cabral M V 1978 Agrarian structures and recent rural movements in Portugal. *Journal of Peasant Studies* 5: 411–45

Cairncross A (ed) 1974 *Economic Policy for the European Community: the way forward*. Macmillan, London

Carney J, Hudson R, Lewis J (eds) 1980 *Regions in Crisis: new perspectives in European regional theory*. Croom Helm, London

Castells M 1978 Urban social movements and the struggle for democracy: the citizens' movement in Madrid. *International Journal of Urban and Regional Research* 2: 133–46

Castells M 1978 *City, Class and Power*. Macmillan, London

Castells M 1983 *The City and the Grassroots*. Arnold, London

Castles S 1984 *Here for Good: Western Europe's new ethnic minorities*. Pluto, London

Castles S, Kosack G 1985 *Immigrant Workers and Class Structure in Western Europe* 2nd edn. Oxford University Press, Oxford

Catudal H M 1975 The plight of the Lilliputians: an analysis of five European microstates. *Geoforum* **6**: 187–204

Cavazzani A 1976 Social determinants of part-time farming in a marginal region of Italy. In Fuller A M, Mage J M (eds) *Part-time Farming: problem or resource in rural development*. Geo Abstracts, Norwich, pp 101–13

Cecchini P 1988 *The European Challenge*. Wildwood, Aldershot

Cerase F P 1974 Migration and social change: expectations and reality. A study of return migration from the United States to Italy. *International Migration Review* **8**: 245–62

Cherki E 1973 Le mouvement d'occupation de maisons vides en France. *Espaces et Sociétés* **9**: 63–91

Cheshire P, Carbonaro G, Hay D 1986 Problems of urban decline and growth in EEC countries. *Urban Studies* **23**: 131–49

Chisholm M 1986 The impact of the Channel Tunnel on the regions of Britain and Europe. *Geographical Journal* **152**: 314–34

Christaller W 1964 Some considerations of tourism locations in Europe. *Regional Science Association Papers* **12**: 95–105

Church A 1988 Urban regeneration in London Docklands. *Environment and Planning* **6**: 187–208

Church A, Hall J 1986 Discovery of Docklands. *Geographical Magazine* **58**: 632–9

Churchill R 1980 Revision of the EEC's Common Fisheries Policy. *European Law Review* **5**: 3–37 and 95–111

Churchill R 1981 Specific sectors: fisheries. *European Law Review* **6**: 478–81

Clark G 1979 Farm amalgamations in Scotland. *Scottish Geographical Magazine* **95**: 93–107

Clout H D 1968 Planned and unplanned changes in French farm structure. *Geography* **53**: 311–15

Clout H D 1971 *Agriculture*. Macmillan Studies in Contemporary Europe, London

Clout H D 1974a Population changes in the Auvergne region of central France. *Erdkunde* **28**: 246–59

Clout H D 1974b Agricultural plot consolidation in the Auvergne region of central France. *Norsk Geografisk Tidsskrift* **28**: 181–94

Clout H D 1976 Rural–urban migration in Western Europe. In Salt J, Clout H D (eds) *Migration in Post-War Europe: geographical essays*. Oxford University Press, Oxford, pp 30–51

Clout H D (ed) 1978 *Changing London*. University Tutorial Press, Slough

Clout H D 1984 *A Rural Policy for the EEC?* Methuen, London

Clout H D (ed) 1987a *Regional Development in Western Europe* 3rd edn. Fulton, London

Clout H D 1987b Rural space. In Clout H D (ed) *Regional Development in Western Europe*. Fulton, London, pp 87–108

Clout H D 1987c The neighbourhood project for urban rehabilitation in France. *Planning Outlook* **29**: 70–8

Collingridge D 1984a Lessons of nuclear power: US and

UK history. *Energy Policy* **12**: 46–67

Collingridge D 1984b Lessons of nuclear power: French 'success' and the breeder. *Energy Policy* **12**: 189–200

Collins D 1975 *The European Communities: the social policy of the first phase* 2 vols. Martin Robertson, London

Commission of the European Communities 1968 *First Guidelines for a Common Energy Policy*. Brussels

Commission of the European Communities 1973 *Report on the Regional Problems in the Enlarged Community*. Brussels

Commission of the European Communities 1976 Environment Programme, 1977–81. *Bulletin of the European Communities, Supplement*, **6/76**

Commission of the European Communities 1980 *Outlook for the Long-term Coal Supply and Demand Trend in the Community*. COM(80) 117/final, Brussels

Commission of the European Communities 1981a The development of an energy strategy for the Community. *Bulletin of the European Communities, Supplement* **4/81**: 7–20

Commission of the European Communities 1981b The European automobile industry. *Bulletin of the European Communities, Supplement* **2/81**

Commission of the European Communities 1981c *The Regions of Europe: first periodic report on the social and economic situation in the regions of the Community*. Brussels

Commission of the European Communities 1982 *Commission Communication to Council on a Mediterranean policy for the enlarged Community*. COM(82) 353/final

Commission of the European Communities 1984 *The Regions of Europe: second periodic report on the social and economic situation and development of the regions of the Community*. Luxembourg

Commission of the European Communities 1985 Advanced manufacturing equipment in the Community. *Bulletin of the European Communities, Supplement* **6/85**

Commission of the European Communities 1987a The European energy policy. *European File* **2/87**

Commission of the European Communities 1987b The European Community and environmental protection. *European File* **5/87**, 3–11

Commission of the European Communities 1987c *Third Periodic Report from the Commission on the Social and Economic Situation and Development of the Regions of the Community*. Brussels

Commission on Energy and the Environment 1981 *Coal and the Environment*. HMSO, London

Constantinides P 1977 The Greek Cypriots: factors in the maintenance of ethnic identity. In Watson J L (ed) *Between Two Cultures: migrants and minorities in Britain*. Basil Blackwell, Oxford, pp 269–300

Cooke P, da Rosa Pires A 1985 Productive decentralization in three European regions. *Environment and Planning A* **17**: 527–54

Coull J R 1972 *The Fisheries of Europe*. Bell, London

Couper A D 1972 *The Geography of Sea Transport*. Hutchinson, London

Courgeau D 1978 Les migrations internes en France de

1954–1975: vue d'ensemble. *Population* **33**: 525–45

Courgeau D, Lefebvre M 1982 Les migrations internes en France de 1954–1975: migrations et urbanisation. *Population* **37**: 341–69

Cowan P 1969 *The Office: a facet of urban growth*. Heinemann, London

Croxford G J, Wise M, Chalkley B S 1987 The reform of the European Regional Development Fund; a preliminary assessment. *Journal of Common Market Studies* **26**: 25–38

Culot M 1974 The rearguard battle for Brussels. *Ekistics* **37**: 101–04

Damesick P J 1979 Offices and inner urban regeneration. *Area* **11**: 41–7

Damesick P J, Wood P A (eds) 1987 *Regional Problems, Problem Regions and Public Policy in the United Kingdom*. Oxford University Press, Oxford

Daniels P W 1975 *Office Location: an urban and regional study*. Bell, London

Daniels P W (ed) 1979 *Spatial Patterns of Office Growth and Location*. Wiley, Chichester

Daniels P W 1982 *Service Industries: growth and location*. Cambridge University Press, Cambridge

Daniels P W 1983 Service industries: supporting role or centre stage? *Area* **15**: 301–10

Daniels P W 1985 *Service Industries: a geographical appraisal*. Methuen, London

Daolio A 1975 Les luttes urbaines en Italie. *Espaces et Sociétés* **15**: 105–15

Dawson J A (ed) 1979 *The Marketing Environment*. Croom Helm, London

Dawson J A (ed) 1980 *Retail Geography*. Croom Helm, London

Dean C J 1982 The trans-Mediterranean gas pipeline. *Geography* **67**: 258–60

Dean K G 1986 Counterurbanization continues in Brittany. *Geography* **71**: 151–4

Dean K G 1987 The disaggregation of migration flows: the case of Brittany 1975–82. *Regional Studies* **21**: 313–26

De Barros A 1980 Portuguese agrarian reform and economic and social development. *Sociologia Ruralis* **20**: 82–96

De Benedictis M 1981 Agricultural development in Italy: national problems in a Community perspective. *Journal of Agricultural Economics* **32**: 275–86

De Clercq M, Naert F 1985 Regional economic disparities in Belgium and regional, national and supra-national policies: an analysis of collective failure. *Planning Outlook* **28**: 13–20

De Lannoy W 1975 Residential segregation of foreigners in Brussels. *Bulletin de la Société Belge d'Etudes Géographiques* **44**: 215–38

Dematteis G 1982 Repeuplement et revalorisation des espaces périphériques: le cas de l'Italie. *Revue Géographique des Pyrénées et du Sud-Ouest* **53**: 129–43

Department of Energy 1974 *United Kingdom Offshore Oil and Gas Policy: Cmnd. 5696*. HMSO, London

Department of Energy 1976 *Development of the Oil and Gas Resources of the United Kingdom, 1976*. HMSO, London

Department of Energy 1982 *Development of the Oil and Gas Resources of the United Kingdom, 1982*. HMSO, London

Department of Energy 1987 *Development of the Oil and Gas Resources of the UK 1987*. HMSO, London

Department of the Environment 1975 *The Flixborough Disaster: report of the Court of Inquiry*. HMSO, London

Department of the Environment 1981a *Coal and the Environment*. HMSO, London

Department of the Environment 1981b *The Vale of Belvoir Coalfield Inquiry*. HMSO, London

De Rougemont D 1979 *The State of the Union of Europe*. Pergamon, Oxford

De Smidt M 1985 Relocation of government services in the Netherlands. *Tijdschrift voor Economische en Sociale Geografie* **76**: 232–6

De Smidt M, Wever E (eds) 1984 *A Profile of Dutch Economic Geography*. Van Gorcum, Assen and Maastricht

Despicht N 1980 Centre and periphery in Europe. In De Bandt J (ed) *European Studies in Development*. Macmillan, London, pp 38–41

Deubner C 1980 The southern enlargement of the European Community: opportunities and dilemmas from a West German point of view. *Journal of Common Market Studies* **18**: 229–45

Devavry J 1977 Les rues pietonnes en France. *Hommes et Terres du Nord* 45–61

De Vries B, Dijk D 1985 Electric power generation options for the Netherlands to 2000: an evaluation of government's and environmentalists' scenarios. *Energy Policy* **13**: 230–42

Dicken P 1976 The multi-plant business enterprise and geographical space: some issues in the study of external control and regional development. *Regional Studies* **10**: 401–12

Dicken P 1986a *Global Shift: industrial change in a turbulent world*. Harper and Row, London

Dicken P 1986b Multinational enterprises and the local economy: some further observations. *Area* **18**: 215–21

Dicken P, Lloyd P E 1981 *Modern Western Society: a geographical perspective on work, home and well-being*. Harper and Row, New York

Dimitras E 1967 Greece prepares for the return of her intra-European migrants. *Migration News* **16**: 1–3

Dokopolou E 1986a Foreign manufacturing investment in Greece, competition and market structure. In Hamilton F E I (ed) *Industrialization in Developing and Peripheral Regions*. Croom Helm, London, pp 188–204

Dokopolou E 1986b Multinationals and manufacturing exports from the enlarged European Community: the case of Greece. In Hamilton F E I (ed) *Industrialization in Developing and Peripheral Regions*. Croom Helm, London, pp 205–31

Donnay J P 1985 Méthodologie de la localisation des bureaux. *Annales de Géographie* **94**: 152–73

Donnison D, Middleton A (eds) 1987 *Regenerating the Inner City: Glasgow's experience*. Routledge and Kegan Paul, London

Douglass W A 1971 Rural exodus in two Spanish Basque villages. *American Anthropologist* **73**: 1100–14

Dovring F 1965 *Land and Labour in Europe in the Twentieth Century*. Nijhoff, The Hague

Dower M 1965 Fourth wave: the challenge of leisure. *Architects' Journal* 20 January 1965, 122–90

Dower M et al 1981 *Leisure Provision and People's Needs*. HMSO, London

Drewett R 1979 A European perspective on urban change. *Town and Country Planning* 48: 224–6

Drudy P J 1978 Depopulation in a prosperous agricultural sub-region. *Regional Studies* 12: 49–60

Duclaud-Williams R 1978 *The Politics of Housing in Britain and France*. Heinemann, London

Dupuy G 1981 Le téléphone et la ville. *Annales de Géographie* 90: 387–400

Ellington A, Burke T 1981 *Europe: environment*. Ecobooks, London

Environmental Resources Ltd 1983 *Acid Rain: a review of the phenomenon in the EEC and Europe*. Graham and Trotman, London

Erz W 1979 Katalog der Naturschutgebiete in der Bundesrepublik Deutschland. *Naturschutz Aktuell* 3

Esher V 1969 *York: a study in conservation*. HMSO, London

Etzioni A 1967 Mixed-scanning: a third approach to decision-making. In Faludi A (ed) 1973 *A Reader in Planning Theory*. Pergamon, Oxford, pp 217–29

European Coal and Steel Community 1964 *Study on the Long-term Energy Outlook for the European Community*. High Authority of the ECSC, Luxembourg

European Free Trade Association 1981 *EFTA Bulletin* 1981–1, 2–12

European Investment Bank 1980 EIB support for energy investment. *Information* 23: 1–11

European Investment Bank 1982 *Annual Report, 1981*. EIB, Luxembourg

European Investment Bank 1987 *Annual Report, 1986*. EIB, Luxembourg

Evans D 1978 *Western Energy Policy*. Macmillan, London

Evenson N 1981 The city as an artifact: building control in modern Paris. In Kain R J P (ed) *Planning for Conservation*. Mansell, London, pp 177–98

Everling U 1980 Possibilities and limits of European integration. *Journal of Common Market Studies* 18: 217–28

Falk T 1978a Urban turnaround in Sweden: the acceleration of population dispersal 1970–75. *Geo Journal* 2: 27–33

Falk T 1978b Urban development in Sweden 1960–75: population dispersal in progress. In Hansen N M (ed) *Human Settlement Systems*. Ballinger, Cambridge, Mass, pp 51–83

Federici N, Golini A 1972 Les migrations entre les grandes régions des six pays du Marché Commun. *Genus* 28: 27–68

Fel A 1974 Types d'évolution démographique de la France rurale. *Geographia Polonica* 29: 55–62

Fennell R 1979 *The Common Agricultural Policy of the European Community*. Granada, London

Fennell R 1982 Farm succession in the European Community. *Sociologia Ruralis* 21: 19–42

Fennell R 1985 A reconsideration of the objectives of the Common Agricultural Policy. *Journal of Common Market Studies*. 23: 257–77

Ferrarotti F 1972 Rome: capitale à la périphérie. *Espaces et Sociétés* 5: 31–62

Festy P, Prioux F 1975 Le divorce en Europe depuis 1950. *Population* 30: 975–1017

Fielding A J 1975 Internal migration in Western Europe. In Kosiński L A, Prothero R M (eds) *People on the Move: studies on internal migration*. Methuen, London, pp 237–54

Fielding A J 1982 Counterurbanization in Western Europe. *Progress in Planning* 17: 1–52

Fielding A J (1986) Counterurbanization in Western Europe. In Findlay A, White P E (eds) *West European Population Change*. Croom Helm, London, pp 35–49

Flockton C H 1982 Strategic planning in the Paris region and French urban policy. *Geoforum* 13: 193–208

Flowerdew R, Salt J 1979 Migration between labour market areas in Great Britain, 1970–71. *Regional Studies* 13: 211–31

Fofi G 1970 Immigrants in Turin. pp. 269–84 In Jansen C J (ed) *Readings in the Sociology of Migration*. Pergamon, Oxford, pp 269–84

Fontaine A 1971 The real divisions of Europe. *Foreign Affairs* 49: 302–14

Ford L 1978 Continuity and change in historic cities: Bath, Chester and Norwich. *Geographical Review* 68: 253–73

Frank H J 1966 *Crude Oil Prices in the Middle East*. Praeger, New York

Franklin S H 1969 *The European Peasantry: the final phase*. Methuen, London

Franklin S H 1971 *Rural Societies*. Macmillan Studies in Contemporary Europe, London

Franko L G 1976 *The European Multinationals: a renewed challenge to American and British big business*. Harper and Row, London

Freeman C (ed) 1984 *Long Waves in the World Economy*. Frances Pinter, London

Frémont A 1978 L'aménagement régional en France: la pratique et les idées. *L'Espace Géographique* 7: 73–84

Fröbel F, Heinrichs J, Kreye O 1977 The tendency towards a new international division of labour. *Review* 1: 73–88

Fröbel F, Heinrichs J, Kreye O 1980 *The New International Division of Labour*. Cambridge University Press, Cambridge and Maison des Sciences de l'Homme, Paris

Fuerst J (ed) 1974 *Public Housing in Europe and America*. Croom Helm, London

Fuller A M 1975 Linkages between social and spatial systems: the case of farmer mobility in northern Italy. *Sociologia Ruralis* 15: 119–24

Galt A H 1979 Exploring the cultural ecology of field fragmentation and scattering in the island of Pantellaria. *Journal of Anthropological Research* 35: 95–108

Gasson R 1974 Mobility of farm workers. *Department of Land Economy Occasional Paper no. 2*. University of Cambridge

Georgakopoulos T A 1980 Greece and the EEC. *Three Banks Review* 128: 38–50

George P 1972 Questions de géographie de la population en République fédérale allemande. *Annales de Géographie* **81**: 523–37

George V, Lawson R (eds) 1980 *Poverty and Inequality in Common Market Countries*. Routledge and Kegan Paul, London

Gibb R A 1986 The impact of the Channel Tunnel rail link on south-east England. *Geographical Journal* **152**: 335–50

Gillespie A E, Goddard J B 1986 Advanced telecommunications and regional economic development. *Geographical Journal* **152**: 383–97

Glyptis S A 1981 Leisure life styles. *Regional Studies* **15**: 311–26

Goddard J B 1975 *Office Location in Urban and Regional Development*. Oxford University Press, Oxford

Goddard J B, Champion A G (eds) 1983 *The Urban and Regional Transformation of Britain*. Methuen, London

Gokalp C 1973 L'émigration turque en Europe et particulièrement en France. *Population* **28**: 335–60

Goldfield D R 1979 Suburban growth in Stockholm and the United State. In Hammarström I, Hall T (eds) *Growth and Transformation of the Modern City*. Swedish Council for Building Research, Stockholm, pp 139–56

Goosens M, De Rudder J 1976 Management centres and location of top management in Belgium. *Bulletin de la Société Belge d'Etudes Géographiques* **45**: 121–33

Gorbachev M 1987 *Perestroika. New Thinking for our Country and the World*. Collins, London

Gordon R L 1970 *The Evolution of Energy Policy in Western Europe: the reluctant retreat from coal*. Praeger, New York

Gordon R L 1987 *World Coal: economics, policies and prospects*. Cambridge University Press, Cambridge

Gottmann J 1950 *A Geography of Europe*. Holt, Rinehart and Winston, New York

Goursolas J M 1980 New towns in the Paris metropolitan area. *International Journal of Urban and Regional Research* **4**: 405–18

Green A E, Howells J 1987 Spatial prospects for service growth in Britain. *Area* **19**: 111–22

Greene R P, Gallagher J M 1980 *Future Coal Prospects: country and regional assessment*. Ballinger, Cambridge, Mass.

Greenwood D 1976 The decline of agriculture in Fuenterrabia. In Aceves J B, Douglass W A (eds) *The Changing Faces of Rural Spain*. Schenkman, New York, pp 29–44

Guedes M 1981 Recent agricultural land policy in Spain. *Oxford Agrarian Studies* **10**: 26–43

Guilmot J, McGlue D, Valette P, Waeterloos C (eds) 1986 *Energy 2000: a reference projection and alternative energy outlooks for the European Community and the World*. Cambridge University Press, Cambridge

Guilmot P 1978 The demographic background. In Council of Europe *Population Decline in Europe: implications of a declining or stationary population*. Edward Arnold, London, pp 3–49

Guruswany L D, Papps I, Storey D J 1983 The development and impact of an EEC Directive: the control of discharges of mercury into the aquatic environment. *Journal of Common Market Studies* **22**: 71–100

Guttesen R, Nielsen F H 1975 Regional development in Denmark. *Geografisk Tidsskrift* **75**: 74–87

Haigh N 1986 *European Community Environmental Policy in Practice, Volume 1, Water and Waste in Four Countries*. Graham and Trotman, London

Hajdu J G 1978 The German city today. *Geography* **63**: 23–30

Hajdu J G 1979 Phases in the post-war German urban experience. *Town Planning Review* **50**: 267–86

Hajdu J G 1981 Pedestrian precincts in Germany. *Town and Country Planning* **50**: 173–4

Hall P G 1967 Planning for urban growth: metropolitan area plans. *Regional Studies* **1**: 101–34

Hall P G 1977 *The World Cities* 2nd end. Weidenfeld and Nicolson, London

Hall P G 1981a *The Inner City in Context*. Heinemann, London

Hall P G 1981b Regional development in the EEC: a look back and a look forward. *Built Environment* **7**: 229–32

Hall P G 1984 *World Cities* 3rd edn. Weidenfeld and Nicolson, London

Hall P G, Cheshire P 1987 The key to success for cities. *Town and Country Planning* **56**: 50–3

Hall P G, Hay D 1980 *Growth Centres in the European Urban System*. Heinemann, London

Hall P G, Markusen A 1985 *Silicon Landscapes*. Allen and Unwin, London

Hall R 1976 Demographic and social change in the EEC. In Lee R, Ogden P E (eds) *Economy and Society in the EEC*. Saxon House, Farnborough, pp 85–107

Hall T 1979 The central business district: planning in Stockholm 1928–78. In Hammarström I, Hall T (eds) *Growth and Transformation of the Modern City*. Swedish Council for Building Research, Stockholm, pp 181–232

Hamilton F E I 1976 Multinational enterprise and the European Community. *Tijdschrift voor Economische en Sociale Geografie* **67**: 258–78

Hamilton F E I 1978 Multinational enterprise and the European Economic Community. In Hamilton F E I (ed) *Industrial Change: international experience and public policy*. Longman, London, pp 24–41

Hamilton L, Just W D 1981 The evolution of regional disparities in the European Community: an ethical perspective. *Ecumenical Research Exchange (Rotterdam), Discussion Papers* **288**: 1–38

Hammar T (ed) 1985 *European Immigration Policy: a comparative study*. Cambridge University Press, Cambridge

Hamnett C 1983 The condition in England's inner cities on the eve of the 1981 riots. *Area* **15**: 7–13

Hamnett C, Williams P R 1980 Social change in London: a study in gentrification. *Urban Affairs Quarterly* **15**: 469–87

Harris R C 1977 The simplification of Europe overseas. *Annals of the Association of American Geographers* **67**: 469–83

Harrison A 1982 Land policies in the member states of the European Community. *Agricultural Administration* **11**: 159–74

Hartke W 1956 Die Sozialebrache als Phänomen der geographischen Differenzierung der Landschaft. *Erdkunde* **10**: 257–69

Hartner P, Jones G 1986 *Multinationals: theory and history*. Gower, Aldershot

Harvey D R, Thomson K J 1985 Costs, benefits and the future of the Common Agricultural Policy. *Journal of Common Market Studies* **24**: 1–20

Haskins G, Gibb A, Hubert A (eds) 1986 *A Guide to Small Firm Assistance in Europe*. Gower, Aldershot

Hass-Klau C H M 1982 The housing shortage in Germany's major cities. *Built Environment* **8**: 60–70

Hass-Klau C 1986 Berlin's 'soft' urban renewal in Kreuzberg. *Built Environment* **12**: 165–75

Hayter R 1982 Truncation, the international firm and regional policy. *Area* **14**: 277–82

Health and Safety Executive 1978a *Canvey: an investigation of potential hazards from operations in the Canvey Island/Thurrock area*. HMSO, London

Health and Safety Executive 1978b *Canvey: summary of an investigation of potential hazards from operations in the Canvey Island/Thurrock area*. HMSO, London

Health and Safety Executive 1979 *Advisory Committee on Major Hazards, Second Report*. HMSO, London

Health and Safety Executive 1981 *Canvey: a review of potential hazards in the Canvey Island/Thurrock area*. HMSO, London

Hebbert M 1982 Regional policy in Spain. *Geoforum* **13**: 107–20

Hebbert M 1987 Regionalism: a reform concept and its application to Spain. *Environment and Planning C* **5**: 239–50

Hechter M, Brustein W 1980 Regional modes of production and patterns of state formation in Western Europe. *American Journal of Sociology* **85**: 1061–94

Heinritz G, Lichtenberger E (eds) 1986 *The Take-off of Suburbia and the Crisis of the Central City*. Steiner, Stuttgart

Hengchen B, Melis C 1980 Contribution to the study of the Brussels urban social movement. *International Journal of Urban and Regional Research* **4**: 116–26

Her Majesty's Stationery Office 1969 *Bath: a study in conservation*. HMSO, London

Herbert D T, Smith D M (eds) 1979 *Social Problems and the City: geographical perspectives*. Oxford University Press, Oxford

Hervo M, Charras M 1971 *Bidonvilles*. Maspero, Paris

Herzfeld M 1980 Social tension and inheritance by lot in three Greek villages. *Anthropological Quarterly* **53**: 91–100

Hill K 1974 Belgium: political change in a segmented society. In Rose R (ed) *Electoral Behavior*. Free Press, New York, pp 29–208

Hirsch G P, Maunder A M 1978. *Farm Amalgamation in Western Europe*. Saxon House, Farnborough

Hodgson R D, Smith R W 1979 Boundary issues created by extended national maritime claims. *Geographical Review* **69**: 423–33

Hoffmann G W (ed) 1953 *A Geography of Europe*. Ronald, New York

Hoffmann-Nowotny H J 1974 Immigrant minorities in Switzerland. *Current Sociology* **1**: 1–24

Hoffmann-Nowotny H J 1978 European migration after World War II. In McNeill W H, Adams R S (eds) *Human Migration: patterns and policies*. Indiana University Press, Bloomington, pp 85–105

Holland S H 1976a *Capital versus the Regions*. Macmillan, London

Holland S H 1976b *The Regional Problem*. Macmillan, London

Holland S H 1980 *The UnCommon Market*. Macmillan, London

Home R K 1982 *Inner City Regeneration*. Spon, London

Horner A A, Parker A J (eds) 1987 *Geographical Perspectives on the Dublin Region*. Geographical Society of Ireland, Dublin

House J W 1978 *France: an applied geography*. Methuen, London

House of Lords Select Committee on the European Communities 1986 *Single European Act and Parliamentary Scrutiny 12A Report. Session 1985–86*. HL 149. HMSO, London

Houston J M 1964 *The Western Mediterranean World: an introduction to its regional landscapes*. Longman, London

Hudman L E 1978 Origin regions of international tourism. In Sinnhuber K, Jig T (eds) *Studies in the Geography of Tourism, vol. 2*. Ferdinand Hirt, Vienna, pp 43–9

Hudson R, Lewis J R (eds) 1982 *Regional Planning in Europe*. Pion, London

Hudson R, Lewis J (eds) 1985 *Uneven Development in Southern Europe*. Methuen, London

Hudson R, Rhind D, Mounsey H 1984 *An Atlas of EEC Affairs*. Methuen, London

Hume I M 1973 Migrant workers in Europe. *Finance and Development* **10**: 2–6

Ilbery B W 1984 Core–periphery contrasts in European social well-being. *Geography* **69**: 289–302

Ilbery B W 1986 *Western Europe: a systematic human geography* 2nd edn. Oxford University Press, Oxford

Inglehart R 1971 Changing value priorities and European integration. *Journal of Common Market Studies* **10**: 1–36

Ingram D R 1983 Changes in the size and age structure of London's population: 1971–1981. *Geography* **68**: 56–60

Insall D and Associates 1969 *Chester: a study in conservation*. HMSO, London

International Energy Agency 1980a *Energy Policies and Programmes of IEA Countries*. OECD, Paris

International Energy Agency 1980b *Energy Research Development and Demonstration in the IEA Countries*. OECD, Paris

International Energy Agency 1984 *Energy Policies and Programmes of IEA Countries*. OECD, Paris

International Tanker Owners' Pollution Federation 1980 *Measures to Combat Oil Pollution*. Graham and Trotman, London

Ion D C 1977 The North Sea countries. In Mangone J G (ed) *Energy Policies of the World, vol. 2.* Elsevier, New York, Oxford and Amsterdam, pp 121–216

IUCN 1974 *United Nations List of National Parks and Equivalent Reserves.* Morges

IUCN 1986 *United Nations List of National Parks and Equivalent Reserves 1985*: Gland

Jacoby E H 1959 *Land Consolidation in Europe.* International Institute for Land Reclamation and Improvement, Wageningen

Jallade J P (ed) 1981 *Emploi et chômage en Europe.* Economica, Paris

Jarrett R J 1975 Disincentives: the other side of regional development policy. *Journal of Common Market Studies* 13: 379–90

Jenkins J R G 1986 *Jura Separatism in Switzerland.* Oxford University Press, Oxford

Jensen-Butler C 1982 Capital accumulation and regional development: the case of Denmark. *Environment and Planning A* 14: 1307–40

Jensen-Butler C 1987 The regional economic effects of European integration. *Geoforum* 18: 213–27

Johnson J H, Salt J 1981 Population redistribution policies in Great Britain. In Webb J W, Naukkarinen A, Kosiński L A (eds) *Policies of Population Redistribution.* Geographical Society of Northern Finland, Oulu, pp 77–92

Johnson S P 1979 *The Pollution Control Policy of the European Communities.* Graham and Trotman, London

Johnston D 1976 *Marine Policy and the Coastal Community: the impact of the Law of the Sea.* Croom Helm, London

Johnston R J, Doornkamp J C (eds) 1982 *The Changing Geography of the United Kingdom.* Methuen, London

Jolliffe W 1977 Farming in the rural–urban fringe in Britain. In Gasson R (ed) *The Place of Part-time Farming in Rural and Regional Development.* Centre for European Agricultural Studies, Wye, pp 35–41

Jones D T 1981 *Maturity and Crisis in the European Car Industry: structural change and public policy.* Sussex European Research Centre, Brighton

Jones P 1984 Retail warehouse developments in Britain. *Area* 16: 41–6.

Jordan T G 1973 *The European Culture Area.* Harper and Row, New York

Jung H-U 1982 Regional policy in the Federal Republic of Germany. *Geoforum* 13: 83–96

Kade G, Schiller G 1969 Gastarbeiterwanderungen: ein neues Element in der Wirtschaftspolitik der Mittelmeerlander. *Weltwirtschaftlich Archiv* 102: 333–55

Kain R J P 1981 Conservation planning in France: policy and practice in the Marais, Paris. In Kain R J P (ed) *Planning for Conservation.* Mansell, London, pp 199–233

Kain R J P 1982 Europe's model and exemplar still? The French approach to urban conservation. *Town Planning Review.* 53: 403–22

Kariel H G, P E 1982 Socio-cultural impacts of tourism: an example from the Austrian Alps. *Geografiska Annaler (Series B)* 64: 1–16

Karpat K H 1976 *The Gecekondu: rural migration and urbanization.* Cambridge University Press, Cambridge

Kayser B 1977 European migrations: the new pattern. *International Migration Review* 11: 232–40

Kearns K C 1979 Intraurban squatting in London. *Annals of the Association of American Geographers* 69: 589–98

Kearns K C 1982 Preservation and transformation of Georgian Dublin. *Geographical Review* 72: 270–90

Keating M, Jones B (eds) 1985 *Regions in the European Community* Oxford University Press, Oxford

Keeble D, Owens P L, Thompson C 1981 EEC regional disparities and trends in the 1970s. *Built Environment* 7: 154–61

Keeble D, Owens P L, Thompson C 1982 Regional accessibility and economic potential in the European Community. *Regional Studies* 16: 419–31

Keeble D, Owens P L, Thompson C 1983 The urban–rural manufacturing shift in the European Community. *Urban Studies* 20: 405–18

Kerr A J C 1977 *The Common Market and how it works.* Pergamon, Oxford

Kerr A J C 1986 *The Common Market and how it works* 3rd edn. Pergamon, Oxford

Kiljunen M L 1980 Regional disparities and policy in the EEC In Seers D, Vaitsos C (eds) *Integration and Unequal Development: the experience of the EEC.* St Martin's Press, New York, pp 199–222

King R L 1970 Structural and geographical problems of south Italian agriculture. *Norsk Geografisk Tidsskrift* 24: 83–95

King R L 1973 *Land Reform: the Italian experience.* Butterworth, London

King R L 1976 The evolution of international labour migration movements concerning the EEC. *Tijdschrift voor Economische en Sociale Geografie* 67: 66–82

King R L 1977 Italian migration to Great Britain. *Geography* 62: 176–86

King R L 1978 Shifting progress in Portugal's land reform. *Geography* 63: 118–19

King R L 1979 Return migration: a review of some case studies from southern Europe. *Mediterranean Studies* 1: 3–30

King R L 1982 Southern Europe: dependency or development? *Geography* 67: 221–34

King R L 1984 Population movement: emigration, return migration and internal migration. In Williams A M (ed) *Southern Europe Transformed.* Harper and Row, London, pp 145–78

King R L 1987a *Italy.* Harper and Row, London

King R L 1987b Italy. In Clout H D (ed) *Regional Development in Western Europe.* Fulton, London, pp 129–63

King R L, Bridal J 1982 The changing distribution of Cypriots in London. *Studi Emigrazione* 65: 93–120

King R L, Mortimer J, Strachan A J 1984 Return migration and tertiary development: a Calabrian case-study. *Anthropological Quarterly* 57: 112–24

King R L, Took L J 1983 Land tenure and rural social change: the Italian case. *Erdkunde* 37: 186–98

Klaasen L H 1987 The future of larger European towns. *Urban Studies* **24**: 251–7

Klaasen L H, Drewe P 1973 *Migration Policy in Europe: a comparative perspective*. Saxon House, Farnborough

Klatte E 1986 The past and future of European Environmental Policy. *European Environmental Review*. **1**: 32–4

Klein L 1981 The European Community's regional policy. *Built Environment* **7**: 182–9

Kliot N 1987 Maritime boundaries in the Mediterranean: aspects of co-operation and dispute. In Blake G (ed) *Maritime Boundaries and Ocean Resources*. Croom Helm, London, pp 200–26

Kofman E 1982 Differential modernization, social conflicts and ethno-regionalism in Corsica. *Ethnic and Racial Studies* **5**: 300–12

Kormoss I B F 1976 Urban extensions in Belgium. In Laconte P (ed) *The Environments of Human Settlements* vol 1. Pergamon, Oxford, pp 177–86

Kosiński L 1970 *The Population of Europe*. Longman, London

Kouvelis K 1979 Description d'une nouvelle stratégie de rénovation: le cas du quartier Kreuzberg à Berlin. *Espaces et Sociétés*, **30–31**: 109–42

Kromarek P 1986 The Single European Act and the environment. *European Environmental Review* **1**: 10–12

Kunzmann K R 1981 Development trends in the regional and settlement structure of the Federal Republic of Germany. *Built Environment* **7**: 243–54

Kuper J 1979 The third world comes to the Netherlands. *New Community* **7**: 469–73

Labasse J 1984 Les congrès, activité tertiaire de villes privilégiées. *Annales de Géographie* **93**: 687–703

Lambert A M 1963 Farm consolidation in Western Europe. *Geography* **48**: 31–48

Lambert J 1971 The Cheshire cat and the pond: the EEC and the Mediterranean area. *Journal of Common Market Studies* **10**: 37–46

Landes D S 1969 *The Unbound Prometheus: technological change and industrial development in Western Europe from 1750 to the present*. Cambridge University Press, Cambridge

Lane D 1980 Mini-farming in the Italian south. *Geographical Magazine* **53**: 177–9

Law C M 1980 *British Regional Development since World War I*. Methuen, London

Law C M 1986 The geography of exhibition centres in Britain. *Geography* **71**: 359–62

Lawless P 1981 *Britain's Inner Cities*. Harper and Row, London

Lebon A, Falchi G 1980 New developments in intra-European migration since 1974. *International Migration Review* **14**: 539–79

Lee R, Ogden P E (eds) 1976 *Economy and Society in the EEC*. Saxon House, Farnborough

Leigh M, Van Praag N 1978 The Mediterranean challenge: 1. *Sussex European Papers no. 2*. Sussex European Research Centre, Brighton

Lenon B 1987 The geography of the big bang: London's office building boom. *Geography* **72**: 56–9

Lewis J R, Williams A M 1981 Regional uneven development on the European periphery: the case of Portugal. *Tijdschrift voor Economische en Sociale Geografie* **72**: 81–98

Lichtenberger E 1970 The nature of European urbanism. *Geoforum* **4**: 45–62

Lichtenberger E 1976 The changing nature of European urbanization. In Berry B J L (ed) *Urbanization and Counter-urbanization*. Sage, Beverly Hills and London, pp 91–107

Limouzin P 1980 Les facteurs de dynamisme des communes rurales françaises. *Annales de Géographie* **89**: 549–87

Ling J J 1973 Early state building and late peripheral nationalisms against the state: the case of Spain. In Eisenstadt S N, Rokkan S (eds) *Building States and Nations vol 2*. Sage, Beverly Hills, pp 32–116

Lodge J 1986 The Single European Act: towards a new Euro-dynamism? *Journal of Common Market Studies* **24**: 203–23

Lopreato J 1967 *Peasants no more*. Chandler, San Francisco

Lopriano N 1986 Radiation knows no frontiers: Chernobyl's challenge to science and government. *European Environmental Review* **1**: 2–9

Lowenthal D 1968 The American scene. *Geographical Review* **58**: 61–88

Lucas N J D 1979 *Energy in France: planning, politics and policy*. Europa Publications, London

Lucas N J D 1985 *Western European Energy Policies: a comparative study of the influence of institutional structure on technical change*. Clarendon Press, Oxford

Madge C, Willmott P 1981 *Inner City Poverty in Paris and London*. Routledge and Kegan Paul, London

Mallet S 1975 *The New Working Class*. Spokesman Books, Nottingham

Manganara J 1977 Some social aspects of the return movement of Greek migrant workers from West Germany to rural Greece. *Greek Review of Social Research* **29**: 65–75

Manne A S, Roland K, Stephan G 1986 Security of supply in the Western European market for natural gas. *Energy Policy* **14**: 52–64

Manners G 1981 *Coal in Britain: an uncertain future*. George Allen and Unwin, London

Mansholt S 1979 *The Common Agricultural Policy: some new thinking*. Soil Association, London

Marceau J 1977 *Class and Status in France: economic change and social immobility 1945–75*. Oxford University Press, Oxford

Marmot A F, Worthington J 1986 Great Fire to Big Bang: private and public designs on the City of London. *Built Environment* **12**: 216–33

Marquand J 1980 Spatial changes and economic divergence in the EEC. *Journal of Common Market Studies* **19**: 1–20

Marsh J S 1979 Agriculture. In Tsoukalis L (ed) *Greece and the European Community*. Saxon House, Farnborough, pp 68–83

Marshall J N 1985 Services and regional policy in Great Britain. *Area* **17**: 303–8

Marstrand P (ed) 1984 *New Technology and the Future of Work and Skills*. Frances Pinter, London

Martin R, Rowthorn B 1986 *The Geography of Deindustrialization*. Macmillan, London

Martins M R, Mawson J 1980 Regional trends in the European Community and revision of the common regional policy. *Built Environment* **6**: 145–52

Martins M R, Mawson J 1982 The programming of regional development in the EC. *Journal of Common Market Studies* **20**: 229–44

Massey D 1979 In what sense a regional problem? *Regional Studies* **13**: 233–43

Massey D, Meegan R 1982 *The Anatomy of Job Loss*. Methuen, London

Matthiessen C W 1980 Trends in the urbanization process: the Copenhagen case. *Geografisk Tidsskrift* **80**: 98–101

Maull H 1980 *Europe and World Energy*. Butterworth, London

Mayhew A 1970 Structural reform and the future of West German agriculture. *Geographical Review* **60**: 54–68

McDermott P J 1979 Multinational manufacturing firms and regional development: external control in the Scottish electronics industry. *Scottish Journal of Political Economy* **23**: 279–94

McDonald J R 1965 The repatriation of French Algerians, 1962–63. *International Migration* **3**: 146–57

McElrath D 1962 The social areas of Rome: a comparative analysis. *American Sociological Review* **27**: 376–91

Mead W R 1982 The discovery of Europe. *Geography* **67**: 193–202

Mellor R E H, Smith E A 1979 *Europe: a geographical survey of the continent*. Macmillan, London

Mendosa E L 1982 Benefits of migration as a personal strategy in Nazare, Portugal. *International Migration Review* **16**: 625–45

Mendras H 1970 *The Vanishing Peasant: innovation and change in French agriculture*. MIT Press, Cambridge, Mass

Mennell S 1976 *Cultural Policy in Towns*. Council of Europe, Strasbourg

Mény Y, Wright V (eds) 1985 *Centre–Periphery Relations in Western Europe*. Allen and Unwin, London

Merlin P 1971a *L'Exode Rural*. Presses Universitaires de France, Paris

Merlin P 1971b *New Towns*. Methuen, London

Metton A 1982 L'expansion du commerce périphérique en France. *Annales de Géographie* **91**: 463–79

Michael R 1979 Metropolitan development concepts and planning polices in West Germany. *Town Planning Review* **50**: 287–312

Minet G, Siotis J, Tsakaloyannis P 1981 Spain, Greece and Community politics. *Sussex European Papers no. 11*. Sussex European Research Centre, Brighton

Ministry of Agriculture, Fisheries and Food 1981 *Atlas of the Seas around the British Isles*. MAFF, London

Minshull G N 1978 *The New Europe: an economic geography of the EEC*. Hodder and Stoughton, London

Mitchell B 1976 Politics, fish and international resource management: the British–Icelandic Cod War. *Geographical Review* **66**: 127–38

Molle W 1979 *Regional Economic Development in the European Community*. Saxon House, Farnborough

Molle W and Cappelin R 1988 *Regional impact of Community policies in Europe*, Avebury, Aldershot

Molle W, Paelinck J 1979 Regional policy. In Coffey P (eds) *Economic Policies in the Common Market*. Macmillan, London, pp 146–71

Molle W, Wever E 1984a *Oil Refineries and Petrochemical Industries in Western Europe: buoyant past, uncertain future*. Gower, Aldershot

Molle W, Wever E 1984b Oil refineries and petrochemical industries in Europe. *Geo Journal* **9**: 421–30

Monke J 1986 Portugal on the brink of Europe: the CAP and Portuguese agriculture. *Journal of Agricultural Economics* **37**: 317–31

Monkhouse F J 1959 *A Regional Geography of Western Europe*. Longman, London

Morris A 1985 Tourism and town planning in Catalonia. *Planning Outlook* **28**: 77–82

Morris A, Dickinson G 1987 Tourist development in Spain. *Geography* **72**: 16–25

Morris C N 1980 The Common Agricultural Policy. *Fiscal Studies* **1**: 17–35

Moseley M J 1980 Strategic planning and the Paris agglomeration in the 1960s and 1970s: the quest for balance and structure. *Geoforum* **8**: 179–223

Musto S A 1981 Regional consequences of the enlargement of the European Community. *Built Environment* **7**: 172–81

Mutton A F A 1961 *Central Europe: a regional and human geography*. Longman, London

Nature Conservancy Council 1982 *National Nature Reserves*. NCC, London

Naylon J 1967 Tourism: Spain's most important industry. *Geography* **52**: 23–40

Naylon J 1981a Spain, Portugal and the EEC: a troublesome enlargement. *Bank of London and South America Review* **15**: 122–30

Naylon J 1981b Barcelona. In Pacione M (ed) *Urban Problems and Planning in the Developed World*. Croom Helm, London, pp 223–57

Naylor E L 1987 EEC dairy policy. *Geography* **72**: 239–41

Netting R McC 1981 *Balancing on an Alp: ecological change and continuity in a Swiss mountain community*. Cambridge University Press, Cambridge

Newby H 1979 *Green and Pleasant Land? Social change in rural England*. Penguin, Harmondsworth

Nicholson B 1975 Return migration to a marginal area: an example from north Norway. *Sociologia Ruralis* **15**: 227–45

Nicholson B M 1981 The role of the inner city in the development of manufacturing industry. *Urban Studies* **18**: 57–72

Noble M K 1985 Reconstructing Naples. *Geography* **70**: 246–9

Noreng Ø 1980 *The Oil Industry and Government Strategy in the North Sea*. Croom Helm, London and the International Research Center for Energy and Economic Development, Boulder, Colorado

North J, Spooner D 1977 The great UK coal rush. *Area*
9: 15–27

North J, Spooner D 1978 The geography of the coal
industry in the UK in the 1970s. *Geo Journal*
2: 25–72

Nuclear Energy Agency 1986 *Severe Accidents in Nuclear
Power Plants*. OECD, Paris

Öberg S, Oscarsson G 1987 Northern Europe. In Clout
H D (ed) *Regional Development in Western Europe*.
Fulton, London, pp 319–51

Odell P R 1981 The energy economy of Western Europe: a
return to the use of indigenous resources. *Geography*
66: 1–14

Odell P R 1986 *Oil and World Power* 8th edn. Penguin,
Harmondsworth

Odell P R, Rosing K 1976 *The Optimal Development of the
North Sea Oilfields*. Kogan Page, London

Offshore Promotion Services 1980 *European Continental
Shelf Guide and Atlas*. OPS, Maidenhead

O'Flanagan T P 1982 Land reform and rural modernization
in Spain: a Galician perspective. *Erdkunde* **36**: 48–53

Ogden P E 1980 Migration, marriage and the collapse of
traditional peasant society in France. In White P, Woods
R (eds) *The Geographical Impact of Migration*.
Longman, London, pp 152–79

Ogden P E 1985a France: recession, politics and migration
policy. *Geography* **70**: 158–62

Ogden P E 1985b Counterurbanization in France: the
results of the 1982 population census. *Geography*
70: 24–35

O'Loughlin J 1980 Distribution and migration of foreigners
in German cities. *Geographical Review* **70**: 253–75

Openshaw S 1982 The geography of reactor siting policies
in the UK. *Transactions of the Institute of British
Geographers* **7**: 150–62

Organization for Economic Cooperation and Development
1964 *Oil Today*. OECD, Paris

Organization for Economic Cooperation and Development
1977 *The OECD Programme on Long-range Transport of
Air Pollutants: measurements and findings*. OECD, Paris

Organization for Economic Cooperation and Development
1979a *The Siting of Major Energy Facilities*. OECD,
Paris

Organization for Economic Cooperation and Development
1979b *The State of the Environment in OECD Member
Countries*. OECD, Paris

Organization for Economic Cooperation and Development
1980a *OECD Economic Surveys: Norway*. OECD, Paris

Organization for Economic Cooperation and Development
1980b *OECD Economic Surveys: the Netherlands*.
OECD, Paris

Organization for Economic Cooperation and Development
1980c *The Impact of Tourism on the Environment*.
OECD, Paris

Organization for Economic Cooperation and Development
1981 *International Investment and Multinational
Enterprises; recent international direct investment trends*.
OECD, Paris

Organization for Economic Cooperation and Development

1983 *Environmental Effects of Energy Systems*. OECD,
Paris

Organization for Economic Cooperation and Development
1984 *Emission Standards for Major Air Pollutants from
Energy Facilities in OECD Member Countries*. OECD,
Paris

Organization for Economic Cooperation and Development
1985a *Transfrontier Movements of Hazardous Wastes:
legal and institutional aspects*. OECD, Paris

Organization for Economic Cooperation and Development
1985b *Petroleum Industry: energy aspects of structural
change*. OECD, Paris

Organization for Economic Cooperation and Development
1987a *OECD Economic Surveys: Norway*. OECD, Paris

Organization for Economic Cooperation and Development
1987b *Tourism Policy and International Tourism in
OECD Member Countries*. OECD, Paris

Organization for Economic Cooperation and Development
1987c *Review of Fisheries in OECD Member Countries*.
OECD, Paris

Orlando G, Antonelli G 1982 Regional policy in the
European Community and Community regional policy.
European Review of Agricultural Economics **8**: 213–46

Pacione M 1974 The Venetian problem: an overview.
Geography **59**: 339–43

Pacione M 1977 Tourism: its effects on a traditional
landscape in Ibiza and Formentera. *Geography*
62: 43–7

Pacione M 1979 Housing policies in Glasgow since 1880.
Geographical Review **69**: 395–412

Pacione M 1982 Economic development in the
Mezzogiorno. *Geography* **67**: 340–3

Pacione M 1985 Inner-city regeneration: perspectives on
the GEAR project. *Planning Outlook* **28**: 65–9

Pacione M 1987 Socio-spatial development of the south
Italian city: the case of Naples. *Transactions, Institute of
British Geographers* **12**: 433–50

Pahl R E 1965 *Urbs in Rure: the metropolitan fringe of
Hertfordshire*. London School of Economics, London

Palmer J 1988 *Trading Places*. Radius Hutchinson, London

Papageorgiou-Venetas A 1981 Conservation of the
architectural heritage of Greece: means, methods and
policies. In Kain R J P (ed) *Planning for Conservation*.
Mansell, London, pp 235–58

Parish W L 1973 Internal migration and modernization: the
European case. *Economic Development and Cultural
Change* **21**: 591–609

Parker S 1976 *The Sociology of Leisure*. George Allen and
Unwin, London

Parsons J J 1973 Southwards to the sun: the impact of
mass tourism on the coast of Spain. *Association of Pacific
Coast Geographers, Yearbook* **35**: 129–46

Pathe D C 1986 Simulator key to successful plant start-up.
Oil and Gas Journal **84**: 49–53

Pearson L F 1981 *The Organization of the Energy Industry*.
Macmillan, London

Peck F W, Townsend A R 1984 Contrasting experience of
recession and spatial restructuring: British Shipbuilders,
Plessey and Metal Box. *Regional Studies* **18**: 319–38

Peet R 1980 Capital accumulation and regional crisis in Western Europe. *Environment and Planning A* **12**: 1317–24

Pepelasis A A 1963 *Labour Shortage in Greek Agriculture.* Centre of Economic Research, Athens

Pepelasis A A et al 1980 The Tenth Member: economic aspects. *Sussex European Papers no. 7.* Sussex European Research Centre, Brighton

Perroux F 1955 Note sur la notion de pôle de croissance. *Economie Appliquée.* Appears in English translation in McKee D L, Dean R D, Leahy W H (eds) 1970 *Regional Economics.* Collier Macmillan, London and New York

Perry P J 1969 The structural revolution in French agriculture: the role of Sociétés d'aménagement foncier et d'établissement rural. *Revue Géographique de Montréal* **23**: 137–51

Petroleum Economist. A monthly survey of developments in the oil, gas and petrochemical industries

Pickvance C G (ed) 1976 *Urban Sociology: critical essays.* Tavistock, London

Pieroni O 1982 Positive aspects of part-time farming in the development of a professional agriculture: remarks on the Italian situation. *GeoJournal* **6**: 331–6

Pilat J F 1980 *Ecological Politics: the rise of the green movement.* Sage, Beverly Hills and London

Pinder D A 1976 *The Netherlands.* Dawson, Folkestone, Hutchinson, London and Westview Press, Boulder, Colorado

Pinder D A 1978 Guiding economic development in the EEC: the approach of the European Investment Bank. *Geography* **63**: 88–97

Pinder D A 1981 Community attitude as a limiting factor in port growth: the case of Rotterdam. In Hoyle B S, Pinder D A (eds) *Cityport Industrialization and Regional Development: spatial analysis and planning strategies.* Pergamon, Oxford, pp 181–99

Pinder D A 1983 *Regional Economic Development and Policy: theory and practice in the European Community.* George Allen and Unwin, London

Pinder D A 1986 Small firms, regional development and the European Investment Bank. *Journal of Common Market Studies* **24**: 171–86

Pinder D A, Hoyle B S 1981 Cityports, technologies and development strategies. In Hoyle B S, Pinder D A (eds) *Cityport Industrialization and Regional Development: spatial analysis and planning strategies.* Pergamon, Oxford, pp 323–38

Pinder D A, Husain M S 1987a Innovation, adaptation and survival in the West European oil refining industry. In Chapman K, Humphrys G (eds) *Technical Change and Industrial Policy.* Blackwell, Oxford, pp 100–20

Pinder D A, Husain M S 1987b Oil industry restructuring in the Netherlands and its European context. *Geography* **72**: 300–08

Pollock E E 1981 Free ports, free trade zones, export processing zones and economic development. In Hoyle B S, Pinder D A (eds) *Cityport Industrialization and Regional Development: spatial analysis and planning strategies.* Pergamon, Oxford, pp 37–45

Postan M M 1977 The European economy since 1945: a restrospect. In Griffiths R T (ed) *Government, Business and Labour in European Capitalism.* Europotentials Press, London, pp 23–39

Pounds N J G 1953 *Europe and the Mediterranean.* McGraw-Hill, New York

Pourcher G 1970 The growing population of Paris. In Jansen C J (ed) *Readings in the Sociology of Migration.* Pergamon, Oxford, pp 179–202

Prescott J V R 1975 *The Political Geography of the Oceans.* David and Charles, Newton Abbot

Puchala D J 1971 Patterns of West European integration. *Journal of Common Market Studies* **9**: 117–42

Pugliese E 1985 Farmworkers in Italy: agricultural working class, landless peasants or clients of the welfare state? In Hudson R, Lewis J (eds) *Uneven Development in Southern Europe.* Methuen, London, pp 123–39

Ray G F 1976 Impact of the oil crisis on the energy situation in Western Europe. In Rybczynski T M (ed) *The Economics of the Oil Crisis.* Macmillan, London, pp 94–130

Ray G F, Uhlmann L 1979 *The Innovation Process in the Energy Industries.* Cambridge University Press for the National Institute of Economic and Social Research, Cambridge, London and New York

Reid G L, Allen K, Harris D J 1973 *The Nationalized Fuel Industries.* Heinemann, London

Reitel F 1976 Les bourses de valeurs. *Mosella* **6**: 1–72

Richmond A H 1969 Sociology of migration in industrial and post-industrial societies. In Jackson J A (ed) *Migration.* Cambridge University Press, Cambridge, pp 238–81

Rijnmond Public Authority 1983 *Risk Analysis of Six Potentially Hazardous Industrial Objects in the Rijnmond Area.* Reidel, Dordrecht, Boston and New York

Riley R C 1976 *Belgium.* Dawson, Folkestone and Hutchinson, London

Ritson C 1982 Impact on agriculture. In Seers D, Vaitsos C (eds) *The Second Enlargement of the EEC: the integration of unequal partners.* Macmillan, London, pp 92–108

Robert S, Randolph W G 1983 Beyond decentralization: the evolution of population distribution in England and Wales 1961–1981. *Geoforum* **14**: 75–102

Rodwell D G 1975 Conservation legislation: a European survey. *European Heritage* **5**: 32–7

Rokkan S 1980 Territories, centres and peripheries. In Gottmann J (ed) *Centre and Periphery: spatial variation in politics.* Sage, Beverly Hills and London, pp 163–204

Romanos A 1969 Illegal settlements in Athens. In Oliver P (ed) *Shelter and Society: new studies in vernacular architecture.* Barrie and Jenkins, London, pp 137–55

Romanos M C 1979 Forsaken farms: the village-to-city movement in Western Europe. In Romanos, M C (ed) *Western European Cities in Crisis.* Lexington Books, Lexington, pp 3–19

Rose A M 1969 *Migrants in Europe: problems of acceptance and adjustment.* University of Minnesota Press, Minneapolis

Rose R (ed) 1974 *The Management of Urban Change in Britain and Germany*. Sage, Beverly Hills and London

Roussel L 1977 Démographie et mode de vie conjugale au Danemark. *Population* 32: 339–59

Roussel L 1987 Deux décennies de mutations démographiques (1965–85) dans les pays industrialisés. *Population*. 42: 429–48

Routledge I 1977 Land reform and the Portuguese revolution. *Journal of Peasant Studies* 5: 79–98

Russett B M 1971 Interdependence and capabilities for European co-operation. *Journal of Common Market Studies* 9: 143–50

Rustow D, Penrose T 1981 Turkey and the Community. *Sussex European Papers no. 10*. Sussex European Research Centre, Brighton.

Sallnow J, John A 1982 *An Electoral Atlas of Europe 1968–81*. Butterworth, London

Salt J 1976 International labour migration: the geographical pattern of demand. In Salt J, Clout H D (eds) *Migration in Post-War Europe; geographical essays*. Oxford University Press, Oxford, pp 80–125

Salt J 1981 International labor migration in Western Europe: a geographical review. In Kritz M M, Keely C B, Tomasi S M (eds) *Global Trends in Migration*. Center for Migration Studies, New York, pp 133–57

Salt J 1984 High level manpower movements in north-western Europe and the role of careers. *International Migration Review* 17: 633–51

Salt J 1985a West German dilemma: little Turks or young Germans? *Geography* 70: 162–8

Salt J 1985b Europe's foreign labour migrants in transition. *Geography* 70: 151–8

Sampson A 1968 *The New Europeans*. Hodder and Stoughton, London

Savery J 1984 *French Multinationals*. Frances Pinter, London

Saville J 1957 *Rural Depopulation in England and Wales, 1851–1951*. Routledge and Kegan Paul, London

Schaller C, Motamen H 1985 Structural changes in the UK energy market. *Energy Policy* 13: 559–63

Schipper L 1983 Residential energy use and conservation in Denmark, 1965–80. *Energy Policy* 11: 313–23

Schipper L 1987 Energy conservation policies in the OECD – did they make a difference? *Energy Policy* 15: 538–48

Schmid J 1982 The family today: sociological highlights on an embattled institution. *European Demographic Information Bulletin* 13: 49–72

Schoonenboom J 1979 Ethnic minorities. *Planning and Development in the Netherlands* 9: 36–57

Schubnell H 1978 Law affecting contraception, abortion and sterilization in Europe. In Kirk M (ed) *Law and Fertility in Europe*. Ordina, Dolhain, pp 31–61

Seabrook J 1985 *Landscapes of Poverty*. Blackwell, Oxford

Secchi C 1980 The effects of enlargement on the EEC periphery. In De Bandt J (ed) *European Studies in Development*. Macmillan, London, pp 42–8

Seers D 1979 The periphery of Europe. In Seers D, Schaffer B, Kiljunen M L (eds) *Underdeveloped Europe*. Harvester Press, Hassocks, Sussex, pp 3–34

Seers D, Schaffer B, Kiljunen M L (eds) 1979 *Underdeveloped Europe: case studies in core–periphery relations*. Harvester Press, Hassocks, Sussex

Sheehan S 1980 The impact of EEC membership on Irish agriculture. *Journal of Agricultural Economics* 31: 297–310

Sidenbladh G 1965 Stockholm: a planned city. *Scientific American* 213: 106–21

Simmons I G 1975 *Rural Recreation in the Industrial World*. Edward Arnold, London

Sinfield A 1981 *What Unemployment Means*. Martin Robertson, Oxford

Sivini G 1976 Some remarks on the development of capitalism and specific forms of part-time farming in Europe. In Fuller A M, Mage J A (eds) *Part-time Farming in Europe: problem for resource in rural development*. Geo Abstracts. Norwich, pp 274–83

Skovgaard J A 1978 Conservation planning in Denmark, *Town Planning Review* 49: 519–39

Slater M 1979 Migrant employment, recessions and return migration: some consequences for migration policy and development. *Studies in Comparative International Development* 14: 3–22

Smidelius B, Wiklund C 1979 The Nordic Community: the ugly duckling of regional co-operation. *Journal of Common Market Studies* 18: 59–75

Smith G 1978 The reintegration of the state in Western Europe. In Kolinsky M (ed) *Divided Loyalties*. Manchester University Press, Manchester

Smith N, Williams P (eds) 1986 *Gentrification of the City*. Allen and Unwin, Winchester, Mass.

Smith R W 1980 Trends in national maritime claims. *Professional Geographer* 32: 216–23

Sortia J R, Vandermotten C, Vanlaer J 1986 *Atlas Economique de l'Europe*. Société Royale Belge de Géographie et Université Libre de Bruxelles, Brussels

Spooner D 1981 The geography of coal's second coming. *Geography* 66: 29–41

Spooner D J 1984 The southern problem, the Neapolitan problem and Italian regional policy. *Geographical Journal* 150: 11–26

Stamp L D 1965 Land-use statistics for the countries of Europe. *World Land-use Survey Occasional Paper no. 3*. Bude

Steed G F P 1978a Global industrial systems: the case of the clothing industry. *Geoforum* 9: 35–47

Steed G F P 1978b Product differentiation, location protection and economic integration: Western Europe's clothing industries. *Geoforum* 9: 307–18

Stephens M 1978 *Linguistic Minorities in Western Europe*. Gower, Llandysal

Stephenson G 1972 Cultural regionalism and the unitary state idea in Belgium. *Geographical Review* 62: 501–23

Stern J 1986 After Sleipner: a policy for UK gas supplies. *Energy Policy* 14: 9–14

Stöhr W, Tödtling F 1978 An evaluation of regional policies: experiences in market and mixed economies. In Hansen N M (ed) *Human Settlement Systems*. Ballinger, Cambridge, Mass, pp 85–119

Stungo A 1972 The Malraux Act. *Journal of the Royal Town Planning Institute* 58: 357–62

Talbot R B 1977 The European Community's regional fund: a study in the politics of redistribution. *Progress in Planning* 8: 183–281

Tangermann S 1979 Germany's role within the CAP. *Journal of Agricultural Economics* 30: 241–54

Taylor D, Diprose G, Duffy M 1986 EC environmental policy and the control of water pollution: the implementation of Directive 76/464 in perspective. *Journal of Common Market Studies* 24: 225–46

Taylor E, Davey W G 1984 Energy in Western Europe. *Energy Policy* 12: 409–24

Taylor M J, Thrift N (eds) 1986 *Multinationals and the Restructuring of the World Economy*. Croom Helm, London

Teumis H B 1978 The early state in France. In Claessen H J M, Skalnik P (eds) *The Early State*. Mouton, The Hague, pp 235–56

Thoman G R 1973 *Foreign Investment and Regional Development: the theory and practice of investment incentives, with a case study of Belgium*. Praeger, New York

Thompson I B 1970 *Modern France: a social and economic geography*. Butterworth, London

Thompson K 1963 *Farm Fragmentation in Greece*. Centre for Economic Research, Athens

Thwaites A T 1978 Technological change, mobile plants and regional development. *Regional Studies* 12: 445–61

Tilly C 1975 *The Formation of National States in Western Europe*. Princeton University Press, Princeton

Tommel I 1987 Regional policy in the European Community: its impact on regional policies and public administration in the Mediterranean member states. *Environment and Planning C* 5: 369–81

Torre J de la, Bacchetta M 1980 The uncommon market: European policies towards the clothing industry in the 1970s. *Journal of Common Market Studies* 19: 95–122

Tovias A 1979 EEC enlargement: the southern neighbours. *Sussex European Papers no. 5*. Sussex European Research Centre, Brighton

Townsend A 1980a The role of returned migrants in England's poorest region. *Geoforum* 11: 353–69

Townsend A 1980b Unemployment geography and the new government's regional aid. *Area* 12: 9–18

Townsend A R, Peck F W 1985 The geography of mass redundancy. In Pacione M (ed) *Progress in Industrial Geography*. Croom Helm, London, pp 174–218

Townsend A R, Peck F W 1986 The role of foreign manufacturing in Britain's great recession. pp. 282–310 In Taylor M J, Thrift N (eds) *Multinationals and the Restructuring of the World Economy*. Croom Helm, London, pp 282–310

Townsend P 1987 *Poverty and Labour in London*. Low Pay Unit, London

Trébous M 1980 Moslem workers in France and the practice of their faith. In De Bandt J (ed) *European Studies in Development*. Macmillan, London, pp 142–8

Tsoukalis L 1981 *The European Community and its Mediterranean Enlargement*. George Allen and Unwin, London

Tugendhat C 1987 *Making Sense of Europe*. Penguin, Harmondsworth

Tuppen J 1977 Redevelopment of the city centre: the case of Lyon–Part Dieu. *Scottish Geographical Magazine* 93: 151–8

Tuppen J, Bateman M 1987 The relaxation of office development controls in Paris. *Regional Studies* 21: 69–74

Tuppen J N 1988 *France in recession, 1981–86*, Macmillan, London

Tuppen J N, Mingret P 1986 Suburban malaise in French cities, *Town Planning Review*, 57: 187–201

Turner B, Nordquist G 1982 *The Other European Community: integration and co-operation in Nordic Europe*. Weidenfeld and Nicolson, London

Uhrich R 1987 *La France inverse? Les régions en mutation*. Economica, Paris

Unger K 1986 Return migration and regional characteristics: the case of Greece. In King R L (ed) *Return Migration and Regional Economic Problems*. Croom Helm, London, pp 129–51

United Nations Economic Commission for Europe 1983 *An Efficient Energy Future: prospects for Europe and North America*. Butterworth, London

Van Doorn J 1975 European regional policy: an evaluation of recent developments. *Journal of Common Market Studies* 13: 391–401

Van Hoogstraten P 1985 Stages in Dutch regional policy, 1945–1984. *Planning Outlook* 28: 20–8

Vanhove N, Klaasen L H 1979 *Regional Policy: a European approach*. Saxon House, Farnborough

Vanhove N, Klaasen L H 1987 *Regional Policy: a European Approach* 2nd edn. Avebury, Aldershot

Van Praag C S 1981 Dispersion and dispersal policy. *Planning and Development in the Netherlands* 13: 27–49

Van Valkenburg S 1959 Land use within the European Common Market. *Economic Geography* 35: 1–24

Van Valkenburg S 1960 An evaluation of the standard of land use in Western Europe. *Economic Geography* 36: 283–95

Van Valkenburg S, Held C C 1952 *Europe*. Wiley, New York

Van Voorden F W 1981 The preservation of monuments and historic townscapes in the Netherlands. *Town Planning Review* 52: 433–53

Verrière J 1982 L'actualité démographique en République d'Irlande. *Annales de Géographie* 91: 70–86

Verrips J 1975 The decline of small-scale farming in a Dutch village. In Boissevain J, Friedl J (eds) *Beyond the Community: social process in Europe*. Department of Educational Science of the Netherlands and European Mediterranean Study Group of the University of Amsterdam, The Hague, pp 108–23

Vickerman R W 1986 Economic implications of the Channel Tunnel. *Economic Review* 3: 2–6

Vickerman R W 1987 The Channel Tunnel: consequences for regional growth and development. *Regional Studies* 21: 187–97

Vidal de la Blache P 1903 *Tableau de la géographie de la France*. Hachette, Paris

Vielvoye R 1985 Future gloomy for refining industry in Western Europe. *Oil and Gas Journal* **83**: 41–6

Vincent J A 1980 The political economy of Alpine development: tourism or agriculture in St Maurice. *Sociologica Ruralis* **20**: 250–71

Von Krosigk F 1971 A reconsideration of federalism in the scope of the present discussion on European integration. *Journal of Common Market Studies* **9**: 197–223

Wabe J S 1986 The regional impact of deindustrialization in the European Community. *Regional Studies* **20**: 23–36

Wagstaff J M 1968 Rural migration in Greece. *Geography* **53**: 175–9

Walter I 1975 *International Economics of Pollution*. Macmillan, London

Warnes A M (ed) 1982 *Geographical Perspectives on the Elderly*. Wiley, Chichester

Waterhouse A 1979 The advent of localism in two planning cultures: Munich and Toronto. *Town Planning Review* **50**: 313–24

Webb K 1978 *The Growth of Nationalism in Scotland*. Penguin, Harmondsworth

Webb M 1985 Energy policy and the privatization of the UK energy industries. *Energy Policy* **13**: 27–36

White P E 1976 Tourism and economic development in the rural environment. In Lee R, Ogden P E (eds) *Economy and Society in the EEC*. Saxon House, Farnborough, pp 150–9

White P E 1980 Migration loss and the residual community: a study in rural France 1962–75. In White P E, Woods R (eds) *The Geographical Impact of Migration*. Longman, London, pp 178–222

Whysall P, Benyon J 1981 Urban renewal policies in central Amsterdam. *Planning Outlook* **23**: 77–82

Wilkes K 1983 The 1980 Swiss Census. *Geography* **68**: 61–4

Wilkinson P F 1978 The global distribution of national parks and equivalent reserves. In Nelson J G, Needham R D, Mann D L (eds) *International Experience with National Parks and Related Reserves*. University of Waterloo, Canada, pp 603–24

Williams A 1981 Portugal's illegal housing. *Planning Outlook* **23**: 110–14

Williams A M (ed) 1984 *Southern Europe Transformed*. Harper and Row, London

Williams A M 1987 *The Western European Economy: a geography of post-war development*. Hutchinson, London

Williams A V, Zelinsky W 1970 On some patterns in international tourist flows. *Economic Geography* **46**: 549–67

Williams C H 1980 Ethnic separatism in Western Europe. *Tijdschrift voor Economische en Sociale Geografie* **71**: 142–58

Wise M 1984 *The Common Fisheries Policy of the European Community*. Methuen, London

Wise M 1987 European, national and regional concepts of fishing limits in the European Community. In Blake G (ed) *Maritime Boundaries and Ocean Resources*. Croom Helm, London, pp 117–32

Wood P A 1976 Inter-regional migration in Western Europe: a re-appraisal. In Salt J, Clout H D (eds) *Migration in Post-War Europe: geographical essays*. Oxford University Press, Oxford, pp 52–79

Wood P A 1987 United Kingdom. In Clout H D (ed) *Regional Development in Western Europe*. Fulton, London, pp 257–83

Woods S 1987 *Western Europe: technology and the future*. Croom Helm, London

Wynn M 1980 Conserving Madrid. *Town and Country Planning* **49**: 53–4

Wynn M (ed) 1984 *Housing in Europe*. Croom Helm, London

Wynn M, Smith R 1978 Spain: urban decentralization. *Built Environment* **4**: 49–55

Yannopoulos G N, Dunning J H 1976 Multinational enterprises and regional development: an exploratory paper. *Regional Studies* **10**: 389–99

Young S, Hood N 1980 *European Development Strategies of US-owned Manufacturing Companies Located in Scotland*. HMSO, Edinburgh

Yuill D, Allen K, Hull C 1980 *Regional Policy in the European Community*. Croom Helm, London

Index